Legal Services for the Community

Legal Services
for the Community

MICHAEL ZANDER
Professor of Law at the
London School of Economics

Temple Smith · London

First Published in Great Britain 1978
by Maurice Temple Smith Ltd
37 Great Russell St London WC1

© Michael Zander 1978

ISBN 0 85117 155 9 Cased
ISBN 0 85117 156 7 Paperback

Set in 11/12pt Bembo by
Input Typesetting Ltd, Wimbledon
Printed in Great Britain by
Billing & Sons Ltd
Guildford, London & Worcester

Contents

List of Tables

Preface

Interest and concern around the world about legal services has probably been greater in the past fifteen years than in the previous five hundred years put together. Suddenly, in the 1960s and 1970s, the subject seemed to touch a raw nerve which, in country after country, sparked criticism, research, reports, reform proposals and innovation through legislation and other means. The literature grew immensely. There were national and international colloquia, symposia and conferences. Experts were flown from continent to continent to advise and consult with professional bodies, and official committees.

England has a venerable legal system, a strongly entrenched legal profession and a legal aid scheme the basic outlines of which were established a quarter of a century ago. Nevertheless, the ferment of ideas and developments has been as great there as anywhere. In the past fifteen years there have been no less than four statutes dealing with aspects of legal services, the report of an official committee on criminal legal aid, three reports of the Prices and Incomes Board, four reports of the Monopolies Commission and a special report of the Lord Chancellor's Legal Aid Advisory Committee, not to mention innumerable articles, studies, parliamentary questions and debates, and the annual reports of the Law Society and the Lord Chancellor's Advisory Committee on the civil legal aid system. The culmination of this period of development came on 12 February 1976 with the announcement by the Prime Minister, Mr Harold Wilson, that a Royal Commission would be set up with wide terms of reference to investigate all aspects of legal services in England and Wales.[1] The establishment of similar inquiries for Scotland and Northern Ireland followed almost immediately.

The purpose of this book is to consider the problems of providing adequate legal services by lawyers and others.

Since, inevitably, one knows one's own system best, it grows primarily out of experience with the English system, though there is a good deal of reference also to that of other countries. But, in this field, the problems in one country are very similar to those in others. Certainly the debates in England seem to have raised most of the issues that have aroused concern in other countries too. It should, perhaps, be said that the author has himself participated in many of the debates in this field over the past decade or so and does not, therefore, write from the vantage-point of a totally disinterested spectator. The reader will no doubt make appropriate allowance for the possible resulting clouding of judgment.

The book was completed in October 1977 by which date virtually all the written evidence to the Royal Commission had been submitted. I am indebted to the Trades Union Congress, the Legal Action Group, the National Association of Citizens' Advice Bureaux, the National Consumer Council, and the Law Centres Working Group for access to drafts of the whole or part of their evidence before it was made public. The manuscript has been brought up to date to the end of January 1978 but, the Law Society's remuneration survey was unfortunately not available by final proof stage and could not therefore be included. The important American Bar Association – American Bar Foundation national survey *The Legal Needs of the Public* was being completed during the autumn of 1977 and I am much in the debt of Barbara Curran, its chief author, for sending me unpublished chapters as they were finished.

For reasons of economy of space, the simple word *Evidence* in the Notes signifies *Memorandum of Evidence to the Royal Commission on Legal Services 1977*.

In the course of preparing the book I sought information and guidance from a wide variety of individuals, organisations and official bodies. I would wish to record my gratitude to all those who gave me so much invaluable assistance and, in particular, to the Lord Chancellor's Office, the Home Office, the Senate of the Inns of Court and the Bar, and the Law Society.

It also gives me the greatest pleasure to express my thanks to my secretary Miss Betty Lias who has uncomplainingly borne the burden of this book in addition to her ordinary work. She performed prodigies in producing order out of seeming chaos.

Finally, I would apologise to the reader for errors of both commission and omission. The book is longer than either I or my publisher would have wished and therefore demands the reader's kind indulgence. On the other hand, I am conscious that at almost every point there is much more that (had one but world enough and time) could be said. There is hardly a chapter that could not itself be the basis of a book. For the expert in the field there will inevitably therefore be too little, whilst for the non-expert the fault may lie somewhat in the opposite direction. In mitigation I would plead only the difficulty of fully satisfying both kinds of reader at the same time.

Michael Zander
London, 1978

Introduction

Legal services in England, as throughout the Western world, have until recently been provided by lawyers in private practice, members of a self-governing profession. The state played little part in assisting or controlling the provision of lawyers' services. Today the situation is transformed. The state provides massive funding for legal services and is increasingly concerned to ensure that the public gets the service it needs in this field.

This growing involvement of the state represents a revolution in the conceptual framework of the subject. The legal profession is still grappling with the implications of the change. When the legal aid scheme was first introduced in England in 1949, many of the judges clearly disapproved. Within a year Lord Justice Singleton said he was 'rather appalled at the number of assisted persons there are'. He hoped 'that it will not mean the disappearance of the ordinary litigant'.[1] The Lord Chief Justice, Lord Goddard, said in 1951 he found there was 'very little gratitude among persons who get [legal] aid'. He was beginning to believe 'that it would be far better to leave many of these people to defend themselves'.[2] Even twenty years later he clearly remained unreconciled to this new development. In an eight-line Foreword to a book on the Inns of Court, he referred, sourly, to only one matter – the growth of legal aid. When he took his first brief in the reign of Queen Victoria there had been no legal aid scheme. 'Half a century later, in 1948, the Legal Aid Act was introduced. How far that has been an advantage to the Bar may be doubted'.[3] But the extent of the revolution may be judged from the fact that the Bar now draws about half its income from state funds.[4]

The growth of the state's involvement in legal services has been traced in a major scholarly article by Professor Mauro Cappelletti.[5] He identified four main historical periods: the

Roman world; the Mediaeval world; the French Revolution and the nineteenth century; and the modern period.

A class of advocates (*advocati* or *patroni*) developed first in the classical period of the Roman Republic. Prior to that, there had been the magistrates and the learned jurists whom they consulted, but who did not represent the parties.

Insofar as the poor received their legal rights in the ancient world, it was more likely to be through the system known as *clientela*, under which the poor attached themselves to a powerful man, a *patronus*, and in return for services and political support, were assisted by him in many matters including, where necessary, litigation. When this system eventually waned in post-classical times, little appears to have come to replace it, though there are references to the practice of the court assigning an advocate to women, minors and weak persons.[6] But it seems doubtful whether such help was, in reality, available on any considerable scale. The Roman world seems to have been unable to suppress lawyers' fees or to provide any proper machinery for assisting the poor with their legal problems. In this area, as in others, Rome permitted great differences of wealth and power to determine the outcome of disputes.

One of the first manifestations of public institutions assisting in the provision of legal services was the establishment, under the Emperor Valentinian, in the second half of the fourth century AD, of the office of *defensor* to 'defend the towns, the churches, and the *humiliores* [lower classes] against the powerful and the public functionaries'.[7] According to a historian of the period, the system represented an attempt by the Emperor to gain the support of the lower classes against the rising power of a sort of pre-feudal nobility. One of the tasks of the *defensor* was to act as advocate of the poor. The office was frequently held by the local bishop. But after about half a century it fell into disuse after the office fell into the hands of the very men it was supposed to control.[8]

The second stage, that of the mediaeval period, created legal aid to the poor as part of the apparatus of the feudal Christian community.[9]

> Legal aid, like other assistance to the *miserabiles personae* of Christendom, was a form of *charitas*. It was given by the Church and by Christian men as a pious work, in much the same way as they

honoured The Peace of God during war, built hospitals for the sick or furnished bread during famine.[10]

Partly this help came from the spontaneous charity of individuals. But the canon law eventually created an official, known as the *advocatus pauperum deputatus et stipendiatus*, whose job it was to represent the poor in ecclesiastical courts. The institution subsequently spread to the secular courts in several parts of France and to many of the free communities of Italy. Under the name *avvocatura dei poveri* this system was still flourishing in Italy in the nineteenth century.

In addition, the church, on several occasions, commanded magistrates to waive the court fees of the poor and sometimes to assign a private lawyer to help them without charge. In England, it was recognised by the time of Henry III that the poor should not pay for writs, and in 1495 in a statute of Henry VII the judges were required to assign counsel to the poor. A similar system was adopted in Milan, Tuscany and Naples.[11] In Germany, decrees in the late fifteenth and sixteenth centuries regulated the practice of assignment of counsel to the poor.[12]

The motive force for these initiatives, therefore, was either Christian charity or secular courtly notions of nobility and chivalry in which protection of the oppressed played an important part. Not unnaturally, however, the performance of these essentially altruistic ideals left much to be desired. One *advocatus pauperum* would be expected to provide for a whole city or even region. No remuneration was provided for the lawyers, and in practice, only some would make their services available. There was no structure or organisation for providing such services. The instincts of one ruler would not always be shared by his successors or even by his followers. The system itself was often ambivalent as to how far it wished to pursue charitable inclinations – the judges of England appear to have allowed the flogging of defendants who received aid but lost their cases and to have construed the statute of Henry VII to apply only to plaintiffs.[13]

The third stage was that from the French Revolution to the twentieth century. The French Revolution marked the moment when, for the first time, primary significance was attached to the role of the state in preserving the natural rights of the governed, one of which was access to justice. Both the

American Bill of Rights and the French Declaration of the
Rights of Man gave attention to the securing of justice. The
Bill of Rights provided for a right to counsel and a law of 1790
in France for the *gratuité de la justice*. But lawyers in both
countries continued to demand fees that could not be afforded
by the poor. In the second half of the nineteenth century
legislation in many Western countries provided for the waiving of court fees and the gratuitous provision of lawyers for the
indigent. Such legislation was passed in France in 1851, in Italy
in 1865, and in Germany in 1877. In England, in 1883, the *in
forma pauperis* procedure was enlarged by the raising of the
capital limit for receipt of aid from £5 (at which it had been
fixed in 1495) to £25. The procedure, which had been limited
to plaintiffs, was made available to defendants. In 1914 the
previous requirement of a solicitor's letter attesting to the
merits of the case was abolished and lawyers were made available through a Poor Persons Department instead of by the
previous method of assignment by the judges. In 1925 these
functions were transferred to the Law Society.

In America, in 1892, the federal judges were authorised to
assign attorneys to represent the poor with sufficiently
meritorious cases. In 1910, the Act was extended to criminal
proceedings, to defendants as well as plaintiffs and to appellants as well as proceedings.

Thus, as Professor Cappelletti says: 'during the era of
laissez-faire, all major nations of the West sought distinct
national solutions to the legal problems of the poor; yet the
resulting solutions all depended on the same central elements.'[14] In each country legal aid was provided by the same
mechanism as in the mediaeval period – waiving of court fees
and the assignment of private lawyers to the needy without
charge to the client or remuneration to the lawyers. But,
although charity was still the essence of the service, the new
element was the action of legislatures to establish a route to
legal services by positive law and to support it with at least a
minimal administrative structure. At least in theory, a poor
person could now invoke the machinery of the state to help
him secure his legal rights.

But, although the rhetoric had changed, the reality was still
somewhat as it had always been. Systems that depended
mainly on the goodwill and devotion of individual practition-

ers were inevitably limited in their scope and effectiveness. To quote Cappelletti again:

> Actual equality requires that all citizens have effective access to comparable legal services and cannot exist in a system in which some legal services are rendered to paying clients and others are given gratuitously to the recipients of a quasi-charity. In the first place, in a free market economy, a lawyer will necessarily tend to concentrate his time, effort and skill on the remunerative business, the source of his livelihood and reputation. Secondly, the highly skilled and financially successful lawyer will tend to avoid matters of little financial importance, leaving them to the young and inexperienced or to the unsuccessful. Finally, a steady diet of non-remunerative work is distasteful, even to the charitably minded, and there will be a tendency to keep the volume of such work at a low level, whether more formally, through a demanding admissions procedure, or less formally, through a failure to publicise the programme, or a simple tendency of practitioners to be unsympathetic to non-paying clients.[15]

The most recent of the four periods was the first in which there was a real attempt to close the gap between theory and reality. Hitherto, it had been sufficient to proclaim moral and then legal obligations. Now it was seen that, in order to make the slogans about equal access to justice effective, state action and, in particular, state funding, was indispensable. The start of this movement came in England – with the Poor Prisoners Defence Act 1930 for criminal cases, and the Legal Aid and Advice Act 1949 for civil cases. Under both these Acts legal services were provided by private practitioners at the state's expense. Under the 1930 Act the lawyers worked on a fixed scale of charges, regarded by the profession as being wholly unremunerative. But the 1949 Act provided for remuneration at first at 85 per cent and later at 90 per cent of the full rate applicable for ordinary clients.

Legislation involving the commitment of state funds for legal aid programmes has, in the past few years, been introduced, to name only a few, in the United States (1964 and 1974); Ontario (1966); Zambia (1967); South Africa (1969); Manitoba (1971); England (1972); Sweden (1972); West Germany (1972); Quebec (1972); France (1972); Italy (1973); Saskatchewan (1973–4); British Columbia (1975); Newfoundland (1975); and Nova Scotia (1977). All these schemes are variations on two main themes – the payment out of public funds to private practitioners or the employment of state-salaried lawyers. Each system prescribes the financial and other conditions that make applicants eligible for legal aid and the procedures for handling applications. Each establishes a bureaucracy to administer the system. Their common feature is the recognition that legal services are becoming, or have indeed become, part of the bundle of benefits that modern states are expected to provide. In a growing number of countries token implementation is no longer politically acceptable. More is required, and although there is (and will probably always remain) a great gap between the promise and the fulfilment, states now feel morally committed to applying substantial resources to meeting the need for the services of lawyers.

England, which was the first country to develop a modern legal aid system, now devotes very considerable resources to its maintenance. In 1977–8 estimated public expenditure for legal aid, including salaried law-centres, was some £87m.[16] The fact that so much public money is now spent on legal services is one of the chief causes of the increasing public scrutiny of the work of lawyers, of which the inquiries of the Prices and Incomes Board, the Monopolies Commission and now of the Royal Commission are the most dramatic examples.

The growth of public scrutiny has also been seen in the sustained criticism to which the profession has been subjected in the past twenty or so years in the press. Lawyers have, of course, always been unpopular. But in recent years in England they have had to face not only ill-informed general grumbling, but detailed and, on the whole, informed criticisms. The five-week campaign leading to the establishment of the Royal Commission in January and February 1976 started with the publication on 2 January 1976 of the writer's study of lawyers' fees in criminal legal aid cases.[17] But it was quickly broadened by the press into more general issues. Between 15 January and 21 February 1976 there were editorials supporting the call for an inquiry in *New Society*, *The Sunday Times*, *The Times*, the *Daily Mirror*, *The Guardian*, *The Observer*, and *The Economist*.[18] They raised a long list of problems requiring investigation whether the profession should remain self-governing, the costs of going to law, the division of the profession into barristers and solicitors and other restrictive practices and monopolies, the system for handling complaints against lawyers, and the quality of legal education and of legal services. *The Times* said that the question was whether the legal profession provided an adequate service to the public. Royal Commissions, it suggested, ought not to be lightly advocated. They were appropriate only if there were solid reasons to think that there was something seriously amiss in a field of real public importance, and if exhaustive inquiry was indicated by the need to clarify the issues and to focus attention on the means of reform. Both criteria were satisfied in this instance. 'Regrettably, both branches of the legal profession have been reluctant or unable seriously to look into, and reform, their own affairs.'

Nor was the critical chorus confined to the lay press. The *New Law Journal*, one of the profession's three weeklies, argued editorially (5 February) that an inquiry was needed in order to quell public disquiet. The questions being asked (about management, availability, quality and cost of legal services) were too firmly implanted in the public mind for their investigation to be put off any longer. The extent to which there had already been a loss of public confidence was 'apparent to anyone who keeps his ears and eyes open'. In the existing climate of public opinion 'delay can only reinforce the suspicion that the questions to which we have referred are not being investigated because the answers would be unpalatable to those with a vested interest in the established order'. The case for a Royal Commission should not, however, be conceded for public relations reasons. We lived in an age of great social and economic change to which the legal system had responded in various ways. There had, however, been no comprehensive stock-taking, 'no all-embracing re-appraisal of the relationship between what society wants and what the legal shop has to offer'. If there were discrepancies between one and the other 'as beyond all shadow of doubt' there were, they needed to be put right for the sake of society and for the sake of the legal system, irrespective of the difficulties and inconveniences that would be involved for lawyers or indeed others. 'Lawyers particularly have nothing to gain from being involved in an institution that is out of phase with society's reasonable and necessary requirements.'

The call for a Royal Commission was echoed early by the Legal Action Group,[19] a major lobby in the poverty law field, by the Society of Labour Lawyers, and by the chairman of the British Legal Association, a right-wing ginger group of solicitors.[20] More surprising, however, was the cautious welcome given to the Commission by the official representatives of the profession. On the day before the Prime Minister made his announcement (11 February) the Chairman of the Bar, Sir Peter Rawlinson, and the President of the Law Society, Sir Edmund Liggins, in a joint public statement said 'both the Bar and the Law Society wish[ed] to make it clear that, far from seeking to avoid a Royal Commission, they would welcome the opportunity to participate in a comprehensive examination of the structure of the profession, its functions, its remuneration and the services it provides'. No doubt the statement was dictated to some extent by force of circumstances. The leaders of the profession were aware of the imminence of the Cabinet decision to set up a Royal Commission. Yet at the same time, the profession's statement undoubtedly reflected a feeling widely held in the legal profession that, although there might be things to criticise, the basic structure was sound. The setting up of the Royal Commission, as Sir Peter Rawlinson said only a few hours after the announcement, would 'give the profession the chance to expose the falseness and superficiality of the current fashionable criticisms'. It would be the first occasion for the full range of criticisms to be met and answered and for an impartial and authoritative assessment of the truth.

The Royal Commission, under its chairman Sir Henry Benson, had its first meeting on 2 July 1976. It set up subcommittees on needs for legal services, on the cost and duration of legal procedure, on conveyancing, on legal education and on fees and charges payable to lawyers. It distributed more than 2,500 copies of a general circular inviting evidence, and long, detailed questionnaires to more than 100 bodies and individuals. The Commission has been deluged by the voluminous written evidence that has poured in from all sides. Press advertisements provoked communications from more than 1,500 individuals and organisations. Both branches of the profession commissioned remuneration surveys. Empirical studies were launched by a variety of bodies including the

Citizens' Advice Bureaux and the Consumers' Association. The Commission itself initiated studies of law centres, legal advice centres, national advisory organisations, earnings of barristers' clerks, and legal procedures and costs in other countries.[21] The inquiry is unique. No legal profession has previously been subjected to so detailed or so broad an investigation.[22] The results will be relevant to legal professions all over the world. The setting up of the Royal Commission with its wide terms of reference[23] is an opportunity for those concerned with the problems of legal services to collect and to articulate their thoughts. The book that follows is offered as a contribution to the debate.

1 The Private Profession

The foremost providers of legal services are lawyers. Over centuries they have established their position in the community as the leading experts in a complex field which affects every citizen. They play a variety of roles – as advisers, negotiators, draftsmen, litigators, advocates, referral agents, arrangers of finance and other accommodations as well as general aides and comforters. They act for the most powerful elements in society and for the least powerful.

In most countries they seem to be the target for a good deal of abuse. This is understandable and probably inevitable. They earn their living out of other people's troubles; their way of conducting business often heightens conflict between the parties; they affect peculiar modes of speech; their services tend to be costly; they are felt to be (and often are) more than usually conservative; they are held responsible for defects in the legal system over which they have little control; they are blamed for the unsuccessful outcome of proceedings even when this is due to shortcomings in the client's own case. Even the best legal profession is therefore likely to be the object of much negative feeling.

But although in some ways the profession has a bad image, in others it has a very good one. Most surveys show that the great majority both of the general population and of those who have used lawyers, speak well of them. In 1973, for instance, the Law Society reported on a survey it had commissioned based on interviews with a random sample of 920 respondents. No less than 73 per cent said their impressions of solicitors were 'very favourable' or 'fairly favourable', while only 7 per cent said they were fairly or very unfavourable. (Very favourable or fairly favourable ratings were given by 95 per cent in relation to nurses, with doctors close behind. The only other group with higher rating than solicitors were bank managers with 79 per cent. Immediately below solicitors came clergymen (70 per cent), accountants (65 per cent), architects (57 per cent), barristers (45 per cent), Members of Parliament (40 per cent) and estate agents (36 per cent).) Of the 687 individuals who replied to a question on the quality of legal services received from solicitors, 52 per cent said they were 'very satisfied', 34 per cent 'fairly satisfied', 5 per cent 'fairly dissatisfied' and 4 per cent 'very dissatisfied'.[1]

Interviews with a random sample of 651 respondents in Scotland showed very similar results. (More than 92 per cent of those who had used solicitors said they were satisfied with the way lawyers conducted their business and the 'extremely high regard in which solicitors are held was also found in people who may never have met a solicitor personally'.) The only occupational group that rated a higher reputation than solicitors was the medical profession.[2] The Consumers' Association, in a survey of some 1,200 members who had used solicitors since September 1975, found that almost all thought their solicitors friendly. Only one in ten said they were dissatisfied overall.[3] In a survey of 1,651 respondents in three poor London boroughs it was found that 59 per cent of respondents thought that 'lawyers have a good understanding of the problems of the ordinary man' (as against 18 per cent who disagreed and 23 per cent who had no view); and 68 per cent agreed that 'you can expect to get a fair and sympathetic reception in a solicitor's office' (only 6 per cent disagreed and there were 25 per cent who had no view).[4]

The response to lawyers is, therefore, both strongly negative and strongly positive. Moreover, it appears to be greatly affected by the nature of the problem taken to a lawyer. The recent major study of a national random sample by the American Bar Association and American Bar Foundation found that American lawyers, too, were extremely well regarded overall by their clients. 83 per cent of users gave their lawyer the top rating for competence. 13 per cent thought he had done a moderately competent job and 4 per cent judged the lawyer as incompetent. On each of seven more detailed criteria of assessment the overwhelming majority said lawyers were 'excellent' or 'good' (promptness, 87 per cent; interest in the client, 85 per cent; honesty, 90 per cent; explaining fully, 87 per cent; keeping client informed, 79 per cent; paying attention, 89 per cent; fair and reasonable charges, 82 per cent).[5] But when satisfaction was tested by reference to the nature of the problem, important differences emerged. Users who went to lawyers for real property matters, estate planning or estate settlement were most satisfied. Those who went on personal injury, property damage, problems with governmental agencies, consumer difficulties or criminal charges were more likely to be negative about their lawyers. The report says that it is also clear from the data that the types of problem taken to lawyers by sub-groups such as blacks, latinos, younger persons, the under-educated, or the less affluent are 'more likely to result in situations in which the lawyer consulted will not handle the case, does not complete work on it, or is unable to achieve the desired results; in addition, the lawyer appears to be unconcerned about or uninterested in the client's problem'.[6]

Organisation and size

The English profession is divided into barristers and solicitors. The basis of the functional distinction today is that solicitors are the first-tier advisers and barristers are the second-tier or specialist service. Barristers are brought in to perform two main functions – to advise and to appear as advocates. Solicitors have a monopoly over the right of direct relations with the client, whilst barristers enjoy a virtual monopoly over the right of audience in the higher courts. (In the lower courts and tribunals barristers and solicitors have an equal right of audience.) By tradition, the Bar is the senior branch. Solicitors have, in the past fifty years, made great advances educationally, socially and professionally, but although official rhetoric now proclaims that the two branches have equal status,[7] the Bar remains the senior of the two branches – if only by definition of the system. The solicitor attends on the barrister, not vice versa. The sense of superiority of barristers and of inferiority of solicitors may be less than in the past, but it is still real.[8]

For most of this century the size of the profession was more or less static, at just under 20,000 solicitors and 2,000 barristers. From 1960 onwards there has been an extraordinary growth in the numbers on both sides of the profession. The number of barristers in practice rose from 1,919 in 1960 to

4,076 in November 1977 (including 336 women) – an increase of more than 100 per cent; the number of solicitors with practising certificates rose in the period 1960 to 1976 from 18,438 to 31,250 – an increase of 69 per cent. (The proportion of women in the profession has been increasing slowly but steadily. In 1971 the proportion of women barristers was 6.1 per cent and in 1976 it was 8.7 per cent. On the solicitors' side, in 1971 it was 6.0 per cent and in 1976, 9.6 per cent.) One cause of this great expansion has been the enormous growth in representation financed out of public funds through legal aid. In 1960 there were 5,648 grants of legal aid in magistrates' courts; in 1976 the number of proceedings had doubled but the grants of legal aid had risen nearly fifty-fold to 269,883.[9] In 1960 there were 9,136 grants of legal aid for proceedings in quarter sessions and assize courts; in 1976 the equivalent number for cases in crown courts was 91,184. In 1960 there were 23,085 grants of civil legal aid; in 1975–6 the figure was 207,977. These figures obviously represent a greatly increased work-load for the profession and especially for barristers, a high proportion of whose work consists of advocacy. (The increase is even greater than appears from the figures for legal aid for defences since the prosecution is of course also usually legally represented.) In the case of the solicitors' branch the increase in numbers is probably connected mainly with the great growth in home ownership and the resulting develop-ment in conveyancing work. The number of mortgages granted by building societies in 1960, 1965, 1970, 1975 and 1976 respectively (to the nearest thousand) was 387,000, 389,000, 544,000, 660,000 and 715,000.[10]

The English legal profession is divided into various compo-nent elements. On the barristers' side there are Queen's Coun-sel (also known as QCs or silks) who are normally about 10 per cent of those in practice, and juniors. One result of the vast recent expansion of the Bar has been the relative growth of the proportion of young members of the profession. Those under ten years from Call were one-third of the Bar in 1966, but more than half in 1976. This tendency has been aggravated by a great increase in the numbers of full-time and part-time judges needed to cope with the greater volume of cases being heard in the courts. The ranks of senior counsel in the middle 1970s began to get a little thin.

Barristers are not allowed to form partnerships or to have any other profit-sharing arrangements,[11] though they do pool expenses by working in chambers. Each chambers is required to have a clerk who functions as office manager. He also negotiates fees on behalf of his principals (the senior clerk is normally paid on a commission basis). The total number of sets of chambers has not greatly altered over the years. In 1960, when there were 1,919 barristers in practice, there were 269 sets of chambers with an average of seven barristers per set. By 1976, with 3,881 in practice, the number of sets of chambers had only risen to 287 – an average of thirteen barristers per set.

On the other side of the profession, solicitors work either as partners or as employees (assistant solicitors). But there are also a large number of unadmitted personnel – formerly called managing clerks and now more usually referred to as legal executives. There are almost as many of these as there are qualified solicitors. Although legal executives are not technically qualified, much of the work they do is 'legal' – see pp. 299–302 below. Solicitors' firms also use trainee solicitors (articled clerks). Like legal executives, articled clerks, according to their abilities and the policy of their firms, do a good deal of legal work.

Most firms of solicitors are comparatively small. The National Prices and Incomes Board (PIB) calculated that in 1967 about two-fifths of all firms had only one partner and 70 per cent had only one or two partners. Only 10 per cent of firms had more than five partners.[12] But the larger firms delivered most legal services. Thus, the PIB found that 56 per cent of bills nationally were delivered by the 30 per cent of firms with three or more partners and that 28 per cent of all bills were delivered by the 10 per cent of firms with five or more partners.[13] The larger firms also employed the majority of solicitors – the 30 per cent of firms with more than three partners had 59 per cent of all solicitors, and the 10 per cent of firms with more than five partners had 32 per cent of the solicitors.[14] The PIB also found that larger units were generally more profitable because they were more economical. Its figures seemed to indicate 'that an increase in the size of practices, which enables the practice to organise its work on a more specialised basis, leads to a more effective use of manpower and, therefore, to a reduction in expense'.[15] Small firms, it thought, would therefore do well to amalgamate. But a later Birmingham study took issue with this recommenda-tion. It found that even small firms could make good profits provided they had a large turnover of work and were 'geared up' by having sufficient junior staff.[16]

Geographical distribution

Barristers are highly concentrated – 188 of the 287 sets of chambers are in a small area of London. The Bar's annual report for 1976–7 stated that of 3,881 barristers in practice only 1,127 (29 per cent) practised wholly or mainly outside Lon-don. There are twenty-six towns with one or more sets of chambers. But many barristers whose chambers are in London appear in courts outside the capital.

Solicitors, of course, are much more dispersed than barris-ters. The number of actual firms is not known precisely, but it is about 7,000. There are, for instance, 6,850 firms insured under the Law Society's compulsory insurance scheme. (By way of contrast, there were some 9,000 general practitioners' medical practices in 1975.[17]) Their distribution is, however, not even. A study by Ken Foster, based on the 1971 Law List, showed that the national average was one solicitor per 2,418 of the population and one solicitors' firm per 4,732 of the popula-tion.[18] But a ranking of all the counties and boroughs in England and Wales on both measures showed a wide spread, ranging from Bournemouth, with one solicitor for every 913 of the population and one firm per 1,993 of the population, to Bootle, with one solicitor per 24,736 and one firm per 37,104 of the population. The study showed that most solicitors practise in urban areas rather than in the country. Nearly half of all solicitors practised in the main conurbations which have only one-third of the total population, while no less than two-thirds of all solicitors practised wholly or mainly in towns or conurbations with populations of over 100,000.

Foster tested the distribution of solicitors against that of doctors and dentists and found it was very similar. When he looked at various factors to explain this distribution he found that most of the possible explanations were not borne out by the statistics. Five socio-economic indicators were investi-gated in two counties, Lancashire and Cheshire. There proved to be no significant correlation between distribution of solicitors or their offices and the number of owner-occupiers. Though there was some correlation with the level of freehold housing, there was a higher correlation with the age of the population. Thus, a middle-class, but young, town would have fewer solicitors than a working-class, but older, town of the same size. But by far the highest correlation was between the distribution of solicitors and their firms and the level of retail sales per head. The correlation proved to be as high for the rest of the country as for Cheshire and Lancashire. In other words, the distribution of solicitors in England (as in the USA and Australia[19]) seems to be mainly determined by the level of economic activity. This also explains the fact that solicitors have to some extent followed retail business from the central urban areas to new shopping centres in the suburbs. A study in Birmingham showed that, whereas in 1951 only 13 per cent of solicitors' offices were located in the suburbs, the proportion in 1971 was 23 per cent. New offices were located primarily in areas where they would attract conveyancing work rather than in areas of lower socio-economic status.[20] But, notwithstanding the drift towards the suburbs, most solicitors still practised in the centres of urban areas. Moreover, the larger towns had a significantly higher concentration of solicitors than surrounding smaller towns. Thus, whereas Birmingham had an average of one solicitor per 2,133 of the population, the equivalent figures for the surrounding towns of Wolverhampton, Walsall, Warley, Dudley, West Bromwich, Sutton Coldfield and Solihull were, respectively: 3,021; 3,356; 4,085; 4,883; 5,375; 6,394; and 7,641.[21]

The authors of the Birmingham study explained the concentration of solicitors in certain places or areas by reference to various factors. One was that solicitors serve organisations that are themselves centralised. Thus, it was inevitable that London, being the financial, commercial and administrative centre of the country, should have a high concentration of lawyers. Solicitors naturally collected close to certain kinds of institution with which they commonly did business, such as banks, insurance companies, building-societies and courts. Secondly, centralisation enabled work to be handled in bulk where decentralisation would require less efficient or less economical handling.

Centralisation is obviously beneficial – at least in terms of ease of access – to those who work in the urban centres or who can get there relatively easily. Even for those who may find it somewhat difficult to get into the centre this may not be fatal – going to a solicitor is so rare an event in an individual's life that there may be no great hardship in having to exert oneself somewhat beyond the ordinary. Most people are prepared to make a special effort to go even considerable distances for special occasions such as family outings, shopping expeditions for major purchases (or an away football-match). But the further people have to go to see a solicitor, the more they may find reasons for not going. Those who are absolutely clear in their minds that they need a solicitor's help may not be deterred, but those faced with situations where the need for a solicitor is less obviously essential could be affected by the extent to which effort is needed to get there.

There is little reliable information as yet on the economic and social pros and cons of locating solicitors' offices more or less centrally. Do clients prefer to have their solicitor, as it were, at their own street corner, or do they prefer the relatively anonymity of the main street for visiting solicitors over the more conspicuous visit closer to home?[22] Presumably, other things being equal, it is cheaper to handle work in greater bulk centrally. On the other hand, to what extent are the cost savings of the more economical centralised service passed on to the consumer? Are the savings from centralised and bulk handling cancelled by higher rents and other overheads in the main urban areas? What numbers and kinds of clients fail to visit solicitors who would do so if they were more accessible, and for what kinds of problems? In the ABA/ABF study it was found that, of those who had thought of consulting a lawyer but had not done so, only 3.5 per cent cited problems over finding a lawyer as their reason. This was 0.7 per cent of the entire sample.[23] But even if the same were true in England, the accessibility of local firms may still be an important source of work, if only because it is a means of communicating knowledge about the existence of firms. In the study of three poor London boroughs, those who knew of a firm of solicitors within one hour of their home or their place of work (30 per cent of the sample) were asked how they first heard of them. No less than 31 per cent said they passed the name-plate in the street.[24] This suggests that solicitors may be able to attract some custom by opening inexpensive skeleton offices in under-solicitored areas. A lawyer and a receptionist-secretary might function successfully as a first line of advice and assistance, feeding clients into the main office if their problems required further action.

It does not seem likely that ways will be found to *direct* solicitors to set up in under-solicitored areas, but various forms of encouragement might be devised. The Manchester Law Society and the Nuffield Foundation are experimenting with a form of subsidised practice. The Foundation has underwritten the capital and running costs of a new, two-solicitor practice in an area with no such firms. It is guaranteeing up to £50,000 over a three-year period. The firm, which opened in May 1977, does not advertise and operates in every way like an ordinary firm.[25] The experiment is designed to test how large a subsidy is needed to set up an ordinary private firm existing from whatever work it can get in a poor neighbourhood. It does conveyancing, if any comes its way, but there is an understanding that it would refer commercial work to the nearest private firms. Doctors in the National Health Service are paid extra rates and allowances for practising in little-favoured areas.[26] Application of this principle in the legal field might be a way of attracting more lawyers to poor areas, but the method is unlikely to be easily adopted.[27] There would obviously be strenuous objection from local private practitioners if public moneys were used to subsidise some private firms but not others. The same subsidies would presumably have to be paid to all firms in such areas. But custodians of public moneys are unlikely to be attracted to the idea of offering a general subsidy to lawyers who are working for their own profit. It is one thing to pay for items of work done by such lawyers for the poor. It is something rather different to pay certain capital costs and guarantee a minimum level of income for firms that may derive a significant portion of their work from paying clients. It would be surprising if this system of financing proved successful.

But, even if solicitors decline to set up offices in areas where there are presently an insufficient number of firms, there may still be ways of bringing in the potential clients. For many the most difficult step in seeking help with a problem is probably the first. Means need to be found for bringing clients who need expert help or assistance into 'the system'. One method would be to develop local advice points manned by lay advisers and/or solicitors from which cases could be referred to solicitors' offices. In Southampton and Birmingham there is now a 24-hours-a-day emergency telephone legal service manned by lawyers through which clients can get the help they need. In the Southampton scheme the rota is arranged so that a solicitor is on duty every evening from 6 p.m. until the morning, and from 6 p.m. on a Saturday to Monday morning. The name of the duty solicitor is available to the public via a telephone answering machine. The tape is changed each day. The number to call is advertised regularly in the local evening paper. The solicitors pay £8 as their subscription to cover the costs of the advertisements and of the answering machine. The first interview given under the scheme is free of charge. Of the first 1,000 or so people advised under the scheme, about two-fifths subsequently applied for legal aid.[28] Experiments with mobile advice units and other forms of facility for providing legal services in areas not adequately served are currently being tried in various parts of the country.

The legal aid scheme

The legal aid scheme in England has from the start been channelled through the private profession – what in the United States is known as Judicare. It has three component parts – the criminal scheme, the civil scheme and the legal advice and assistance scheme (known also as the Green Form or '£25 scheme').

The *criminal legal aid scheme* is run by the courts under the general control of the Home Office. It began in 1903, with the Poor Prisoners Defence Act which provided for representation in the higher criminal courts for defendants who could show that they had a serious defence. (The Lord Chief Justice, Lord Alverstone, said the Act was passed 'in the interests of innocent persons'.[29] In 1930, criminal legal aid was extended to trials and committal proceedings before magistrates. It was made no longer obligatory for an accused person to reveal his defence in advance. The test was simply whether the grant of a defence certificate was 'desirable in the interests of justice'.[30] The interests of justice remain the merits test today.[31] For proceedings in crown courts, whether the defendant plans to plead guilty or not guilty, both the merits test and the means test are regarded as satisfied in virtually all cases. Of those who appeared in crown courts for trials in 1976, 96 per cent were represented on legal aid. For those committed by magistrates for sentence alone, the proportion was 97 per cent.[32] For trials before magistrates' courts, the applicant has to show that he needs to be represented because the case threatens him with a real risk of losing his liberty or reputation or because there is a substantial question of law at issue or he cannot follow the proceedings through some physical, mental or language disability.[33] There is also a means test. The court can, but rarely does, ask the defendant who has legal aid to make a contribution to the cost.[34] The application is first vetted by the court clerk, who has the power to grant, but not to refuse, legal aid. If he declines to grant it, the application must go to the court itself. There is no right of appeal from a refusal of criminal legal aid, though an application can be repeated at the same court.

The *civil legal aid scheme*[35] is run by the Law Society under the authority of the Lord Chancellor's Office. The scheme dates from the 1949 Legal Aid and Advice Act, which implemented the recommendations of the Rushcliffe Committee.[36] The Act provided for application to be made to local committees of barristers and solicitors with a right of appeal against refusals to a similarly constituted area committee. The local and area committees apply, as the merits test, the question whether a reasonable solicitor, advising a reasonable client who had the means, would advise him to use his own money in taking (or defending) the proceedings. The applicant must meet two tests – that he has a reasonable chance of winning *and* that it is not unreasonable for him to have legal aid in the particular circumstances of the case.[37] Thus legal aid must be refused under the first limb in cases that are brought to test the law when the prospects of success are slight.[38] Legal aid is likely to be refused under the second limb, for instance, if the costs of securing victory would be out of proportion to the anticipated fruits. It is for this reason that legal aid is not normally available in small claims.

There is also a means test which creates three categories of individuals – those eligible for legal aid without having to pay anything, those eligible subject to payment of a contribution, and those altogether ineligible. Although the means test limits have been raised from time to time,[39] they have gradually fallen behind inflation. It has been estimated that between 1964 and 1974 the proportion of households, with children, eligible for legal aid declined from 64 per cent to 23 per cent. When individuals rather than households were considered it was estimated that at the end of 1973 some 41 per cent of the population were eligible for legal aid – ranging from 21 per cent of couples where the household head was under 65 to 78 per cent for one-parent families. The increasing proportion of elderly people in the population is one of the reasons why there is still a sizeable section of the community eligible for legal aid.[40] The Lord Chancellor's Legal Aid Advisory Committee said, in its report for 1975–6, that the scheme had become more and more limited and now only covered the legal problems of those with little or no income.[41]

But for those who get legal aid it provides great protection. Once the applicant has paid his contribution (if any) he will normally not have to pay more for his own costs, even if the case ultimately goes to the House of Lords. If he loses he will only be required to pay, in respect of his opponent's costs, the same amount he has already been required to pay towards his own costs.[42] If he is on a nil contribution he will pay nothing towards his successful opponent's costs. Admittedly, the scheme requires that any damages or other proceeds of the litigation must first be paid into the legal aid fund which recoups itself in full for the costs incurred on behalf of the plaintiff before paying out to him, but this normally leaves a profit for the assisted party. The total number of legal aid certificates issued in 1976–7 was 218,857.[43] In its first twenty-six years the scheme succeeded in recovering total damages of £194m. and had retained contributions from litigants of £23.5m.[44] But throughout its history, the overwhelming bulk of services provided by civil legal aid – four-fifths or over – has been in the matrimonial field. One reason is that the means of husbands are not aggregated with those of wives in this situation and most wives therefore qualify.

The third part of the legal aid scheme, *legal advice and assis-*

tance (the Green Form scheme) was the last to be developed. The 1949 Act permitted solicitors to give only oral advice subject to a severe means test. In 1968, the Law Society proposed a new approach by which a solicitor would be able to do up to £25 worth of work – oral or written advice, negotiation, vetting of documents, in fact anything short of actual advocacy – for clients who qualified on the means test.[45] The work could be done anywhere. If the problem required more than £25 worth of work, the solicitors could get permission from the legal aid authorities to exceed the £25 limit. This proposal was implemented in the 1972 Legal Advice and Assistance Act and came into effect in April 1973. In the overwhelming majority of cases the assistance given is within the £25 limit. (In 1976–7 there were 300,807 claims for payment and 15,868 applications for authority to exceed the limit. Of these 79 per cent were granted.[46]) The record for services obtained under the Green Form scheme appears to be held by the Adamsdown law centre which secured services amounting to some £1,800 worth to fight planning proposals made by the local authority.[47]

In most countries legal aid is primarily provided by young practitioners. It is one of the great virtues of the English system that it involves so large a proportion of the profession at all levels of experience. In fact, legal aid is, for most practitioners at the Bar of all levels of seniority a greater source of income than private work, and for those who specialise in criminal defence work, legal aid work is virtually the sole source of income. Again, in many countries the lawyer who does legal aid is assigned to the client, whereas under the English scheme the client is free to select any lawyer willing to take his case. If he does not know of any, he will be assisted to find one, but none can be foisted on him against his will.

The legal aid scheme embraces civil and criminal proceedings in all the courts, and legal advice and assistance of any kind including oral and written advice, drafting documents, negotiating and even preparing an argument for the client to present at an oral hearing. The only significant categories of court cases now excluded from the scheme are defamation, relator actions, and election petitions. A Working Party set up by the Lord Chancellor's Office recommended, in 1975, that these be brought within the scheme.[48] Legal aid does not, as

yet, extend to tribunals apart from the Lands Tribunal and the
Employment Appeal Tribunal. The Lord Chancellor's Legal
Aid Advisory Committee recommended, in 1974, that legal
aid be extended to cover all tribunals.[49] Most of those who
gave evidence to the Royal Commission supported this proposal.[50]

It has already been seen that virtually all defendants in the
crown courts are represented on legal aid. The proportion
represented privately in trials and proceedings relating to sentence in 1976 were a mere 2.9 per cent and those unrepresented
were 0.6 per cent.[51] There are no equivalent figures for magistrates' courts, but it is obvious that the more than tenfold
increase between 1966 and 1976 in grants of legal aid for
proceedings in magistrates' courts means that many of those
needing representation now get legal aid. Some no doubt pay
for their own representation, and some are represented
through the Automobile Association, the Royal Automobile
Club and the other private organisations. A study in magistrates' courts in 1976, covering 782 cases in 76 courts, showed
that the defendant was represented in 46 per cent of the cases.[52]
In personal injury cases it seems that about half the cases that
come to trial in the High Court are financed by legal aid[53] and
most of the rest by trade unions.

The work done by the profession

The Bar
There has never been any systematic study of the work of the
Bar, but there can be no doubt that it consists mainly of
advocacy. Some barristers spend much of their time on advising, drafting and other non-court work. This is true, for
instance, of those who do commercial work, tax, trusts or
company law. But these are highly specialised, small fields.
The great majority of the Bar are engaged in criminal, matrimonial and personal injuries work, all of which involve a
great amount of advocacy. Some specialise in one of these
classes of work but most do a mixture. All criminal cases and
all divorce cases have to come to court, and although most
personal injury cases settle before trial, these cases form the
overwhelming majority of those tried in the Queen's Bench

Division. (More than 70 per cent of actions set down for trial in the Queen's Bench Division are for the recovery of damages in personal injury cases.) In addition to advocacy in the higher courts, where barristers have a virtual monopoly over the right of audience, they also appear a great deal in magistrates' courts, county courts and tribunals where they have an equal right of audience with solicitors. There are no official figures for the volume of work done here respectively by the two branches of the profession.[54] The fact that the Bar, which still attracts most of the ablest people in the profession, should be so massively involved in advocacy provides a fascinating contrast with the position in the United States. There, on the whole, the ablest lawyers go to practise in the Wall Street or equivalent firms engaged in corporate and commercial work. Most of the best English lawyers deploy their talents mainly in handling criminal and personal injuries cases on behalf of individuals; the best American lawyers tend to work for large corporations.

Two of the three main classes of work handled by the Bar (crime and matrimonial cases) are dominated by legal aid and the third (personal injury work) is greatly affected by it. The Bar's remuneration survey conducted for the Royal Commission showed that barristers earned 43 per cent of their income from public funds (16 per cent for prosecution work, 19 per cent from criminal legal aid and 8 per cent from civil legal aid); 48 per cent from private work (4 per cent criminal and 44 per cent civil); and 9 per cent from miscellaneous sources (including 2 per cent from judicial work and 2 per cent from overseas clients).[55] But some parts of the Bar were much more dependent on publicly funded work than others. For London Chancery and Specialist Bars, public funds represented only about 5 per cent or less of their gross income, whereas on the circuits the figure was some 65 per cent. Even QCs with circuit practices earned more than 60 per cent of their income from public funds.[56]

The solicitors' branch

Whereas the work of the Bar is primarily advocacy in courts and tribunals, that of the solicitors' branch is mainly property transfers. The report of the National Prices and Incomes Board (PIB) in 1968 showed the extraordinarily high proportion of the profession's income earned from this single class of work. Property work accounted for a total of 71.3 per cent of income: conveyancing (55.6 per cent), probate and the administration of estates (13.6 per cent), leases (2.1 per cent). Litigation and related work brought in 17.4 per cent of income, and the balance of 11.3 per cent was made up of all other non-litigation business, including advice, negotiation and drafting for the business and commercial communities and for ordinary individuals.[57]

A study in 1977 based on interviews with a random sample of 103 partners in different kinds of firms in the West Midlands gave additional colour to these findings. They were asked to rank nine categories of work in order of importance for the firm, on a seven-point scale ranging from 'extremely important' (scored as 7) to 'not at all important' (scored as 1). Importance was to be judged by the time spent on that class of work rather than on the revenue derived from it. Property and conveyancing were said to be scale 7 or 6 in 90 per cent of the practices. Wills and probate work were the next most important class of work, with 58 per cent of firms placing it in scale 7 or 6. The third class of work was matrimonial matters. The mean scores for the nine categories are shown in Table 1.1.

Table 1.1

Importance of different categories of work in
103 West Midlands practices

	Mean score*
Property and conveyancing	6.65
Wills, Probate, etc.	5.41
Matrimonial	5.18
Other litigation	4.68
Personal injury	4.60
Criminal	4.52
Company and commercial	4.03
Tax matters	3.61
European and International	1.60

*7 = the maximum (extremely important)
 1 = the minimum (not at all important)

Source: David Podmore, 'The Work of the Solicitor in Private Practice', *Law Society's Gazette*, 20 July 1977, p. 636.

Although the mean scores of the four next categories of work were much the same, the spread across the seven categories of importance differed. For personal injury work and 'other litigation' there was a fairly even spread with a very small number of practices in which these types of work were 'not at all important'. Criminal work and company and commercial work 'bunched' at both ends of the scale with some firms regarding them as very important and others as not at all important. In these fields it appears that some firms do a great deal of the work and others very little. Tax work seemed to be of some importance to most firms.

The West Midlands study also threw some light on the extent to which individual solicitors specialised within firms. Analysis showed that whereas the work of firms was fairly broadly spread across the seven categories of importance, the work of solicitors tended to be polarised to a much greater extent between the extremes of 'extremely important' and 'not at all important'. Interviews confirmed, over and over again, the need for the firm to have a broad range but for individual solicitors to specialise. But although most firms may offer a broad range of services, there is also a considerable degree of specialisation even between firms. The big City firm specialises in the work of the business community and of wealthy individuals. At the other end of the spectrum some firms specialise in the legal problems of the poor. The official civil legal aid statistics show, for instance, that in 1975–6, 5 per cent of offices received one-third of the payments made under the fund, 14 per cent had three-fifths of the payments, and 24 per cent of the offices received four-fifths of payments.[58] The average receipt per office in 1975–6 was £4,908, but there were 332 offices that received between £20,000 and £40,000 that year, 51 that collected between £40,000 and £60,000 and 22 that got over £60,000.[59]

Detailed study of firms in the Birmingham areas confirmed the extent to which legal aid work is done by a relatively small number of firms. Half the legal aid work in the area appeared to be handled by one-tenth of the firms, about a fifth of the firms did some legal aid work and 70 per cent did hardly any.[60] But even the firms that did the greatest volume of legal aid work also had substantial revenue from conveyancing.[61] The Birmingham study reported that some forms of work, notably crime, were unpopular. Almost half the firms in that study never, or almost never, dealt with it.[62] Almost a fifth of all firms appeared reluctant to take on litigation of any kind except for established clients.[63] The authors thought this might have the effect of discriminating against clients in the poor areas – few of whom may qualify as 'established' for these purposes.[64] Firms that got work they did not handle referred the client to other firms known to deal with that class of work.[65]

It had been hoped by some that the introduction of the Green Form scheme in 1973 would broaden the work done by solicitors. Clients with new kinds of problem might now feel able to consult solicitors, and solicitors, for their part, might be able to make a profit out of advisory work that had previously been unremunerative. New offices might even be opened in under-solicitored areas.[66] These hopes have not been realised. The number of claims for payment under the scheme has been rising steadily each year, from 109,000 in 1973–4. It was 199,000 in the second year, 253,000 in the third and 301,000 in the fourth. But the matters dealt with under the Green Form scheme are largely the same as those handled under the main legal aid scheme. Matrimonial problems have dominated, being between 56 and 59 per cent of the total in each of the three years from 1974. The next largest category in each year has been criminal matters (between 12 and 15 per cent), and no other class of problem has accounted for more than 5 per cent of the total.[67] There is therefore no indication as yet that the new scheme has significantly altered the nature of work handled by solicitors as a whole.

The private sector is, by definition, dependent on profits to survive. Time must be spent on administration, training of students, professional self-improvement and other non-billable activities. But it would be surprising if any great proportion of lawyers' time was consciously devoted to non-fee-generating work. There was a moment in the early 1970s when it seemed in the United States as if there might be a major shift of emphasis among private practitioners toward voluntary (pro bono) work.[67a] The leading firms in New York, Chicago and other large cities were having to offer their new recruits time off from work to serve in offices in the slums. Some of the firms themselves financed poverty law offices, or donated the full-time services of members of their own staff.[67b] But the rhetoric of this development was probably much greater than its true extent and by the mid-1970s the mood had changed and interest in pro bono work had somewhat subsided. A survey of the pro bono activities of American lawyers in 1973–4 based on a nationwide, randomly drawn sample of 1,450 US lawyers showed that, on average, 6 per cent of a lawyer's billable time was devoted to unpaid legal work, mainly for individuals in traditional fields such as matrimonial, family and criminal law. Thirty per cent said they did no such work in billable hours. Outside billable hours, the American profession did an average of twenty-seven hours of such work per year – about half an hour per week. Nearly two-fifths reported that they did no such work out of hours. The work done out of office hours was mainly for organisations – usually charities, churches, civic organisations and educational institutions. There was little work done either in or out of hours in the fields of poverty law, welfare, employment, civil rights or minority problems, nor in work directed to changing the law or the legal system. The smaller, lower-status firms did most of the unpaid work that was done for the poor or disadvantaged.[68].

In 1975, at its annual meeting the House of Delegates of the American Bar Association passed a resolution that 'it is a basic professional responsibility of each lawyer engaged in the practice of law to provide public interest legal services'. Such service was defined as being work 'without fee or at substantially reduced fee' in the fields of poverty law, civil rights law, public rights, representation of charitable organisations, or activity designed to increase the availability of legal services or the administration of justice.[69] It would be pleasant to think that the passage of such a resolution would significantly increase the volume of unpaid work done by the profession, but realism suggests that this is unlikely.

Means of expanding the profession's work

Both sides of the English profession currently face threats to their economic future. The Bar is threatened chiefly by the proposals of the Pearson Royal Commission on Civil Liability which are likely to have the effect of reducing the personal injury work available to lawyers by making compensation available through insurance instead of common law claims. On the solicitors' side this will drastically affect the relatively small number of firms that handle this work in bulk, but for barristers the effects will be much more general, since a much higher proportion of barristers do this work and it involves a much larger slice of the Bar's income. Barristers could also lose work if the Royal Commission on Legal Services were to recommend expanded rights of audience in the higher courts for solicitors (see p. 181 below). Solicitors, for their part, face the possibility that the Royal Commission will recommend the abolition of the solicitors' conveyancing monopoly or, at least, its extension to include a new category of licensed conveyancers (see p. 191 below). Even if proposals to allow others to compete with solicitors over conveyancing were implemented, it does not follow that the profession would necessarily lose a large share of the work, particularly in the short run. But it would probably lose some.

In other fields, however, the profession either is, or could be, expanding its work. Crime will, presumably, continue to boom. The number of divorces will probably continue to rise. It rose from 25,000 in 1960 to 126,700 in 1976,[70] and although legal aid has now been withdrawn from the actual hearings in most instances and do-it-yourself divorce is being officially encouraged (see p. 326 below), there will always be a great deal of work for the legal profession arising out of broken marriages and broken homes. The importance of representation in tribunals is increasingly recognised, and the work for the legal profession there is likely to increase considerably, especially in Industrial Tribunals – the more so, of course, if legal aid is extended to cover tribunal work. But the greatest likely expansion of services provided by solicitors in private practice is through the growing knowledge of potential clients and of lay advisers of the value of using laywers (see Chapter 9). Hitherto, the services of English lawyers have been used by individuals (as opposed to businesses) mainly for five classes of work – conveyancing, probate, personal injury cases, matrimonial disputes and crime. If lawyers are to provide fuller services, they will have both to attract more clients in presently well developed fields and, also, to open up new areas of work, in which lawyers have not traditionally been much used. (For methods of financing a broader range of legal services see pp. 213–32 below.)

Institutional advertising

There are a variety of ways of attempting to expand the work done by the profession. One obviously is institutional advertising. The Law Society has, over the years, done a great deal to inform the public about the services that lawyers can provide. It has produced film strips, wall charts and a book for use in schools, ten paperback books in a series entitled 'It's Your Law', designed for the man in the street, and a set of free leaflets under the general title 'See a Solicitor'. It has a senior official responsible for Professional and Public Relations, and a chief press officer, with supporting staff.[71]

Advertising has been used with some apparent success by the Central Office of Information in campaigns to make legal aid better known to the public. In 1972, a two-month pilot campaign was conducted in the Newcastle upon Tyne area using a television commercial backed by press advertising, posters and leaflets. Clients wanting the help of a solicitor were encouraged to send a coupon (printed in newspapers), stating the nature of the problem, to a specified address from which they would be sent the name and address of a suitable firm. A new logogram was devised for the campaign and has been used ever since for legal aid.[72] In March 1973 the Central Office of Information financed a more ambitious campaign for a few months to advertise the new Green Form scheme. The campaign used television, radio, the national press and some two million leaflets, posters and pamphlets.[73] The campaign continued subsequently on a much reduced scale in the press only. In 1977, the Law Society raised the practising certificate by £10 in order to finance an experimental National Information Campaign from October 1977 to February 1978 using 45-second advertisements to be shown on commercial television at weekends, and cartoon strips for use in national daily and Sunday newspapers.[74] There were to be before-and-after surveys to test the impact of the campaign.

The main problems with institutional advertising are its expense and its cost-effectiveness. In mid-1977, a quarter-page advertisement in a national newspaper cost about £1,500 and in a provincial paper some £400. Television cost some £10,000

per half minute.[75] The Law Society's £10 a head for the
National Information Campaign raised £300,000, which in
this context is therefore not a large sum and which, it was felt,
could not be stretched beyond a five-month period. Yet it is
difficult to imagine the profession being willing to produce
larger sums unless there were felt to be clear dividends. Previous research results in this regard are mixed.

Research conducted before and after the campaign in Newcastle upon Tyne showed a dramatic increase in the proportion
of people interviewed who said they would seek help from a
solicitor. 200 people in social classes C2, D and E were asked
whether they would use solicitors for their problems. Before
the campaign only 1 per cent said they would; after the campaign the proportion rose to 28 per cent.[76] But this huge
increase in the proportion prepared to use solicitors contrasts
with the test reported in May 1976, conducted by advertising
agencies for the Young Solicitors, in the Leeds area. An advertisement was published in a prominent position in three successive issues of the *Yorkshire Post* on the business page. The
target audience was ABC1 householders aged 24 or over who
claimed to read the paper at least once a week. Interviews
before and after showed that there was no apparent shift
during the four months of the campaign in the attitude of the
public to solicitors, and the campaign did not succeed in
persuading people to accept the suitability of solicitors on tax
matters (specifically the Capital Transfer Tax).[77] It may be
that the higher social classes aimed at in this survey are more
resistant to such advertising than the lower social classes tested
in the Newcastle upon Tyne study.

Surveys conducted on behalf of the Central Office of Information suggest that, although some improvements can be
made in public awareness through institutional advertising, it
may not be the best way to use scarce resources. A study in
May 1973 by Metra Oxford Consulting Ltd inquired into the
effectiveness of the intense publicity campaign that Spring to
launch the new Green Form scheme. It showed that in March
1973 before the campaign, awareness of the scheme among the
general public was 24 per cent and in May it had increased to 48
per cent.[78] (Both before and after, the level of awareness was
greater in the higher than in the lower social classes – 29 per
cent for the ABC1 group, 23 per cent for the C2 and 19 per cent .

for the DE before the campaign, went to 54 per cent, 47 per cent and 44 per cent respectively.[79]) Research a year later indicated that 84 per cent of respondents were aware that there was *some* way of getting help on legal matters without having to pay the full legal costs, but awareness of the Green Form scheme by name had slipped from 48 per cent in May 1973 to 27 per cent. Knowledge of the Green Form scheme was especially low amongst those eligible to use it. On the other hand, 79 per cent had some knowledge of legal aid – though it was greater among men than women (82 per cent against 76 per cent) and among higher social classes (87 per cent for ABC1, 83 per cent for C2 and 65 per cent for DE).[80]

Both of the studies done for the Central Office established that, not surprisingly, referral agencies are more knowledgeable than ordinary members of the public. In 1973 a sample survey amongst six categories of recommending individuals and agencies showed that the overall average of awareness of the Green Form Scheme was 76 per cent in May, compared with 53 per cent before the five-week intensive advertising campaign in March.[81] By the following year, this proportion had slipped to 62 per cent, but 98 per cent of recommenders (compared with 79 per cent of clients) had heard of legal aid.[82] The survey organisation that conducted the 1974 study suggested that the best strategy was probably to keep the key terms – New Legal Aid, the Green Form Scheme, Legal Aid, Legal Advice – in the public eye and to devote most effort to increasing the efficiency with which recommenders handled cases with a legal component. Even though recommenders had heard of the legal aid scheme and even though they identified many of their clients' problems as having a legal aspect, they did not seem quick to refer them to providers of legal help. (The report suggested the hypothesis 'that recommenders tend to be deterred from referring their clients to direct sources of legal help, except in cases of obvious need, by psychological barriers'.[83])

The Lord Chancellor's Advisory Committee is therefore likely to be right in concluding that 'mass publicity for the legal aid scheme ... is not good value for money'.[84] Unless the individual who sees an advertisement about legal aid or legal services has a felt need for the help of a lawyer at that moment, it seems that the advertising will not make much impact. Saturation coverage in the press and television would no doubt affect the level of public knowledge about the potential uses of lawyers, but this is prohibitively expensive. So far as money spent on legal aid advertising is concerned, the Advisory Committee recommended to the Royal Commission that 'better results are obtained by concentrating on providing information at the point of immediate need' to the advisory workers who come into contact with so many people who need help on legal matters. For those in the population who go to Citizens' Advice Bureaux (CABs), social workers, the police, doctors and the like, advertising directed to lay intermediaries may be effective. But for those who do not, general advertising – so far as it can be afforded – may still be the best hope for increasing the use of lawyers for those with legal problems.

Advertising by individual firms and solicitors

Advertising on behalf of the profession as a whole is, of course, not the only way of reaching the public. There is also advertising by individual firms. Such advertising, however, raises ethical problems. The traditional attitude of lawyers to individual advertising, like that of all professions, is negative. Lord Justice Scott summed it up in a case decided in 1945: 'touting for clients, like advertising, is fundamentally inconsistent with the interests of the public and with the honour of the profession. The function of a solicitor is to advise or negotiate or fight for a client, but only if retained. The client may seek him, but he must not seek the client'.[85] The Law Society's evidence to the Royal Commission stated that the special relationship of trust between the lawyer and his client required the lawyer to refrain from some of the practices acceptable in the market place.

> In particular, while professional men constantly compete with one another in reputation for ability, they do not compete by way of advertisement and other methods familiar and unobjectionable in the business world. The Society believes that self-advertisement by individual solicitors is wholly inconsistent with the proper relationship between solicitor and client.[86]

There are various reasons for the profession's hostility to solicitation of business – the fear that it would undermine the relationship of trust between lawyer and client, that competition and 'shopping around' are irrelevant in the context of professional services, that self-advertisement may be misleading and above all that it is undignified. Partly these arguments are easily countered. Thus it is silly to suggest, as the Law Society's latest *Guide to Professional Conduct* does, that 'advertising can have little or no effect upon the supply of the service, since it does not increase the number of solicitors . . .'[87] The whole point of advertising is to increase demand for the service. If it succeeds, the number of solicitors or at least the extent of their practices will, by definition, increase. It is equally absurd to argue, as the same guide does, that 'the practice of "shopping around", which may save money or yield improved quality in the case of commercial products, is of no relevance when professional services are sought'.[88] A well-advised client will consult as widely as possible as to the relative merits of the available practitioners before deciding where to take his legal work. If solicitors felt themselves under the pressure of informed 'shopping around' it is likely that they would respond with improved standards and lower charges, as in any other field of human activity. Competition and the threat of the loss of custom help to concentrate a man's mind, whether he is a lowly tradesman or of a more exalted station.

It is of course true that the client is not well placed to evaluate either the quality of service provided by a lawyer or the accuracy of any self-advertisement. But the client is not *now* able to judge the quality of service and is nevertheless required to select his lawyer. He is not likely to be worse placed if lawyers are allowed to do more to attract custom and to compete. It is possible that some of the information placed at the public's disposal by lawyers eager to solicit work may be inaccurate or misleading – though the risks of this are presumably less with members of a profession than in the case of the ordinary commercial community. But the information allowed to be communicated can be limited by rules to matters capable of factual statements. There can be a prohibition on advertising that is false or misleading, backed by the possibility of disciplinary action. Moreover, there is already the possibility that a client will be misled into using a firm in the belief that it is competent in the field in question, when it is not, or that its charges are reasonable having regard to the work involved or to those of other firms, when they are not. Little is done by the profession to reduce the incidence of such errors.

The more complex problem is at what point advertising or solicitation of business become so undignified as to erode the public's trust and confidence. No one proposes that lawyers be permitted to take full-page advertisements in national newspapers or to use flashing neon signs. If the standards of ethics of professional men are higher than those of the world of business and commerce, one of the reasons is that there is an expectation that they should be, shared by clients and the members of the profession. A loss of public confidence in the probity of the professions might in turn affect the quality of their ethical conduct and standards. It is right, therefore, to have regard to what the public expects as one of the measures of what ought to be permitted. But this is not the same as saying that standards are immutable. Until recently banks did not advertise. It seems unlikely that the public's confidence in the banking system has been diminished by the advertising now undertaken in this field. Even without laying any special emphasis on the fact that lawyers work in the field of the administration of justice, there can be no doubt that the sense of trust between a client and his professional adviser is important. The question is therefore not whether it ought to be preserved but at what point it is truly threatened. This must necessarily be a question requiring judgment capable of reflecting changing standards.

Rule 1 of the Solicitors' Practice Rules forbids the inviting of instructions for work, advertising and touting. In the past this meant, for instance, that a solicitor who appeared on radio or television or wrote an article in the lay press could give his name or his profession but not both. This rule has recently been abolished. In the past a solicitor was not permitted to accept work where he knew he had been specifically named by a lay referral-agency; the client had simply to be shown a list of names of local practitioners and left to make his own inevitably uninformed choice. This rule has likewise been abolished. A solicitor may still not advertise in the lay press the opening of a new office and may place only one advertisement in the lay press of a change of address of an existing office. Until recently a solicitor's entry in a directory or law list had to be confined to his name, address and description. Now he may also state the work he undertakes (or does not undertake) provided this does not amount to a statement that he or his firm specialises in any class of work.

This development in turn led to the most important form of advertising yet permitted by the Law Society – its Referral or Solicitors' Lists, first published in 1976. These lists were produced at public expense to indicate the firms that undertook legal aid work. They were prepared on a local basis. There were twenty-eight separate booklets covering some 7,000 firms. Each booklet contains the names of the firms in its area that do legal aid, and an indication as to which of the fourteen listed categories of work the firms deal with. The lists also give details of CAB rota schemes, of legal advice centres and of law centres. Some 25,000 copies were distributed, free of charge, to citizens' advice bureaux, public libraries, local authority social service departments, town halls, police stations, and court offices. The lists are to be kept up-to-date and new editions will be published on a regular basis. The second edition, published in December 1977, included two innovations. One was information as to whether firms were willing to give a preliminary interview of up to half an hour, costing not more than £5, inclusive of VAT. 73 per cent of the 7,000 offices on the lists were participating.[89] (Where the contribution under the Green Form scheme is nil or less than £5, the lesser amount applies.) The second change is that firms can indicate an emergency telephone number – either the number of a member of the firm or the office number if arrangements have been made for calls to be intercepted and re-directed to the firms 'duty solicitors'. A message recording machine is not allowed.[90]

The Referral Lists have been criticised on three counts.[91] One is that they only apply to legal aid work. The Law Society is, however, planning to expand the concept to include also non-legal-aid work – though it remains to be seen whether the cost of such additional material (or different lists) will also be met out of public funds. The second criticism made is that, when a firm indicates that it does a certain category of work, there is no guarantee that it actually has any competence in the field. This criticism appears misconceived. An entry in a Referral List showing that a firm does, say, criminal work may carry an implicit suggestion of competence in that field, but there is no way of guaranteeing this without some form of external control (on which see p. 154 below). Referral Lists should be seen for what they are – an indication of willingness to undertake work, not a warranty of ability. In fact, the more solicitors express willingness to do work they have not done before, the more they are likely to expand their service to the public. If clients come in, solicitors will gradually 'gear up' for the new work. No doubt, the first few clients will suffer from the lawyers' relative inexperience in that area of work, but that is true of many services provided by lawyers. It is a normal part of legal practice to have to learn how to handle unfamiliar kinds of work.

The third criticism is that the lists do not contain enough information. Thus, it has been suggested that they should give details not only of firms but of individual solicitors and should show their status in the firm, date of qualification, and age. These criticisms have been met in the proposals of the Law Society of Scotland for a Directory of Services and Specialists. All solicitors in Scotland were circulated in May 1977 and invited to forward details (and £2) for each solicitors' entry for the Directory. This was to include details of the name and address of the firm, its hours of opening, the names of solicitors in the firm (partners and employees), their year of admission, whether they undertook work in the different levels of court and which of twenty-five categories of work they normally handled. The breakdown of work categories is very detailed (e.g. it distinguishes between Divorce, Separation and Custody, Adoptions, Immigration/Racial, Accident claims, Town and Country Planning, Compulsory Purchase, Tax returns, Tax planning, etc.). The Directory also invites firms to show whether they will handle legal aid work and whether their members speak any foreign language. It is to be widely distributed. Scottish solicitors are also asked to indicate on their returns whether any solicitor in the firm 'has a reasonable level of experience' in any of a list of more esoteric specialised fields or in any other such field not listed. The names of such specialists are not to be included in the Directory but will be kept by the Law Society for use in response to specific inquiries from members of the profession or of the public for assistance in finding solicitors with expertise in specialist fields. The categories in this list include Oil and Gas law; Patents, Designs and Trade Marks; Shipping and navigation law; Fishery law; EEC law; Newspaper and publishing law; as well as some more usual fields such as Taxation, Planning, Bankruptcy, Industrial Relations and Trade Union law.

It is inevitable that the present trend of liberalising the rules against advertising will continue. In July 1976, the Monopolies Commission proposed that solicitors be allowed to advertise in any form whatever, subject only to the qualification that such advertisements should not claim superiority over other firms, should not contain inaccurate or misleading statements and should not be such as to be 'reasonably regarded as likely to bring the profession into disrepute'.[92] Subject to these conditions, the Commission thought that firms should be able to advertise in the press or other media or by circulars 'or by any other means'.[93]

The Commission thought there were two main objections to the existing restrictions on advertising. First, they deprived users and potential users of helpful information, and second, they reduced the stimulus to cost-saving, to innovation, to the setting up of new practices and to competition amongst solicitors. The Commission rejected the argument that advertising would undermine either the profession's ethical conduct or the public's confidence. As to the first, it thought that 'the standards of the profession and the sense of responsibility of its members are in our view too strong for this to happen'.[94] It followed that it did not think that advertising would lead to solicitors becoming any less worthy of trust than at present. Nor did the Commission believe that clients would think less well of them. Clients trusted solicitors even though it was 'difficult to believe that solicitors' clients are so naive as not to recognise that there is inevitably a commercial element in their relationship with their solicitors'.[95] There was no serious danger that this trust would diminish 'if solicitors were allowed to advertise within limits', though this could alter if misleading or extravagant claims were made, and, even if this was unlikely, it should be guarded against.[96] (A study based on 651 interviews of a random sample in Scotland showed that the overwhelming majority, far from being scandalised by advertising, said they would welcome a solicitor contacting them to give legal advice, if they were in a hypothetical situation involving a legal problem.[97]) The Commission recommended that advertisements might refer to the qualifications of members of firms (including 'allusions to particular classes of client to whom services were offered or to particular kinds of service which were offered'), the convenience of the firm's location, its expedition in dealing with clients' affairs or the level of fees charged.

The lawyers have so far not been very receptive to the Commission's proposals. The Law Society of England and the Law Society of Scotland both rejected the idea of advertising by individual firms other than through Referral Lists. But the English Law Society's evidence to the Royal Commission, published in February 1978, stated that the Referral Lists, 'should be advertised appropriately in local newspapers', and that individual solicitors should be able to place in local papers summaries of the information in the Lists. This could be a very valuable innovation. A second proposal to be considered was that solicitors be permitted to indicate outside their offices some information about the work they undertake, their charge for an initial half-hour interview and information about the legal aid scheme.[98] There were also signs in autumn 1977 that the Law Society might somewhat relax its very strict rules as to the size and style of nameplates, lettering on windows, window displays and other forms of attracting potential custom from passers-by.

Meanwhile, in June 1977 the United States Supreme Court held in *Bates and Osteen v. State Bar of Arizona*[99] that American lawyers could undertake some forms of advertising. There can be little doubt that this will prove to be a most important decision. Two lawyers opened what they called a 'legal clinic' in Phoenix, Arizona, aiming to provide legal services at modest fees to persons of moderate income who did not qualify for legal aid. They accepted only routine cases such as uncontested divorces for which costs could be kept down by use of paralegal workers, automatic typewriters, and standardised forms and office-procedures. After operating for two years they advertised in a local newspaper that they were offering 'legal services at very reasonable fees' and listed their fees for uncontested divorces, uncontested non-business bankruptcies and other matters. Disciplinary proceedings were brought against them but the US Supreme Court eventually held that the blanket suppression of advertising by lawyers violated the free speech clause of the First Amendment and that lawyers might constitutionally advertise their prices for routine legal services. The court[100] expressly rejected all the well-known traditional arguments against advertising by members of a profession – that such advertising would have an adverse effect on professionalism,[101] would be inherently misleading,[102] would have bad effects on the administration of justice,[103] would produce undesirable economic effects,[104] would have an adverse effect on the quality of legal services[105] and would be difficult to police.[106] It did hold, however, that such advertising if false, deceptive or misleading, could continue to be restrained and that it could be made subject to reasonable restrictions on the time, place and manner of such advertising. The court expressly did not deal with advertising relating to the *quality* of legal services, nor with personal solicitation of business by lawyers or their agents, for instance in hospitals or on the site of an accident.

The *American Bar Association Journal* in its issue of August 1977 said that, in the first four weeks after the decision, there had not been a great rush to advertise. In many cities not even half a dozen ads had appeared in daily papers, though in the *Los Angeles Times* there had been a full page of lawyer ads within days of the decision. Only seven of the seventy advertisements on that page listed prices. Most mentioned rather the kind of work the firm did, sometimes without comment, sometimes as 'emphasis in', 'experienced in', and sometimes with the claim 'specialist in'. (For discussion of the problem of claims to specialist ability see pp. 152—57 below.) Little had happened to 'overthrow professional dignity, undermine justice or con the public'.[107]

Responding to the Supreme Court's decision, the American Bar Association in August 1977 amended its rules to permit lawyers to advertise by print or radio, but not television, in their own areas – name, address, age, fields of law in which the lawyer or his firm practises or specialises, educational background, date of admission to the profession, public offices held, foreign language ability, whether credit cards are accepted, fee for an initial consultation, availability on request of a written fee schedule or estimate, hourly rate or fixed fees for specific legal services. The rules state that, with permission of the client, lawyers may advertise their names. But advertisements must not contain a 'false, fraudulent, misleading, deceptive, self-laudatory or unfair statement or claim'.[108]

The effect of the *Bates* decision will be felt on many continents. The English profession predictably reacted critically to the Supreme Court's decision.[109] In its evidence to the Royal Commission the Law Society said that 'there are no degrees of touting and that all soliciting of potential clients should continue to be prohibited'.[110] But its deeds speak larger than its rhetoric. Nameplates, business cards, entries in law lists, professional directories, telephone directories and Referral Lists (not to mention joining the golf club, the Rotarians or other similar bodies), are all forms of touting and solicitation of business. They are, however, officially approved and thereby cease to be *called* touting and solicitation. The line of what is officially approved has been considerably extended in the past decade. The Lord Chancellor's Advisory Committee on Legal Aid in its evidence to the Royal Commission said that although the new Referral Lists were a start in the right direction, 'a great deal more can yet be done'. If lawyers were to be sufficiently accessible, and if reluctance to consult them were to be reduced, 'the public must know more about them: where and who they are, how they can be contacted, what services they do and do not provide'. To the extent that restrictions on advertising unduly prevented the spread of information on these matters, the Committee said: 'we think that the restrictions should be relaxed'.[111] There is little doubt that the process of relaxation will continue.

New techniques for providing legal services by private practitioners
Several techniques have been developed to enable the profession to provide a fuller legal service. The Law Society in February 1978 suggested to the Royal Commission that anyone who thought he had a legal problem should be able to dial an advertised phone number for taped information as to how to find a suitable lawyer. Another approach has been the legal advice facility manned by lawyers in the evening or at other out-of-office times, usually on a voluntary basis. This form of charitable work has in fact been known in the profession for many decades. What is new is the extent to which it has re-

cently grown. In October 1972 the Legal Action Group published a report entitled 'Legal Advice Centres – an explosion'. This said that, at that date, it had found 61 legal advice centres. Of these only 13 had been in existence prior to 1968. There is no current figure for the number of such centres today, but there is no doubt that it has greatly increased – probably to well over 200. The extent of the service they can provide is obviously limited. They lack funds; an adviser at one session may not attend again for several weeks; clients who need continuing help must normally be sent on to the private profession; and there are ethical rules which limit the work that barristers and solicitors can do in such centres basically to oral advice confirmed by a written note or the drafting of letters to be signed by the client.[112] The main value of such centres is for diagnostic consultations, referral and the handling of problems that only require oral advice.

Solicitors in private practice who take part in voluntary advice schemes are severely restricted by the Practice Rules in the extent to which they can take clients who need continuing help back to their own offices.[113] The Law Society has the power to grant waivers from these Practice Rules. In the past few years a large number of waivers have been granted – mainly for advice schemes run on a rota basis in citizens' advice bureaux. The clients are referred to the solicitor's advice session with the client. The interview in the bureau is free of charge. If the client then needs further help from a solicitor, the solicitor who has already seen him is permitted to take the case back to his own office on the normal basis – either paying or on legal aid, depending on the client's financial situation. The number of Law Society waivers for such schemes has risen rapidly. In April 1972 there were 5; by September 1975, 87; by October 1976, 169; and in autumn 1977 there were some 200 such schemes in operation. The Law Society estimated in 1976 that there might be some 4,000 solicitors involved in rota schemes up and down the country dealing with 80,000 bureau interviews each year, of which probably about one-third would be referred back to solicitors' offices for further help.[114]

Another variation on the rota system has been the duty solicitor scheme started in magistrates' courts. This was first seriously proposed in 1971 by Justice (the British Section of the International Commission of Jurists) as a means of assisting the unrepresented defendant on his first court appearance.[115] The duty solicitor's main function would be to advise the defendant as to his plea; if he decided to plead guilty, the duty solicitor would make a plea of mitigation; if he chose to plead not guilty, the duty solicitor would help him with an application for legal aid, make a request for bail and ask for an adjournment. When the report was first published, it did not evoke much positive response, but gradually the idea has caught on. The first scheme was started in Bristol in 1972. By September 1975 there were 29; a year later there were 61 and in February 1977 the number had risen to 79. The Law Society's evidence to the Royal Commission stated that the schemes had 'proved successful and should be supported and extended'.[116]

The next stage of development is likely to be through the combination of waivers from the Practice Rules with fuller use of the legal aid and the advice and assistance schemes. The present expanding systems of rotas in magistrates' courts and citizens' advice bureaux could be applied equally well in prisons,[117] hospitals, accommodation for the elderly, social service departments or indeed any form of community or neighbourhood advice facilities. The only limit is the willingness of the local legal profession to man such services. Provided such work pays sufficiently well to make it economically viable, these schemes could offer a potentially useful source of new work for the profession.

The chief problem with the Green Form scheme for the purpose is the very steep contribution required of all but the poorest, and the cut-off point which excludes most people in ordinary work.[118] The new fixed fee scheme of half an hour's diagnostic advice for £5 or so, negotiated with Local Law Societies by the CABs, promises to be a major breakthrough. But at present it is not only new but voluntary. It should be incorporated in the Green Form scheme so that for the first half hour's advice the client pays either nothing (if on supplementary benefit) or a flat rate of, say, £5 irrespective of means. The state would pay the lawyer £5 for each client to whom advice is given for nothing. For the rest it could either pay nothing (leaving it to the profession to provide the service at a slight loss as a form of public service or loss leader), or, if this becomes too burdensome for solicitors, it could supplement the client's basic £5 to make it up to some more appropriate figure. A low, flat-rate non–means-tested fee for a diagnostic interview could have an important impact in removing the public's reluctance to go to a lawyer for fear of the cost.[119] Even more important sources of work may develop through new techniques in the financing of legal services discussed in Chapter 7 (pp. 213–32 below).

Another approach to increasing legal services to the public is the type of law practice whose advertisements led to the Supreme Court's decision on advertising. A cut-price lawyer's service on the supermarket model may be both feasible and of adequate quality. Provided the lawyers who operate such a service select their cases with some care and handle only routine transactions, they may be able to combine professional standards with lower fees. A Committee of the American Bar Association has recommended that experiments with such clinics might be tried in non–contested domestic relations cases, individual bankruptcies, traffic cases, landlord-tenant and social security problems and simple wills. The crucial question was whether the work could be standardised and whether forms and para-professionals could be utilised. The ABA itself in 1975 approved the basic idea of such clinics and encouraged local bar associations to ask it for funding of pilot projects. In June 1976 it approved a grant of $60,000 for an experimental clinic in Philadelphia.[120]

The professional man's natural reaction may be sceptical. Such a service, he will say, must be defective since professional work is, by definition, incapable of routinisation. Yet, in reality, much lawyers' work is routine and is in fact treated as such by good as well as by bad lawyers. In most firms of solicitors, conveyances, wills, leases and other standard documents are taken from precedents used over and over again in the office. Divorces can be handled on a routine basis. So, to an extent, can personal injuries litigation. The firm that can 'gear up' for bulk work and still retain a reputation for competence can, if it chooses, pass on economies of scale to the customer and thereby hope to increase its own practice. By reducing the cost of legal services, it may not merely attract work from competitors but actually increase the total volume of work coming to the profession. This is particularly likely to occur if the firm is permitted to advertise its lower fees – thus inviting new as well as existing custom. (On price competition see pp. 208–10, 253 below).

But it must be recognised that this form of practice will be unattractive to many lawyers. It offers little reward to those looking for intellectual challenge, the stimulus of complex problems or the satisfaction of doing a job worthy of a professional person. Irrespective of its actual quality, it will be regarded by the profession as providing a second- or even third-rate service and will therefore have low prestige or status.[121] If it proves attractive to any large number of practitioners it will either be because they are hungry or because they are committed to the ideal of low-cost services for the general public – or both. First indications from the US were not very encouraging, but latterly it seems as if the idea may be making some headway. One Baltimore office, for instance, was reported in October 1977 to have opened no less than sixteen offices in its first year of operation.[122] But whether such an experiment is successful or not, the English profession does seem generally more open to new ideas than in the past. Law centres, rota schemes in CABs, duty solicitor schemes, a mass of new legal advice facilities have all been started in the past decade. A firm in Bristol in a working-class area asked the Law Society in autumn 1977 to permit it to advertise 'self-help advice sessions' in the evenings. Clients would be able to use the firm's facilities for a fee of £1. They would be provided with a desk, stationery, reference books and would be able to draft their own letters and documents under the supervision of a solicitor who would be in attendance. The firm envisaged that the scheme might be used for small consumer claims, probate, divorce, adoption, social security claims, tribunal cases and even simple conveyancing.[123] The Royal Commission's report is bound to generate ideas for new ways of providing services to the public. The next decade is likely to see further developments.

2 The Public Sector in Legal Services: A New Concept Established

The single most important recent development in the techniques for providing legal services is that public funds should be used to pay salaries to lawyers to do work not being done by private practitioners. For centuries the legal profession has given its services mainly for fees paid by the individual client to private practitioners. The first large scale departure from this tradition was the twentieth-century innovation of the state providing legal aid funds to enable private practitioners to give the poor similar services to those available for those with means. In England, the development of the legal aid scheme provided by private practitioners took nearly three-quarters of a century, from the Poor Persons Defence Act of 1903 to the Legal Advice and Assistance Act in 1972. By comparison with this slow development, introduction of state salaried lawyers has moved with amazing rapidity.

State salaried lawyers have, of course, been known in many countries as prosecutors in criminal cases – District Attorneys in the United States, Procurators Fiscal in Scotland, the Procureur Général in France, the Staatsanwalt in Germany and similar institutions in most countries in the world. There have also, for many decades, been salaried public defender offices in several countries. In the United States the first Public Defender office was established in Los Angeles County in 1914. In succeeding years similar offices were created in several other jurisdictions.[1] By 1965 the number of public defender offices had grown to 117[2] and by 1977 to over 900.[3] In Australia the first Public Defender office was established in 1916 in Queensland.[4] In 1941, New South Wales set up a Public Defender[5] and a similar office exists in Victoria.[6] There were even examples in Australia of state salaried lawyers in the field of civil work. The New South Wales Public Solicitor was established as long ago as 1943 under the Legal Assistance Act of that year to provide legal aid to low income earners.[7] In England, the

Law Society, in 1942, set up a Services Divorce Department staffed by salaried solicitors to conduct matrimonial cases for members of the armed forces. Most solicitors were serving in the forces and there were not enough private practitioners to handle the work. The Law Society's Divorce Department prepared the paper work and at modest fees instructed counsel to appear in court. By the end of the war the Department had 100 employees including 8 solicitors.[8] The Department was gradually run down in the years after the war and was disbanded in 1961.

In fact (something that is not widely known), the concept of a salaried legal advice service was urged by the Law Society in its evidence to the Rushcliffe Committee and was incorporated both in the Rushcliffe Committee's Report and in the resulting legislation. The 1949 Legal Aid and Advice Act s.7 stated that legal advice under the Act meant 'oral advice on legal questions given by a solicitor *employed whole-time or part-time for the purpose*' (my italics). The original Law Society scheme put to the Rushcliffe Committee was for advice centres in some 250 places, staffed by just under 100 solicitors employed whole-time by the Society, reinforced in less populous areas by solicitors in private practice engaged part-time in the work.[9] There were to be no less than 80 advice centres in London alone.[10] The Rushcliffe Report accepted these proposals but it was implemented in stages[11] and the advice part was postponed. In 1958 the Law Society proposed that the advice scheme should be implemented by using solicitors in their own offices instead of salaried solicitors. The Society's own explanation for this change in policy was that it offered a more economical basis for the scheme which otherwise might not have been implemented at all.[12] The Law Society's proposals were accepted and were implemented in March 1959.

The development of salaried legal services in the United States

But the main development of the salaried lawyer concept has come, in the past ten to fifteen years, mainly as a result of pioneering of this mode of delivering legal services in the United States. Before the mid–1960s there had been no governmental scheme for legal aid in the United States at either the federal or the state level. Legal aid depended on the donations of time and money of public-spirited lawyers and bar associations. At the start of the 1960s there were 236 legal aid societies and 100 public defender offices.[13] But in 1962 their combined budget was under $4m., an amount, it has been estimated, that was less than two-tenths of 1 per cent of the nation's total annual expenditure for the services of lawyers.[14]

The motivating philosophy of legal aid was articulated by Reginald Heber Smith, the leader of the American movement, in his seminal book published in 1919: 'In vast tracts of the civil law and in all of the criminal law related to the more severe crimes, equality in the administration of justice can be had only by supplying attorneys to the poor'. Legal aid societies, he said, should be set up in all the main cities, and those already existing should triple their staffs and multiply their case-loads. 'If these things can be done, that part of the denial of justice which is traceable solely to the inability of the poor to employ counsel will be eliminated, and it is only in this way that the great difficulty of the expense of counsel will be completely overcome.'[15] The function of legal aid, therefore, was to provide representation for those who lacked it. This was the traditional view of legal aid throughout the Western world – the poor person should have a lawyer to do battle for him in the adversary process, otherwise there could be no equality before the law.

In the 1960s, however, a different philosophy emerged through the so-called War on Poverty.[16] In 1963 the Ford Foundation, as part of its 'grey areas' programme, set up Community Progress Inc. in New Haven, the object of which was to establish decentralised service centres which would offer residents the assistance of consumer education specialists, social workers, health services, lawyers and similar aid. The lawyers were to work in teams with social workers to diagnose, refer and co-ordinate the legal problems of the poor.[17] In New York in 1964, a legal unit was established as part of the Mobilisation for Youth Programme. Its first director, Edward Sparer, recommended to the Board that the resources of the unit be focussed on 'a demonstration of the value of legal service to the poor in those very basic areas

where the [legal aid] society was not presently giving services'. The chief objective, he thought, should be to achieve
social change primarily through the use of the test case.[18] The
third of the early neighbourhood lawyer programmes, in
Washington, DC, again funded by the Ford Foundation, was
the Neighbourhood Legal Services Project (NLSP). The
NLSP Board decided to focus its resources primarily on consumer credit practices, housing problems, public assistance
and ex-servicemen's problems, juvenile problems and representation of adult criminal defendants in some classes of work.
The objectives were to combat poverty, to complement existing resources, and to develop test cases in areas with potential
significance for the poor. It established a training programme
for lawyers in the poverty field and produced more than a
thousand pages of written materials stressing the different
kinds of legal attack that could be made against laws and
practices affecting low-income tenants, consumers, and welfare recipients. A team of law students was employed to
investigate legal theories that might be used to change the legal
structure as it impinged on the poor.[19]

In July 1964 Jean and Edgar Cahn published their article
'The War on Poverty: A Civilian Perspective' in the *Yale Law
Journal*.[20] They proposed that neighbourhood law firms were
needed as the mechanism for giving the poor some control
over their fate. The War on Poverty was to be in the hands of
professional social workers and local political establishments.
The lawyers could be a countervailing force answerable, as
lawyers traditionally are, to their clients. The neighbourhood
law office was to be the means by which the local poverty
community could control, or at least influence, the agencies
responsible for distributing income and opportunity to the
community. The lawyers could provide a mixture of community service and leadership and could disseminate 'not simply legal knowledge, but more vital, could impart the spirit of
hope, dignity, militant citizenship, and constructive advocacy
which together comprise the civilian perspective' on the War
on Poverty.[21]

The War on Poverty was put onto official federal basis with
the passage of the Economic Opportunity Act 1964, which set
up the Office of Economic Opportunity (OEO). The Act
made no actual mention of legal services for the poor, but

several legal services programmes were funded by OEO under section 205, which authorised grants to 'community action programmes'. In 1965 the Legal Services Programme was created as a separate division within OEO, and in the fiscal year 1966 more than $27m. was committed for financing legal services around the country. By September 1966 programmes had been funded in 37 of the country's 50 largest cities. There were 551 offices manned by some 1,100 lawyers. In July 1967 there were 800 offices with 1,600 full-time staff attorneys in 46 of the 50 states. By June 1968 there were 2,000 lawyers. In 1972 this had increased to 2,660 in some 850 offices.[22] In the following years, the financial drain of the Vietnam war and the political unpopularity of the War on Poverty combined to reduce OEO's budget. Most of OEO was reduced in scope. The Legal Services Programme just about managed to survive intact.

The philosophy of the OEO Legal Services Programme was to combine several functions. The two main aims were to give ordinary legal services to the poor, though mainly in the civil law field – assistance to individual clients by way of advice, drafting of legal documents, negotiations with third parties, representation of claims. The second aim was law reform. As the OEO Legal Services Guidelines stated, 'advocacy of appropriate reforms in statutes, regulations and administrative practices is a part of the traditional role of the lawyer and should be among the services provided by the programme'. Test cases were to be used to develop the law for the benefit of the client community as well as the individual. A third aim was community education to inform people about their legal rights. Such education could also serve a preventive function by avoiding the development of legal problems. By March 1967 the Legal Services Programme had decided that of these, its prime objective was to focus on law reform.[23] Earl Johnson Jr., Director of the OEO Legal Services Programme, told the Harvard Conference on Law and Poverty on 17 March 1967 that it was impossible to achieve fully all of the goals of the Legal Services Programme. The 'primary goal of the Legal Services Program should be law reform, to bring about changes in the structure of the world in which the poor people live in order to provide on the largest scale possible consistent with our limited resources a legal system in which the poor enjoy the same treatment as the rich'.[24] The means to achieve the objective[25] included: the foundation of a national newspaper, *Law in Action*, to give publicity about law reform successes; the setting up of the *Clearinghouse Review* to publish abstracts of important decisions in the field; the publication of the *Poverty Law Report* to give detailed treatment to developments in the field of poverty law; the setting up of a national training programme (named after Reginald Heber Smith), to educate the best young poverty lawyers in the special problems of the subject; and the establishment of national law reform centres[26] or 'back-up' centres to research legal problems in the field, to master-mind test case litigation and to support the law reform work of neighbourhood law firms.

Salaried legal services in England – the early debates

The first published mention of neighbourhood law firms in England was in an article by the present writer in September 1966, commending the idea.[27] As a result of the article I was invited by the Lord Chancellor's Advisory Committee to discuss the idea that neighbourhood law firms be introduced in England.[28] The Committee reported in June 1967 that it had not been convinced.

> While we agree that there is considerable ignorance of the law, especially of more recent changes in it, and that consultation with lawyers on such matters is desirable, we are not convinced that the failure to take advantage of the facilities available, including consulting solicitors, is confined to any submerged portion of the population, the poor or the inarticulate, or is due to ignorance of the facilities. We are not satisfied of the need for the radical and expensive alteration in the Legal Advice scheme which [Mr Zander] advocates under the Neighbourhood Scheme ... we do not consider that the case he advocates has been made out.[29]

The Lord Chancellor's Advisory Committee repeated its negative reaction to neighbourhood law firms in its report the following year, published in October 1968. It would only be justifiable to jettison the legal aid scheme in favour of the neighbourhood firms concept, it said, if it was better than our system in reaching those who were unaware of their legal rights. This did not appear to be the case. ('We observe from reports of the American system that it appears to be just as unsuccessful as the English scheme in persuading people to get legal advice before the need for litigation arises.'[30]) In these circumstances it 'remained firmly of the opinion that development of the Citizens' Advice Bureaux provides the best solution to this problem.'[31]

Meanwhile, in January 1967, the Society of Labour Lawyers held a conference on problems of the legal profession. Widespread concern was expressed that, notwithstanding the achievements of the legal aid and advice system, there were serious defects in the provision of legal services to the community. In response to this concern, a sub-committee was set up under Mr Morris Finer, QC, 'to examine the present provision of legal and other advisory services to the community, to consider possible ways of improving such services, and to make recommendations'.[32]

In February 1968, the Law Society published its paper on what eventually became known as 'the £25 scheme' for advice and assistance to replace the existing oral advice scheme. In this the Law Society also suggested that there should be what it called an Advisory Liaison Service to act as a link between potential clients and the practising profession. Referral agencies such as citizens' advice bureaux could hold sessions for their clients at which the Liaison Officer could attend to give simple advice. His main function would be to discover the nature of the client's problem, and to effect a direct introduction to a solicitor able and willing to help. There were dangers in steering clients to particular firms, but it was 'important that clients, particularly of the kind for whom special provision is needed, should be put into direct touch with someone who is accustomed to handling the type of problem involved'.[33] The choice of solicitor would be based on panels drawn up in consultation with local law societies. The client would retain full freedom of choice. The Advisory Liaison officers could also be available on the telephone to advise social workers as to whether a legal problem was involved, and if so, how best to deal with it.

This work could be done by the permanent local legal aid officials, the number of whom would have to be increased for the purpose. Such work would, in fact, build on the original functions of legal aid Local Secretaries. The Secretary in the Manchester area had, for instance, maintained advice facilities at Bolton, Burnley, Bury, Stockport, Salford and Oldham as well as at his Manchester local office. 'He kept closely in touch with the Citizens' Advice Bureaux and took a keen interest in the work.'[34] It was significant, the Law Society said, that the Manchester area had consistently had a volume of applications for legal advice far higher than from London, where it was not possible, under the permitted staff establishment, to undertake such additional work. It would be the object of the Service to co-operate with all social agencies providing assistance to the lay public.

The next development was the completion by the Society of Labour Lawyers committee of its draft report. The committee took evidence from a wide variety of witnesses, and in August 1968 presented its draft conclusions to a week-end conference in Oxford of some 150 members of the Society. The draft report welcomed the Law Society's proposed £25 scheme and the Advisory Liaison Service, but it thought these did not go far enough. The chief recommendation of the draft report was that local legal centres, staffed by salaried lawyers and model-led on the American neighbourhood law centres, should be established in poverty areas. Nothing less than the introduc-tion of a new public service to operate alongside, and in supplement to, the private profession would suffice to deal adequately with the problem of providing proper legal ser-vices to those sections of the public who went short of them. Local legal centres were needed to provide high-quality legal services to those parts of our cities where the existing need was greatest. What was needed was centres sited in areas where there were few solicitors. Such centres could develop services in ways that were impracticable or even undesirable for private practitioners. They would be able to open in the evenings and at week-ends. They could undertake education of the public about legal services generally and the uses of the legal system. By promoting public knowledge about legal rights they could begin to overcome the barriers and inhibitions which ham-pered the existing system. Lawyers in legal centres could develop expertise in the legal problems of the poor. To run the public service there should be a new national independent management committee consisting of representatives of the profession, the citizens' advice bureaux, the lawyers work-ing in publicly financed legal services and the clients themselves. At the local level there should be committees, again consisting of a mixture of the profession, the staffs of the centres and members of the local community.

In the early part of the week-end conference participants showed some unease at the concept of a state salaried sector in legal services. The Labour Party, in its evidence to the Rush-cliffe committee, had, after all, argued that it would be wrong for the state to administer legal advice offices, or even the legal aid scheme as a whole, since the state would be directly or indirectly affected by many of the claims for which the scheme would provide legal assistance.[35] Twenty years later the idea of state salaried lawyers was still alarming to many of the barristers and solicitors who attended the meeting. But as the week-end went on the mood changed, first from doubt to tentative support and finally to strong endorsement of the idea.[36] Experts from the housing, social work and community services fields confirmed the sub-committee's view that pri-vate practitioners were unable to meet the whole of the great need of the poor for legal services and that a specialised and committed salaried service could help to fill the gaps.

By the end of the conference the only sour note was that of the Law Society. Earlier that year, in February, the Law Soci-ety, in its memorandum *Legal Advice and Assistance*, had expre-ssed strongly critical views about the idea of neighbourhood law firms. The memorandum said that it had been suggested that the answer to the problem of the unmet need for legal services was to set up 'a parallel and quite distinct legal service ... manned by salaried solicitors paid by the state or out of charitable funds, who build up a legal practice by being where the need lies and by an active, and even aggressive, social service directed at searching out cases of need and persuading people to take advantage of the help the law can give them'.[37] It might, at first sight, seem that this development would represent an advance, but 'on closer consideration, it [is] seen to compare unfavourably with an extension of the present scheme'.[38] The Law Society gave five reasons:

(a)   It contemplates a radical departure from the concept of legal aid as so far developed in this country and, by introducing a separate and distinct legal service, it would exercise a divi-sive social influence.

(b)   It is based on notions of indigency and charity constituting a step backwards towards a poor person's procedure.

(c)   It eliminates, and would introduce confusion over, the legal aid principle of obligation to contribute, wherever reasonable to expect this.

(d)   It would be expensive both in overheads and remuneration of the solicitors involved, unless they were those who were too young or old or incompetent to attain the higher salary levels.

(e)   As public money would be involved it would be necessary to set up an organisation to control its application.[39]

In the view of the Law Society, a 'simpler, more practical and more effective means of meeting the problem' was to set up its own Advisory Liaison service. In particular, private practitioners were likely to be more effective than salaried lawyers: 'the existing advice service, based on the practitioner in his office, already accustomed to advising, has proved more beneficial than the method originally contemplated of basing advice on salaried solicitors would have been'.[40] Departure from this would be a serious mistake.[41]

The draft report of the Finer Committee dealt highly critically with this section in the Law Society's February 1968 memorandum.[42] In order to give the Law Society the chance to reply, and to have the benefit of its views more generally, the Law Society was invited to send a spokesman to the Society of Labour Lawyers' Oxford Conference in August 1968. It sent Mr Seton Pollock, who was responsible for guiding the Law Society's policy in the field of legal aid over many years.[43] Mr Pollock delivered a speech from a prepared text. He made it clear that the Law Society basically disapproved of the proposal to establish local legal centres as a separate system, separately managed. It was wrong to think that the existing scheme could not be adapted to the needs of the community. 'Our task, surely, is not to use legal aid as an instrument in a crash action programme to meet a current evil, which ought to be met by other more appropriate means, but a legal aid scheme developing as quickly as the necessary funds can be made available to provide a permanent answer to that problem.'[44] It was true that there was a scarcity of solicitors in some places, but no good was done by exaggerating the problem. 'We do not suffer from the situation prevailing in

America, in which solicitors are normally situated downtown in a world remote from the poor who need their services. We have our solicitors on Lavender Hill, in Whitechapel and Stratford.'[45] It was one of the purposes of the Law Society's £25 scheme 'to create a situation in which it will be economically possible to extend normal legal services in accordance with where the need lies instead of, as hitherto, where the money lies'.[46] A large proportion of the profession took part in the legal aid scheme.[47] Publicity for the legal aid scheme in Crown Post Offices would be more effective in reaching the public than even a score or more neighbourhood law firms.[48]

Mr Seton Pollock said that the situation in America was very different from that here. Our 'war on poverty' had not just started. Their law of contract lacked the protective character of ours. Poverty lawyers were needed in small civil actions there because American civil procedure lacked devices like the default and judgment summons procedure to enable the courts to protect debtors. In America there was nothing like the citizens' advice bureaux and the lawyers had to fill this gap. The geographical area served by neighbourhood law firms had to be very circumscribed. Individual clients were sometimes sacrificed in favour of others whose problems presented important issues for test cases. It was not even true that salaried services were cheaper than those provided by private practitioners. The comparative figures that tended to suggest this were misleading, as much of the work done by American lawyers would be done here by social workers, or the citizens' advice bureau.[49]

In his own published account of the conference Mr Seton Pollock described the draft report as 'essentially a propaganda document aiming at the introduction into this country of the American neighbourhood law firm approach'.[50] The contribution made to the discussion on behalf of the Law Society, he said, 'was to urge the importance of producing a document which could not be subjected to valid adverse criticism'.[51] From this the reader of Mr Seton Pollock's book might assume that the Law Society's attitude was, broadly, that of the somewhat pained but avuncular critic whose main concern is to see that a report with which he basically agrees is written in such a way as to present its ideas in the most effective form. This, however, was hardly the style of Mr Pollock's contribution. In a lengthy address (in mimeographed form it runs to nearly seventeen pages) there was not one sentence that indicated support of any kind for the concept of local legal centres as proposed in the draft report.

Mr Pollock has vehemently and repeatedly denied that the Law Society in 1968 was against a salaried component in the legal aid scheme itself. The Law Society had, after all, envisaged a salaried element in the legal advice scheme in its original recommendations to the Rushcliffe Committee. 'What was opposed was the conception of an entirely separate Legal Aid System confined in scope to the very poor as contrasted with the fundamental legal aid principle of ensuring that all sections of the community should have the benefit of the protection of the law and legal services on equal terms.'[52] But this ignores the content of the Law Society's 1968 memorandum (cited above) which stated, in terms, that the advice scheme based on private practitioners was 'more beneficial' than the originally contemplated scheme based on salaried solicitors and that a departure from this would be a 'serious mistake'.

The truth appears to be that the Law Society in 1968 was actively against the idea of salaried solicitors providing legal services out of public funds. Naturally, it was particularly hostile to the suggestion that salaried solicitors should be managed by a new structure in which the Law Society would play only a modest role. But it was also opposed to the idea of state salaried lawyers as such. There was no contemporaneous published (nor, so far as I am aware, unpublished[53]) word which suggests that at that time the Law Society favoured state salaried lawyers. Its attitude was made clear in the address of the incoming President of the Law Society, Mr H. E. Sargant, at the Society's National Conference in October 1968. He referred critically to the Labour Lawyers' draft report which 'favoured the setting up, on the American plan, of Neighbourhood Law Firms manned by fully-paid full-time lawyers'.[54] 'Not only would free advice be given to the poor and needy, but a full-scale legal service would be available including the taking of any proceedings which might be necessary on behalf of the clientele.'[55] The idea was clearly unacceptable. 'Such a plan would be the thin edge of the wedge. It would mean a loss of the independence of the profession and could lead to a total nationalised legal service.'[56]

The attitude of the Law Society to state salaried lawyers contrasts strikingly with that of the American Bar Association. In February 1965 the ABA House of Delegates at the Association's annual meeting passed, *without a single dissenting vote*, a resolution affirming the ABA's complete support for the then new idea of federally funded salaried lawyers in poverty areas. Delegates resolved that the Association reaffirmed 'its deep concern with the problem of providing legal services to all who need them and particularly to indigents' and resolved that the ABA would co-operate with the OEO 'in the development and implementation of programmes for expanding availability of legal services to indigents and persons of low income'.[57] The leaders of the ABA had decided that they were not going to repeat the mistake made by the American Medical Association in bitterly opposing Medicare and thus seriously damaging its public and political standing.

In the recent book on the American legal profession co-edited by Ralph Nader it was said that 'the ABA leadership has consistently supported and actively lobbied for expansion of the responsibilities of legal services lawyers, for their independence from political pressures and for their unhampered ability to provide full and effective representation of their clients, much to the consternation of some local bar associations'.[58] The support of the ABA for the legal services movement was an important bulwark during the battles with the political Right in the Nixon years and during the difficult gestation period of the Legal Services Corporation. Today it is virtually taken for granted. In England the story has been very different.

The Society of Labour Lawyers' pamphlet *Justice for All*[59] was published in December 1968, tidied and sharpened up, but substantially unchanged in its main lines from the draft considered at the Oxford meeting. By a strange but genuine coincidence, the Conservative Lawyers produced their own pamphlet, *Rough Justice*, in the same month. It favoured two main solutions to the problem of the unmet need for legal services: capital grants and higher rates of remuneration for lawyers working in the slums,[60] and more schemes whereby private practitioners assisted on rotas in citizens' advice bureaux. But if these failed, 'as a last resort', experiments with salaried neighbourhood law firms 'could be tried'. The Conservatives approached this proposal with caution, however, 'for the scheme would involve the setting up of a considerable administrative machinery, and might well suffer from the inflexibility and bureaucratic control associated with so much of the machinery of the welfare state'.[61]

In March 1969, Mr Seton Pollock, writing in the *Law Society's Gazette*, again expressed his views on why neighbourhood law firms on the American pattern were not the answer in England. But this, he said, 'leaves open the question as to whether local legal centres should form part of English legal aid'.[62] To this he gave an answer which, though ambiguous, was distinctly less categorically negative than in 1968.

> The Council believe it would be a mistake, however, to regard such centres as the sole or even the primary need at the present time. In our present state of ignorance, both as to the extent and character of unmet need, it would be foolish to take up positions over the pattern of remedies which may need to be developed.[63]

The Society of Labour Lawyers had not, of course, suggested that legal centres were the sole or even the primary need – rather that they should be established to complement private practice.

Four months later, in July 1969, the Law Society revealed that it had completely changed its policy. Instead of being absolutely opposed to state salaried solicitors, it now wished to have permission to employ them itself as part of its Advisory Liaison Service. In February 1968 it had proposed that the Advisory Liaison Service should advise local agencies and their clients about the nature of clients' problems and should help to steer lay clients to solicitors. In the July 1969 memorandum, the duties of the Advisory Liaison Office had been expanded to include:

> ...(d)   to maintain, where this is found to be required, permanent advisory centres in particular districts to give advice and to perform services similar to those falling within the category of advice and assistance ...
>
> (e)   to set up permanent local centres similar to those maintained during the early days of legal aid (which dealt with the special problem of divorce) but adapted to the general needs of the district including, if necessary, rep-

resentation in magistrates' courts and county courts and
the conduct of litigation so far as this cannot be absorbed
by solicitors' firms.[64]

No explanation has ever been given of this *volte face*, but it
seems probable that two main factors explain it. One was that
officials at the Law Society had broadly come to accept that the
idea of salaried solicitors would not go away and that, properly controlled, it even had some merit as a mechanism for
solving some of the problems in the legal services field. Secondly, the Law Society feared that if a Labour Government
were to win the then forthcoming General Election, it would
be likely to implement the proposals of the Society of Labour
Lawyers, and the Law Society would then lose control of this
new development in the provision of legal services. If state
salaried solicitors were to be established, the Law Society
wanted to be in charge.

This *démarche* appeared to have been successful when, in
January 1970, the Lord Chancellor's Legal Aid Advisory
Committee, in a special report, recommended that the Law
Society should be given the right to run law centres.[65] The
Advisory Committee said it had considered both of the Law
Society's memoranda, and the proposals from the Society of
Labour Lawyers and from the Society of Conservative
Lawyers. The Law Society's revised proposal to allow the
Advisory Liaison service to run advice centres and even law
centres, it said, now looked like the proposals of the Society of
Labour Lawyers. But there were important differences.
Under the proposals of the Society of Labour Lawyers, local
legal centres would be a new public service financed by the
state which would directly employ the lawyers manning the
centres. A management committee would insulate the lawyers
from governmental or other pressures. The Advisory Committee said it doubted whether an *ad hoc* body of this kind
'could really succeed in managing the centres or in insulating
them from pressure'.[66] It would be preferable to have the
centres run by the Law Society. Responsibility for administration of all forms of legal aid and advice should be concentrated
in one body. The Law Society had shown itself fit to be that
body, though it 'would be well advised to consult regularly
with relevant local organisations and services over the prob-

lems that may arise and the needs which have to be met'.[67] Moreover, it would not be right to enable centres to litigate on behalf of the poor in some situations where legal aid was not now available. This would have the undesirable effect of producing two legal aid schemes – one for the deprived areas and one for the rest.[68] The Committee therefore preferred the view of the Law Society.

This approach was translated onto the statute book in the 1972 Legal Advice and Assistance Act. The then Conservative Government, with Lord Hailsham as Lord Chancellor, put through this Act, Part II[69] of which gave the Law Society power to employ salaried solicitors to give legal advice or assistance and to act for individuals with legal aid, and to assist advisory agencies in giving advice to their clients.

But although the Act came into force in April 1973, Part II has remained a dead letter and seems unlikely now ever to be put into effect. The Law Society has never been given any money with which to set up any part of the advisory liaison service – other than the appointment of one liaison officer in June 1969, three years before the 1972 Act, and a second in 1977. The Law Society, not surprisingly, has complained about this from time to time. At first the complaint was echoed by the Lord Chancellor's Legal Aid Advisory Committee which, in its annual report for 1972–3, deplored the failure to implement Part II as 'both serious and short-sighted'.[70] In the following year the Committee reiterated the 'crucial importance' it attached to the early implementation of the section of the 1972 Act which empowered the Law Society to establish law centres and to employ advisory liaison officers.[71] But the Advisory Committee's enthusiasm for the idea of Law Society law centres thereafter appeared to wane. In the annual report for 1974–5 the Committee said that, although it had in the past placed on record its support for Law Society law centres, it was its firm view 'that the provision of what is needed on the ground is of much greater importance than the question as to who should be responsible for its administration'.[72] In the 1975–6 annual report the Committee confirmed that it remained of the opinion that the Law Society had a role to play in the running of law centres. But the precise way for this to be done would require investigation. For one thing the statute only permitted salaried solicitors to act for legally aided clients and did not normally contemplate representation in criminal matters. These were serious limitations, especially whilst there was no legal aid in tribunals and the legal aid financial limits remained as narrow as they were. The Committee said it would report at a later stage as to what it thought should be done.[73] But in its evidence to the Royal Commission the Advisory Committee did not refer to Law Society centres at all.

In *its* evidence, the Law Society agreed that the statutory provisions permitting it to run law centres were too narrow. Solicitors would only be able to act for those who qualified for the Green Form scheme (whose eligibility level was far too low) or who had obtained a legal aid certificate. Thus, centres could not provide help for clients before most tribunals, or undertake criminal cases. The statute allowed the Law Society to employ solicitors but it was unclear whether this extended also to barristers and social workers. Thirdly, there was no means under the statute of involving local organisations or other representatives of the community in the management of a law centre or of delegating powers to such a management committee.[74] It urged that it should be given the power to run some such centres.[75] It also envisaged an expanded role for liaison officers – attached to the new proposed legal services committees (see pp. 258–9 below) – to service such committees and to help orchestrate local resources.[76]

The only manifestation of the public sector in legal services run by the Law Society, therefore, was Mr Simon Hillyard who, from his appointment in 1969, was for eight years the sole Advisory Liaison Officer. In July 1969 the Law Society said his job would be to start in the London borough of Camden and to participate there in the work of legal aid offices and in citizens' advice bureaux 'collecting, meanwhile, relevant information about the Borough, its needs and resources, and co-operating with the Holborn Law Society and the Local Authority'.[77] His work, it was said, 'must be regarded primarily as in the nature of a probe into the extent and type of need that must be met, but this will be most effectively done if he is not simply an observer but is deeply involved in what is already going on'.[78] It was intended that, having gained valuable experience, he would then move on to some other neighbourhood less well provided with facilities than Camden. His task there would be to promote the advisory liaison concept there and to evaluate the extent of need for legal services.[79]

However, Simon Hillyard's work has been relatively little focused on these objectives. For the first year or so he did in fact have an office in a deprived area (Brixton) and worked mainly to help social workers and other lay advisers to steer clients with legal problems to the right private practitioners, but it soon became obvious that one liaison officer could hardly cope with the problems at the grass-roots level. He retreated to the Law Society's building in Chancery Lane and has ever since dealt with problems at the macro rather than at the micro level. As the only liaison officer for the entire country he devoted his efforts mainly to getting schemes established that might have national relevance. So he played a leading part in the establishment of duty solicitor schemes in magistrates' courts and rotas of solicitors for citizens' advice bureaux. He was much involved in the promotion of the referral lists published by the Law Society to advertise the availability of legal aid solicitors and what work they do. He helped to negotiate the principle of information about fixed fee interviews to be included in the referral lists. His functions have been more in the field of policy, devising new schemes and working to get them implemented, than in giving legal advice either to clients or to lay advisers, or in investigating unmet needs.

Law centres are established

The law centre movement has, meanwhile, taken firm root. The first law centre was established in North Kensington in 1970 as the result of the initiative of local lawyers and community workers. Ironically, considering its opposition to law centres, the actual opening ceremony on 17 July 1970 was performed by the President of the Law Society, Mr Godfrey Morley. Messages of support were read from the Lord Chancellor, Lord Hailsham, and from the chairman of the Law Commission, Sir Leslie Scarman. Those present included the outgoing Labour Attorney-General, Sir Elwyn Jones, Mr Edward Gardner, QC, MP, for the Conservative Lawyers, and Mr R.E.K. Thesiger representing the Lord Chancellor's Office. The press release put out by the Law Society said that the centre, operating from a converted butcher's shop in a seedy neighbourhood of West London, was intended to provide first-class legal advice and legal representation for the local inhabitants:

> The scarcity of solicitors in poor areas, plus the mistaken belief that lawyers exist only to benefit the landlord, the finance company, the police, but not the poor citizen, as well as the ignorance of many of their legal rights, combine to create a barrier between those most in need of legal advice and representation, and the lawyers whose job it is to provide those services. This is the barrier the centre is attempting to break down.

The centre was to be run by Mr Peter Kandler, thirty-five years old, an experienced private practitioner who had for years been involved with various moves to improve legal services for the citizens of North Kensington. There was to be a full-time community social worker to provide a link between the lawyers and the community. The money for the centre was raised mainly from two charitable trusts, the City Parochial Foundation and the Pilgrim Trust, which between them made grants totalling £4,000. (In the first year the centre earned a further £4,000 from legal aid.) There was a local management committee consisting of four lawyers and six non-lawyers. All four lawyers were friendly to the concept of the law centre. One represented the local law society and one was Simon Hillyard of the Law Society.

For a while after the establishment of the North Kensington centre no others were set up. But from 1973 onwards the movement gathered momentum. Thirteen were set up in 1973 and 1974 and since then another dozen or so have been established.[80] By mid-1977 the number was 25 and growing. Some were set up by local authorities, some by the Urban Aid Programme administered by the Home Office on the basis of 75 per cent funding from central funds and 25 per cent from local authority funds. The Home Office's Community Development Project, financed on the same mix of central and local funds, had twelve projects, of which six employed lawyers and two had actual law centres. The Nuffield Foundation established an experimental centre in one London borough[81] and another subsequently, as has been seen (p. 31 above), in Manchester. In July 1974 the Lord Chancellor, Lord

Elwyn-Jones, who has spoken repeatedly in support of law centres,[82] announced that he had obtained £50,000 to support law centres; this was increased in 1975 to £100,000 and in 1976 to £150,000. Most centres derived a portion of their finance from legal aid, receiving payment under the ordinary scheme, as private practitioners would. (The budget of a typical 2-3 lawyer centre in 1977 was some £50,000.)

Law centres are different in a variety of ways from private firms of solicitors. On the most obvious level, they look different. Instead of the formality and staid dignity of the typical solicitor's office, law centres go out of their way to present an informal, casual atmosphere. They are normally at street level in main shopping centres. Instead of the usual discreet nameplate, they have a large sign in the window, 'LAW CENTRE'. Their shop fronts and interiors are plastered with posters and notices about legal rights, campaigns for racial equality, meetings of the local tenants' association, and information as to what to do about bad housing, wife-battering, or harassment from landlords. They have large, open-plan offices with desks in every corner. The furniture is usually somewhat dilapidated. Lawyers, secretaries, receptionists, all tend to wear jeans and unconventional hair styles. Volunteer workers mill about. In several centres lawyers take their share of filing, receptionist and telephone-operator work and even typing. Law centres commonly have evening and Saturday sessions. Many have a 24-hour telephone emergency service, used mainly in criminal and harassment cases. Their services are free and they are permitted to advertise.

But the centres are different not only in the way they provide their services, but also in the services they actually provide. One difference is the nature of the work they do. Most private firms of solicitors depend for the bulk of their income on conveyancing and probate work. Law centres typically devote the largest proportion of their time to landlord–tenant disputes and other housing problems. In a survey of the first fifteen law centres, housing problems accounted for 40 per cent or more of the total work-load in ten of the centres.[83] Employment, social security and consumer problems played a larger part in the work of the centres than for most firms of solicitors.

Another difference is the type of client. Solicitors in private practice tend naturally to work for individual clients who instruct and pay them. Law centres place great emphasis on the value of helping groups and the community more generally. By concentrating on problems that affect large numbers of people rather than just individuals the law centres believe they are getting the best value out of their own scarce and over-stretched resources. Group and community work are increasingly the dominant mode of service provided by law centres.[84] There are innumerable examples: forming and servicing tenants associations; running campaigns on how to get rents or rates reduced; writing and distributing leaflets, posters, pamphlets and even newspapers about aspects of the law; lecturing in schools, old people's homes, prisons, hostels; running surveys; performing in street theatre entertainment on legal rights.

Many centres have concentrated on particular local problems – bad landlords, breaches of the fire regulations, redevelopment plans of the local authority, relations between the police and the coloured community. Law centres commonly identify a problem and then go out of their way to try to cope with it. A centre may swamp the local county court with cases of illegal evictions as a means of sensitising the judge to the problem, and of alerting bad local landlords that evictions will be effectively resisted. In another area the centre may decide that too many elderly people are failing to get their heating allowance, or that immigrant workers are being exploited by a particular employer or that the harassment office of the local authority requires to be pressured to prosecute landlords who harass their tenants. One centre became aware that the fuel allowance in supplementary benefit payments was inadequate to meet the costs of tenants on a particular estate. It conducted a number of successful appeals, but a report it commissioned under the Green Form scheme from a consulting engineer showed the problem to be common to the estate generally. As a result, it started negotiations with the Supplementary Benefits Commission to get the rate of benefit raised for everyone living on the estate.

Law centres have used test cases in the traditional sense of cases that seek to establish a point of law in the courts. But they interpret the concept more broadly to include any form of legal action that involves community gain. It may be conducted purely at the local level and achieve no more publicity than is available from the local press. Yet if the conduct of one landlord, or employer, or builder, or local authority, is altered as a result, the action may have had its desired effect. Sometimes it is not necessary to achieve *any* publicity. The fact that the action has been started may be enough to achieve a settlement not merely for one person but for a whole group similarly situated. A law centre provides expertise in the special legal problems of the poor. It can take a long view and set priorities for action. It has a means of keeping the community informed of developments and of receiving the views of the community through its management committee and its network of local contacts.

From the start the law centres attracted great press and other media interest and a good deal of political support. Lord Elwyn-Jones, on 21 March 1974, making his maiden speech as Lord Chancellor, said he intended that the government should concentrate on the provision of more law centres. 'I intend to do all I can to support the existing centres and encourage the creation of new ones.'[85] Two months later, on 15 May 1974, he elaborated on this theme. It was not reasonable to expect private practitioners to set up and operate profitably in the poorest areas. In such areas there tended to be 'a gulf between the outlook, and sometimes even the language (particularly in the case of immigrants), of ordinary professional men and their prospective clients'. In the deprived urban areas, 'I believe that the only effective solution is the provision of law centres'. Some solicitors in private practice had the necessary knowledge of social welfare to win the confidence of people at this level of need, 'but in the nature of things, many cannot do so'.[86]

> In the areas I have in mind it is, I believe, only law centres that are likely to be able to meet people's needs ... Moreover, such centres – and this is one of their values – are not limited to assisting individual clients but ... can offer a wider range of help ... By working in this way for groups of individuals, centres can and frequently do achieve more than can be achieved by the conventional individual casework approach with which we are all familiar.[87]

Salaried lawyers in citizens' advice bureaux

A parallel development to that of law centres has been that of salaried lawyers paid out of public funds in other agencies – citizens' advice bureaux, community development projects, consumer advice centres and the like. The first full-time lawyers in the citizens' advice bureaux were appointed in February 1973 with the establishment of the Paddington Neighbourhood Advice Bureau and Law Centre.[88] The centre is financed by the City of Westminster and the staff are all employed by the Greater London Citizens' Advice Bureaux. In 1977 there was a staff of four lawyers and support staff in the law centre and five advice workers in the CAB. The two worked closely together. A solicitor, for instance, is always on duty during office hours to advise CAB workers and their clients. Cases that need continuing help or more expert assistance than the CAB can provide are referred direct to the law centre. A similar Advice Bureau and Law Centre was opened in Hackney in May 1976.

There are also a number of 'community solicitors' employed by citizens' advice bureaux. The Lewisham Community Lawyer, for instance, set up and supervises three legal advice centres in particularly deprived areas. He acts as a resource not only for the CABs in the area, but also for other community organisations such as the local Housing Aid Centre, tenants associations and similar community organisations. In North Kensington the citizens' advice bureaux have employed a community lawyer as part of the Information and Aid Centre opened in 1974 under the elevated motorway. The centre represents a spread of local authority services (social services, community relations, information) and independent agencies (housing action centre, voluntary workers bureau and citizens' advice bureau). Although the lawyer is technically employed by the CAB, he is integrated into the centre as a whole, and serves as a resource for any of its parts. His main objective has been not only to advise on individual problems but also to 'raise the legal expertise of the maximum number of lay advisers'.[89] In Waltham Forest a community lawyer took up the job in June 1974, funded, in this case, by the local authority. He works at one CAB and takes advice sessions at two weekly sessions in other parts of the borough. In

December 1977 there were ten bureaux in all employing salaried lawyers at an approximate cost of £10,000 per annum per lawyer.

Several of the units set up by the Community Development Project (CDP) have included salaried lawyers. The CDP began in 1970 as an action-research experiment involving central and local government, voluntary agencies and the universities in 'a concerted search for better solutions to the problem of deprivation than those we now possess . . . including the establishment of more valid and reliable criteria for allocating resources to the greatest social benefit'.[90] Twelve local authorities collaborated with the Home Office in the programme. Six of the twelve employed lawyers. Four of these (Benwell, Coventry, Liverpool and Birmingham) had separate legal facilities; two more (Canning Town and Southwark) had lawyers on their staffs. In Coventry, for instance, a community lawyer was appointed in 1973. The advertised job description stated that his task would be to offer legal advice to clients, to give legal help to community groups such as tenants associations and adventure playgrounds, and to liaise with statutory and voluntary agencies such as the CABs, the Council of Social Service, social workers and community workers. He was to make properly documented referrals to solicitors in private practice and to 'explore ways and means whereby a legal service can become an instrument of betterment for disadvantaged individuals, groups and communities'.[91]

It is clear that the use of salaried solicitors in the CAB service is regarded by all concerned as an important new addition to its strength. The Council of the National Association of Citizens' Advice Bureaux (NACAB) resolved in September 1977 to continue and indeed to develop the innovation. NACAB's evidence to the Royal Commission said that there was substantial scope for experimentation with different methods of providing the services of lawyers to assist lay agencies.[92] The availability of a staff lawyer 'inevitably leads to an improvement in the extent and quality of the legal services which non-lawyer advice workers are able to provide'.[93] Staff lawyers working within agencies such as CABs 'would multiply the "productivity" of the advice workers to a dramatic extent'.[94] This had always been the function of the Honorary Legal Adviser – usually a local solicitor in private practice who assisted the workers. But with a salaried lawyer available, bureaux could in practice draw much more readily and frequently on such skills. It had been estimated, for instance, that the Paddington Advice and Law Centre solicitors helped Paddington CAB workers in more than 2,000 cases a year and the 24-hours-a-day duty solicitor service available on the telephone to CAB workers throughout London dealt with a further 3,500 cases a year.[95] Also staff lawyers could play an important role in training bureau workers, and in producing leaflets, legal do-it-yourself kits, posters and other means of helping clients and potential clients to cope with legal problems. It was hoped to have a network of full-time staff lawyers throughout the country available to CABs and to other advisory agencies especially in areas where there was no law centre. In addition to advising agency workers and helping with training they could appear as tribunal advocates, become involved in relevant research projects and act as liaison links between the agencies and the private profession.

Experience in other countries

In the past few years lawyers whose salaries are paid by the state or other public funds have been established not only in this country but in many other countries as well. In the United States the Legal Services Corporation was set up by Federal statute in 1974 to take over OEO's neighbourhood law firms. In December 1977, the Corporation had some 300 programmes with about 750 neighbourhood offices and some 3,500 salaried lawyers. They were said to be handling about one million matters. The law reform or 'back-up' centres were retained to assist the neighbourhood offices but because of the terms of the Legal Services Corporation Act (s.1006(a)(3)(A)) they are now confined to research on actual cases rather than general legal problems. The Corporation is able to command significant Congressional support. In 1971 the Congressional appropriation was $71m. Through the Nixon years funding was static. In 1975 the first appropriation for the Corporation was $92.2m; in 1976 it was $125m, and in 1977 $140.3m. For 1977–8 the appropriation was $205m, only a little under the sum asked for by the Corporation ($217m). It was expected that by the end of 1978 there would be some 900 offices and over 5,000 lawyers. The Corporation stated in its first annual report for 1976 that its plan was that, by the end of 1980, every 10,000 poor persons would have access to legal assistance by the equivalent of two legal services lawyers – compared to 11.2 lawyers per 10,000 persons in the population generally.[96] The longer-term objective was the equivalent of four lawyers per 10,000 poor persons.[97]

In Australia, the Australian Legal Aid (ALAO) Office was established in July 1973 by executive act of the Labour Government. At the opening of ALAO's offices, the Labour Attorney General, Lionel Murphy, QC, said:

> A nation-wide Federal salaried service, operating in conjunction with the private profession, is necessary to discharge that responsibility, particularly to disadvantaged persons and in remote areas of Australia. The service should present a new image of accessibility to the law by such means as local 'store front' offices. The lawyers of the Federal salaried service should have, and be seen to have, a role in conducting cases on behalf of disadvantaged persons in the community.[98]

The ALAO, in 1976, employed some 150 lawyers and 210 administrative staff. It operated in each of the States, in the Capital and in the Northern Territories. The head office was in Canberra, with branch offices in each State capital, Canberra and Darwin. Twenty-five regional offices, mainly of two lawyers, had been opened in suburban and provincial centres throughout the country.[99] The offices were located in shopfronts in busy shopping streets. An important difference between the Australian and the American conception of the salaried sector was that ALAO favoured referrals to private practitioners as a matter of principle. (In 1976–7, ALAO's financial allocation was $20m. for its network of offices, including $9.5m. for payments to private practitioners.[100])

The Labour Government fell in December 1975 and the precise future of ALAO remains somewhat unclear. There was a cut-back in ALAO's staff in 1976.[101] But the incoming Attorney-General, Mr R. J. Ellicott, QC, had indicated before the General Election that he favoured the continuation of the salaried sector in legal services – though it might be provided more on the State than on the Federal level. He said in Parliament that his party would encourage the establishment in each

State of a Legal Aid Commission which would have within it the necessary salaried service to the extent to which that was thought prudent.[102] Salaried services in Australia appear to be both solidly established and fully accepted in principle.[103] The Law Council (the Australian equivalent of the Law Society), in a press statement in February 1975, said: 'The legal profession considers that the provision of a comprehensive legal aid service to the public should include salaried services ... organised in such manner as best suits the needs in each locality.'[104] Discussions in 1976–7, held between the Attorney-General and Attorneys-General of the States, have been on the basis of a model statute which provided for each State having its own statutory Commission which would provide legal aid through salaried lawyers and by referral of cases to private practitioners in accordance with policies determined by each Commission.[105] The first such Commission was established in Western Australia in 1977.[106]

In Sweden, the Public Legal Aid Law of 1972 provided for citizens to get legal aid services either from private practitioners or from salaried lawyers. Section 2 of the Act said 'legal aid is rendered by advocates or by assistant lawyers employed by public law offices or private law firms or where stated in the law, by other persons'. In Zambia, the Government set up a department of salaried lawyers to provide legal aid shortly after gaining independence in 1964.[107] In 1972 the Legal Aid Department consisted of ten qualified counsel and six unqualified assistants, plus the director.

In British Columbia, the Legal Services Commission Act 1975 provides for legal aid services by a mixed system of private practitioners and salaried advocates. Wherever possible, the client is given a choice. In Nova Scotia the Legal Aid Planning Act 1970–1 has operated through 26 salaried lawyers and 600 private practitioners on panels.[108] In Manitoba, the bulk of legal aid services is provided by salaried lawyers under the Legal Aid Services Society of Manitoba Act.[109] In Quebec, clients have a choice between private practitioners and salaried lawyers, and in 1976–7 three-quarters of the work went to salaried lawyers and one quarter to advocates in private practice. In Manitoba free choice, by contrast, has led to three-quarters of legal aid cases going to private practitioners.[110] The Secretary to the Legal Aid Directors of Canada said, in

October 1976, that according to many observers the trend appeared to be 'towards the mixed delivery system'.[111] The various Canadian provincial legal aid plans, in August 1976, employed a total of 446 salaried advocates.[112]

There can be no doubt, therefore, that publicly funded legal services are now fully established as a proper part of the system for providing legal services. In England, the final seal of official approval was bestowed by the Lord Chancellor's Legal Aid Advisory Committee which in the 1960s had expressed serious reservations about neighbourhood law firms. In three annual reports from 1972–3 it affirmed its support for law centres.[113] In 1975–6 it went even further. Law centres, it said, were 'playing a vital part in making legal services available in the most deprived areas, and on matters on which the poorer sections of the community most strongly feel the need for those services'.[114] More centres should be established and existing centres should be supported where necessary. Centres had 'established themselves as an integral and essential branch of legal services'. The law centres movement formed 'a kind of public sector of legal services'.[115] With these sentences, law centres were fully embraced as part of the English legal system.

3 The Public Sector: Its Scope, Role and Management

A legal aid scheme based solely on private practitioners or solely on state salaried lawyers is naturally simpler than one which seeks to mix the two systems. Yet, increasingly, it is felt that the mixed system is best; the problems which this poses are varied.

Relations between the public and private sectors

Much of the past hostility towards law centres from English solicitors and the Law Society has resulted from a fear that they represent an economic threat. Since the legal aid scheme provides assistance for any client with a legal problem who qualifies under the means test, every law centre client is, *in theory*, a potential client of a private practitioner. Law centres have, naturally, been set up mainly in poor neighbourhoods. Solicitors who practise in such areas may be struggling for their own economic position. They are, in any event, unlikely to be at the affluent end of the spectrum of solicitors' earnings. It is therefore understandable that they might view with concern the establishment in their midst of a law centre permitted to advertise for work and to offer free services. On the face of it, the law centre could result in a significant loss of custom.

In practice, however, this does not appear to have happened. To some extent, this might be because law centres attract clients who would not otherwise have gone to solicitors in private practice. The Law Society, in its evidence to the Royal Commission, conceded that law centres 'act as a magnet to attract a wide variety of people with legal problems. Many of these people are unlikely to have been to a solicitor before'.[1] Even more, the Law Society said that 'law centres are making a large number of referrals to solicitors'.[2] Most law centres provided 'substantial evidence of this (Paddington Centre, 492 referrals in 1975/6; Camden, 684 referrals during the same period)'. The Law Society continued:

It appears that there is considerable evidence to suggest that solicitors have opened offices in the vicinity of centres since those centres were opened. For instance, at least one office has been established in each case in the vicinity of the North Kensington, Manchester and West Hampstead centres while no less than four offices each have been established near the Camden and Islington centres.[3]

The matters referred on to private practitioners fall into two main categories – work that the centres do not handle at all, and work that they might handle, but which they refer out in order to reduce their own case-load, or for other pragmatic reasons. Certain classes of work are excluded by most law centres. Conveyancing, divorce, commercial, or substantial probate work are all more or less automatically referred on to private practitioners. Personal injury cases are normally referred on. Many law centres decline to act for landlords, even for those who are people of small means.[4] Most law centres favour a policy of acting in cases that involve group or community problems and accordingly often refer on cases that raise only individual ('case-work') problems. Referrals due to pressure of work are also common. Most of the law centres have found themselves with more work than they can handle and have resorted to a variety of expedients to reduce the problem, including narrowing the range of cases they take and thus referring more on to local practitioners. The pattern of law centre work has, therefore, to a considerable extent been different from that of local private practitioners. As has been seen, most law centres do primarily housing work for tenants; relatively few private practitioners have any significant volume of such work. Law centres appear to do more consumer work, eviction cases, tribunal representation, immigration and employment work than solicitors in ordinary private practice. The main area of overlap between law centre work and that of the private profession has been in the fields of crime, personal injury cases and matrimonial work other than divorce.

Waivers from the Practice Rules

In order to offer free legal services, law centres have needed a waiver from the ordinary Practice Rules which make it professional misconduct to attract business by unfair means. Waivers from these rules are granted by the Law Society, and the waiver system has been treated by the Law Society as the means to control the establishment of law centres and what they should be permitted to do. The history of the negotiations over waivers is an unhappy story involving a great deal of acrimony.[5] Partly this was in the nature of the situation – those wishing to set up law centres were bound to chafe at any controls emanating from a Law Society that was felt to be either fundamentally hostile or, at best, ambivalent toward the very concept of state salaried lawyers. Even, therefore, if the Law Society had followed a clear, consistent and reasonable policy, there would have been difficulties. In fact the Law Society's attitude altered from time to time, was applied inconsistently and, for the first few years, was based on an analysis of the problem which has since been conceded to be unacceptable.

The policy of the Law Society was initially shaped by its traditional attitude to the giving of services by solicitors in Poor Man's Lawyer services – notably the well-known services at Toynbee Hall in the East End of London, the Mary Ward Settlement in Tavistock Square and Cambridge House in Camberwell. The conditions for waivers for such services were set out by the Law Society in 1951. They applied both to solicitors working on salaries and to those who came to the centres on a voluntary, unpaid basis, whose clients required further continuing assistance. The 1951 rules stated that the Law Society would consider applications for waivers on a number of conditions. These related mainly to the private practitioner who wished to take clients from the free legal advice centre to his own office. The arrangement had to be genuinely 'in the interests of the person for whom the advice was available'. There could be no arrangement aimed at unfairly attracting business to any solicitor. Before acting for a client in his private office, the solicitor had to have *written* confirmation that the client wished the solicitor to act 'at the normal charges'. The client who needed the help of a solicitor had to be given a list with the names of a number of solicitors and had to be advised to make his own selection. No particular solicitor was to be recommended by the centre.[6] Waivers could also be granted to enable a salaried solicitor to accept instructions without making any charge – but this did not apply to work done for a person in receipt of legal aid. The main thrust of these various conditions was to ensure that solicitors did not gain any unfair advantage over fellow practitioners by attending free legal advice centres and there scooping up lucrative cases that they would take back to their own offices. The system of controls was based on a cynical view of the motives of those who worked in such centres. The extent to which it served the interest of clients of such centres was purely accidental. Its chief purpose was to serve the interests of the profession.

The waivers saga went through several stages. When the first law centre was set up in 1970, the Law Society had not formulated any coherent policy to cope with the problem. The waiver for North Kensington's centre was granted without trouble. At that time the chief requirements for a waiver were that there was an unmet need for legal services, that the centre had a responsible management committee including representation of the local law society and that it had a constitution. But by early 1973, when a number of new law centres had started, or were starting, the Law Society did seek to impose certain more formal conditions. Thus, in January 1973, the Law Society tendered a draft undertaking to be signed by the solicitors in one centre in which they would agree not to undertake any conveyancing, commercial or company work, and not normally to accept instructions in probate or divorce matters, litigation arising out of personal injuries, or criminal cases tried on indictment for 'professional and/or habitual criminals'. This led to negotiations with what became the Law Centres Working Group.

In July 1973 the Law Society produced a document that would have excluded law centres from certain categories of work but permitted them to do consumer protection and work for charitable and other non-profit-making concerns. Further discussions were to be held. Nothing happened until February 1974 when the Law Society produced a wholly different and much more contentious draft. This gave clear precedence to private practitioners. It specified that waivers would only be granted if 'a defined and apparent need' was demonstrated which the legal profession could not meet. Centres had to operate 'under the control of the Law Society'.

A seat on the management committee had to be kept for a representative of the local law society which had to approve the constitution. Centres must only do work which local solicitors were 'unable or unwilling to undertake'. Waivers would be revocable at will by the Law Society; for instance, if there was evidence 'that a centre is retaining cases which could properly be referred to solicitors in private practice'. The records of the centre would have to be submitted to the Law Society at six-monthly intervals showing the number of referrals to private practitioners.

This draft provoked a furious reaction. The Law Centres Working Group refused even to discuss it. The Legal Action Group, to whom it had been sent for comment, wrote a blistering critique of both its tone and its content.[7] At a meeting held in June 1974 the Law Society agreed to withdraw the draft and to prepare a new one. A month later, on 30 July 1974, the Lord Chancellor, Lord Elwyn-Jones, announced in the House of Lords that the Law Society had agreed that the existing system for dealing with waivers was not satisfactory and that 'as an interim measure' it would in future work in close consultation with his office in deciding whether waivers should be granted and on what terms.[8] This was a major new development, for it inserted the Lord Chancellor for the first time into the process of the Law Society's decision-making. He was, in effect, claiming a right of governmental intervention between the warring factions. Machinery was agreed whereby the Law Society would report to the Lord Chancellor on delays in processing waiver applications and the Lord Chancellor would receive appeals against refusals or 'unreasonable conditions' and would 'advise' the Law Society.

In April 1976, a draft document was circulated which had been agreed between the Law Society and the Lord Chancellor's Office. But this time it went not simply to the Law Centres Working Group but (at the suggestion of the Lord Chancellor's Office) also to a number of other voluntary agencies – the Legal Action Group, the National Association of Citizens' Advice Bureaux and the Greater London CABs. These voluntary agencies thereby became involved in the long and somewhat sticky negotiations that then ensued.

The April 1976 draft was, in some ways, very different from the February 1973 document. Instead of control by the local

law society there was to be participation by the local profession. There was no mention of a non-competition clause.
Instead the Law Society was to impose conditions, depending
on the needs of an area. There was no requirement that need
for a centre be proved, but the Law Society was to make
inquiries to establish whether the service was needed. The
Lord Chancellor would act as referee and court of appeal. But
at a meeting between all concerned on 3 May 1976 this draft
was unceremoniously rejected by the voluntary agencies.
Their main objection was that it gave to the Law Society a task
for which it was manifestly not fitted – that of determining
(albeit subject to the Lord Chancellor's approval) whether and
where law centres should be set up. For one thing, it lacked the
technical know-how to investigate the unmet need for legal
services, but even more it was in a situation of an impossible
conflict of interest. The main opposition to law centres came
from the private profession. The Law Society, as the chief
spokesman of the private profession's interests, could hardly
be the impartial arbiter between those who wanted a centre
and the local law society. Moreover, it was, in any event, not
for a private profession to veto expenditure of public moneys.

The debate was given point by a then current controversy
which precisely illustrated the problem. The local council in
the London borough of Hillingdon, with the support of a
variety of community organisations, decided to establish a law
centre. The local law society opposed the centre on the ground
that this was not a poor, under-solicitored area, but one in
which there were in fact quite a number of private firms which
could do all the local legal work. There was therefore no need
for a law centre. The Law Society sided with the local solicitors. The decision produced a considerable volume of critical lay and legal press comment.[9] The centre appealed to the
Lord Chancellor under the new machinery. The parties to the
discussions on 3 May 1976 all anticipated that the Lord Chancellor would advise the Law Society to grant the waiver and so
indeed it proved, only nine days later.

The Lord Chancellor wrote that the Law Society should not
concern itself with the question of need. That was a matter for
the funding agency. The test for the grant of a waiver was
whether the centre was properly constituted and whether 'its
services will not duplicate those normally provided by private

practitioners to such a substantial extent as to amount to unfair competition'. The Law Society duly gave its consent to the Hillingdon waiver and at the same time agreed to abandon the attempt to assess need. The basis of the negotiations which then began again in earnest was that a waiver would be granted for centres with an appropriate constitution and management committee, provided they gave an undertaking not to engage in unfair competition. Agreement took an unconscionable time to achieve but in August 1977 the Law Society was finally able to publish the agreed text of the settlement.[10] This provided that, apart from 'initial advice and assistance', law centre lawyers would not normally act in cases of conveyancing, commercial matters, divorce, probate (save for personal applications in small estates), personal injury cases where the claim was for an amount more than that covered by County Court Scale 2 (in 1977, £500), and criminal matters where the accused was over twenty-one. But it was recognised that in certain exceptional circumstances these restrictions would not apply: in cases of emergency; where the conduct of the client's case required his professional business to be conducted by the salaried solicitor; where a private practitioner was not 'reasonably available'; where the confidence of the client 'would be eroded by referral of the case'; and depending on local conditions. The Law Society would be concerned to consider the revocation of the waiver only where the number of cases within the prohibited categories undertaken by the centre 'was so disproportionate to the total number of cases done by the centre that the services normally provided by solicitors in private practice were being unnecessarily duplicated'. In cases of dispute the Lord Chancellor would 'advise'.

To a great extent the deal between public and private sectors reflects the existing situation in that law centres on the whole have no ambition to do conveyancing, commercial or ordinary divorce work. But a particular law centre that wanted (or whose management committee wanted it) to do a considerable volume of, say, adult criminal cases in magistrates' courts or substantial personal injury cases would find its way barred by the concordat. It clearly represents a 'carve-up' between the public and the private sector. Is this in the public interest? (The writer was a party to the negotiations on behalf of the Legal Action Group, and is perhaps therefore not in an ideal position to judge this question.)

One objection is that the concordat protects the private sector from the stimulus of competition from the public sector which might have the effect of reducing charges. Another objection is that it deprives clients of the advantage of being able to seek a complete legal service from law centres. Instead, if they come with certain problems, they must be referred on. Also, it might be said to deprive the custodians of public money of the right to use it for the purpose of providing services without regard to the possibility that this may deprive the private sector of profitable work.

On the other hand, there are reasons that support such an arrangement. The chief one is that public funds are scarce and should be used only where it seems that necessary services cannot be, or at least are not being, provided by the private sector. Public funds for law centres should, therefore, not be used to do what the private sector is already capable of doing; they should instead aim at doing work that is not being done. From this it would follow that the services of law centres should complement, not duplicate, those of private practitioners. Secondly, the specialisation of function implicit in the arrangement should ensure that the services are provided more efficiently and economically than if law centres tried to duplicate the work of private practitioners. Thirdly, if the public and the private sectors do not feel themselves to be in competition with each other, it is likely to promote better working relations between them.

Law centre work and means tests

There is one problem that has not so far received adequate attention – namely, whether it is right that law centres should be able to offer their clients free services without any means test whilst, in systems like that in England, legally aided clients of private practitioners may have to pay a contribution. There is an obvious inequality in the fact that a law centre client can get a free legal service for which another client in precisely the same financial position would have to pay a contribution if he went to a private practitioner. The fact that law centres offer free services might be said to be a further reason for a non-competition arrangement between the public and private sectors. Law centres would be the offices where the public went with 'welfare law' problems for which there would be no charge. But this ignores the fact that the non-competition arrangement is designed to limit the work done by law centres but not the work done by private practitioners. In other words, there is nothing to prevent private practitioners from handling the kinds of work done by law centres and, to some extent, this does in fact occur. Some solicitors maintain a practice that overlaps with the work of law centres. Why should the client of the one receive a free, fully subsidised service whilst the other must pay? The question is the more important if it is intended to increase not only the number of law centres but also the number of private practitioners willing and able to undertake 'welfare law' work. This is especially true since many matters handled by law centres for the poor also afflict the not-so-poor. Some kinds of matters primarily affect the poor – supplementary benefits and small probate matters are obvious examples. But members of all social class and income groups in the community may have landlord–tenant disputes, small personal injury cases, industrial injuries and other welfare benefit problems, consumer or immigration cases. Law centres may specialise in certain kinds of work, but many who would not qualify as poor also need such expertise. If they cannot go to law centres they ought to be able to get competent advice from private firms.

Law centres obviously value the fact that they can provide free services without any formal means test. It avoids administrative work and the awkwardness of referring-on clients for whom the law centre would be able to provide a valued service. The assurance that the service will be free may attract clients who would otherwise not venture into a lawyer's office at all. The law centre may feel that the client cannot, in truth, afford the contribution that he would have to pay under the ordinary legal aid scheme. But these reasons in themselves can hardly justify the continuing discrimination in favour of law centre clients, since all of them would apply to private practitioners as well. Moreover, the exemption of law centre clients from means tests must surely be based on the assumption that most such clients would, if assessed, be eligible to legal aid on a nil contribution. If a significant proportion of the clients of law centres could, according to the ordinary rules, pay contributions, there is no obvious reason why they should not do so – unless the work done by law centres is such that it ought to be free of charge even to those who can pay contributions – in which case the same work done by private practitioners ought also, perhaps, to be free of the means test and contribution. Nothing is known about the proportion of law centre clients whose means would make them liable to pay a contribution in the ordinary legal aid scheme, but having regard to the very low means test limits, it would not be surprising if the proportion was quite high. It is true that most law centres are sited in poor areas, but even in such areas most of those in ordinary work would, at best, be subject to a contribution and many would be outside the limits of the legal aid scheme altogether. The Law Society's evidence to the Royal Commission said that 'only a quarter of the working population is now eligible for legal aid'.[11]

For these reasons the differentiation between law centres providing 'welfare law' services without a means test and private practitioners providing the full range of services, including welfare law, subject to a means test is illogical. So far, the problem has largely been ignored since the original rhetoric supporting the establishment of law centres so clearly indicated that their services should be free of charge. But at some point this nettle will have to be grasped.

There are three alternative solutions. One is to extend contributions to law centres; another is to extend exemption from contributions to private practitioners. Both would have advantages and disadvantages. If means testing were extended to law centres, it would mean that the public purse would benefit from any excess of contributions over the administrative costs of assessing and collecting them. Secondly, there would be the benefit of equalising the position of the client of the law centre with that of another, similarly placed, client who went to a private firm. Thirdly, there might be some gain in placing the private and the public sectors on the same footing and thus, in effect, promoting healthy competition between the two and offering a genuine choice to the public. On the other hand, means testing would take up valuable time, would deter some clients and annoy others. Insofar as some clients would then be asked to pay contributions they felt they could not afford, the centre would lose those clients and the clients would lose the opportunity of having the problem solved with the help of lawyers. Unless special rules were developed, it would cripple the work of law centres for groups since these would become ineligible for the services of law centres just as they are outside the means test limit for ordinary legal aid. Since work for groups is one of the most important aspects of the role of law centres, special rules would have to be developed to permit groups to receive services from law centres. The benefit of such rules should, however, be applied also to groups who seek help from private practitioners.

Alternatively, the principle of non-means-tested work in the welfare law field could be extended to private practitioners. The main problem here would be the cost; otherwise, this might be a most desirable development. Moreover, the principle would not be so radical an innovation as might at first sight appear. Virtually all defendants in crown courts receive legal aid and hardly any are asked to pay a contribution (p. 33 above). The abolition of the means test in this field might actually *save* the Treasury money, since the cost of administering the means test and contribution system probably exceeds the total of the relatively insignificant sums paid by way of contribution[12] plus the costs that would then be incurred in providing free services for the few who now pay for their own representation.[13]

It is clearly right that defences in criminal cases in the higher level of courts should be the first category of legal services made free of charge to all, regardless of means. There could be no more grave situation for any person than to face serious criminal charges. But after such cases, difficult value judgments inevitably arise as to the relative social priority of different kinds of legal services. In the present context the question is whether law centre work should be done by private practitioners free of charge regardless of means. The idea poses one obvious problem in that it would be difficult, if not impossible, to arrive at a satisfactory definition of law centre work for this purpose. But even if such a definition could be agreed, it is by no means clear that all the matters covered would necessarily have the first priority for inclusion on the list of free services to be provided by private firms regardless of means. Thus, advice on loss of a home would certainly have a claim to such priority, but small consumer claims might not. The idea of attempting to define law centre work and of making it all available, at the expense of tax-payers, from law centres or private practitioners is, therefore, conceptually difficult and socially of doubtful validity. It is also financially impracticable, since it is inconceivable that the Treasury would be prepared to move at one step to such a vast extension of free legal services.

Here, therefore, is a dilemma. If the means test and contributions were extended to law centres, the special quality of law centre practices might be endangered; if they were abolished for private practitioners, there would be an unacceptably costly expansion of the legal aid scheme. If law centres continue to operate without the means test which applies to the private sector, there is arbitrary discrimination in favour of their clients, as against clients with the same problems and in the same financial situation who go to private firms.

There is no tidy solution of this problem. Any of the possible solutions are open to some objections. Any massive expansion of free services paid for out of public funds is plainly a non-starter in the foreseeable future, so the alternative of enabling private firms to do *all* law centre work without any means test can be eliminated as a serious suggestion. The choice then appears to lie between leaving the situation as it is at present, and applying the means test to law centre clients. If the latter solution were adopted, it might reasonably be argued that the non-competition clause would then be inappropriate. Law centres and private firms would be on the same basis as regards fees charged to legally aided clients and there would be a strong case for saying they should be permitted to compete right across the board. This is precisely the solution adopted in both Sweden and Quebec. Thus under the 1972 Swedish Act a client entitled to legal aid has the choice of going either to a private practitioner or to a public law office manned by state salaried lawyers. The fees that he pays are the same in either case. The intention is that the public law offices should be self-financing. The client's means are assessed and, if the costs of the case exceed his contribution, the office sends its bill to the legal aid authorities just like a private firm.[14] This avoids financial discrimination in favour of one class of clients as against another. It may also help to avoid the danger that the public sector will (fairly or unfairly) be identified in the public mind as a second-class service for the poor. If welfare law problems are dealt with free of charge by the public sector and all other services are handled subject to a contribution, there is the obvious possibility that some will conclude that one is, by definition, a less good service than the other. If both are charging the same, this is less likely.

But the defect of this solution is that it would make it difficult for the public sector to play its role of promoting a different kind of service to that offered by private practitioners. If law centres were required to be self-financing, they might be dominated by the profit motive just like private practitioners. Even if they were relieved of the full burden of the need to cover their costs they would probably tend to work mainly for individual clients with individual problems – just as private practitioners do. The whole range of more broadly focused work for groups and the community as a whole which the law centres in England increasingly regard as their chief concern would then be lost.

In order to determine which alternative policy to follow it is desirable to isolate what indeed are the most valuable elements in the public sector model of providing legal services. One, unquestionably, is the fact that it becomes possible to place an office where it is needed. If private practitioners will not set up in a particular area which has a need for lawyers, the only solution is to use public funds for the purpose. To achieve this objective, however, there is no need for the public sector firm to be any different from a private firm. A second objective is to bring in clients who need the help of lawyers but who would not, for one or another reason, go to private firms. This objective is usually said to be met by the fact that law centres are able to offer free services and that they can advertise. In reality, they do little advertising since they have more than enough work. Moreover, if the recommendations of the Monopolies Commission on advertising[15] were implemented, private practitioners too would be allowed to do more to make themselves known to potential clients. Any difference between public and private would then depend on which had the best image in the community. It may be that law centres, with a distinct bias toward community and group problems, would have an advantage in such competition – but

it might be somewhat marginal. The availability of free services as a means of bringing in clients may be important, but
there is no obvious way to measure its importance other than
by controlled experiments which would be difficult to mount.
It may prove that certain clients will come in to law centres
who could not be persuaded to come in to private practitioners, but this in itself would not necessarily justify the expense
of setting up large numbers of law centres. There might be
much cheaper ways of attracting that submerged clientele.

The best reason for the establishment of law centres (other
than the fact that they can be sited where they are needed) is the
distinct contribution they make in a type of legal service that is
different in style and content from that of private practice. The
fact that this service is free and non-means-tested *may* be an
essential ingredient in projecting the image and playing its
particular role. In the writer's view, it is above all for this
reason that there is a strong case for a network of law centres
around the country to complement the services provided by
private firms and for their relatively narrow range of services
to be provided without charge and subject only to a very
rough and ready means test, if any at all.

The siting of law centres

The size of the public sector must depend on the availability of
money and manpower. At the end of 1977 there were only 27
law centres. But while it is obvious that there ought to be
many more than this, it is impossible to form any concluded
view as to how many more – 100, 200, 500, or more? One
hopes to see a steady development in their numbers in smaller
towns and even rural areas, as well as in the largest cities where
they have, hitherto, mainly been established. From a political
point of view there is probably much merit in the American
Legal Services Corporation's proposal that it hopes to see at
least the equivalent of two lawyers (and later of four lawyers)
for every 10,000 poor persons. Such a target may be artificial
but (suitably adjusted to the needs and possibilities of different
countries) it provides at least some criterion of measurement
and of future expectations.

The exact positioning of law centres poses the question of
relative priorities of areas. In 1974 the Lord Chancellor
announced that he had invited Mr Richard White of Birming-

ham University to undertake an urgent examination of the nature and extent of the need for legal services. Unfortunately, the fruits of these labours have never been published. The only glimpse of the contents of the White report was when the same Lord Chancellor said in June 1976 that the report he had received identified the areas of greatest need and confirmed that there was 'an urgent need for the setting up of more law centres. . . .'[16] There was no doubt that the law centres were 'playing a vital part in making legal advice available in the areas of greatest need and on matters on which the poorer sections of the community most strongly feel the need for legal assistance'. But the Lord Chancellor said they were needed not only in the areas of greatest need, because even in places where there were plenty of solicitors there was a need for law centres – since the ordinary solicitors tended 'to confine themselves to matrimonial and criminal matters'.[17] On this analysis, there would be a case for a law centre almost anywhere. But since Richard White's Report has not been published it is not known what criteria he used to identify the areas of greatest need nor how he suggested that decisions should be taken as between several places with strong claims for a law centre. The National Association of Citizens' Advice Bureaux in its evidence to the Royal Commission suggested that the siting of law centres might be guided by reference to the level of unemployment, the percentage of elderly citizens, the percentage of houses in multiple occupation, the numbers of immigrants whose mother tongue is not English or who were born abroad, the take-up levels of means-tested benefits, the proportion of single-parent families, the rate of juvenile crime and of truancy, and the number of solicitors in full-time private practice. 'A significant departure from the national or even the regional norm on any 3 or 4 criteria in a definable urban neighbourhood with a population between, say, 20,000 and 100,000 should cause thought to be given to a law centre rather than a less intensive form of supplementary legal service.'[18] This seems, broadly, to be the right approach.

The manning of the public sector

If the public sector is to flourish, it is obvious that it must attract (and continue to attract) recruits of adequate quality. Experience so far on both sides of the Atlantic suggests that

law centre and similar work is likely to draw mainly young
lawyers. The typical law centre lawyer, in the early years of
the movement at least, was in his twenties rather than his
thirties or forties.[19] This has the advantage that the lawyers are
energetic and enthusiastic and the disadvantage that they lack
experience. It would, of course, be desirable to have some
directors of law centres who were in their mid-thirties or even
their forties, but so far, in England, few such lawyers have
come forward. It also remains to be seen whether those who
start in law centre work in the 1970s will still be there ten years
on.

In the United States too the legal services programme has
been dominated by young lawyers. A survey has shown that
in 1967, 40 per cent of the lawyers in the OEO programme
were new or recent graduates; only a quarter of the total had
graduated more than seven years before. By 1972, more than
three-quarters of the 1967 vintage Legal Services Programme
lawyers had gone[20] – suggesting a rapid 'burn-out rate'. Law
centre work is probably more demanding in terms of hours
and conditions of work, low pay and stress than work in
ordinary private practice and it is therefore not surprising that
the turn-over is fairly rapid. From some points of view this is
unfortunate, but there are compensating factors. One is that
the life-blood of the public sector is the recently qualified
lawyer. Provided they continue to come forward in sufficient
numbers,[21] and provided those in charge of law centres have a
minimum of experience (preferably at least five or so years in
the profession), the public sector will continue to be viable. It
is unrealistic to suppose that many will continue to work in the
front line for very long periods. But if law centre work is
regarded as valid experience for those ultimately going into
private practice, experience so far suggests it should be able to
attract enough recruits.

The public sector is too new in England for there to be any
experience of the turn-over problem. The survey of Legal
Services lawyers in the United States, however, shows that
those most likely to stay are the older lawyers, who are also the
least likely to join. Once they joined, they stayed. The popular
belief was that those who went into the Legal Services movement tended to be from the best law schools and to be moti-
vated by a strong sense of idealism or even radicalism. The

survey found that they were in fact recruited from a great variety of backgrounds and from many types of law school. 'The "radical" character of the program did not lie so much in the personnel, but rather in what they were being hired to do, that is, represent individuals and groups that were virtually unheard-from previously and who were taken advantage of by others who had greater access to legal resources.'[22] When they went on into private practice it was not to the kind of private practice which attracts most money and status. 'Former Legal Services lawyers in private practice have a less prestigious practice (as measured by the traditional indicators of type of clients, type of work setting, and professional income), and they do more pro bono work oriented to social reform than do other lawyers of comparable background and experience.'[23] Those who did not go into private practice were heavily concentrated in non-business pursuits – public defender's offices, public interest law firms, social reform-oriented foundations, teaching, or working for a government department.[24] This then is the second main compensating fact of the turn-over in personnel – that lawyers who have worked in the public sector take their experience with them. It influences their choice of later occupation and, even more important, it probably affects the way they do their work, whatever it may be.

Central or local management and funding for law centres?

There must be some way of determining at any moment in time how many law centres there should be, and where. Hitherto, these decisions have been taken by a variety of bodies – chiefly local authorities, the Urban Aid Programme, the Community Development Project, and, in a sense, the Lord Chancellor's Office insofar as its reserve funds have been used to provide continuing financial support for centres that would otherwise have succumbed for lack of money. It would be administratively more rational if such decisions were taken by one agency at the national level. A national structure for law centres would also have other advantages. It would give cohesion to the public sector and would strengthen it politically. It would make it possible to have a single annual report of statistics and developments. (The flow of annual reports from individual centres is already too great to be absorbed and digested.) A national structure might raise the level of office efficiency – an area which has been somewhat neglected in law centres. It would also help to create a better career structure for the lawyers working in the public sector. It is true that a unified system might hamper the flowering of local initiatives, but this risk could be reduced by retaining both the present local management committees consisting of lawyers and laymen, and the right of local authorities to finance law centres where the national system decided not to provide such a facility in that area.

A national system should provide a better buffer against indignant politicians and others whose sensibilities are offended by an activist public sector. Its proper work necessarily includes the duty to take up the cudgels against public authorities, central and local. This may provoke calls for the reduction or withdrawal of funding for the lawyers engaged in such activities. It is likely to be easier for such pressures to be resisted at the national level than in town halls and council chambers up and down the country. Officials and members of the national organisation are apt to be better informed and more in touch with the leaders of opinion in the field, including the lay and legal press, and therefore less susceptible to the appeals of the backwoodsmen. Local political leaders and their officials are less likely than their equivalents at the national level to be convinced of the value of having public sector lawyers. It is true that, if there is only one national money-tap, it is easier to turn it off than if there are many local ones. A government determined to destroy the public sector or even merely to clip its wings has the means available through control of the purse. But, on balance, the danger of benighted political interference with the proper work of public sector lawyers seems less at the national than at the local level.

Public sector lawyers and independence

There are, of course, those who believe that state salaried lawyers are, by definition, apt to be supine and to lack the vital quality of independence which lawyers rightly regard as of crucial importance. The most extreme way of expressing this sentiment is that only lawyers in private practice can be relied on at times of crisis to do their duty to resist actual or potential tyranny. In reality, even courageous lawyers are unlikely to make the difference between a successful or an unsuccessful take-over by a real dictator. But in situations short of this the extent of the lawyers' true independence could be of genuine significance. The difficulty with the argument that equates state salaries with a lowered capacity to resist improper pressure from the state is that judges, Members of Parliament and officials such as Ombudsmen have shown in many countries that they are capable of being independent, notwithstanding that they depend for their salaries on the public purse. In South Africa, for instance, some private practitioner members of the legal profession have an honourable record for resistance to government policies in the political field – but so do some South African judges. The 3,500 or so federally funded neighbourhood lawyers in the United States probably bring as many actions against public authorities, federal, state and local, as the entire American private profession put together.

It is, of course, possible that lawyers whose economic future is dependent on salaries paid out of the public purse will be less than conscientious in representing their clients in conflicts with the state or other authorities – but the same is true of private practitioners. There are, for instance, private practitioner defence lawyers who are less energetic on their clients' behalf than they should be.[25] A salaried public sector, led by strong lawyers with a clear sense of their role, may provide a service that is in every respect as independent (and competent) as that of the private profession. By the same token, it could be lax, incompetent and craven. The chief ingredient of independence is the willingness of the lawyer to do his full professional duty for his client without regard to consequences for himself. Private practitioners are as likely as salaried lawyers to take the easy way. Barristers, for instance, frequently complain in private about the poor quality of the instructions they receive from solicitors. How often do they make such complaints direct to the solicitors who brief them? How often do solicitors refrain from seeking a writ of habeas corpus on behalf of a suspect in the police station through a mixture of laziness and reluctance to disturb a comfortable working relationship with the local police? Solicitors refuse cases that they think may damage their image with their existing clients. Barristers, whilst defending, sometimes 'pull their punches' in cross-examining the police for fear, conscious or unconscious, that they will not get prosecution work. It is, in fact, easier to do one's duty as a lawyer in the dramatic confrontation between citizen and the state than in the day-to-day, humdrum business of representing clients in ordinary cases. Independence, like competence, depends mainly on the values and qualities of those who provide the service, not on whether they happen to be paid salaries from public moneys or fees by the case.[26]

This is not to say that organisation is wholly irrelevant; merely that a fully independent service may function even if it is salaried out of public funds. But it is obviously sensible to build in additional safeguards. Thus, it is better for public-sector lawyers to be employed by the law centre as a separate entity than by the local authority direct. It may be better still for them to be employed by some form of Legal Services agency, established separately from government, like the University Grants Committee. Such Commissions have now been established in many jurisdictions: British Columbia,[27] Manitoba,[28] Newfoundland,[29] Nova Scotia,[30] Quebec,[31] Saskatchewan[32] and the United States.[33] It has been proposed, and seemingly accepted, in Australia, both at the federal and the state level,[34] and by an official report for Ontario.[35] Such a Commission can provide support, political muscle, and leadership to help the lawyers in the service remain wholly independent. (See further, pp. 269–71 below). Lawyers in the public sector should also, of course, be able to look to their professional association and the profession as a whole for support in any situations of conflict between their duty as lawyers and improper pressures from without.

Should the legal aid scheme be taken away from the Law Society?

If there were a Legal Services Commission it would, presumably, receive an annual grant of public funds to provide legal services. It should be responsible for the entire public sector based on salaried services. But what of services provided by private practitioners out of public funds – through the ordinary English legal aid system (known as Judicare in the United

States)? The Law Society has been managing the legal aid scheme since its inception in 1949. Should this responsibility now be taken away and given to a new Legal Services Commission?

The Legal Action Group (LAG), in its evidence to the Royal Commission, has answered this question in the affirmative, and so in Ontario did the Osler Committee in 1974. LAG said:

> In the structure we propose, the Law Society would hand the administration of the Legal Aid Scheme over to the Legal Services Commission. This is an essential corollary of our scheme for making legal services more responsive to local needs, which involves a network of area legal services councils ... charged with planning and organising legal services nationwide. Clearly, it would be quite inappropriate for the Law Society – a professional association – to be such a body.[36]

The time had come for the Law Society to cede responsibility for the legal aid scheme, notwithstanding its competent administrative record. It was in modern times increasingly 'inappropriate for one organisation to try to exercise the dual role that the Law Society currently plays: that of professional association on the one hand, and watchdog of the public interest on the other'.[37]

The Osler Committee recommended that the supervision and management of all legal services funded out of the public purse be taken away from the Law Society of Upper Canada and entrusted, instead, to a new independent Corporation consisting of lawyers and laymen, 'with a singleminded determination to provide legal services to the public, uninhibited by control or direction in that regard by any agency of government or the Law Society'.[38] But the Osler Report has not yet been implemented and it is not yet certain that it will be. The problem of shifting control over legal aid from the Law Society in England is probably even greater politically than in Ontario. If the Rushcliffe Committee were sitting today, it would almost certainly recommend (as the equivalent Canadian and Australian committees have) that legal services be run by a body independent of the profession. The Irish equivalent of the Rushcliffe Committee, for instance, whose report was published early in 1978, recommended an independent commission to run legal aid.[39] Attitudes to these issues have greatly changed since the early post-war years. But it does not follow that this is necessarily the right answer in England today. There is a natural governmental reluctance to offend so powerful a group as the lawyers' professional organisation by taking away statutory management responsibilities, especially when on the level of strict management efficiency there is no serious criticism of the system. It was not surprising that the Lord Chancellor's Legal Aid Advisory Committee in its evidence to the Royal Commission should have thought that no sufficient case had been made out for divesting the Law Society of its stewardship of the scheme.[40]

But the question whether the Law Society should continue to run publicly funded legal services is, on analysis, not as crucial as it may at first appear. In reality, the Law Society, under the English system, has very little real power. It 'manages' a legal aid budget of more than £40m., but in order to be allowed to establish one law centre, or even to appoint one extra Advisory Liaison Officer, it has to get Treasury approval – and in both cases it has petitioned for several years in vain. It cannot decide that a private firm should open in a particular area. It has little control over the level of fees paid out of the legal aid fund. It has no influence over the volume of cases brought to legal aid certifying committees – this depends entirely on the number of individuals in the community who come forward with problems eligible for legal aid. It cannot prevent a person who qualifies on the means and merits test from receiving legal aid – improper refusal of a certificate can be challenged by application for an order for *certiorari* and *mandamus*. The Law Society cannot extend the scope of the legal aid scheme nor decide, as the Lord Chancellor recently did,[41] to withdraw legal aid from undefended divorce hearings and redistribute the estimated £6m. to be saved by raising the means test limits and setting up more law centres. If there were a Legal Services Commission, it would be limited in precisely the same ways. More especially, it seems inconceivable that any government would permit such a Commission to take the kinds of decision that would be the main purpose of having such a body – notably the allocation of funds as between legal aid through the private sector and legal services through the salaried sector. These decisions would either remain with the government (e.g. how much money to give the salaried sector and the scope and extent of legal aid given by private practitioners) or with the legal aid certifying committees deciding on individual applications for legal aid.

The areas in which it is vital that decisions are not left to the profession alone are, above all, the level of state funding of legal services, the mode of provision of such services, controls over fees paid and the professional rules of etiquette governing the provision of legal services. In the English context all this can be achieved whilst leaving the Law Society with its existing stewardship of the legal aid scheme, subject to the participation of laymen (see pp. 258–67 below). (The level of funding and the scope of the legal aid scheme are clearly a governmental responsibility. For control of fees see pp. 200–13 below; for controls over the rules of etiquette see pp. 267–69 below.)

The body or agency responsible for the public (salaried) sector would have to determine how best to use its moneys. Since there are at present very few law centres (in 1977 less than thirty) with a total budget of little more than £2m., it is not necessary to make unduly heavy weather of the running of the public sector. The Law Centres Working Group and the Lord Chancellor's Office appear to contemplate a small secretariat, drawn from the law centres movement but financed and approved by the Lord Chancellor's Office. If the public sector becomes large enough to justify a full-blown Legal Services Commission, there will be time enough to set it up then. In countries offering legal services through private practitioners and salaried lawyers it is obviously tidier and better for the management structure to encompass both models. If, however, as in England, the political battle to unify the structure appears too great to contemplate, the main objectives of such a scheme can nevertheless be achieved by other means. There should, however, be a small office, including a national director, for the public sector to give leadership, stimulate new ventures, liaise with official bodies and generally play a promotional role for the development of the public sector.

Should the public sector be transformed into a national legal service?

The discussion hitherto has been based on the assumption that there will continue to be both a private and a public sector in state financed legal services. But since there is in England a functioning national health service, it is logical to ask whether there should not equally be a national legal service, and the more so since the public moneys applied to legal services now run into tens of millions of pounds a year. By a national legal service is usually meant a system for providing legal services out of general taxation. Most of those who use the term envisage that the services are provided by lawyers who are state salaried, though the question of state salaries is separate from that of legal services financed out of the public purse. (One might have salaried lawyers offering services for which the public had to pay the full market fee or, conversely, private practitioners financed by the state to provide free services to individual clients.)

There are various reasons, however, for believing that the analogy between legal and medical services is not apt. First, a great range of legal services are sought and obtained by business concerns that have no counterpart in the medical field. Only individuals can seek the help of a doctor; companies, partnerships, unincorporated bodies and groups all have legal problems. It may be reasonable to say that all individuals, irrespective of means, should be entitled to state subsidised medical services; it makes far less obvious sense to apply the same approach to the entire business community. But even comparing only individuals, it does not seem likely that any government would conclude that the general body of tax-payers ought to finance legal services to those fortunate enough to be able to buy or sell their own homes or to inherit property. Such a policy would be considered highly regressive rather than progressive. It follows that free legal services could not be offered to the business community or for property transfers. *But these make up the bulk of present legal services.* The proposed national legal service would therefore exclude most legal services currently provided.

The national legal service could only operate insofar as there were lawyers willing and able to do that work. If most lawyers are engaged in serving private clients, there will be correspondingly few to assist clients of the national legal service. Of course, lawyers might be won away from private clients to work for the public sector by the ordinary inducements of the marketplace. Thus, if national legal services were paid for at a higher rate than those offered by private clients, lawyers would presumably move from the private to the public sector. But there is little hope of the public sector ever paying better than the private – at present in all countries the levels of remuneration in the public sector appear to be lower.[42] At best, the two might pay somewhat equivalent rates, but even this seems unlikely.

Certainly, most lawyers would rather work in the public sector than not work at all, at least if the conditions of work are acceptable. Both sides of the English profession are massively involved in providing state-funded services to defendants in criminal cases – virtually without a means test or contribution – because it is sufficiently well paid and there is hardly any private work in this field. But, although the money for this work comes from the state, it is perceived by the profession as being essentially in the private sector because of the all-important fact that the lawyers are paid by the case and not salaries. If all lawyers who wished to be paid for undertaking criminal legal aid work had to agree to become state salaried, some might prefer to leave the profession or to do other legal work, if there were any. The conditions of work would then have become unacceptable to them. Whilst, however, most of the legal profession continue to earn a more or less satisfactory living from serving the business and property-owning classes, there would be no real incentive for them to shift to other, even to non-salaried, state-financed work – especially, of course, if it paid less. Any substantial provision of new free legal services by lawyers paid for out of general taxation would, therefore, require either a corresponding increase in the size of the legal profession or a substantial re-deployment of existing lawyers towards new classes of work. Both would be difficult to achieve without economic costs that would probably be regarded as too high to be feasible. (The suggestion that the new free legal services should be provided mainly by less costly para-professionals would doom the national legal service to the appearance, and probably the reality, of second-class standards. This hardly seems the best way to maximise the role of para-professionals.) On the present basis, relatively few lawyers would therefore be available for the public sector because of the counter-attraction of the private sector.

Assuming that most lawyers continued to prefer the private

sector, would it nevertheless make sense to require that all state-funded work be channelled to the public salaried sector? Private practitioners would then have to make their choice. If they opted for the private sector, they could not also enjoy the benefit of state-funded work. The converse of this question is whether, in countries such as the United States, state-funded legal aid should be channelled to private practitioners through Judicare or whether it should be directed wholly, or at least mainly, to salaried lawyers. This question has been the subject of intense debate there. The Legal Services Corporation is charged with the statutory duty to report to Congress on the advantages and disadvantages of different modes of delivering legal services and has in hand a massive comparative study of Judicare and the Salaried or Staff model which includes comparison of costs.[43]

One crucial factor seems, however, to have been largely overlooked. It is meaningless to compare costs per unit of work done or overheads without taking into account the fact that firms of private practitioners already exist whereas salaried services have to be established. It may well be true that, so far as direct overheads are concerned, the salaried system can handle cases at lower cost per item of work – for a variety of reasons including higher case-loads, lower salaries and lower rents. But to obtain a fair comparison it is necessary to include also the capital cost of establishing the salaried offices. Thus in the English context, if legal aid work now done by private practitioners were re-directed instead to law centres it would mean that enough law centres would have to be set up to handle some £40m. worth of civil work (without even counting another £40m. worth of criminal work). It is virtually certain that, in practice, this could not be done, since it seems unlikely that there would be enough lawyers willing to shift from the private to the public sector to staff a national network of law centres to handle that volume of work. But, even if the lawyers were willing to make the switch, it would hardly make economic sense from a governmental point of view. The capital cost of establishing that number of law centres would obviously be very high and this would be public money largely thrown away since it would simply replace private sector funds.

Moreover, legal aid work is highly decentralised. In 1975–6

there were payments to 8,159 offices for civil legal aid work and magistrates' court criminal work. (The statistics relate to offices; a firm may have more than one office.) Of these, 2,228 offices (27 per cent) received under £500, 1,945 (24 per cent) received between £500 and £2,000, 1,640 (20 per cent) had between £2,000 and £5,000, and 1,207 (15 per cent) between £5,000 and £10,000. The remaining 1,139 firms (14 per cent) received over £10,000.[44] It would be economic madness to establish law centres to handle the business now done by all these 8,000 offices. No doubt, it could be done by a much smaller number of law centres organised efficiently to handle legal aid work in bulk – but, even then, the bill would be gigantic, not to speak of the inconvenience to the public of having to travel great distances to the much smaller number of legal aid firms.

Private practitioners should be used for public sector work so far as they can be used – subject to proper controls as to levels of fees, etc. The more members of the private profession become involved in serving the poor, the better for both the profession and the public. The part of the population eligible for legal aid is clearly better served in having access to the large number of private firms (as well as law centres), rather than being limited simply to the much smaller number of law centres. But the broader scope of work is beneficial also to the lawyers themselves – giving them the opportunity to serve the whole community, not only those able to pay for their services. The role of the salaried or public sector should be to fill the gaps. This makes maximum use of the available resources. The doctrinal struggle, especially in the United States, between supporters of the staff or salaried model for legal services on the one hand and of Judicare on the other has been bitter and prolonged.[45] It is time for the two factions to declare a truce. There is a need for both models. In countries with a free legal profession and a mixed economy the majority of the profession will probably continue in the future, as in the past, to serve clients with money and property. Even if it were desirable, there is no acceptable way of preventing this. The level of governmental funding of legal services will go on rising, perhaps as dramatically as in the past decade or so. If the private profession devotes a growing proportion of its time and effort to serving the poor who are eligible for services that the state is prepared to finance, so much the better for the public. It is pure political dogma that holds this to be wrong.

It has been argued by some advocates of the public sector that it is likely to be more efficient, more competent, more cost-effective, more attractive to clients as well as being more reform-oriented. It is possible that all or any of these claims might be validated in a particular locality or even a particular country – at a given time. But there is nothing in the nature of the two models of providing legal services that makes it inevitable. Thus the American neighbourhood law firms and more especially the 'back-up centres' may have concentrated considerable efforts on law reform. But the Australian Legal Aid Offices have operated more as referral points to private firms and English law centres have hitherto done more case-work than test-case or other law reform work. It is perfectly possible to imagine that the public sector would be 'better' than private practice and that in the same country or locality a few years later the position would be reversed. More is likely to depend on the quality of the lawyers in each service than on the fact that they are in private practice or paid state salaries. Certainly the public sector may be better able to cope with problems on a group basis than private practitioners, but, comparing like with like, it seems improbable that either the private or the public sector will *necessarily* be the superior form of practice, even in such matters as cost-effectiveness. If client opinion is any guide there is evidence that at least in some circumstances clients prefer to go to private practitioners,[46] but in other circumstances they may prefer the services of the public sector lawyers.

There can be no serious doubt that in any event there will be ample work for both private practitioners and public sector lawyers. Private practitioners are at present the dominant mode of providing legal services, but they must be supplemented by the public sector. The Lord Chancellor's Advisory Committee said in 1975, that while it was important that full emphasis should be given to the work of private practitioners under the legal aid scheme, it had become apparent 'that at least for the forseeable future, private practice cannot provide all that is needed nor would it be reasonable to complain at its failure to do so'. There was 'a clear case for salaried solicitors to be appointed to assist in doing the work, particularly in urban areas of special need: for lack of such provision many people are being wholly deprived of their legal rights in such essential matters as housing, social security, employment and consumer difficulties'.[47]

The right development is, therefore, not towards the abolition of the private sector and its replacement by a state salaried system, but an expansion of publicly financed legal work done partly by a growing salaried sector and partly by the private profession. Each has its strengths. Increasingly, for instance, the Treasury may be prepared to recognise that certain kinds of legal service are so important as to constitute 'basic legal rights', justifying their provision without regard to means both by the salaried sector and by private firms. Thus, it might be said that every citizen should have the right, at the state's expense, to consult a solicitor once or twice or three times a year for half an hour on any legal problem. In its evidence to the Royal Commission the Law Society suggested that an initial free diagnostic interview should be available to those who qualified under the means test for the Green Form scheme. If this were too expensive it might be limited to tenants or occupiers facing a threat of eviction.[48] This would be a start. As public funds for legal services and public support for their use in such ways grew, the idea could be gradually expanded. The Society of Labour Lawyers and The Legal Action Group have said that eventually we ought to move to a situation where 'basic legal rights' available free to every citizen should cover a great multitude of situations presenting legal problems. Suspects in police stations, children and parents involved in custody disputes, battered wives, aliens threatened with deportation, employees facing threatened loss of a job, even victims of accidents might all be candidates for free legal services provided as of right by the state without regard to means. Obviously it will be extremely difficult to persuade governments to advance rapidly down this road. Yet *any* step taken in this direction would be valuable and the most important, by far, will be the first. After that it will only be a matter of developing an existing concept as resources permit. The precise priorities for the gradual development of such an approach would vary according to taste and judgment. Its potential costs could be tested by experiment. It would be subject to periodic review and adjustment as economic conditions altered. It offers the best prospect for the next stage in the growth of publicly funded legal services.

4 The Quality of Legal Services: Discipline and Complaints

It is inevitable that the work of lawyers should sometimes provoke complaint from clients. The problems that people bring to lawyers are commonly tangled and frequently involve affairs that have a high emotional content. Often a successful outcome of the matter is of great importance to the client. If it involves litigation or other court proceedings, one party has to lose and may be inclined to blame his lawyer more than the weaknesses of the case. Some of those who become involved with lawyers are of a belligerent disposition and may be more complaint-orientated than the average member of the community. Some complaints verge on the frivolous and vexatious; some are simply misconceived; others are perfectly well founded. The legal profession's approach, broadly, has been that, if a complaint discloses misconduct which is 'unprofessional', it will act. But if it falls short of unprofessional conduct the client will be left without a remedy, other than an action for negligence. The profession's traditional view is that its function is primarily to discipline its own rather than to provide any redress to the aggrieved client.

Each side of the profession has elaborate machinery for dealing with allegations of misconduct.

The machinery for handling discipline and complaints

The Bar
Traditionally, at the Bar the disciplinary function was exercised by the benchers of the four Inns of Court. Each Inn disciplined its own members according to its own standards. When the Bar Council was first established in 1895 it tried to obtain jurisdiction over discipline but it was repulsed by the Inns which determined that the Bar Council should not 'interfere with the property, jurisdiction, powers or privileges of

the Inns of Court'.[1] This position continued until after the Second World War. But in the past decade or so power over discipline has gradually shifted away from the Inns and towards the practising Bar. From 1966, with the setting up of the Senate of the Four Inns of Court, complaints against barristers were dealt with first by the Bar's Professional Conduct Committee, which consisted entirely of practitioners. If they thought the complaint was sufficiently serious, they referred it to the Senate's Complaints Committee, most of whose members were also practitioners. That committee decided whether the complaint was sufficiently serious to go before the Disciplinary Committee (which consisted of a judge and six practising barristers) or only to the barrister's Inn. In 1974, implementation of the Pearce Committee's Report (see p. 246 below) led to the establishment of new machinery. All complaints against barristers go first to the Professional Conduct Committee of the Senate of the Four Inns of Court and the Bar. This consists of fourteen practising barristers, at least one non-practising barrister and a Lay Member drawn from a panel first appointed in 1975 by the Lord Chancellor. It is a sub-committee of the Bar Council (which consists purely of practising barristers) and not of the Senate (a significant number of whom are judges, retired barristers and other non-practitioners).

The procedure for handling complaints[2] is for a member of the Professional Conduct Committee to examine each complaint, and to report to the Committee. The Committee, in deciding what, if anything, to do, may ask the barrister for his written comments. It can seek further information from the complaining individual, the solicitors in the case, the barrister's clerk or any other person. This information is brought to the notice of the barrister complained of and, if the complaint is rejected, of the complainant.

The consideration of the complaint by the Committee takes place without any oral hearing. Neither the barrister complained of, nor the complainant, is present. The Bar told the Royal Commission that complaints from lay persons are never rejected without the agreement of the lay representative on the Committee. (A decision on a complaint requires the participation of at least five members of the Committee.) The complainant can ask for the case to be reopened. When he does, it

starts afresh. But complainants are not seen – according to the
Bar, many complainants are unavailable because they are in
prison, and moreover committee members give of their time
voluntarily. Neither of these reasons appears in itself entirely
persuasive. In appropriate cases even a person in prison could
be seen. In view of the small number of cases handled per year,
the burden of seeing the occasional dissatisfied complainant
would not seem insuperable. The Committee has power (in
ascending order of gravity) to admonish the barrister, to
report the matter to the Treasurer of his Inn, or to present a
charge before the Disciplinary Tribunal. Charges are only
pressed to the point of a case before the Disciplinary Tribunal
if the complaint appears to justify suspension or disbarment.

The Disciplinary Tribunal is not appointed by the Bar
Council but by the Senate from its own members, who are not
members of the Professional Conduct Committee. It consists
of between five and seven members, one of whom is a judge,
and one is a Lay Member drawn from the same panel that
serves the Professional Conduct Committee. Hearings before
the Disciplinary Tribunal are adversary in nature. The case for
the Senate is presented by counsel, sometimes instructed by
solicitors, and the defendant is normally represented. Evidence is taken. The hearing is, however, not open to the
public, nor is the complainant permitted to attend. The Tribunal has power to disbar, suspend, or reprimand the barrister
or to order him to repay or to forego his fees in the case. There
is a right of appeal to the judges of the High Court sitting as
visitors to the Inn of the barrister concerned. The judges are
nominated by the Lord Chancellor. As many as five may sit.[3]

The Bar's evidence to the Royal Commission gave some
details of the types of complaint in the recent past. Table 4.1
shows the nature of complaints received. Some two-thirds
concerned allegations of poor-quality work by barristers.
The Bar also gave details of the source of complaints. Of
304 complaints in the three-year period, 59 (19 per cent)
came from prisoners and 111 (36 per cent) came from other
lay clients. The next largest categories were courts (45 complaints, or 15 per cent) and solicitors (40, or 13 per cent).
Other barristers brought a total of 17, the Professional Conduct Committee 19 and the Law Society 6.[4] Between two-
thirds and three-quarters of the complaints each year are dis-

Table 4.1
Nature of complaints against barristers, 1972–6

	1974	1975	1976	Total
Quality of work done (bad advice, acting without instructions, or contrary to instructions, lack of courtesy, inadequate representation, undue influence, conduct of the proceedings, late returns of briefs, delay, absence)	66	61	75	202 (66%)
Etiquette (advertising, touting, abuse of qualifications, refusing to act, chambers matters)	7	24	15	46 (15%)
Fees	3	–	–	3 (1%)
Miscellaneous (withholding information, unrelated to practice	20	16	17	53 (17%)
Total	96	101	107	304 (100%)

Source: Bar, *Evidence, Submission No.* 7, p. VIII.6, Table 1.

missed either by the Committee or by the Tribunal. There are no figures which show the relationship between the nature of the complaint and the likelihood of its being upheld. But the Secretary of the Senate has given a strong indication that it is breaches of the rules of conduct and etiquette, rather than incompetence, delay, or undue costs that are likely to result in action against a barrister. In an article about the new procedures in 1976, he divided common complaints into the two main categories. Breaches of the rules of etiquette 'could well result in disciplinary action whereas, for the second group, – inefficiency, delay, undue cost, etc. – such action would almost certainly be inappropriate ... A barrister's success or failure may well govern whether or not he gets work, but as a general rule it cannot be a matter for disciplinary action'.[5] In November 1972, the former Senate of the Four Inns of Court adopted the proposition that 'such professional incompetence on the part of a member of the Bar as would be likely to be detrimental to the proper administration of justice or otherwise to bring the profession into disrepute should attract disciplinary sanctions'.[6] But it was stated in May 1977, nearly five years later, that no disciplinary proceedings had ever been brought on these grounds.[7]

Solicitors
For the first several hundred years of their history, the discipline of solicitors and attorneys was in the hands of the judges. In successive Acts of Parliament (in 1403, 1605 and 1729) the judges were given duties of control and discipline. But the system worked badly. The judges did not discharge their functions of examining candidates for admission.[8] They exercised powers of control if the offence was committed in their very courts, but not much otherwise. There was no system for the public to make complaints. Moreover, standards were relatively lax. The Court of Appeal ruled in 1893 that 'the mere fact of a man being convicted for a criminal offence punishable with imprisonment and hard labour is not itself sufficient to justify his being struck off or even suspended from practice'.[9]

From the latter part of the nineteenth century the Law Society increasingly became involved in the process. In 1874 it was given the right to be heard on an application to the court for the striking off of any solicitor from the Roll. Under the 1888 Solicitors Act the inquiry as to whether disciplinary proceedings were warranted was to be conducted not as before on behalf of the court, but by a committee nominated by the Master of the Rolls from the members of the Council of the Law Society. The Solicitors Act 1919 provided that the actual hearing of the charges should be by a Disciplinary Committee appointed by the Lord Chancellor from past or present members of the Council of the Law Society, with the role of the court now confined to that of appeal tribunal.

This meant that the Law Society first investigated complaints, then prosecuted and then adjudicated. The officials were from the Law Society; the Committee were Council members; it sat in the Law Society's Hall. This multiplicity of roles played by the Law Society was criticised both from within and outside the profession, depending on the vantage-point of the critic, as being either too partial or too hard on solicitors.

The Law Society resisted the suggestion that any changes

were needed, but in 1972 the occasion of a new Solicitors' Bill forced reforms. A Labour backbench MP, Mr Michael English, used parliamentary procedures to block progress on the Law Society's Bill[10] until he got acceptable concessions regarding the complaints machinery.[11] One was the establishment of a Lay Observer to supervise the handling of complaints by the Law Society. The Disciplinary Committee became the Disciplinary Tribunal and its members, for the first time, included laymen appointed by the Lord Chancellor. The requirement that the solicitor members should always be past or present Council members was dropped. The Tribunal sits with three members, two of whom are solicitors and one a layman. The idea of lay involvement in the disciplinary process was not, in fact, entirely new since regulations made under the 1967 Criminal Justice Act had provided for a lay member of the Complaints Tribunal to handle complaints against a barrister or solicitor arising out of criminal legal aid. The Home Secretary, Mr Roy Jenkins, insisted on this innovation against the adamant opposition of both branches of the legal profession. The Law Society had also experimented voluntarily for a year (in 1971–2) with its own lay observer of the complaints system.[12]

The Law Society receives in the region of 5,000 complaints each year. Table 4.2 shows the actual number of complaints, their source, and the number of complaints expressed as a proportion of the total number of solicitors with practising certificates. The figures for each year are remarkably uniform.

Table 4.2

Complaints against solicitors

	Solicitor complaints	Lay complaints	Total	Total as % of all solicitors
1973	623	4,230	4,853	16.8
1974	626	4,116	4,742	15.8
1975	731	5,021	5,752	18.4

Source: Law Society, *Evidence, Memorandum No. 3*, Part 1, p. 56.

The complaints, which have to be in writing, are processed by the Law Society's staff in the Professional Purposes

Department. [13] The Department is the largest in the Law Society. The staff decide, in the first place, whether the complaint is one over which the Law Society has jurisdiction. An important exclusion (considered further below) is that the Law Society will not normally handle complaints that appear to allege negligence by a solicitor. In such cases the complainant is told that he should seek advice from another solicitor with a view to considering taking legal proceedings. If the complaint is within the Law Society's jurisdiction, and not manifestly frivolous, the staff may then correspond with the complainant to get further details. In very rare cases the complainant will be interviewed by a staff member. If the matter appears to require explanation from the solicitor, he will be asked to give his version of the facts. With the consent of the complainant, the letter from the client will be sent to the solicitor. If, in view of the staff, the solicitor deals with the matter adequately, his letter of explanation will be sent to the client complainant. If the staff are satisfied with the solicitor's explanation, but the complainant is not, the matter is automatically referred to the Professional Purposes Committee, whose members are members of the Council of the Law Society. If they confirm the view of the staff that there is no ground for pursuing the matter further, the client is told that he can still appeal to the Lay Observer.

The staff may, however, take the view that the solicitor's explanation is not adequate. In that event, the case goes to the Professional Purposes Committee. The Committee considers the matter on the papers, without any oral hearing. If it finds against the solicitor, it has a variety of possible punishments, none of which, however, include any power to order compensation for the complainant. The mildest is a reprimand. If the allegation is one of delay, the solicitor may be ordered to report monthly to the Law Society on the progress of the matter. The Committee can impose conditions until further notice on the grant of the annual practising certificate – for instance, that the solicitor practise only with a partner or only as an employee. In a case of serious delay the Committee can also order the solicitor to hand over the papers in the case to enable the client to instruct another solicitor. (The threat of such action is usually sufficient to expedite matters.) The Committee can order the inspection of any solicitor's accounts. In certain circumstances it can resolve to take over a solicitor's bank accounts. It can appoint an agent to take over a practice with a view to returning the papers to clients as quickly as possible. If necessary, these powers can be exercised at short notice. The Committee's most serious weapon is to institute formal disciplinary proceedings before the Disciplinary Tribunal. (In the case of complaints arising out of criminal legal aid the statutory regulations provide, similarly, that it is the Law Society (or, as the case may be, the Bar Council) which makes the complaint to the Tribunal.) The procedure at this stage becomes adversary as in a court. The solicitor is entitled to be, and normally is, represented, by solicitor and counsel. The Law Society's case is presented by a solicitor or counsel. The hearing is in private. Evidence is taken on oath. Proof of guilt is required to be beyond a reasonable doubt, as in a criminal case. The complainant is not entitled to be present.

If the case is proved, the Tribunal can strike the solicitor off the Rolls, which prevents him practising as a solicitor until such time, if ever, as he succeeds in persuading the Tribunal to restore him to the Rolls. He can practise as an unadmitted person in the employment of a solicitor, but he must inform the prospective employer of his status as a struck-off solicitor and the would-be employer must then first obtain the written permission of the Law Society. Lesser penalties include suspension from practice for up to five years, a fine of up to £750, or simply a reprimand. The solicitor can also be ordered to pay the costs of the proceedings. There is a right of appeal against the decision of the Tribunal to the Divisional Court of the Queen's Bench Division. The proceedings are normally limited to consideration of the transcript of the hearing by the Tribunal and the materials considered by the Tribunal. Fresh evidence is rare. The court usually upholds the Tribunal.

The judges still retain their inherent jurisdiction to deal with misconduct by solicitors as officers of the court – but this power is now used very infrequently. If the court believes that a solicitor may have committed some professional offence it normally refers the matter to the Law Society. Occasionally, however, a solicitor is ordered to pay the costs of a stage in the proceedings where his own default has caused costs to be wasted.

At the time of the debate on the Solicitors Act 1974, the Law Society analysed complaints received from November 1972 to May 1973. In this period there were 529 letters making 712 separate complaints. The breakdown is given in Table 4.3.

Table 4.3
Breakdown of complaints against solicitors

Complaints found to be justified

Breakdown:		
Delay	140 (66.9% of 209)	
Complaints about third party solicitor	19 (9.0%)	
Costs	7 (3.3%)	
Conflict of interest	18 (8.6%)	
Failure to keep informed	5 (2.3%)	
Negligence	20 (9.7%)	209
Found either unjustified or outside Law Society's powers		503
Total examined		712

Source: Law Society, *Evidence, Memorandum No. 3*, Part 1, p. 54.

Of the complaints that were found to be justified, two-thirds concerned excessive delays. Costs were the subject of complaint in only 3 per cent of cases. It appears that the proportion of cases found justified is usually around 30 per cent, but nothing is known about the cases that are not upheld or which are deemed to fall outside the Law Society's powers. There has not hitherto been any information even as to the types of complaint that were deemed to be outside the Law Society's jurisdiction, but since January 1977 the Society has been keeping records, which will make such analysis possible. Nor are there any figures as to what are the matters that lead to disciplinary proceedings. But it is certain that the overwhelming majority arise out of failures by solicitors to comply with the very stringent accounts rules.[14] Just as in the case of the Bar, the solicitors' disciplinary procedures are used mainly to penalise professional misconduct rather than complaints from clients over the way in which their cases have been handled.

Since February 1974 a client whose complaint is rejected by the Law Society has been able to 'appeal' to the Lay Observer appointed by the Lord Chancellor under the provisions of the 1974 Solicitors Act, s.45. His duty is to examine 'any written allegation by or on behalf of a member of the public concerning the [Law] Society's treatment of a complaint about a solicitor or an employee of a solicitor'. His offices are in the Royal Courts of Justice, not in the Law Society. In his first annual report the Lay Observer said he had received complaints from 437 individuals. Some two-thirds (275) raised matters outside his jurisdiction – requests for legal advice and the like. The number of complaints received for examination was 162. In his second year of operation he had received complaints from 305 individuals and had investigated 127. The breakdown of problems in the two years was fairly similar, as appears from Table 4.4. In both years, most complaints arose from disputes as to property, divorce and matrimonial proceedings and the administration of wills and estates. There were few complaints about the conduct of criminal proceedings – in contrast with the complaints against barristers, almost a fifth of which came from prisoners.[15] The first report stated that the complaints which were outside the Lay Observer's competence indicated 'a very similar proportion'.

The reports also showed the nature of the complaints. Again they were much the same in both years, though the proportions varied, as shown in Table 4.5. In both years, about half the complaints related to delay or incompetence. Clients complained that they were not sufficiently kept in the picture, that they were given estimates of costs that turned out to be much too low, that matters dragged on too long. Sometimes, however, the complaint was based on a failure by the client to understand the law or its limitations. Both the Lay Observer's two reports 'found relatively little cause for criticising the way in which the Law Society had carried out its responsibilities within its powers'.[16] Most complaints alleged that the Law Society's decision had been wrong,

Table 4.4

Type of matters referred to Lay Observer
1976 and 1977

	1976 (%)	1977 (%)
Miscellaneous property disputes (boundaries, buildings, patents, motor cars, stocks and shares, etc.)	38	21
Matrimonial	18	28
Administration of estates	14	14
Landlord and tenant	10	2
Conveyancing	4	10
Professional negligence (architects, doctors, solicitors)	2	2
Criminal proceedings	2	3
Contractual disputes	2	5
Personal injury cases	2	2
Miscellaneous	7	12
Total	100 (162)	100 (127)

Source: *First and Second Reports of the Lay Observer,* 1976 and 1977,
Appendix II.

often coupled with criticisms that its investigations should have been broader, for instance by questioning witnesses. (The Law Society has no power to summon witnesses.) Some complainants felt aggrieved by the Law Society's unwillingness to give legal advice or opinions on questions of law. In his first report the Lay Observer said he had criticised the Law Society's handling of the complaint in thirteen cases (9 per cent of the 140 cases in which the investigation was completed). In the second report the number was eleven (again 9 per cent). Taken as a proportion of all the 5,000 or so complaints handled by the Law Society, the dozen or so in which the Lay Observer makes criticisms is obviously tiny. As a proportion of the matters handled by the profession, it is infinitesimal.

Table 4.5

Nature of complaints to Lay Observer
1976 and 1977

	1976 (%)	1977 (%)
Delay	43	24
Withholding documents or information, exercise lien	25	10
Negligence or incompetence	7	27
Accounts	7	21
Disclosing confidential information	7	5
Conflicts of interest, collusion	6	9
Complaints regarding unqualified staff	6	2
Total	100(191)	100(127)

Source: *First and Second Reports of Lay Observer* 1976 and 1977, Appendix II.

Evaluation of the weaknesses of the existing system and some proposals for reform

The Lay Observer's two reports reveal the central flaw in the approach of both sides of the profession to the whole problem of complaints. The profession's procedures are geared basically to serious issues of professional misconduct and not to the ordinary complaints of clients. In his second report the Lay Observer, Admiral Place, said: 'In the considerable majority of matters referred to me it is not the propriety of the solicitor's conduct that is in question, but rather is there criticism of how he has done his work in the broadest sense. Complaint may be levelled at any part of the whole range of his activity: the time taken, explanations given, the quality of the advice, the fees charged'.[17] Where the propriety of conduct was in question it tended to be something 'which would, if substantiated, be more likely to merit deprecation or rebuke rather than disciplinary proceedings'.[18] It is symptomatic that the relevant committees are entitled the Professional Conduct and Professional Purposes Committees, and Disciplinary Tribunal. The profession has been interested in dealing with lax standards only if they amount to professional misconduct. Moreover, even in the case of more serious complaints, if they allege mere negligence the profession again has told the lay complainant that he must find his remedy, if at all, through the courts by way of an action for negligence. This is not only burdensome in itself, but often the lay client finds he must settle the account of the first set of solicitors before they will release his papers in order to instruct a second firm. He may also have difficulty in finding solicitors to take on the case against another firm.

The Lay Observer's recommendations

The Lay Observer has advanced various proposals to improve the situation. First, the Law Society and local law societies ought to assist those wishing to consider actions for negligence by drawing up lists of local firms willing to act in such cases. ('It seems to me that lists of solicitors who have the skill and experience for professional negligence litigation should be compiled and available to the public on demand.'[19]) If such lists could be prepared and circulated to citizens' advice bureaux and similar advisory agencies they might be of some value. There were indications in autumn 1977 that the Law Society might accept this suggestion[20] and even possibly go beyond it to establish some new system at the local level for assisting clients wishing to sue their former solicitors for negligence.

Then, in his first report, the Lay Observer suggested that 'there ought to be a system of control to prevent solicitors dealing with matters of which they have little experience'.[21] There seems little hope that this would be feasible. Since a solicitor (or barrister) is entitled to take any work, it would be difficult for the professional bodies to become involved in judging whether the lawyer's experience justified his taking a case. Even if a rule were promulgated making it professional misconduct to take cases beyond one's experience or competence, it is safe to predict that it would rarely, if ever, be enforced. The American Bar Association has, in fact, promulgated just such a rule but to little apparent effect.[22]

The Lay Observer had a more practical proposal on the subject of the solicitor's lien on documents, which gives him the right to hold the papers until he is paid. The lien, he said, was unjustified. ('In my view a client should have his papers returned when he needs them to pursue further action on which he is seeking other advice. The solicitor can always take proceedings for his charges, in which the client is at risk for costs, but for the client to be obliged to incur delays and charges in taking legal action for the recovery of documents seems to me unfair'.[23]) The Society of Labour Lawyers, in evidence to the Royal Commission, agreed. The effect of the lien, it said, was that either a client had to pay what he regarded as an excessive bill, having regard to the work, or he had to contest the bill, thus losing time and money, or he had to stay with solicitors with whom he was, by definition, dissatisfied.

The Society suggested that a solicitor ought to be under a professional duty to hand over the papers to the client on receiving an undertaking from a second firm that its proper charges would be paid when the matter was concluded. This should be the rule in any event. Better still, however, would be legislation simply abolishing the solicitor's lien. It seems wrong in principle that a professional person should be given so disproportionate an advantage over his client. No doubt the solicitor wishes to be paid, but he can sue for his fees in the ordinary way. He does not need, nor should he have, any greater protection than a claim for his fair and reasonable costs.

Intervention by the professional associations on negligence and neglect

The central problem, however, is whether the professional bodies should be prepared to intervene in regard to allegations of negligence, incompetence or neglect. This nettle has recently been grasped for the first time by the Bar. The matter came up in the course of preparing evidence for the Royal Commission. A statement on behalf of the Senate and the Bar Council said that under bye-laws adopted in April 1977 the Professional Conduct Committee had been given new powers to deal with minor breaches of good professional behaviour.[24] There was 'a natural repugnance to employing disciplinary sanctions against persons whose shortcomings stem from no moral turpitude but from inexperience, excusable ignorance, or even innate inability'. On the other hand, 'those who feel such repugnance will agree that the profession has a duty to prevent manifestly incompetent persons offering their services to the public'. To this end the Professional Conduct Committee now has the power to *advise* a barrister (as opposed to admonishing him) where it finds that a complaint discloses incompetence or a breach of professional etiquette falling in either case short of professional misconduct. The intention is to provide for machinery for warnings or cautions.

The Law Society has had similar powers since 1972.[25] In its evidence to the Royal Commission it stated that although office efficiency was not in itself regarded as a matter of professional conduct, a solicitor's attention might be directed to evidence from complaints that his office was inefficient. The solicitor would be asked for an explanation. The Law Society might inspect his books. If no satisfactory explanation was given he might be rebuked or even severely rebuked. If the inefficiency persisted, the Council would have a discretion over the issue of the practice certificate or its issue subject to conditions. In the final resort, disciplinary procedures could be considered.

These powers sound as if they meet the point, but they are so rarely exercised as to be largely theoretical. It was for this reason, no doubt, that the Lay Observer urged the Law Society to do more in this regard. In his second report, issued in June 1977, he said that in many cases the Law Society could act without prejudicing the client's right to take legal proceedings for negligence. Thus 'where office error is apparent, such as a date missed, witnesses not warned, promised follow-up action not taken and so forth, I believe the Law Society should at least ensure that the senior partner of the firm is informed so that he may take corrective action in his office administration: the facts of office error are rarely in dispute. Delay is pernicious. It should be the subject of Law Society comment if only in the form of an opinion'.[26] Presumably he intended that the Law Society should give advice not merely to the firm under criticism, but to the profession as a whole through published rulings or guidance. 'Whilst redress for the client can only be awarded by the courts, it seems to me very desirable, in the interests of the profession and of the general public, that lessons from mistakes are learnt.'[27] But his focus was still clearly on working through individual complaints. 'I have given some thought to whether the Law Society would perform a useful function by considering complaints about competence and I believe the Society would be wise to look through this window on the world.'[28]

Standards might be raised generally if the experience could be translated into admonitions to the profession at large. The Bar Council publishes rulings on individual cases in the annual report and the Law Society does so in its weekly *Gazette*. But it would be unrealistic to expect that such action could make much impact. An incompetent, inefficient or slovenly lawyer is not likely to be greatly improved by reports of proceedings taken against others. At best, such improvements would be marginal. Moreover, they offer no satisfaction to the aggrieved client.

At present the only direct help given to the client is in the case where he is the victim of fraud by the solicitor. The Law Society has had a Compensation Fund since 1942 to which all solicitors with a practising certificate must contribute. If the client has no other recourse (against the defaulting solicitor's partners or through insurance) he may claim against the fund. The fund is on a compensation, not indemnity, basis. Under the compensation system there is no legal entitlement to the payment, but all admitted claims are paid in full, plus costs, whereas under the indemnity system which operates in some countries there is normally limited liability which can, however, be pursued in the courts. The total number of solicitors involved in claims in the years 1971 to 1975 was 60 – an average of 12 per year.[29] The amounts claimed in each of those years varied from £496,444 in 1971 to £1,135,080 in 1975.[30] Claims rejected for one or another reason in those years ranged in aggregate amount from £32,241 in 1975 to £78,558 in 1973.[31] The great bulk of claims, therefore, are admitted. But apart from the rare complaint of financial dishonesty, clients cannot look for any direct redress from the professional bodies.

There are further things that might be done – both to improve the situation of the aggrieved client and to raise standards of work more generally. The first, simplest, and least controversial would be to extend the jurisdiction of the Lay Observer to complaints against barristers. This requires no discussion. It would surely be accepted as right without much difficulty. The second would be to persuade the professional bodies to take on the task of dealing with allegations of negligence or neglect. Neglect might be defined as culpable

acts of omission or commission which do not amount technically to negligence – negligence being something more serious
which might form the basis of an action for damages. Both
sides of the profession have the machinery for such action but
they rarely use it. A Committee of the American Bar Association, under the chairmanship of former Supreme Court Justice
Tom Clark, said that it was understandable that disciplinary
proceedings would not be pressed in relation to relatively
minor matters of complaint, but 'the dismissal of complaints
involving minor misconduct, necessitated by the limited
alternatives available to the disciplinary agency, interferes
with effective disciplinary enforcement in several respects'.[32]

> First, dismissal of a matter involving established minor miscon-
> duct subjects the profession to criticism by the public. The com-
> plainant who knows that the accused attorney has been guilty of
> misconduct but is unaware of the limited alternatives available to
> the disciplinary agency may conclude that the dismissal evidences
> the profession's disinterest in effectively policing its members
> . . . If an informal admonition were authorised, the complainant
> could be advised confidentially that his complaint had been sub-
> stantiated and that, although formal charges of professional mis-
> conduct were not being instituted, a permanent record of the
> complaint was being maintained by the disciplinary agency for
> future reference.[33]

A second problem, according to the Clark Committee, was
that the accused lawyer and the profession at large tended to
interpret the lack of interest of the professional bodies in such
cases as evidence that minor failings did not really matter.
Moreover, 'the deterrent effect of an informal admonition
timely given is lost and the attorney may, consequently, later
involve himself in more substantial misconduct'.[34] Thirdly,
where no proper records are kept of dismissed complaints,
'dismissal may immunise the attorney guilty of repetitive acts
of minor misconduct from substantial discipline'.[35]

The relative usefulness of a procedure for warnings in dealing with most complaints is shown by figures produced by the
Association of the Bar of the City of New York for 1968–9. In
that period 13 lawyers were disbarred, 14 were suspended, 3
were censured, 22 were admonished by the committee after a
hearing and 158 were admonished by administrative action on
the part of the committee's officers or staff.[36]

When it comes to more serious failures amounting to possible negligence, the English professional bodies have argued that they should not seek to interpose themselves between the client and the court. Either the client or the solicitor might be prejudiced, it is said, if the Law Society presumed to supplant the court in determining whether there had been a failure to meet the reasonable minimum standard of competence. It is difficult to accept this argument. If the Law Society gave a view as to negligence it would be without prejudice to the right of both parties to reject it. So, if it were said that the solicitor had been guilty of negligence, incompetence or inefficiency, it would be open to the solicitor to refuse to recognise the opinion – leaving it for the client to sue or not to sue. If, on the other hand, the opinion was that no case of negligence had been made out, it would remain open to the client to sue anyway. It might appear that there would be little point in having so 'soft' a remedy. But its value is that it would probably defuse the overwhelming majority of disputes between solicitors and their clients. What the average client with a sense of grievance towards his solicitor wants is to have an impartial opinion from an independent source. Even where he has a genuine and well-founded complaint about the way his case was handled, he is most unlikely to want to go to the trouble and expense of suing his solicitor for negligence. In many cases the solicitor's failure does not amount to negligence in the strict sense, and yet a fair-minded person would say that the solicitor ought to make some amends in the form, say, of a reduced bill. (The taxation process is not open to this line of argument since taxing masters will not consider whether work was well or badly done.) The Law Society does provide just such a service in the area of remuneration certificates (see p. 200 below), even though there is the alternative remedy of a court taxation.

The Society of Labour Lawyers suggested to the Royal Commission that the Law Society should be willing to provide a semi-official view on allegations of negligence or incompetence. Such a service, it admitted, would be burdensome – but so was the existing complaints machinery, and that was not a reason to dispense with it. 'Alternatively and perhaps preferably, from the client's point of view, such reviews might be carried out by solicitors employed for the purpose by the Lay Observer. This would have the merit of offering a review that was seen to be wholly independent of the Law Society.'[37] The proposal deserves support.

Liability of lawyers for professional negligence

A third proposal to assist the client would be legislation to make all lawyers legally liable for negligence in whatever circumstances. The old rule was that barristers could not be sued for any form of negligence, however gross, whereas solicitors could be sued for negligence. In 1967, the House of Lords, in *Rondel v. Worsley*,[38] ruled that a barrister could not be sued for negligence in the course of advocacy or litigation. It suggested that a solicitor could claim the same immunity, but that both barristers and solicitors could be sued for negligence in work not connected with advocacy or litigation. In May 1977 the Court of Appeal applied this ruling to give immunity to a barrister who had advised action against the wrong party, with the result that the plaintiff lost his claim![39]

The rationale of the immunity advanced by the judges is that it is required by public policy. Lawyers, it is said, would not be able to perform their tasks in the field of advocacy (including the preparation of advocacy) if they had to worry about the possibility of an action for negligence. Thus, a competent advocate knew what witnesses need not be called, what questions need not be asked. If he faced the possibility of an action for negligence he would have to waste time and, therefore, money by asking every question, calling every witness. Witnesses, lawyers and the judge all had immunity from proceedings for defamation in respect of anything said in the course of trials. The immunity of advocates from liability for negligence was on a similar basis. Negligence actions would permit convicted men to reopen their convictions. Moreover, it would not be fair to barristers to expose them to the risks of negligence actions when they were bound by the 'cab-rank' rule to take any client.

These arguments can, however, be countered. In the first place, it is not probable that barristers would be influenced to do their work much differently by the thought that they might be sued for negligence. There are already strong pressures to do well – the desire to acquire and retain a good reputation, self-respect, competitiveness and concern for the interests of the client. There are many other occupations that involve complex and delicate operations that are carried on perfectly well in spite of the theoretical threat of negligence actions. (Surgery is an obvious example.) If such liability did result in advocates changing their mode of work it could be that in some cases they would become more prolix, but in others they might be more careful.

The immunity for those taking part in judicial proceedings arising out of what they *say* is quite different from an immunity for negligence. Immunity from defamation is *necessary* to the conduct of the trial process; immunity from negligence actions is not essential – as witness the fact that in most countries it does not exist, and until *Rondel v. Worsley* it did not exist for solicitor-advocates. It is true that negligence actions might permit convicted men to re-open their convictions, but if they have been convicted owing to the negligence of their lawyers this may not be unreasonable. In theory there would be many such actions, but the experience of other countries suggests that this fear is greatly exaggerated. There are many disincentives to litigation – including the costs and the difficulty of getting legal aid unless a case has merit. It is, of course, disagreeable for a professional person to be faced with the possibility of defending such litigation, but this already exists in regard to other professions and there is no good reason why lawyers should be immune. It may appear unfair to subject barristers to such actions and at the same time require them to take any client, but a doctor is liable even where the dictates of his profession require him to give medical services. Moreover, in reality, even if the cab-rank rule did not exist, barristers would not frequently refuse to act for a client. Most instructions are accepted by barristers without ever seeing the client. The barrister knows that the client is represented by a solicitor who has had the chance of refusing him – if he did not, there is no greater reason for the barrister to do so.

There is a tendency on the part of lawyers and judges to regard the work they do as unique and entitling them to special privileges. This tendency (especially the claim to special privileges) needs to be regarded with scepticism. The immunity of the barrister was in fact part of the bundle of privileges that gave him his status. It therefore did not extend to

solicitor-advocates. In *Rondel v. Worsley* the judges, for the
first time, sought to find functional reasons to justify the
immunity which was, for that reason, extended to solicitors.
The judges purported to act in the name of the public interest,
but the press at least was not persuaded. When the Court of
Appeal ruled in favour of the barristers' immunity[40] it
attracted severely critical reaction from *The Times, The Sunday
Telegraph, The Financial Times, The Economist,* and the *New
Statesman*.[41] *The Times* went so far as to say that the courts
should not be surprised if the decision 'provokes the murmur
that the law knows how to look after its own'. Even the
professional journals were critical – the *New Law Journal*,[42] the
Solicitors' Journal,[43] the *Law Society's Gazette*,[44] and the *Journal
of the Law Society of Scotland*.[45] The Society of Labour
Lawyers, the Association of Liberal Lawyers and a majority of
Justice,[46] argued in evidence to the Royal Commission that
lawyer-advocates should be liable for their acts of negligence
like all other professional persons. In practice, such an action
would not often succeed, but the risk of incompetence
amounting to negligence should fall on the professional man
who can insure against the risk, rather than on his client.

If advocates do become liable for negligence it would be
right to require that barristers, like solicitors, have compulsory insurance. In fact, after the House of Lords indicated in
Rondel v. Worsley that barristers could be liable for some forms
of negligence, many members of the Bar obtained insurance
cover. The Law Society's compulsory insurance scheme for
solicitors came into force as from 1 September 1976.[47] There
would appear to be no valid reason why barristers equally
should not be required to protect their clients (and themselves)
by taking out some form of approved minimum policy.

Research as a means of improving the quality of work

But improved procedures for handling complaints and better
remedies for aggrieved clients are unlikely to make any real
impact on the quality of work done by lawyers. There are
three main reasons. One is that hardly any clients have the
energy or inclination to complain even if they feel there is
something to complain about. It is too much trouble, it is
embarrassing to criticise one's professional adviser and,
moreover, it is unlikely to bring any results. An inquiry into

the stories of a sample of forty-five clients in Michigan all of whom had serious complaints against their lawyers showed that not one had taken his case to the disciplinary system and only one had approached the organised bar in any way.[48] Even in criminal cases where the defendant has the time and nothing to lose by alleging that his lawyers have misconducted themselves, such complaints are rare. Thus, the criminal legal aid complaints tribunal, established in 1967, appears *never* to have sat although hundreds of thousands of criminal cases have been dealt with in the period. It would be ludicrous to suggest that there have not been cases in which serious criticisms could not have been made of the way the cases were handled by the lawyers. But any system which relies on clients to take the initiative inevitably means that only a tiny minority of cases will ever be brought to the attention of the authorities. Nor is there any guarantee that they will be the most serious cases. Many complaints are, in fact, wholly misconceived – brought by troublesome or disturbed clients, whereas reasonable clients with genuine grievances may feel inhibited from complaining – and the more so if the complaint involves a potential claim for negligence with all the attendant difficulties and disincentives of legal proceedings, especially against a lawyer.

Secondly, the failure to complain is often because the client is unaware of the fact that the work has been badly done. It is of the nature of many professional services that the client cannot evaluate what has been done for him and therefore cannot know its quality. A client who reads through even a simple will before signing it is unlikely to have much idea whether it fully carries out his instructions and provides for various contingencies as he would have wished. There will be many expressions and clauses he will not understand. If, as is normal, the lawyer has simply adapted a form of precedent used in his office, the client will have no idea whether the adaptation has been successful. Are there other clauses that should be included? Is the drafting clear and 'judge-proof'? The client cannot know. If the lawyer negotiates a settlement for £3,000 in an accident claim, and recommends acceptance, the client has no idea whether this represents reasonable advice or whether a more competent or more experienced accidents lawyer might have got £5,000. The same ignorance affects virtually every aspect of a lawyer's work. Serious errors may be made by lawyers without the client ever realising the fact.

A third reason for viewing complaints and disciplinary procedures as marginal to the problem of maintaining professional standards is that instances that are penalised are regarded by all concerned as exceptional. The presumption is that they are deviations from the norm, and the ordinary practitioner is, therefore, unlikely to be much influenced by reading or hearing that his colleague has been criticised for such failure. If they are exceptional this attitude is legitimate. But what if they are in fact fairly typical? Reliance on complaints in isolated cases makes it likely that the profession and its governing bodies will remain unaware of any general problems.

The only way to meet this difficulty is to have some mechanism for conducting research into the way in which legal services of different kinds are *normally* provided.

One way to conduct such research is to invite the views of those who have experienced legal services as clients. Such research is valuable and some has in fact been done.[49] Clients' statements of fact as to how their cases were handled may be mainly accurate, and the views expressed may throw light on certain features of the way in which lawyers do their work.[50] But inevitably clients are not well placed to evaluate reliably whether the work has been done well or not. Neither their satisfaction nor their dissatisfaction can necessarily be regarded as based on accurate perception. This is not to say that the opinions of clients on such issues should be regarded as worthless – as would, for instance, be implied by the comment of Mr David McNeill QC, Chairman of the Bar, when he dismissed 121 long tape-recorded interviews with convicted defendants about plea bargaining as merely 'the tittle-tattle of the cells'.[51] Such contempt for the views of clients reveals something important about the attitude of lawyers toward their clients and does the profession little credit. But it is obvious that the views of clients alone cannot normally be regarded as sufficient on the question whether work is adequately done or not.

The views of lay intermediaries, such as CAB workers, may also be worth collecting,[52] but again, since such workers lack detailed knowledge both of the individual cases and of the 'proper' way to handle them, such opinions must be treated with some reserve. The most promising technique is to have competent researchers investigate random samples of actual cases – looking at files, talking to the lawyers involved and to their clients, and then assessing the quality of the work done, if possible with the help of experts in the field. Such research, if properly conducted on validly drawn samples, makes it possible to advance general conclusions about the way in which that particular category of work is actually done by the profession *as a whole*. Assertion and counter-assertion, anecdotes and counter-anecdotes, can be replaced by facts, or at least by more soundly-based impressions.

The Urban Institute in Washington, DC, working for the Legal Services Corporation, has pioneered a form of peer review of lawyers' work whereby teams of lawyers from a variety of professional backgrounds attempted to assess the quality of work done by other lawyers by detailed interviewing.[53] It found in the pilot study that both private practitioners and state salaried lawyers were generally willing to co-operate with such research. The verdict on the performance of lawyers studied was not unduly flattering. On a five-point scale from 'poor' to 'outstanding', 54 per cent were in the middle range of 'adequate', 6 per cent were 'poor', 21 per cent were 'marginal', 19 per cent were 'effective and competent' and none was 'outstanding'. The lawyer interviewers tended to agree on their overall ratings. Consensus was reached on 88 per cent of the ratings – in most cases before the team of assessers discussed the case.[54] In a New York study of personal injury cases, by Douglas Rosenthal, the performance of the lawyers was again reviewed by experts in the field. The verdict was harsh – 'In 77 per cent of the cases (44 out of 57), clients did worse than they should have according to the arithmetic mean of the values assigned to their claim by each of the panelists. Even allowing for a conservative error factor of 30 per cent . . . 42 per cent of the clients (24 out of 57) received poor recoveries.[55] A study by staff of the American Bar Foundation suggested that 'between 12 and 27 per cent of all persons who have contracted with an attorney have experienced a problem' in regard to the quality of work done.[56]

The great merit of research based on anonymous random samples is that it can tackle general standards without identifying black sheep. If general deficiencies emerge, it becomes possible to tackle them without the tangle of emotional and practical problems inevitably generated when individuals are singled out as deviants. The approach is then systems-oriented and the search for a better system should be capable of being conducted without undue acrimony or defensiveness.[57]

Recent experience, it is true, suggests that the English legal profession is depressingly over-sensitive about research that reveals any blemishes in its service to the public.[58] But a more mature attitude might be expected to emerge as it comes to understand the value of external inquiry. This method of proceeding ought to be a normal feature of the life of the profession especially in classes of work largely financed out of public moneys. But there is no valid reason why such research should not also be directed at work done in the private sector.

Obviously such a research system would have to be independent of the profession. The mere fact that neither the Law Society nor the Bar appear *ever* to have conducted research into any issue bearing on the extent, scope or quality of legal services is indication enough that, if it were left to the profession, it would not be done. The indolence of the profession in this regard, in spite of lip-service paid to its concern for the level of standards (and in spite of known 'problem areas' in the work of the profession such as the unmet need for legal services or late preparation of cases by barristers), amounts to culpable neglect. The offence has not infrequently been compounded by obstruction of research mooted by others from outside the profession or petulant responses to problems revealed by such researches.

The task of monitoring the state of legal services must be given to an official body, not merely to express the importance of the issue, but also to ensure a reasonable level of co-operation from the profession. Individual researchers, however well recommended, inevitably find it difficult to get lawyers to co-operate in research on aspects of practice. The research team need not be large but it must have sufficient staff and funds to do a competent job. It would probably be best to separate it from any government department, lest its research integrity be compromised by disputes over the policy implications and decisions that flowed from its reports. Perhaps the best home for such an activity would be the office of the Lay Observer. He already has the task of monitoring quality of work in one small field by ensuring that the Law Society handles complaints properly. His conclusion – not surprisingly – is that, given its terms of reference, there is little reason for criticism, but he has also indicated that the complaints system does not deal with the majority of matters of which lay clients complain. It would be entirely appropriate to develop the concept of his office, giving him the task of tackling the problem of maintaining an adequate level of work by the profession. The average quality of work may in every aspect prove to be adequate, in which case the profession has nothing to fear from occasional reports that bear witness to the fact. On the contrary, it will greatly benefit from public recognition of the fact. If, however, as is more likely, there is, here and there, room for improvement, the profession can hardly complain if an independent and fair research unit identifies the problems that appear to require attention.

5 The Quality of Legal Services: Education and Training

The main problem with English legal education is that, although it may be said to be improving, at each of its three stages it is not as good as it should be. The three stages are: (1) academic, (2) vocational and (3) training on the job.

The academic stage

There is now virtual agreement that an entrant to the legal profession should normally first study law as an academic subject at a university or polytechnic, and this is what most entrants to the profession now do. The Bar told the Royal Commission that in 1975, 87 per cent of intending practitioners called to the Bar were graduates of British universities, and of that number, 81 per cent were law graduates.[1] The Law Society's equivalent figures were 77 per cent and 78 per cent.[2] Neither side of the profession has yet taken the final step of making a law degree compulsory, but it is clear that the law degree is now established as the normal form of basic training.

This is entirely new. In most Western countries law has for centuries been treated as a learned discipline requiring university study, but in England this was not so.[3] The ancient universities of Oxford and Cambridge did not start to teach law on any meaningful scale until the late nineteenth century. They had, of course, taught Roman law, but the teaching of English law was left to the Inns of Court. The Inns provided a high standard of instruction until the mid-seventeenth century when, during the Civil War, their courses collapsed, not to be revived until two hundred years later. During this long fallow period the universities provided virtually no legal training. Blackstone delivered his famous course on the Common Law at Oxford from 1753, but after his resignation, the teaching of the subject languished. In 1800, the Downing Chair of the Laws of England in Cambridge was founded, but the subject did not flourish there either. When a Select Committee inquired into the state of legal education in 1846, it reported that 'no legal education worthy of the name is at this moment to be had'.[4] Legal education here, it said, exhibited a 'striking contrast and inferiority' to that 'at present in operation in all the more civilised states of Europe and America'.[5] Whereas in Berlin, for instance, there were fourteen professors teaching some thirty branches of the law to hundreds of students, in Oxford and Cambridge there appeared to be neither lectures, nor examinations, nor even any students in law.[6]

The Select Committee's criticisms led to changes. Both the universities and the profession began to bestir themselves. In 1852 Oxford established a B.C.L. degree, and in 1855 Cambridge started an LL.B. degree. Law faculties began at London University and in provincial universities as they were set up. By 1908, there were eight law faculties. They taught English law as one of the liberal arts, concentrating primarily on jurisprudence and common law subjects, with a strong admixture of Roman law. They were still at the stage of establishing that law was a fit subject for university education. They were short of funds and had difficulty in attracting students. Most of those who went to the Bar tended to read classics or some other non-law subject; solicitors were unlikely to go to university at all. The reputation of the law faculties in the profession was not high.

During the twentieth century, however, the position has gradually changed and in the past decade or so it has been transformed. The number of students undertaking law degrees in England and Wales rose from some 1,500 in 1938 to 3,000 in 1960, to 5,300 in 1970 and over 7,000 in 1974.[7] A survey published in 1975 showed that there were thirty university law schools in the United Kingdom, plus nineteen polytechnics and other local authority maintained institutions offering degree courses in law.[8] The Ormrod Committee Report in 1971 recommended that the law faculties should expand so as to produce some 2,000 graduates per year.[9] In fact, by 1974–5, the universities and polytechnics in England and Wales were producing some 2,500 graduates[10] and by 1980 the figure was expected to be close to 4,000.[11]

Also, the quality of legal education in the law faculties has improved. Until recently the liberality of legal education was thought to depend chiefly on the subject-matter taught. Thus, Roman law, jurisprudence, international law, legal history or common law subjects were fit topics for a liberal education; company law, labour law, tax law and statute-dominated subjects were not. This view has now been largely rejected. Increasingly, it has been accepted that, as Samuel Alexander said, 'Liberality is a spirit of pursuit not a choice of subject'. If a subject is one in which principles can be discovered and reasons for facts and decisions can be related to the principles, such a subject can be made the basis for liberal education. The most 'practical' of legal subjects can be taught so as to illuminate the workings of society and the clashes of social, economic, political and philosophical values implicit in legal rules. Equally, the most 'academic' of subjects can be taught in a dry, pedantic, narrow manner which is the antithesis of the spirit of liberal education.

Practical subjects are now normal ingredients in the law school menu. Moreover, the range of optional subjects has in recent years been broadening very considerably. The survey of legal education published in 1975 showed that law faculties were offering courses in such subjects as common market law, comparative law, planning law, welfare law, human rights and sociology of law.[12] The quality of legal textbooks has risen noticeably in the past generation. Some teachers are trying to involve their students in real-life problems – mostly through legal advice services run by students under the supervision of staff and to a lesser extent through studies of the legal system.[13] The profession unquestionably feels that legal education at the university is more relevant than in the past.

Its main defect, however, is that, in spite of the undoubted improvements, legal education in most universities and polytechnics is somewhat pedestrian. Worthy, but dull, is probably a not unfair description of the average course. In most law faculties students are never required to write anything longer than the weekly three or four page essay. They therefore never learn the skill of using the library for a piece of research. The few universities where a 6,000 – 8,000 word essay is required, (or at least available in some optional subjects) find that students both enjoy and benefit from the discipline of undertaking a longer piece of work. Mock formal legal arguments ('moots') as a means to develop confidence in public disputation are normally optional rather than compulsory and are not undertaken by most students. Student surveys and studies of the legal system in action are rare. Law journals edited by law students, normal in North America, are virtually non-existent. Even the new moves towards involvement in the provision of actual legal services and tentative steps towards some form of clinical legal education affect only a tiny number of students. The style or method of teaching in many instances still leans too heavily on requiring mastery of 'black letter law' – rules as rules rather than as illustrations of principles. The great American law schools have the advantage that they do not have to teach the law of their own states since the students come from all over the country. Teachers can focus on the fundamentals of their subject by reference to practice and results of that practice in different jurisdictions. The English law teacher is much more likely simply to teach the law of England without reference even to comparison with Scotland. Even at the best institutions, therefore, the general level of the education offered does not deserve more than moderate praise. It is distinctly better than even twenty years ago, but there is still a long way to go before the general standards of our best courses match the intellectual quality of the courses offered by the twenty or so leading American law schools.

If that is the position of those fortunate to go to university or a polytechnic, legal education of those who are not law graduates is considerably worse. There are four categories. For both branches there is the graduate who has read some subject other than law, and the mature entrant (over 25) who has some non-legal experience or qualifications. For the solicitors' branch there are also former Fellows of the Institute of Legal Executives and school-leavers. The non-law graduate or mature entrant can complete the academic stage of training by taking the new Common Professional Examination (CPE) in six 'core' subjects. The Ormrod Committee recommended that the CPE be based on a two-year course, but both sides of the profession (and the Lord Chancellor's Legal Education Advisory Committee) decided that a one-year course would suffice. The course will be taught by the College of Law and a number of polytechnics and technical colleges. Fellows by examination of the Institute of Legal Executives who wish to become solicitors gain credit for 'core'[14] subjects they have already taken and have to take any others not yet taken. The Law Society announced in 1975 that from 1980 school-leavers would not be eligible for admission entry into articles.[15] But, under pressure from City firms and other elements in the profession that resented the cost of putting a son or daughter through university, it withdrew and in 1977 announced that school-leavers would, after all, be able to come into the profession direct.[16] The proposed scheme of training for school-leavers was announced in December 1977.[17] They were to have the same 'A' level qualifications as would be necessary to get into university. They would then be required to take the first year law degree course at a polytechnic and pass four 'core' subjects. This would be followed by study (at a polytechnic, or privately or through a correspondence course) for an examination consisting of another four law subjects – the remaining two 'core' subjects plus two others. They would then be ready to take the Final and two years of articles like graduates.

It is inevitable that the courses for those not studying for law degrees will be considerably inferior in quality to those for degree courses. They will, for one thing, be significantly shorter in time. (The one-year CPE course clearly cannot be the equivalent of a three-year degree course. Even the six core subjects to be taught in the CPE course will receive less time than in the degree course.) The teachers will be less able – the quality of teachers in polytechnics is generally lower than in universities and that in technical schools is generally lower than in polytechnics. At institutions teaching for both the law degree and the CPE, the latters' students are likely to be treated and regarded as second-class citizens. Whatever arrangements are made for the academic training of school-leavers, they are likely to be no better than for those who take the CPE – and may be worse. On figures presented to the Royal Commission, entrants to the profession who will not have law degrees will be some 30 per cent of those becoming barristers and some 40 per cent of those becoming solicitors.[18] They are likely to have a decidedly inadequate legal education at the academic stage.

The vocational stage

Examinations and courses

The vocational courses and examinations run by the Inns of Court Council of Legal Education and by the Law Society's College of Law have, in the past, been of very poor quality. For most of this century teaching at the Bar's Council of Legal Education was provided on a part-time basis by practising barristers and academic lawyers. It was wholly academic in style and content – save that subjects were treated with extreme superficiality. Lectures were not compulsory and most of those who intended to practise qualified by attending crammers. Criticism of the system became widespread[19] and in the decade from 1968 significant reforms were introduced. Full-time teachers were appointed. And under a scheme which came into force in 1969 the syllabus became more practical and the Part II course, for the first time in some three hundred years, became compulsory for those intending to enter practice. The changes introduced since 1969 have consolidated these reforms.

The Inns of Court Council of Legal Education has been developing a serious attempt at vocational training – with drafting exercises, classes in advocacy, supervised court attendances and simulated real-life problems, in addition to lectures. The objective is to train young barristers for the work they will meet in the first years of practice. The Bar announced in July 1977[20] that from 1978 a three-week introductory course of lectures would include an intensive series of lectures on procedure, practice and drafting. The three weeks at the end of the course (which lasts from September to late June), is devoted to a project to synthesise the various aspects of practical training in advocacy and drafting. Opposing parties of students will see a problem set of facts from start to appearance in court. Ten talks are to be given on courts and practice by judges, practising barristers, court administrators, barristers' clerks and members of the Lord Chancellor's Office. A film unit is to be created to experiment with the best ways of using films in procedure and practical exercises. Students themselves will be filmed when speaking and presenting an argument so as to improve their style by watching themselves on screen. The students will also be required to attend a course of ten lectures in either forensic science and medicine, or company accounts. There will be optional lectures on human rights, and the opportunity to take classes in typing, speed-writing and public speaking. It is expected that some 650 students will be taking the course.

On the solicitors' side the development of a proper vocational training scheme has met with less success. The modern tradition, like that at the Bar, is one of professional examinations which demand prodigious feats of memory and which, therefore, almost inevitably lead to cram-school courses and rote learning. (Students say that at the College of Law, lecturers dictate even the punctuation.) In 1974 the Law Society proposed to the profession that there should instead be a one-year institutional course offering not only lectures but also a series of practical exercises designed to take students through the stages of conveyancing, probate, company, divorce and other basic transactions.[21] This course would replace both the bad old Part II examination and training under articles. Instead of articles, a person who had taken the new course and examination would be subject to a rule that he could not practise on his own until he had served a further three years in a qualified solicitor's office. The scheme foundered – because the profession refused to put up the money, because it refused to give up articles and, perhaps, because solicitors suspected that the result might be that the profession would lose control over entry.[22]

The Law Society found itself forced to adopt a second-best plan – to devise an improved course without the practical skills training which would have made the course genuinely vocational. By autumn 1977 (three and a half years later) the details of the new course had still not been published. It appeared, however, that instead of dividing the course into the traditional subjects (Conveyancing, Family Law, etc.) there would be four main sections – the Solicitor and his Practice; the Solicitor and his Business Client; the Solicitor and his Private Client; and Litigation. The course would be some 36 weeks long with 250 hours of lectures and 50 hours of tutorials and discussion groups. The object would be to ensure that articled clerks had a grasp of the law, practice and procedure that they were likely to meet. Wherever possible, students would work with actual documents and mock transactions (a partnership

agreement, balance sheets, company memorandum and articles, the documents used in conveyancing, draft wills, litigation forms, etc.). Students would have drafting exercises. The
objective was to be the teaching of practice rather than of rules.

Such a course should be a considerable improvement on the
old one. But there will be two serious and probably insur-
mountable problems. One is the fact that the course will have
little in the way of exercises. In spite of the leavening of
drafting work, it will be mostly lectures and tutorials in which
students are taken through existing materials. It is clearly
better that students should study actual documents relating to
real transactions than that they learn the rules of law relating to
that field. It would be better still if they could also have
experience of drafting the documents themselves under supervision. The second, much more serious, problem is how to
achieve a satisfactory level of teaching. The course, catering
for over 2,000, is to be given by the College of Law and seven
polytechnics.[23] The teaching at all the eight institutions will be
to specifications laid down by the Law Society. But it will be
difficult to achieve a genuine practical orientation to the
course. The teachers, especially at the polytechnics, will be
mainly academics, many of whom are likely to have inadequate knowledge of practice. The Bar's course supplements
the team of full-time academics with some 65–80 part-time
practising barristers. This is difficult enough to organise even
in the Inns of Court with hundreds of practitioners working
close by. In the eight scattered centres where the Part II course
for solicitors is to be provided it will be virtually impossible to
secure the participation of large numbers of practitioners. Yet,
without practitioners, the Law Society's new scheme is
unlikely to be a genuine form of vocational training.

A majority of the Ormrod Committee proposed that the
vocational stage of institutional training be provided from
within the universities and the polytechnics rather than by the
profession. A minority on the Committee, representing the
profession, disagreed and, as has been seen, they have pre-
vailed. On this occasion it would appear that the profession
was right. Vocational training for the legal profession is more
likely to be effective if under the general management of the
professional bodies rather than under that of the English universities and the polytechnics, which have always tended to be

too far divorced from practice. The programme now in process of being developed at the Council of Legal Education for Bar students is aimed at the right objectives. The main problem now is to make its execution as effective as its design. But on the solicitors' side of the profession, if the funds cannot be found to finance a proper institutional practical skills course, the education of solicitors will continue to be seriously deficient. The fortunate few will learn what they need to through well-rounded articles, but the majority will, inevitably, have a less balanced and less smooth transition into practice for the lack of a carefully orchestrated course of practical skills instruction.

Training on the job

However good the basic academic and vocational courses, there is no substitute for real-life experience as a form of education in law. No one can regard himself a competent practitioner who has not himself been in practice. Both sides of the profession are therefore right to insist that some form of apprenticeship should continue to be an essential element in the process of qualification. At the Bar, the requirement is for one year's pupillage, six months of which must be completed before taking any case on one's own. A solicitor must undergo a period under articles, the length of which varies depending on the prior qualifications of the student, and he cannot practise on his own or become a partner until he has worked in an office for three years after qualifying. It is, of course, true that attachment of a beginner to an older practitioner provides no guarantee that he will be properly trained. The pupil master or principal may be too busy to provide any real supervision, or not busy enough to keep his pupil occupied; he may lack the taste or talent for the role of educator; he may himself be incompetent; his practice may be one-sided; he may exploit the cheap labour of his pupil/articled clerk by using him for menial tasks. It is also true that the requirement of articles and the limited practice certificate for three years after qualification in effect gives the profession the power to control numbers. Nevertheless, in order to protect the public it is right to require that a new entrant to the profession be exposed to the discipline of working with someone more experienced before he is allowed to practise on his own. The medical student must complete not only his full period as a student in a teaching hospital, but a further year as a houseman before he is completely qualified. He is paid a salary throughout his houseman's year. Provided the problem of financing the young entrant during pupillage or articles can be solved (see pp. 177–81 below), the same approach ought to apply to the law.

The Ormrod Committee agreed with the Law Society that a one-year institutional practical skills course plus a period of restricted practice for three years after qualification would be better than articles.[24] But in the absence of a full practical skills course it now seems inevitable that articles will continue. It is therefore important to take such steps as can be devised to improve training under articles. The Institute of Chartered Accountants uses a number of techniques that would seem worth copying. It publishes a Training Guide for principals, setting out their duties and suggesting how they can be carried out. It requires that a weekly training record be maintained by students showing the experience they have had. This is inspected by the Institute at stated intervals. Principals who wish to take students have to satisfy a Board of Accreditation that the firm has appropriate arrangements for training. In 1977, the Institute laid down minimum standards of student training that would have to be met.[25] The British Institute of Architects has a similar scheme, including detailed Guidance Notes on training for students and principals and a requirement that students complete a daily log which must be signed every month by a principal in the office designated as Office Supervisor, and shown to the examiners in the final examination. Students must be given not less than ten days' paid leave per year for professional activities, which have the educational objective of broadening practical training. Similar requirements could be made part of training for solicitors. They would not work miracles but might help to improve the quality of the average period of articles. There may also be scope for some use of placements – in law centres or attached to citizens' advice bureaux – for limited periods during articles.

Post-qualification training and the certification of specialists

At present the only formal method of testing competence of lawyers is through the various processes that lead to the initial licence to practise. Yet it is obvious that this is hardly enough to ensure adequate standards of work by members of the profession. Practitioners probably forget in a short time most of what they learnt for their examinations. The law may greatly change during their practising life-times. Their practice may be in fields not covered at all or covered only superficially in their formal courses and examinations. The system proceeds on the assumption that all lawyers have the necessary competence to hold themselves out to practise in all fields unless they can be shown to have conducted themselves so badly as to warrant excommunication. This is hardly an exacting standard.

There are however courses offered to practitioners. The Bar in England takes little advantage of these opportunities. The Bar's evidence to the Royal Commission said simply: 'Little or no post-qualification education or training is undertaken on a formal basis. It is not generally appropriate to the circumstances of practice at the Bar.'[26] Those who were specialists had to absorb the latest developments in their subjects in order to retain their reputations. ('They could not afford to wait for a seminar or course.'[27]) But even the less specialised, according to the Bar, would not be greatly assisted by such courses. It was a feature of general practice at the Bar that a barrister must be prepared at short notice to become expert in a particular part of any one of a great number of fields. The most efficient way to achieve this was to apply oneself intensively as and when the problem came to him, assisted by general awareness of new developments through reading of journals and law reports and regular contact with fellow members of chambers and the Inn. The Bar's attitude seems unduly complacent. It is difficult to believe that standards could not be improved by some attendance at lectures and seminars designed for practitioners.

Solicitors, by contrast, are more aware of the value of courses designed for practitioners. The Law Society's evidence to the Royal Commission gave details of a great variety of post-qualification courses and seminars[28] – courses of several weekly lectures, half-day, one-day, two-day or even longer courses and seminars in a wide variety of fields. Often the lectures were then sold in booklet form or as cassettes. Some 10,000 cassettes had been sold; sales of lectures from a two-day 'crash refresher course' ran to some 30,000–40,000 per year at 70p per lecture; more substantial 80–100-page booklets used in courses sold between 2,000 and 4,000 copies at £2 each. In 1976 there had been some 40 courses or seminars in different parts of the country for which over 7,500 tickets had been sold. In addition, there are a substantial number of similar courses run by private organisations for which high fees are charged and which appear, nevertheless, to achieve large attendances. The Law Society announced in October 1977 that it was setting up a committee 'to consider the introduction of a more comprehensive and improved system of post-qualification education and training'.[29]

The Report of the Ormrod Committee recommended that urgent consideration be given by all concerned to ways of stimulating more continuing education for members of the legal profession. It drew the analogy with the medical profession where post-graduate training was a *sine qua non* of professional advancement. This had 'undoubtedly raised the standards in all the specialities in medicine to an impressive degree'.[30] There was no equivalent tradition in the law. In the United States, by contrast, continuing training had been expanding very rapidly at all levels of the profession, including the judiciary,[31] and had acquired a complex and highly expert organisation. There ought to be an Institute of Professional Legal Studies to promote the subject. The Practising Law Institute in the United States ran a large number of courses for practitioners and was self-financing. A committee should be set up, perhaps on the initiative of the Lord Chancellor, to prepare a detailed scheme. But this proposal of the Ormrod Committee fell on deaf ears and it seems improbable that it will now come to fruition. There is no interest in the idea at the Bar, and although the Law Society is concerned to promote continuing education for practitioners, it may not care to lose its own identity as the organiser of such courses in a more broadly based body including the Lord Chancellor's Office, the Home Office, both sides of the profession and the law faculties.

The only realistic prospect for some such development is if the profession decides to follow the American lead in the direction of certification of specialists. The public wants reliable information as to the particular interests and capacities of lawyers. How is this need to be met? The traditional approach of the legal profession has been not to allow lawyers to communicate any information as to their specialities. This negative approach has now been relaxed by the Bar to permit barristers to state in law lists the areas of work in which they are prepared to practise.[32] As has been seen, the Law Society of England and Wales has produced referral lists, at present limited to legal aid work, intended to communicate this information to the general public. The Law Society of Scotland plans referral lists that will be much more detailed and will include all work, not just that handled under legal aid. Probably in due course the English lists will follow the more comprehensive Scottish form. As has also been seen, the Law Society told the Royal Commission it was prepared to contemplate that the information in the referral lists might be published by the local law society in the local press.[33] But this new liberty (as is also the case with the Bar's entries in law lists), expressly stops short of permitting claims to any specialist expertise or competence. No doubt the entry inevitably carries some suggestion of special competence, especially to the ordinary, uninformed layman. But, strictly, an entry means only that the solicitor is prepared to undertake that class of work. There must be many solicitors who indicate that they are prepared to undertake work in fields in which they have little or no real experience – in the hope of attracting work.

The referral list as at present conceived does not, therefore, certify expertise. In the United States there are now a number of States that have made moves in the direction of permitting notification by lawyers of their specialities. There are two main variations on this theme. One is certification after satisfying externally applied criteria of specialist competence. This is the system developed, for instance, in California. The second is some form of self-certification as applied, for instance, in New Mexico. In California[34] the system has been in operation since 1973. Participation in the scheme is entirely voluntary and non-exclusive. Practitioners who have not qualified as specialists may, therefore, continue to practise in the field. Specialism can be claimed in one of three fields – criminal law, workmen's compensation law and taxation. A lawyer may be certified a specialist in more than one field. In order to become certified, a practitioner must fulfil several different tests. These vary as between 'grandfathers' (e.g. those actively engaged in the field at the time when the new system began) and 'non-grandfathers'. A person could qualify as a grandfather if he had been engaged in full-time practice for more than ten years, at least six of which must have been spent in practice in California. In addition, an applicant had to show 'substantial involvement' in the field by attesting that he had been instructed in not less than a specified number of different categories of proceedings in that field, and that within three of the preceding five years he had spent a minimum of one-third of his time in the practice of that field in California. Grandfather certification was only open to those who applied within two years of the commencement of the scheme. Non-grandfathers must have been in full-time practice for not less than five years in California, must have taken part in a specified number of different kinds of proceedings in that field of work, must have devoted one-third of their time in three of the past five years to that field, and must have attended and completed the prescribed educational course for specialists, plus a written examination. Both grandfathers and non-grandfathers must produce five references, attesting to their proficiency as specialists – four from fellow-practitioners and one from a judge before whom the applicant has appeared. Certification lasts for only five years. A request for re-certification must show continued involvement in the field as a specialist, plus either not less than seventy-five hours of attendance at approved courses, or the passing of an examination. The scheme is intended to be self-financing. The initial application costs $100, the fee for certification is another $100 and annual dues amount to $50.[35] Lawyers who had qualified as specialists were only permitted to list the fact in the telephone classified section and in legal directories – though this will no doubt change under the Supreme Court's new ruling on advertising (see pp. 52–53 above).

The New Mexico system[36] is very different. A practitioner

there has, since 1973, been permitted to state on his letterhead, his business card and in recognised lists and directories that he specialises in one of some sixteen areas of law. In order to claim speciality status a practitioner must affirm in an affidavit that he has devoted not less than 60 per cent of his time to that field for each of the preceding five years. The Bar Association plays no part. A similar approach where the Bar Association, however, plays some role is that in Florida[37] where the Bar has to approve applications. An application must state that the lawyer has been in practice for not less than three years and that during the three preceding years he has had 'substantial experience' in the field in which he wishes to be listed as a specialist. No objective criteria are laid down as to what constitutes substantial experience. He must also state that 'he will earnestly continue his legal education in the designated field through conscientious reading and research and through continuing legal educational programmes or by some other method approved by the Florida Bar'. Once approved by the Bar, the lawyer may (in a tasteful and dignified manner) inform the public of his new status on his letterhead, business card or office door, and in telephone directories, approved law lists and other media as from time to time approved by the Bar.

It is clear that more specialisation schemes will develop in the US, especially in view of the Supreme Court's decision on advertising. The Monopolies Commission, in its 1976 report on advertising by solicitors, appeared to be favouring the less formal (New Mexico) approach to the very restrictive (California) model. ('We see no reason why solicitors, if they were allowed to advertise individually, should not announce that they specialise in some particular branch of the law (provided that such claims are not unfounded).'[38]) But it is by no means obvious that the balance of advantage favours moves in this direction.

The objective of specialisation certification programmes is to assist the public in two distinct ways – first, by providing better information about what lawyers do well, and second, by encouraging lawyers to improve their own standards through additional study. Both are valid and useful objectives. But even if they are achieved there are counter-effects that are less beneficial. First, the public will be misled to the extent that it may assign non-specialist status to practitioners who are in fact experts but who, for one or another reason, chose not to participate in the scheme. Second, and more significant, the likely effect of being able to claim to be a specialist is an increase in fees. The benefits in higher standards and better information may not be worth the extra charges. Third, any process of certification of specialists may make it more difficult for new entrants to establish themselves. Young lawyers or lawyers who come from unpopular minority backgrounds may, for instance, find it difficult to muster the necessary support from 'respectable' colleagues to satisfy a requirement of acceptance of specialist status. Fourth, the process of certification may be costly and time-consuming. Fifth, if the system relies instead on self-certification, it is open to abuse and spurious claims of specialisation. Even if it is based, as in California, on a series of externally applied tests, there is no real guarantee that it will always succeed in passing the expert and failing the non-expert. Moreover, certification of specialism is not in itself any guarantee of competence or skill. On balance, the advantages of such schemes would appear to be considerably outweighed by their disadvantages. It is better to permit lawyers to state only what they do and not to allow them to add that they are specialists.

Relations between lawyers and clients

Most lawyers probably give little thought to the problem of talking with clients – of finding out what the client knows, feels and wants, and of ensuring that the client understands what the lawyer is doing and intends to do. If asked, most lawyers would probably agree that good communication between lawyer and client is important, but how many recognise this to be a 'problem area'? There is little literature on the subject and it is virtually ignored in legal education, both in the universities and in vocational training. Yet we know enough to be sure that there is likely to be much wrong in this field.

There is, at the outset, the problem of language and of the client's difficulty in following what has been said. Nor will the client necessarily indicate when he has not understood. Fear of appearing foolish or ignorant will often be a much stronger influence than the desire to follow what has been said. Often the client may think he understands when in reality he has missed the point. Or he may grasp it for a moment and then find later he cannot recall what has been said to him. The ordinary problems of accurate communication between humans are greatly compounded in the field of law by the extent to which lawyers and other actors in the process (judges, police officers, insurance assessors, etc.) use jargon, the meaning of which is so familiar to them that they fail to realise the need for translation for the benefit of the layman.[39]

A second difficulty may be the lawyer's lack of skill in managing one of the basic tools of his own trade. Competent interviewing of clients and witnesses is one of the most important functions of the lawyer's job, yet he receives little or no training or even guidance in the art. Probably there is no lawyer who could not benefit from some education in the problems of communication. What difference is made if the lawyer comes to greet his client as opposed to remaining behind his desk? What is the effect of sitting during the interview behind a desk? Is the client inhibited by seeing his lawyer writing notes? What happens to the client's flow of words when the lawyer interrupts to ask him to keep to what he, the lawyer, sees as the point? How should one best probe aspects of the client's story that he may find awkward, embarrassing or unpleasant? Should the lawyer smile and be encouraging, or remain impassive and remote? Are lawyers aware of their individual mannerisms – the drumming fingertips, the faraway look, the nervous smile, grunts consciously intended to indicate understanding but unconsciously signalling boredom or irritation? (Most lawyers would benefit from seeing a video-tape of themselves conducting a mock interview. Even a tape-recording could be helpfully revealing of some idiosyncrasies.) These are not trivial matters nor are they marginal to the lawyer's 'real' work. They are part of the business of conducting an effective practice. Performance is often handicapped by personal inadequacies. (The National Association of Citizens' Advice Bureaux in its evidence to the Royal Commission said 'solicitors ... would benefit from training in interviewing and effective communication'. Many complaints about solicitors could be avoided 'if solicitors were more sensitive to their clients' views of their cases'.[40]

The lawyer's tendency will be to attempt to marshal the

questions and therefore the answers in some form of logical and coherent sequence, whereas the client will probably want to tell the story in his own way and resent being told how to present it. (The typically strict handling of witnesses in courtroom examination and cross-examination is hardly a satisfactory model for relations between lawyer and client at an interview.) Controlled experiments have shown that free narration is more accurate than a story obtained by questioning, but questioning is needed to bring out information omitted from the narrative. While questioning broadens the coverage of information, it reduces accuracy. If 10 per cent of free narration is inaccurate, the proportion under questioning will rise to, say, 25 per cent. Forcing the memory by questioning tends to produce distortion, exaggeration and false recollection. Leading questions are a notorious source of error.[41]

There has never been a proper study of the social background of English lawyers, but it is clear that the overwhelming majority are distinctly middle-class, or even upper-middle-class. (The only attempt to survey the origins of university law students found that no less than 84 per cent came from Social Classes I and II.[42] A recent study by the College of Law showed that 77 per cent of solicitor students and 84 per cent of barrister students were from the professional or managerial, executive or administrative class.[43]) There are some who assert that middle-class advisers are, by definition, incapable of understanding and being understood by those of inferior economic or social backgrounds. This is as much nonsense as the contrary thesis that differences in social or economic class make no difference to the freedom and ease of communication. There is little empirical evidence on the problem, but it would be surprising if, at least in some cases, these class differences, especially in speech, did not have an adverse effect on the quality of the relationship between lawyer and client.

There may also be difficulty caused by uncertainty as to what the client really wants or needs. If the lawyer simply responds to what the client states to be the problem, other important issues on which the client 'needs' and would actually welcome assistance may be missed. How far should the lawyer be simply a technician and how far a counsellor in the broader sense of one who seeks to comprehend the problem in the round and advise? To what extent should the lawyer, faced with a client who says he wants a divorce, sensitively explore the possibility of reconciliation? Where a businessman comes to the lawyer wanting to enforce a debt from a customer, is it the lawyer's function to get him to consider the human and business implications of taking legal proceedings? How far should the lawyer take the lead in his relationship with the client – at what point does counsel and advice become manipulation of the client?

This last question raises the fundamental, but usually unnoticed, problem of the balance of power between lawyer and client. The lawyer knows (if he thinks of it) that the client has the power at any time to fire him by withdrawing his instructions. He also knows that his job is to carry out his client's instructions – subject to the limitations imposed by the law and the rules of conduct of his profession. But this knowledge barely impinges on the way in which most lawyers and clients conduct their relationship. Once the lawyer has received his instructions he expects to be allowed to 'get on with it'. He would greatly resent a request from the client to be kept informed of every step taken in the matter. The client who constantly rings up to find out how his case is progressing is regarded as a menace, and ways are soon found to prevent him getting through to the lawyer. It would be simple for a lawyer to send his client a copy of every letter written or received in connection with his problem. Many clients would probably be delighted to be kept informed in this way and would be willing to pay for the extra cost involved. How often is it done? The evidence of the Consumers' Association to the Royal Commission stated that, in a survey of its members who had used solicitors, over half said they were not kept informed about the progress of their case.[44] It is safe to assume that even those who did not make any complaint on this score were kept informed only in very broad terms and at considerable intervals of time. Even the suggestion that solicitors should keep their clients informed in detail would be regarded by most lawyers as offensive – revealing a lack of trust in the lawyer's capacity and diligence. Yet it is obvious that if the client had this means of knowing how his case was proceeding, the lawyer would be under pressure to act more efficiently and more speedily.

More is at stake here than whether the lawyer acts as speed-ily as he should. In the handling of even the most ordinary case a host of questions arise on which policy decisions must be taken. In the ordinary course these are taken by the lawyer without any attempt to consult his client. From the outset the lawyer makes it clear that he expects the client to rely on his professional judgment. Douglas Rosenthal conducted a detailed study of lawyer–client interaction in sixty relatively serious personal injury cases in Manhattan.[45] He found that most clients were not consulted by their lawyers as to the moment in time at which to issue a writ, though this may have important consequences in terms of pressure on the insurance company to settle. Whether the expense of suing was worth-while was almost always regarded as being in the exclusive province of the lawyer. The lawyers normally decided with-out reference to their clients whether to sue in the higher or the lower court, and on the venue, even though the client's con-venience or interests might be different from those of the lawyer.[46] The lawyers decided at what level to pitch the initial settlement demand, at what point to make the first approach for settlement discussion, and with what degree of belliger-ence. These were treated as technical or professional matters on which the client would have nothing relevant to say, and on which it would not even be necessary to keep him informed.

On the basis of his study Rosenthal concluded that lay clients 'are assumed to be virtually helpless in coping with complex personal problems, to be nuisances when they try to involve themselves in the experts' province, and to be incap-able of accepting effective decision-making responsibility'.[47] But, contrary to these assumptions, he also found that those few clients who did involve themselves in the details of their cases did significantly better in the result. Three-quarters of the active clients, compared with only 41 per cent of the passive clients, got what a panel of experts thought were good results, defined as over 70 per cent of the panel's average figure.[48] (The facts of the cases in the sample were evaluated by five personal injury claim experts, who between them represented a balance of experience of work for plaintiffs and insurers. Each determined what he thought the claim was worth, on the basis of the detailed fact sheets. The average of the five estimates was taken as the panel figure.) Clients who participated actively in their cases had statistically significantly better results. Participation took a variety of forms: asking the right questions of the lawyer to get detailed advice on what sort of medical attention to get and what expenses would be recoverable; bringing pressure on the lawyer to get an early settlement where the plaintiff was going abroad and would not be able to return for the trial at short notice; insisting on seeing the top man in the firm rather than allowing the case to be bungled by underlings; checking and finding that the lawyer (an outstanding negligence expert) had neglected to discover that there were co-insurers and that the claim was consequently worth far more than he had advised his client to settle for; changing lawyers and getting a far higher settlement than had been recommended by the first; marshalling evidence to improve the claim.

Rosenthal urges that active participation by the client in the progress of his claim ought to be the norm. Clients should be kept informed in detail of the choices and of the risks involved in their cases and should be treated as partners sharing in the responsibility for deciding such questions. Not all clients would want to take this role; some are more than relieved to hand the whole business over to the lawyer and to let him do all the worrying. But the decision to take a back seat should be the client's, after he has been expressly invited to consider what level of involvement he wishes to have. Client consent to a course of action should be asked for, not simply assumed. Client assistance in preparation of the case should be encouraged, not disregarded.

This model of client–lawyer relationship also fits the prescription of Professor Kathleen Bell on the basis of her inquiries into tribunal hearings. She found that appellants in both Supplementary Benefit Appeal Tribunals and in National Insurance Local Tribunals wanted representation, whether by lawyers or others, that would permit them to play an active role. The ideal type of representative was 'an accessible person with knowledge, experience and skill, but not someone who, in acting for the appellant takes over the case completely and assigns the appellant to a purely passive role. In fact, what emerged was a concept of representation as a joint enterprise of appellant and representative'.[49] Commenting on Professor Bell's finding, Mr Peter Webster QC, in a paper published just before he became Chairman of the Bar, said that the concept of representation as a joint enterprise between lawyer and appellant might 'possibly necessitate a greater identification by the lawyer with his client than is normal in a more traditional practice'.[50] For this model to become normal in the relations of lawyers and their clients, a virtual revolution in the attitudes of clients and lawyers is needed. The ordinary client is unlikely to try to effect such a revolution. Is the lawyer?

6   Monopolies and Restrictive Practices

The problem of monoplies and restrictive practices is common to all professions and in each case the issue is the same – whether the benefits that result from the restriction are greater than the disadvantages. All are agreed that the question must be answered from the point of view of the public interest, but what constitutes the public interest?

The common law has for long had a basic prejudice in these matters – that contracts in restraint of trade are void unless they can be shown to be justifiable as being reasonable from the point of view of both the parties and of the community.[1] This, broadly, is the approach, too, of modern English legislation on monopolies and restrictive practices[2] and of the Monopolies and Mergers Commission. In 1970 the Commission summed up what it took to be the English position:

> In most of the industrial and commercial field it is now generally accepted that collective restrictions on competition are unacceptable unless it can be shown that, in the particular circumstances in which they are operated, they produce positive identifiable benefits that outweigh any disadvantages.[3]

Should this approach extend not only to the supply of goods, but also to the supply of services and more especially to the services given by professions?

The Monopolies Commission, having been asked to consider restrictive practices in the professions, was not persuaded that the basic principles were different. The fact that restrictions (on entry and on competition) were influenced by a concern for standards did not dispose of the business element in the transaction: 'The practitioner earns his living by charging a price for his services. In these circumstances our view is that in examining the effects of collective restrictions on competition in this field we must recognise the relevance of the considerations which are applicable in other fields' of business.[4] Restrictions had adverse consequences, resulting in higher prices, less efficient use of resources, discouragement of new developments and a tendency toward rigidity in the structure and trading methods of those businesses. Such collective restrictions tend to reduce the pressures upon those observing them to increase their efficiency. They may also delay the introduction of new forms of service and the elimination of inefficient practitioners.[5]

The view that restrictive practices are subject to much the same criticism in the professions as in the commercial field has now been accepted by the two leading courts on both sides of the Atlantic. As has already been seen (p. 52 above), the Supreme Court of the United States in June 1977 struck down restrictions on advertising by lawyers and rejected the view that such advertising was inconsistent with the professional ethic. In 1968 the House of Lords ruled[6] that the traditional common law antipathy to restrictions applied to the services of professions (in that case, pharmacists). Lord Upjohn, for instance, said 'I am entirely unable to accept the argument that professional bodies are outside the general doctrine of restraint of trade'.[7] Analysis of earlier judgments, he said, showed that 'there is no exception in favour of a profession from the general rule that the doctrine of restraint of trade applies quite generally'.[8] The House of Lords unanimously held that certain restrictions[9] imposed by the Pharmaceutical Society on its members were in restraint of trade and had not been justified as reasonably necessary for achieving the objects in the society's charter.

The reaction of the professions to such views is basically one of pained distress. To members of a profession it is virtually *lèse majesté* to find any common element between what they do and the activities of those who earn their living in the marketplace.[10] In its evidence to the Royal Commission, the Law Society admitted that professional services, like those of the business world, 'should be carried out efficiently, without delay and at a fair cost', but the Monopolies Commission, it said, was wrong to treat the supply of professional services for reward as a business transaction. It was 'very much more than a business transaction'. The professional man was expected to subordinate his self-interest to that of the client, the client was a bad judge of his own self-interest and the solicitor's position was, therefore, one of trust. Moreover, since he was an officer of the court he had to take into account the danger of acting in such a way as to bring the administration of justice into disrepute. A solicitor had to stand between the citizen and the state; he must preserve his client's confidences. 'Because these duties are required of a solicitor and because he is part of the machinery of justice, he must not behave as though he were carrying on a purely commercial undertaking.'[11]

The way the professions present this point smacks to modern ears somewhat of humbug. It is plain that the fact that a relationship of trust exists between lawyers and their clients or that the lawyer is supposed to make his own interests subservient to those of his client does not *in itself* justify restrictions on services. They can be justified, if at all, only by a careful inquiry into all the relevant pros and cons – which, of course, include the possible effects of the abolition of a restrictive practice on the relationship between professional men and their clients. Professional services *are* different from those provided by the business world because the professions (one hopes) do have a higher standard of service and of ethics. But the question is not whether there are differences between the two but rather whether, in the context of any particular restrictive rule or practice, the differences are material, and whether, granted even material differences, their importance is not cancelled out by other considerations. It might be, for instance, that advertising would lower the professions in the estimation of 'right-thinking members of the community'. It would only follow that advertising should be prohibited, however, if the alleged overall benefits that might result (better access to legal services, easier entry into the profession, and, possibly, lower charges) would be outweighed by the alleged disadvantages (damage to the image of the profession and resulting loss of confidence in its services, promotion of false and misleading claims, and, possibly, higher charges).

Even the fact that a particular restriction is intended to, and does in fact, protect standards does not necessarily justify its retention, for the standards may be higher than is required.[12] A corner delicatessen can offer higher standards of service than a supermarket; it does not follow that shoppers should be denied the right to opt for lower standards of service together with lower prices. The comparison is not made in order to equate professional services with those of businessmen or, worse, tradesmen, but rather because it illustrates the principle of consumer choice and of the relativity of the competing values. It is desirable that professional men serve their clients according both to high ethical principles and exalted standards of service. But if, for instance, this results in the services only being available to the very rich, the price may be too high. Barristers may as a class be better advocates than solicitors and thereby be able to provide a better-quality service to the public in the courts. Nevertheless, solicitors have an equal right of audience in the lower courts and in tribunals and claim enlarged rights of audience in the higher courts, which are opposed by barristers. Solicitors may be better advocates than legal executives and therefore able to provide a better class of service, yet the two share certain rights of audience, and legal executives contend for more, against the opposition of the Law Society. The test in each case is not simply whether standards may fall, but whether there are likely to be compensating advantages. Nor, it should be said, does it follow that standards will fall simply because rules designed for their protection are abandoned. A chastity belt is not a necessary precondition to marital fidelity.

The extent to which, in the field of restrictive practices, everything is relative is illustrated by the remarkable changes the Bar has recently made in the rules of etiquette affecting practice overseas, practice in law centres and representation in tribunals. From 1974, a barrister taking instructions from abroad has been allowed to work without chambers, without a clerk and in partnership with a foreign lawyer. He can accept instructions from a lay client without the intervention of any solicitor. He may negotiate his fees direct with the client. He may take a fixed fee, an annual retainer or even a contingent fee![13] A barrister working in a law centre is now permitted to become a full-time salaried employee and nevertheless retain his right of audience in the courts and his status as a practising barrister, even though he is not in chambers. If he appears in court, he must be instructed by a solicitor in the law centre, but the instructions need consist of no more than 'a back-sheet'. A barrister working in a law centre, whether or not for a fee, may interview and take statements from clients and witnesses, may write and sign letters on behalf of the centre, may negotiate settlements on behalf of clients, and may even allow himself to be described as a barrister on the centre's notepaper.[14] To all intents and purposes, therefore, he is allowed to function virtually as a solicitor. In 1974, the Bar approved arrangements whereby barristers and bar students may represent indigent persons without charge in tribunals without instructions from a solicitor.[15] The barrister may himself take instructions from the lay client. The scheme is run by the Free Representation Unit. (See further, p. 317 below.) The new rules regarding practice for overseas clients were introduced to enable barristers to compete effectively with solicitors for Common Market work;[16] the new rules for law centres and tribunals were adopted under pressure from young barristers wishing to play more of a role in the 'Welfare Law movement'. In each case the new dispensation is completely at variance with the ordinary rules, which inevitably casts doubt on the claim by the profession that the ordinary rules are essential to the integrity and standards of the Bar and of the service it provides to the public.

The force of the profession's arguments in support of monopoly and restriction is also inevitably weakened by the fact that, although there may be room for argument as to whether they are consistent with the public interest, they tend very clearly to be in the interests of the profession. It is *possible* that the public would be better protected if only solicitors could draft wills (as proposed by the Law Society in its 1977 evidence to the Royal Commission), but the self-interest in proposing this monopoly is manifest. The ordinary observer, even if he is innocent of any cynicism about such matters, is bound to be somewhat on his guard. Moreover, experience suggests that a dash of cynicism is not unwarranted. The record shows that the legal profession has over and over again defended not merely the indefensible, but also restrictions that *it itself* later came to accept were contrary to the public interest.

Thus, from the 1870s until 1965 the Bar had a rule that a client wishing to be represented by a barrister who was not a member of the circuit on which the case was being tried had to pay extra fees (£100 for a QC, £50 for a junior).[17] From the latter part of the nineteenth century until 1966 the Bar required that a junior who appeared with a Queen's Counsel had to be paid a fee equal to two-thirds of that paid to the leader, irrespective of the amount of work involved in the case.[18]

From 1850 up to the present day the Bar has resisted every extension of the jurisdiction of the county court where it shares rights of audience with solicitors.[19] At the end of the last, and in the first quarter of the present century, the Law Society fought a masterly rearguard action against compulsory registration of land, which was intended to reduce lawyers' fees. More than forty years after the 1897 Land Transfer Act had introduced compulsory registration the system had still not begun to bite. (An economic historian's account of the battle summarised what happened, applying Max Weber's dictum: 'In England the reason for the failure of all efforts at a rational codification of the law ... was due to the successful resistance against such rationalisation offered by the great and centrally organised lawyers guilds ... They retained in their hands [land transfer] as an empirical and highly developed technology and they successfully fought all moves towards rational law that threatened their social and material position.'[20]) At the same time the Law Society disciplined its members who offered services to the public at fees below those laid down in the statutory scales. ('The powers which had been given to the Society to protect the public from defaulting solicitors were used to protect the profession from competition.'[21]) Both sides of the profession have stoutly defended restrictions on advertising which have subsequently been relaxed. Both sides of the profession had severe restrictions on the services that could be provided to the poor in free legal advice centres which, again, have been greatly liberalised in recent years.[22]

In the field of monopolies and restrictive practices there are no absolutes. A fair evaluation of the public interest, as the Monopolies Commission has said, demands 'a balancing operation'.[23] The benefits of maintaining high professional standards have to be weighed against the disadvantages arising from the restrictions said to be necessary for the purpose. Each case must be judged on its merits.

Examination of the existing restrictions in England shows that they consist of four main categories: (1) those that regulate the organisation and structure of the profession (e.g. division of the profession into barristers and solicitors, or of the Bar into Queen's Counsel and juniors); (2) those that regulate entry into the profession; (3) those that regulate the work that

can be done by its members (e.g. demarcation lines between
members of the profession and between lawyers and non-
lawyers); and (4) those that restrict the way in which the work
can be done (e.g. rules against unfair competition). (Restrictions that concern methods of charging fees are treated separately: see Chapter 7.)

Restrictions that regulate the organisation and structure of the profession

The division between barristers and solicitors

The prime restriction that defines the structure of the profession is, of course, the complex of rules that divide it into
barristers and solicitors. Barristers have a virtual monopoly
over rights of audience in the higher courts, whereas solicitors
have the monopoly of direct relations with the client. A barrister cannot at the same time be a solicitor, or vice versa. The
process of qualification is different. Barristers and solicitors
cannot practise in each other's offices. Their systems of internal government are different. In a sense, they do similar work
– advising, negotiating, drafting and advocacy. But, in
another sense, they perform different functions. Barristers do
not pass any tests that show them to be better, more highly
trained or even more specialised than solicitors. But they
generally work more as specialists and consultants. The lay
client instructs the solicitor, who, if the case demands it,
brings in a barrister. In most situations the solicitor manages
the entire matter from start to finish, but when an expert in
advocacy or an expert in the law is needed the barrister is called
in.

The division is not as ancient as is often supposed.[24] Division presupposes two or more parts of a whole, but it was not
until the seventeenth or even the eighteenth century that the
solicitors could be said to have emerged as a distinct or
identifiable professional group. The Bar had by then had
centuries of development. The distinction until relatively
recently was therefore not between two parts of the same
profession, but between lawyers and sub-lawyers. In 1765
Blackstone set out the hierarchy of the legal profession without even mentioning solicitors. Even a hundred years later

Dicey lectured on legal education without referring to solicitors. Until the late eighteenth and into the early nineteenth century solicitors could be described as 'an unorganised, ill-disciplined, ill-educated category of sub-professional agents, living wholly or partly on the sub-professional trivia of litigation and conveyancing and sharing even this subject matter with court clerks, law students and laymen'.[25]

But in the nineteenth century the solicitors' branch gradually established itself and carved out areas of work in which it specialised. The Bar was persuaded first to give up seeing clients direct and then to cease to do conveyancing. In return the Bar had its monopoly over the rights of audience in the higher courts, its superior status, its role as the consultant branch and a virtual monopoly over appointments to the bench. Lawyers on both sides of the profession have broadly remained in favour of the divided profession. Both the Bar and the Law Society, in evidence to the Royal Commission, argued for its continuation – though the Law Society hoped to see adjustments in its incidents.

There are many arguments both for and against the divided profession.[26] It is said by its advocates that unification would decrease costs by cutting out duplication of work and double-manning. Those who disagree say that costs will rise because work now done by barristers with low overheads would then be done by lawyers working in firms like solicitors whose overheads are much higher. Fusionists maintain that it would increase efficiency because the ultimate advocate would be more likely to be in charge of the preparation of the case; anti-fusionists argue that overall efficiency would decline since more inexperienced advocates would appear in the courts. The heart of the argument is whether unification would weaken specialist services to an undesirable extent. It has been seen that solicitors tend to specialise – in conveyancing, probate, litigation work, company and commercial work, etc. Some solicitors are very great experts in their particular field. The popular view that solicitors are general practitioners and barristers are specialists is, therefore, inaccurate. But it is true that barristers are a specialist service in the sense that they are used as consultants and advisers by solicitors. Many members of the Bar are, in reality, generalists – 'common lawyers' – willing to undertake a considerable range of work. But even they provide a specialist service to their instructing solicitors, and through them to the client by being the expert for the particular case. Whatever the level of expertise in the solicitor's firm, there is usually someone at the Bar to provide more expert guidance than is available in the firm. This is plainly an advantage to solicitors and their clients. If the two branches were merged, obviously there would still be specialists, but would they be equally specialist and equally accessible?

Opponents of fusion argue that it would lead to specialists spending more of their time on generalist solicitor's work and correspondingly less on their speciality. Moreover, they might tend to work mainly for the biggest firms and the biggest clients, and thereby be less available to the general community of clients. Under the present system, they (and their clients) benefit because they get work from many parts of the country. Also, by being in firms they would be more isolated one from another than in chambers and in the Inns, where they see each other daily in close proximity and thereby imbibe both specialist know-how and ethical standards. Advocates of fusion maintain that countries with unified professions have no lack of specialists, and that it is common for lawyers, for instance in the United States and Canada, to refer cases to specialists where they lack the expertise to handle the problem. The objection that lawyers may be reluctant to refer cases for fear of losing the client is to undervalue the lawyers' sense of professional responsibility for the client's interests. The loss of the collegiate atmosphere of the Bar would be compensated by the increased contact between lawyers and their clients. Specialists would not necessarily work for the largest firms – indeed the experience of other countries shows that they may prefer to work as individuals or in very small units. The absence of a separate Bar might reduce the occasions when the client was unnecessarily persuaded to seek and to pay for an expert's opinion simply to spare the solicitor the burden of taking responsibility for deciding what to do. By the same token, it could strengthen the specialist tendencies amongst solicitors which are at present artificially diminished by the convenient availability of the Bar. (Country solicitors, it is often said, use counsel less than those in cities with a local Bar.)

Protagonists on both sides of the fusion debate tend to be

more or less fixed in their respective positions. This has the practical consequence that, whatever the theoretical relative merits of a divided or unified legal profession, it is very difficult to change from one to the other unless practitioners happen to want to change – which usually they do not. Even legislation cannot necessarily achieve fusion if the profession is determined to remain divided. In 1891 the Legal Profession Act in the State of Victoria permitted barristers and solicitors to do each other's work, provided for a new order of 'barristers and solicitors' and constituted a new unified system of legal education for all lawyers. To no avail. Two weeks after the statute became law the Bar Association announced that its members would continue to practise only in the traditional way, and they have continued to do so ever since. The Victorian profession is as divided today as it was in 1890.

In England it is clear that the majority of lawyers and both the main professional organisations would prefer there to be a separate Bar. If there were legislation to unify the profession, the net result would probably be similar to that in the State of Victoria. There would be nothing to prevent individual practitioners from deciding to take instructions only from other lawyers and thus preserving the separate Bar. Most present barristers would be likely to decide to operate in this way. It does not follow, however, that the status quo must be accepted. The ideal would seem to be a situation where the rules permit the profession to organise itself in whatever way seems beneficial to *individual practitioners* in the light of their inclinations and the needs of their clients. There should, therefore, be no rule preventing lawyers from taking instructions only from other lawyers – but equally, legislation should prohibit any rule requiring it. Whilst most lawyers would, therefore, continue as before, some might experiment with new forms of organisation. Some solicitors would take cases in the higher courts (see further, p. 181 below), some barristers would take instructions from clients such as accountants, surveyors, banks and insurance companies, whilst others would be prepared to act directly for clients generally. (Barristers who held clients' moneys would, of course, have to be made subject to the same strict rules as now apply to solicitors.) Given the deep conservatism of the legal profession the probability is that change, if there were any, would be extremely slow. It would move at the speed at which lawyers themselves wanted to go. This at the least should be permitted.

The division between Queen's Counsel and junior barristers

The function of Queen's Counsel is to provide an even more expert service than is available from the Bar generally. They advise or appear as advocates in the biggest or heaviest cases. Hitherto, they have been more or less confined by the two-counsel rule to cases justifying the employment of two counsel and have been prohibited from doing most forms of routine drafting of pleadings and other documents connected with litigation. (Under the rule a QC could not appear in court without a junior, and could not undertake ordinary drafting of pleadings.) The Monopolies Commission recommended in 1976 that the two-counsel rule be abolished as an unjustifiable restriction on the client's freedom of choice, and this was in fact done as from 1 October 1977.[27] But the basic pattern of practice of QCs is likely to continue unchanged. Clearly, there is some advantage to the public in having a specialist class of the top 10 per cent of barristers whose talents are available for the cases that most need their attention. The question, however, is whether there is any need for a separate rank of barristers to achieve a result that is probably achieved in most legal professions without one. The most senior practitioners in any profession tend to devote themselves, on the whole, to the biggest and most difficult problems.

The chief argument against having a bar divided into Queen's Counsel and juniors is that it has a distinct inflationary effect on fees. This is because when the Lord Chancellor bestows the honour of silk on a practitioner, he places him in the position of being able to earn much higher fees. Obviously, senior practitioners in all fields earn more than juniors and lawyers involved in big cases would expect to earn more than those in cases of less complexity or importance. But the fees are higher than they would be if there were no separate rank of Queen's Counsel. This can be seen in the figures for the earnings of practitioners in the Bar's remuneration survey. Table 6.1 shows that there were huge differences in the average earnings of silks as compared with the earnings of senior juniors, *even for silks who had been QCs for less than three years*.

Table 6.1
Median gross and net fees of QCs and senior juniors,
1974–5

	Gross (£)	Net before tax (£)
London specialists		
Juniors 9–15 years from Call	15,478	11,335
Juniors over 15 years from Call	12,540	9,112
QCs appointed after 1972	30,534	23,152
QCs appointed before 1972	29,948	22,229
London common lawyers		
Juniors 9–15 years from Call	11,340	7,776
Juniors over 15 years from Call	11,662	8,089
QCs appointed after 1972	21,839	16,411
QCs appointed before 1972	21,103	14,555
Circuiteers		
Juniors 9–15 years from Call	11,501	7,683
Juniors over 15 years from Call	11,151	7,458
QCs appointed after 1972	20,163	14,158
QCs appointed before 1972	21,193	16,316

Source: Bar Council, *Survey of the Income of the Bar, 1974–5*, Tables 14 and 15.

The average gross fees of QCs in 1974–5 were £26,056,[28] compared with an average of £13,122 for juniors of between 9 and 15 years' experience and £12,958 for those with more than 15 years' experience.[29]

Suppose the effect of abolishing the rank of QC were to reduce the difference between gross fees of QCs and senior juniors by a half, the savings to the clients on the basis of 370 QCs and on the 1974–5 figures would have been in the order of £2.4m. Instead of clients paying a total of some £9.64m. for services supplied by QCs, they would have paid some £7.2m. In addition there would be savings in the fees paid to juniors whose fees when instructed with a QC to some extent reflect the inflated element attributable to the rank of leading counsel.

Moreover, some clients use a QC not because the case justifies one, but because the best way to win, it is thought, is to have a silk. A QC is, by definition of the system, better than a junior – whatever their actual respective merits. He even sits in a different row of benches. (The fact that a barrister must greatly increase his fees immediately on taking silk simply illustrates the point.) The abolition of silks would, therefore, not merely over a period of time somewhat reduce the fees charged by the most senior practitioners, but could also somewhat lessen the tendency to use such practitioners unnecessarily.

Restrictions that regulate entry into the profession

Both sides of the profession make elaborate rules as to the process of qualification that entitles a person to style himself a barrister or solicitor. A barrister[30] must first join an Inn of Court as a student – for which purpose he must be able to show that he has the necessary academic qualifications. He must have a certificate of good character; must not be an undischarged bankrupt, a solicitor, a patent agent or parliamentary agent; must not have been convicted of an offence that in the opinion of the Masters of the Bench of the Inn make his admission 'undesirable'; and must not be engaged in any other occupation which in the opinion of the Masters of the Bench 'is incompatible with the position of a student seeking call to the Bar'. He can also be refused if he is for any other reason considered by the Masters of the Bench 'to be unsuitable for admission'. He must pay the fees.[31] It is then required that he pass or gain exemption from the Part I (or academic stage) of the examination process and that he take the Part II (or vocational stage). He must keep term by dining the requisite number of times,[32] and finally he must be Called. He is then entitled to style himself a barrister or barrister-at-law. If he wishes to practise he must undertake pupillage for a minimum of twelve months and he cannot accept any instructions from a solicitor until he has completed at least six months' pupillage. In order to practise he must be a member of approved chambers with a clerk.

A would-be solicitor[33] must apply to become a student – for which purpose he has to show that he has the requisite educational qualifications.[34] He lodges a statutory declaration nominating three referees and must disclose criminal convictions other than ones for trivial motoring offences. He can be, but rarely is, called for interview as to his fitness to become a student. Once enrolled as a student, he must, like the bar student, take or gain exemption from Part I (the academic stage) of the Qualifying Examination and take Part II (the vocational stage). He must also be enrolled as an articled clerk with a practising solicitor for a period the length of which will depend on his background.[35] When he has completed his articles and his Part II he is eligible to have his name entered on the Rolls and to use the title solicitor, though he may not practise on his own for another three years.

Restrictions in the form of hoops through which would-be entrants to a profession must pass are in themselves unexceptionable. Indeed, they are a necessary part of the very concept of a profession. The question is, therefore, not whether restriction is desirable but whether the particular forms of restriction are open to criticism. The powers to exclude undischarged bankrupts, those who have been convicted of certain kinds of criminal offence and the like do not appear to have given rise to much dispute. Such powers clearly leave great discretion in the hands of the profession to determine what constitutes a character, a conviction, an occupation or other reasons that make a person unfit for membership. But the attempt to eliminate or significantly to reduce such discretion seems doomed to failure.[36] The resulting rules would be long and complex and would at the same time lack the necessary flexibility to be capable of adaptation to changing times and new situations. A vague standard is theoretically open to objection but it actually offers the best prospect of a fair and sensitive system of administration. What *is* lacking, however, is a formal right of appeal against a refusal of admission to a would-be entrant and information generally available as to the number of persons refused admission each year and the reasons for such refusals.

Consideration is given elsewhere to the suitability of the present rules from the educational point of view – see pp. 147–51. The other chief problem raised by the entry requirements is whether they exclude any class or category of person who ought to be able to gain admission to the profession. The one form of restriction that may have such an effect is the cost of qualification. This is substantial, especially for would-be barristers. At the Bar, there are entrance fees, fees for courses and examination, fees on Call or Admission, pupillage fees, the cost of clothes and, above all, the costs of maintenance during the process of qualification estimated at some £1,500 a year in 1977. Even after qualification there may be a period at the Bar before the entrant can expect to support himself completely. Solicitors face tuition fees, examination fees and maintenance costs. The potential sources of funding available are limited to central or local government, the profession and private sources.

Central government funding is not available since the government has always refused to provide financial support for institutions and courses run by a private profession. The apparent exception of teaching-hospitals is not really an exception since they are also hospitals providing medical services.

Local authorities do help to a significant extent by supporting students through various stages of the training but this assistance is patchy. Most of those who enter the profession are law graduates, who are eligible (subject to a means test) for mandatory local authority grants at their university or polytechnic to meet both fees and maintenance during the first, academic, stage of training. Those who enter the profession direct from school can usually get discretionary local authority grants for attendance at compulsory courses for the Part I and Part II. But law graduates cannot necessarily get grants even for the compulsory courses for Part II. Whether any such award is available, and if so, its amount, depends on the discretion of the local educational authority. Non-law graduates find it difficult to get grants for their one-year academic stage course (see p. 146) and have the same difficulties as law graduates in getting grants for the Part II.

It is understandable that those who opt for the relative luxury of a non-law degree before qualifying for the law should have to pay the extra costs involved themselves. There is no valid reason for imposing the cost of their Part I training on the public purse. But there does seem to be an overwhelming case for making grants for the compulsory Part II training mandatory and uniform (though no doubt subject to the usual means test) rather than discretionary. It is patently unfair that the availability and amount of a grant for the one-year Part II courses should depend on the particular area in which a student lives. The importance of mandatory grants for Part II was emphasised by the Ormrod Committee on Legal Education in its 1971 Report: 'If grants are not available for the vocational courses, recruitment will continue to some extent to be limited to those whose parents are able to afford to maintain them during the period of the course, and who are prepared to be dependent on their parents for this part of their training.' The result would be that 'a substantial number of good recruits to the legal profession will be lost to it'.[37] But the Report recognised that, whilst vocational training was conducted in professional schools, there would be a need for new legislation to extend compulsory grants to their students. The likelihood of such legislation was remote, 'for it would raise far-reaching and controversial issues of policy extending well beyond the legal profession'.[38] On the other hand, if the problem was not solved, the profession would have to assist students not able to get grants and whose parents could not support them. If the profession simply went ahead with its own vocational courses, this 'could have disastrous consequences on recruitment for the legal profession'.[39] This prediction has been proved wholly wrong. The profession has gone ahead with courses in its own schools and recruitment has nevertheless boomed. In spite of the cost, there appear to be more than enough who want to enter the profession – at least for the present. But the question remains whether some able but poor recruits are denied entry.

The Bar has *some* means of providing financial support. The Inns dispose of some seventy substantial[40] plus a larger number of small scholarships and prizes. Some are subject to open competition, others to award simply on record and interview. Some are means-tested, others are not. Some are open to all, others only to categories such as Oxbridge students. The total paid out annually amounts to some £140,000.[41] There are also some grants for reading in chambers and limited sums available for interest-free loans to newly called barristers to help them get started. (It is likely that the Report of the Royal Commission when published will show that the Inns have very substantial reserves, at least some of which could reasonably be applied to increase the moneys available for scholarships.)

The Law Society has no equivalent moneys, though there is

a small fund of some £10,000 to assist in cases of financial hardship. Articled clerks, unlike bar students and bar pupils, are, however, normally paid a salary. In former times this was unheard of, but it has now become normal and, although the sums paid are hardly munificent, they can now amount to something approaching a modest living wage. The Law Society's evidence to the Royal Commission suggested that the range was from £750 to £3,000 per annum.[42] A survey of articled clerks at the College of Law conducted in 1976 showed an average weekly gross wage of £38 per week, or £1,975 per annum.[43] But three-fifths of the sample relied on another source of finance apart from their pay – help from parents, earnings of a spouse, or private incomes or savings. The evidence of the Associate Members Group of the Law Society to the Royal Commission stated that most articled clerks suffered from 'a desperate and unjustified lack of income'.[44]

There are no easy solutions to the problem of the costs of becoming a lawyer. Minor irritants such as pupillage fees or premiums for articled clerks are now rare and could easily be abolished. Student fees on Call to the Bar or Admission might be transmuted into some form of annual payment by practitioners. But such suggestions would make no real impact on the problem. Neither central nor local government can be expected to provide the solution. Individual practitioners are understandably reluctant to finance recruits to the profession in the early stages through the medium of levies or similar taxes. If the burden of financing beginners were laid on individual chambers, it would become even more difficult than it already is to obtain a tenancy; if, instead, it were placed on the Bar as a whole, the inevitable screening mechanism to avoid over-subscription might again produce an undesirable restraint on entry.

On the solicitor's side, it would be helpful if the Law Society were prepared to suggest recommended minima of remuneration for articled clerks, based on appropriate estimates of local rates. (There are now some dozen or more local law societies that publish such rates.) The financially marginal recruit would then know what he could expect to earn in his trainee years. It would equally be helpful if there were low-interest or even interest-free loans available to starters on both sides of the profession. The Bar Students Working Party suggested to the

Royal Commission that there might be a scheme of loans financed by the banks and guaranteed by the Inns and the Law Society.[45] But the success of loans depends on whether there is a reasonable prospect of remunerative work to permit repayment. This will depend on general economic conditions. Those most likely to be discouraged by the difficulties of taking on the burden of a loan are precisely those from modest financial backgrounds for whom such a scheme would be primarily designed. More money ought to be made available for loans, but it is improbable that this (or indeed any of the other proposed methods of alleviating financial hardship for would-be lawyers) would be likely to make much of a dent on the existing social class composition of the legal profession. Even if costs were trimmed and methods of financial support in cases of need were improved, it seems probable that the legal profession, (like other professions and like legal professions throughout the world), would remain a predominantly middle-class institution.

Restrictions that regulate the work that can be done by members of the profession

Rights of audience

The problem of rights of audience affects the bar, solicitors, legal executives and non-lawyers. The basic position today is that barristers have a monopoly over most work in the higher courts (House of Lords, Court of Appeal, High Court and crown court), though solicitors have some minor rights of audience in the crown courts; barristers and solicitors have equal rights of audience in the lower courts (magistrates' courts and county courts); and barristers, solicitors, and legal executives have equal rights of audience in proceedings in judges' chambers and before Masters and Registrars. In addition, every court has always had the discretionary power to admit any person as advocate,[46] and this discretion has been massively used to permit police officers to appear in magistrates' courts. In the tribunal system, there are generally no rules that limit rights of audience, and both lawyers and non-lawyers commonly appear as advocates.

In the overwhelming majority of cases heard in the courts, barristers and solicitors have an equal right of audience, for far more cases are heard in the lower than in the higher courts. The trend is also continually to enlarge the jurisdiction of the lower courts. (The jurisdiction of the county courts has, for instance, been increased in successive stages from £200 in 1938 to £2,000 in 1977. The Criminal Law Act 1977 transfers a good deal of business from the crown court to the magistrates' courts.) The debate now is whether there should be any changes in the present rules on rights of audience. Solicitors want increased rights of audience in the crown courts and the High Court; legal executives finally won certain limited increased rights of audience in lower courts in 1977 but want more. The Bar, understandably, opposes the claims of solicitors; solicitors, equally predictably, reject the pretensions of legal executives.

The Bar's evidence to the Royal Commission was, baldly, that 'in general barristers are better advocates than solicitors'.[47] There were some solicitors who showed considerable skill as advocates in the lower courts, 'but the number whose skill matches that of the average barrister is very small'.[48] If solicitors had extended rights of audience, standards in the higher courts would decline. The Bar admitted that, because of its recent great expansion, standards of barristers had somewhat slipped. ('There may, therefore, have been a period during which levels of competence in criminal practice were relatively less high.'[49]) But the expansion had now levelled out and 'a progressive improvement in the standards of advocacy at the Bar is foreseen'.[50] Solicitors could, in any event, refuse to instruct incompetent barristers, whereas lay clients would not be able to judge the competence of their solicitors. It was not true, the Bar said, that extended rights of audience would reduce costs. The work would still have to be done. For the most part the preparatory work now done by solicitors' clerks would still be done by them, and the solicitor-advocate, whose overheads were higher than those of barristers, would need to be paid more rather than less for doing the same work as the barrister (though not necessarily more than a solicitor *and* a barrister). Moreover, the client had the advantage of an independent and fresh view of the case from a barrister. This was especially important in prosecution work. The possibility that crown court prosecutions might be conducted by solicitors employed by local police prosecution departments caused 'grave concern'.[51] Also, if solicitors took a substantial share of the work in crown courts, 'there would no longer be a sufficient demand to justify the continued presence of a local Bar'. The lack of work for young barristers 'would remove the attraction of those Bars and debilitate them'.[52]

The Law Society's case for extended rights of audience in crown courts was made in 1971 in the context of the debate on the Courts Bill then before Parliament. Solicitors, it was argued, ought to be allowed to conduct cases in the crown courts, when they and their clients did not wish to instruct counsel. ('The public cannot understand why the legal system of this country permits a person to be represented by a senior and experienced solicitor–advocate in the magistrates' courts, but precludes that same advocate from appearing in the same type of case in the higher court.'[53]) It would permit cost economies through elimination of duplication of work. It would avoid delays caused by counsel not being available and great inconvenience through late returns of briefs. (The Law Society in 1971 said that a senior prosecuting solicitor in a county council town had more than a third of 1,226 briefs to counsel returned – frequently after 4 p.m. on the day before the trial. Of sixteen briefs delivered by a firm of solicitors in a large town in the south-west, six were returned. In one case, the brief changed hands five times, and the barrister had only twenty minutes to prepare the case before trial.[54])

These problems continue in spite of the recent great increase in the number of barristers. The Law Society's 1977 evidence to the Royal Commission said that 108 local law societies had replied to its request for views about rights of audience. Of these, 36 were content with the existing situation, 2 had no comment and 70 expressed themselves in favour of extensions to existing rights. 'It was in rural areas that the wish for extended rights was strongest.' Many societies had commented on the subject of return of briefs, indicating that in some areas at least the Bar was overloaded. The fact that official complaints had not been frequently made showed not, as the Bar pretended, that there was no problem, but rather that solicitors realised the difficulties faced by barristers and their clerks. It was true that relatively few solicitors had taken advantage of the extension in rights of audience granted in the 1971 compromise package, but this was because, with very limited rights of audience, solicitors could normally only have isolated cases. It was not usually economic for them to do the odd case for which they would have to wait about. Barristers, by contrast, usually had several cases in the same list. (Solicitors also fare badly in the actual ordering of cases on the day – which is done more for the convenience of barristers.) If rights of audience were extended, solicitors would have more cases and would be able to 'gear up' for the work.[55]

The Law Society, in 1977, made three different proposals to the Royal Commission. One was that solicitors should have rights of audience in virtually all cases tried in crown courts. This should extend to prosecution as well as defence solicitors, but only if there were, first, statutory implementation of the proposal that the office of prosecuting solicitor be separated from the police authority. (This question is now being considered by the Royal Commission on pre-trial criminal process, the establishment of which was announced by the Prime Minister on 23 June 1977.) In High Court cases the Law Society only sought the right of audience for very trivial and routine hearings (to mention agreed terms of settlement, to ask for an adjournment or to deal with unopposed applications). Where barristers and solicitors had equal rights of audience, the Law Society also suggested that there be no distinction as to the robes or wigs worn or the benches from which the lawyers addressed the court. ('These distinctions are invidious and tend to confuse the public who may be led to believe that the solicitor has a lower standing in the eyes of the court.'[56]) Secondly, the Law Society suggested that both barristers and solicitors should be confined to advocacy in the lower courts until they had shown, after a period of a few years, that they had sufficient actual experience to justify full rights of audience. No detail was given as to how this might be done. Thirdly, it proposed that the jurisdiction of the High Court should be altered so that only those cases were heard there in which the time and expense involved, and the need for special advocacy skills, were justified. Again, there was no clarification of how this might be achieved.

The case for the extension of rights of audience for solicitors, at least to the crown court, would seem overwhelmingly strong. Most of the cases heard in both the higher and the lower courts could be dealt with by the other.[57] It may be that the average quality of barrister-advocates is higher than that of solicitor-advocates – but this is likely to be due at least partly to the calibre of those who now go into the two branches of the profession. If solicitors had a fuller right of audience, solicitor advocacy would attract more of the best potential recruits for this type of work. Also, if solicitors could handle this form of work in bulk, they would become better at it. About six out of ten crown court cases are guilty pleas, and the great majority of contested cases are short cases that end within a day or so. Experienced solicitor-advocates should be well able to cope with such work.

But the strongest argument for the change in solicitors' rights of audience is that the present system results in such poor preparation in so high a proportion of cases. Research in Sheffield has shown that, in a random sample of higher court criminal cases, barristers saw their clients for the first time on the morning of the trial in 96 per cent of intended guilty pleas and 79 per cent of those pleading not guilty.[58] These figures are a serious indictment of the operation of the divided profession, especially since the work of preparation in the solicitor's office is so often carried out by relatively inexperienced clerks. Neither the Bar nor the Law Society has denied that the figures might be broadly typical, at least in busy courts. But both have denied that this necessarily meant that the service was inadequate.[59] Their basic argument is that it is for the solicitor to decide whether or not to have a conference. The barrister received written instructions. He was trained to prepare a case quickly. The Bar told the Royal Commission: 'In a straightforward case, provided the case has been properly prepared by the solicitor, there should be only a few matters, and there may be none, on which the barrister requires further information: this can be given at the trial conference.'[60] Thus 'in the great majority of cases (even contested cases) where the factual issues are comparatively straightforward, a preliminary conference is neither necessary nor requested or suggested; in more complex cases a preliminary conference is normal practice'.[61] It was, of course, desirable that clients have conferences with their barristers, but there were considerable practical difficulties. Solicitors would have to deliver briefs earlier, the barrister would have to be paid for the time involved in visiting his client in custody. (The Law Society estimated the cost of a pre-trial conference in every crown court case as more than £2½ m.)[62] The lists would have to be organised so as to guarantee that that barrister actually appeared in the case, causing resulting administrative problems and delays. Prior conferences would, therefore, be costly and impracticable. The Sheffield study gave cause for concern, but the fact that the client thought that his case had not been properly presented did not mean that this was correct. The Law Society's evidence to the Royal Commission made substantially the same points.

The argument that most cases do not require a conference between the client and his advocate is unconvincing. First, it is based on an unreal assumption that cases are generally adequately prepared by solicitors. Secondly, even if it were correct that straightforward cases do not require a prior conference, how can it be said that a case *is* straightforward until the advocate has had a proper conference with the client? It seems unlikely that a lawyer charged with an indictable offence would permit his own case to be tried in a crown court without insisting on a full and proper opportunity to talk, well in advance of the trial, with the advocate who was to present the case. He would be aware of all the possible pitfalls of relying on 'the system' to work in his absence. Instructions may be taken by staff who lack experience or skill. Admonitions from the client to search for this witness, or to check that fact, may be ignored – either because the client is taken to be mistaken in thinking the evidence to be important or because time, resources, or financial means are inadequate. The written brief to counsel may be inept – barristers commonly complain about the poor quality of their instructions. Counsel comes to the conference on the morning of the trial having prepared it as presented in his instructions. He is not then in a frame of mind to be told by the client that there are other witnesses who need to be called, further matters to be investigated, or that the client wishes the case to be presented differently. Courts are reluctant to grant an adjournment, especially when everyone is there ready for the case to go ahead. The barrister knows that, even if an adjournment were granted, he might not be available to take the case on the adjourned date. There is overwhelming psychological pressure on the client to allow himself to be processed. Late delivery of briefs by solicitors, late returns of briefs by barristers, resulting last-minute preparation of cases by counsel and consultation with the lay client on the morning of the trial are all endemic to the system. No one has yet suggested convincingly how these defects in the system can be met. But it can hardly be pretended that the system is satisfactory. Nor is the fact that barristers and solicitors have tolerated it for decades evidence that it is working as it should. It would be surprising if a detailed study of how this system actually works in practice did not show that in a significant proportion of cases preparation falls well short of the reasonable mimimum standard of competence.

If solicitors had the right to conduct cases in the crown court, some of these problems might be avoided, or at least reduced. Responsibility for the work would have to be taken by the firm. Preparation and presentation would all be done from under one roof. Even lower-quality advocacy might be more than counter-balanced by better-quality preparation. (It has often been said by experienced advocates that the winning of cases depends much more on good preparation than on the quality of the advocacy.) There is no guarantee that a solicitor's firm would prepare the case better than the combination of a solicitor's firm and counsel instructed at the last moment, but even if it only did so as well at a lower cost there would have been some gain.

It is possible that solicitors might, as a result of a change in rights of audience, come to have a larger share of the available work. If so, the livelihood of the Bar, or at least of some barristers, might indeed be threatened. But, if this happened, it would be because clients and their professional advisers preferred representation by a one-tier system to a two-tier system. They would have rejected the claimed advantages of the independent Bar. If this happened, the Bar would have no right to complain. But this seems unlikely. It is much more probable that, for a variety of reasons, many solicitors would continue to instruct barristers. Some solicitors would run a proper advocacy service and might do it as well as, or better than, their competitors who used the Bar. But most would probably continue much as before. The Bar, in the future as in the past, should be able to hold its own in competition with solicitors.

There is equally a case for giving barristers employed in commerce or industry or in government departments a right of audience at least equivalent to that of solicitors in private practice. At present, barristers who are salaried (with the exception of the Attorney-General and the Solicitor-General and barristers in law centres) may not appear as advocates in any court – though a salaried barrister is allowed to appear for his employer if the employer is allowed to appear by a servant or agent. Solicitors in salaried employment outside private practice do have the same right of audience as those in private practice, and barristers should be treated in the same way. In a recent case Lord Denning, speaking of salaried legal advisers, said they 'are regarded by the law as in every respect in the same position as those who practise on their own account. The only difference is that they act for one client only. They must uphold the same standards of honour and etiquette. They are subject to their client and to the court. They must respect the same confidences. They and their clients have the same privileges'.[63] If this be so, the only remaining basis for denying to salaried barristers the same right of audience as solicitors is protection for the private profession. This cannot provide a sufficient justification for preventing the employer from having the lawyer of his choice to appear for him.

The case for legal executives to have enlarged rights of audience is somewhat different in that they work as employees in solicitors' offices, and the extent to which they would use increased powers would, therefore, be controlled by their solicitor employers. Solicitors would also have responsibility for the standards of work and of ethics of unadmitted persons. But there would seem to be advantage in gradually extending their role in open court. This is in fact now being done in certain uncontested and purely formal proceedings in both county courts and magistrates' courts.[64] The trend will, no doubt, continue – and should, in order to make full use of the present capacities and future potential of this considerable man-power resource. Like the gradual development of solicitors' rights of audience in the higher courts, the rights of audience of legal executives in the lower courts will presumably advance stage by stage so that its success (or otherwise) can be monitored.

The solicitors' conveyancing monopoly

At present, solicitors enjoy statutory monopolies of some

antiquity over conveyancing and probate work for profit. In conveyancing the monopoly does not, in fact, cover the entire transaction, but only the drawing or preparing of the instrument of transfer. It therefore does not include the preparation or exchange of contracts. Breach of the monopoly by an unqualified person makes him liable to a maximum penalty, fixed in 1804 at £50, which is now obviously unrealistically low.

In the past few years unqualified conveyancers have been battling with the Law Society, trying to find a mode of operation that is legal. The Law Society has successfully prosecuted many of these unwelcome competitors, but has not so far managed to drive them out of business. Their share of the lucrative conveyancing market is, however, as yet very small. The Royal Commission was required by its terms of reference to consider specifically 'the rules preventing persons who are neither barristers nor solicitors from undertaking conveyancing and other legal business on behalf of other persons'.

The Law Society devoted no less than sixty-one printed pages of evidence to the Royal Commission to this topic alone.[65] Its case can be briefly summarised in the proposition that the monopoly was in the public interest because non-solicitors could not safely be entrusted with work that was fraught with so many potential hazards and difficulties. The Law Society dealt almost contemptuously with the notion that the monopoly might simply be abolished, leaving anyone eligible to undertake the work. Such a 'free-for-all', it thought, would run wholly counter to the modern trend of providing better consumer protection. 'It would seem strange that while legislation is in prospect for the control of estate agents, any recommendations should be made for relaxing all controls on conveyancing services.'[66] But it dealt at some length with the intermediate suggestion of permitting licensed conveyancers to compete with solicitors, subject to safeguards. The minimum controls, according to the Law Society, would include proper examinations, disciplinary sanctions, accounting rules for clients' moneys and annual accounts, supervisory controls by qualified persons over staff, restraints to eliminate conflicts of interest, compulsory insurance against negligence and a compensation fund for victims of dishonesty.

Whether conveyancing should be left with solicitors, opened also to licensed conveyancers or made a free-for-all, depends on one's evaluation of the difficulty of the tasks involved and of the risks attached to varying degrees of free or freer competition. Solicitors have always been at pains to stress the complexity of conveyancing and its importance to the client – 'the biggest financial transaction of one's life is buying a house'. Others have pointed out that while there are many theoretical and potential hazards in conveyancing, the overwhelming majority of cases are reasonably routine and straightforward. A great volume of conveyancing is in practice done by unadmitted legal executives, many of whom work with little or no supervision. (Advertisements asking for legal executives in conveyancing, as in other fields, commonly indicate that the applicant should be able to work 'without supervision', 'with minimal supervision', 'with little or no supervision'.[67]) An experienced conveyancer, Mr Michael Joseph, has also levelled serious charges of general professional incompetence at solicitors in not, in reality, providing the safeguards for clients that, it is said, are the main reason for using a solicitor.[68]

Given the inevitable controversy as to how complex conveyancing is, it is highly improbable that any government would consider moving from a position of total monopoly to a complete free-for-all. The compromise of opening the field to licensed conveyancers is much more likely to be practical politics. This is the solution adopted more than a hundred years ago in South Australia, where since 1860 licensed land brokers have had the right to compete with lawyers for conveyancing work. Under the previous legislation land brokers were licensed by the Registrar General. The Land and Business Agents Act 1973 provides that this should be the responsibility of a new Board consisting of five members appointed by the Governor. One must be a legal practitioner of at least seven years' standing, one is the Registrar General or his nominee, and one must be a licensed land broker. No one may carry on business as a land broker unless he is licensed under the Act. A licence must be renewed annually by application to the Board. In order to become licensed a person must, after a two-year course, have passed the very demanding Licensed Land Brokers examination set by the Registrar General, or have qualifications deemed to be the equivalent. There are require-ments as to accounts rules. Interest on client accounts in excess of A $2,000 per year has to be paid to the Board which must hold the money to meet claims for compensation for fiduciary default by any land broker. In addition, land brokers must provide a personal bond backed by sureties. The Board has disciplinary powers including power to impose a reprimand or a fine, or to cancel a licence.

The Law Society says that, if licensed conveyancers were subject to examination and financial controls such as compul-sory insurance, fidelity bonds and the like, they would not be able to offer services that were less expensive than those of qualified lawyers. ('The introduction of licensed conveyancers would serve only to lower the standards of conveyancing, or weaken the existing protection of the public without guaran-teeing, or even making probable, that the overall costs could, or would, be diminished.'[69]) The evidence from South Australia does not support this contention. It seems that, not only do land brokers charge significantly lower fees than those charged by solicitors, but solicitors themselves have been obliged, because of this competition, to charge considerably less than solicitors in neighbouring states.

The example of South Australia, therefore, seems worth following. Conveyancing requires expertise but not the full qualification of being a solicitor. Provided there are appropri-ate safeguards as to competence and financial probity, the public should have the right to choose between the full service to be obtained (hopefully) from solicitors' firms and the less full, but adequate and less costly, service obtainable from licensed conveyancers. In practice, the public would probably continue to use solicitors to a great extent, but competition might gradually bring costs down and there might, over a period of time, be a shift of some of the work to licensed conveyancers. These would presumably be legal executives. Surprisingly, the Institute of Legal Executives did not ask the Royal Commission for the right for its members to set up in competition with their solicitor employers. This was not because it doubted the competence of its members to do the work, but rather because it favoured preserving the unity of the legal profession.[70] But it argued that, if an Institute of Conveyancers were to be established, the Institute of Legal

Executives would be the logical body to assume this function.[71] If this were done, it would clearly need to have additional outside members (including a solicitor) appointed by the Lord Chancellor.

Those with the right to do conveyancing should also include barristers. The prevailing statute does in fact permit barristers to do this work,[72] but the Law Society and the Bar reached a private accommodation which was formally concluded in 1903 whereby the Bar agreed not to permit its members to poach on this solicitors' preserve. In 1949 the Bar modified the rule in favour of barristers employed in local government or industry, but, after protest from the Law Society and several years of negotiations, it backed down and in 1955 restored the 1903 self-denying ordinance. In recent years the question has been reopened. The Bar's evidence to the Royal Commission stated that the rule had 'over the years proved highly prejudicial, both as regards recruitment and promotion, to barristers employed in local government'[73] and had created serious problems for the growing number of barristers who sought employment in commerce, finance and industry. Provided barristers doing conveyancing are subject to the same controls as regards competence, client accounts, compensation funds and insurance as apply to others allowed to do conveyancing, there would not appear to be the slightest valid reason to prevent them from doing the work. Moreover, the right to undertake conveyancing should apply to barristers in private practice as much as to those employed. Solicitors do not need (and even if they needed, should not have) protection from competition from barristers.

The probate monopoly and wills

Barristers, solicitors and certificated notaries enjoy a statutory monopoly[74] over the drawing for profit of the two essential documents needed to obtain a grant of probate – the executors' affidavit, swearing they will administer the estate in accordance with the law, and the executors' account, stating the inventory of the deceased's assets. There is nothing to prevent an unqualified person from doing for profit all the other work in probate transactions, including gathering in the estate and distributing it to the heirs. But even a trust corporation such as a bank or an insurance company handling the estate must instruct a solicitor to apply for the executors' affidavit and account. The Association of Corporate Trustees proposed to the Royal Commission that a trust corporation should be entitled to apply for a grant of probate without the intervention of a solicitor. The Law Society opposed the suggestion.[75] Its reasons (other than obvious self-interest) were that 'an application for a grant of probate is an application to a court to exercise its powers'. There was no reason to give trust corporations any special status in regard to applications to the court.

It is true that, in theory, the executors' affidavit is a court document – in the sense that probate of a will is granted technically by the High Court of Justice (Family Division). But the grant is made not by a judge but by the office staff in the Registry. This is an administrative, not a judicial procedure. Only an expert would know that it was notionally a 'court' matter. This point is, therefore, at best, a thin one. It is not strengthened by the little-known fact that in London probably as much as a fifth of solicitor's probate work is actually delegated to 'law agents' who conduct the whole or a substantial part of the transaction, often including the drawing up of the executor's affidavit which goes out notionally under the solicitor's name. Law agents are unlicensed and unregulated private entrepreneurs in the probate field – Oyez Stationers and Waterlows Ltd being by far the largest. They have been plying their craft for a century or more.[76] They act only on the instructions of solicitors, much as do costs draftsmen, and as in the case of costs draftsmen, it is often they rather than the instructing solicitors who are the real experts on the mechanics of probate work. The Law Society's defence of its monopoly is further weakened by the fact that, in tens of thousands of cases each year, the entire probate transaction is completed by ordinary citizens with the help only of the Personal Applications Department (see further, p. 323) – without the help of either solicitors or trust corporations. In short, the Law Society's case for a continuing exclusive monopoly does not stand up to close examination. At the least, a trust corporation ought to be permitted to apply for probate in competition with solicitors. If 'law agents' could form an organisation able to train, test and control their members, they might also be allowed to undertake this work.

If solicitors should not be allowed to retain their monopoly

in the fields of conveyancing and probate, they equally, or
even more, should not be given a new monopoly over the
drawing of wills for profit, as claimed in the Law Society's
evidence to the Royal Commission.[77] According to a survey
in the Probate Registry, out of 37,144 wills admitted to probate in a thirteen-week period in 1966, 77 per cent were drafted
by solicitors, 18.5 per cent were home-made on printed forms
and 4.5 per cent were otherwise home-made.[78] The Law
Society says, rightly, that a badly drafted will can give rise to
many problems, but so can bad legal advice, and that is not
taken, in England at least, as a reason to give lawyers a monopoly in the field of giving legal advice. The public should be
left with the choice to use the cheaper and more accessible
service even though it entails the risk that the printed form
bought from a stationer does not quite meet the needs of the
particular family. If there is real concern about the inaccuracy
of wills made on printed forms, legislation could provide for a
warning to be placed on such forms about the desirability of
seeking advice from a solicitor before signing a will. The Lord
Chancellor's Office could publish a pamphlet on making your
own will – like those on do-it-yourself divorce and suing in the
county courts (see pp. 325–27 below). It would also be desirable, as proposed in 1971 by Justice, that there be official will
forms available from stationers which would have been properly drafted.[79]

The monopoly over the initiation and the handling of court cases

Solicitors have for centuries enjoyed a partial monopoly in
regard to litigation and other court work. The monopoly
covers the issuing of writs, the prosecution or defence of any
action in any civil, or criminal court and the preparation of
'any instrument relating to ... any legal proceeding'.[80] The
ordinary citizen can of course handle his own court case but no
non-solicitor may do court-work for someone else – unless the
court itself exercises its discretion to give such a person a right
of audience. (All courts have an inherent power to regulate
their own procedure – including who appears before them.[81])
The Law Society in its evidence to the Royal Commission said
that the monopoly was justified as it resulted in most litigation

being in the hands of professionals with the necessary expertise, subject to a code of conduct, strict accounting rules and
the control of the court. In the case of solicitors, they were also
covered by compulsory insurance and the compensation fund.
To the extent that the professional weeded out hopeless and
bad claims and defences the court was spared having to process
such cases and opponents were saved from vexatious cases.
The interposing of trained lawyers between the litigant and his
opponent assisted in taking the passion out of litigation,
assisted in concentrating on the real issues, reduced the danger
of unfair tactics and helped to bring about cooperation between litigants. Most cases were settled and the settlement
process was helped by the fact that there were professionals on
each side who trusted each other. Moreover the monopoly
helped to assure the continued existence of the legal profession
and restrained the growth of semi-skilled or unskilled organisations free from controls on conduct, standards and
accounts.[82]

The main controversy arising out of the monopoly in the
past has been over the position of claims assessors who handle
personal injury cases for a percentage. Claims assessors are
active in certain parts of England, notably in the London
docks. The Winn Committee on Personal Injuries Litigation
said that although some of the claims assessors or negotiators
had considerable expertise, claimants might be prejudiced by
using them. This was because negotiators had 'a natural interest in achieving *some* result for their clients since their right to
commission payment depends on it, but they are in a weak
bargaining position because they cannot themselves com-
mence proceedings'.[83] There was evidence that 'settlements
achieved by negotiators for adult plaintiffs are lower, sometimes very much lower, than they should be'.[84] Once a claim
had been compromised for however inadequate a sum, there
would normally be no remedy for the claimant. The Law
Society, not surprisingly, found itself in agreement with the
view of the Winn Committee.[85]

One possible answer to the problem would be to expand the
monopoly on the issuing of process to include recognised
claims assessors who became members of their society and
were bound by certain rules regarding ethics and accounts. If
the claims assessor is a useful addition to the armoury of

services available to the victim of an accident he should be placed in a position to negotiate from the same position of strength as a solicitor. On the other hand, there may be reason to fear that in contentious proceedings, lawyers will not treat claims assessors as equals and the party represented by the claims assessor will, as a result, find that his case is prejudiced. The case for expanding the monopoly to include claims assessors is probably not an overwhelming one nor does their exclusion provoke much interest. (There was virtually no evidence submitted on this subject to the Royal Commission). But the problem of the monopoly over litigation arose in January 1978 in a completely different and much more controversial context. It was reported[86] that the Law Society had brought a successful prosecution against Mr Barry Powell who ran a non-profit making organisation called Assistance in Divorce. It was alleged that he had helped people prepare documents to get undefended divorces and that this infringed the monopoly. (The documents were the petition to the court, the affidavit on the circumstances entitling the petitioner to divorce and an explanation of arrangements for maintenance and the children.) The evidence showed that the organisation had several branches. It had answered some 3,000 inquiries and had seen some 750 couples through their divorce cases. Mr Powell's view was that parties could be helped to remain friends even through a divorce. His organisation had acted for both parties in many of their cases. They charged each side £25 and helped them to fill out all the forms jointly rather than as adversaries. The court found the charges proved but imposed a fine of only £20 on two counts. The chairman of the bench said to Mr Powell – 'We have a certain amount of sympathy with the excellent work you have been doing'.

The principles at stake here are completely different from those relevant in true contentious proceedings. The procedure for undefended divorces has now been simplified to such an extent that a divorce can be obtained without a hearing and even without any personal attendance. Every effort is being made to promote do-it-yourself divorce and legal aid for divorce hearings has been terminated. (See further on these developments pp. 326–27 below). It is therefore entirely appropriate that parties to divorce proceedings should have the help of lay organisations able to assist them with the filling-in of the forms. The prosecution of such agencies by the Law Society seems wholly contrary to the public interest. If the monopoly is to continue generally for litigation there needs to be an exception created for assistance rendered in divorce proceedings to parties who are seeking divorce without a court hearing.

Restrictions on the way in which work can be done or services provided: unfair competition

As has already been seen, in the eyes of the profession, self-aggrandisement is regarded as basically sinful. The ramifications of this attitude have already been considered in relation to advertising (pp. 46–54 above) when it was argued that it was basically ill-suited to the needs of the public. But unfair competition has been defined also to embrace other forms of objectionable conduct. Thus, a solicitor may not, without a waiver from the Practice Rules, take paying instructions from a client whom he has first advised at a free legal advice centre. The rule is based on the fear that the solicitor is 'in a position of advantage to obtain the retainer'.[87] The client may wish that solicitor to act for him, rather than have to go to another solicitor and start all over again, but without a waiver the solicitor may not accept the instructions. Waivers for properly organised schemes, especially in citizens' advice bureaux, are now forthcoming without much difficulty (see p. 55), but the rule remains a hindrance to solicitors who, for one or another reason, do not have waivers. Another example is that a solicitor in salaried employment in commerce or industry is only allowed to act in a conveyancing transaction for a fellow employee if the employer has informed the employee that he is entitled to use a solicitor in private practice on equally advantageous terms. This makes it impossible for employers to offer employees favourable conditions for using solicitors' services as a 'perk'. The benefit to the private profession is clear; that to the client is not.

The same principle prevents a vendor from offering would-be purchasers free or cheaper conveyances if they use the services of a named solicitor. Barristers employed on salaries (other than those who work in law centres) have no right of audience – again to the advantage of those in private practice and to the disadvantage of their employers. A solicitor may not normally share office space, let alone form a partnership, with a member of another profession,[88] even though a multifaceted service provided by, say, a solicitor, an accountant and a doctor or a surveyor could clearly be beneficial to clients. English lawyers have in the past even been forbidden to make such arrangements with foreign lawyers. This prohibition is now beginning to break down. Both barristers and solicitors can form partnerships or other fee-sharing arrangements with lawyers abroad, and a solicitor may even enter a fee-sharing arrangement, short of partnership, with a foreign lawyer in this country. But although the foreign lawyer can now be given a seat in a solicitor's English office, he may not put up a separate name-plate, nor may his name be shown on the solicitor's name-plate.[89]

All these restrictions seem wrong. The concept of 'unfair competition' ought to be abandoned as a basis for the control of private practitioners. In the field of advertising, solicitation of business and touting it is unnecessary. It is enough there to rely on the restrictions suggested by the Monopolies Commission proscribing advertising that is inaccurate, misleading or likely to bring the profession into disrepute. In the field of price competition again it ought to be wholly excluded. There is nothing 'unfair' in reducing prices to the consumer. Participation by private practitioners in free legal advice centres, and in rotas of duty solicitors in magistrates' courts or in citizens' advice bureaux or similar agencies is now regulated through the waiver system. The latest statement of the conditions for the grant of waivers makes it clear that 'unfair competition' is relevant only in the case of law centres and other salaried free legal services. According to the Guide to Professional Conduct, a solicitor in private practice who first saw a client in a free legal advice centre could only continue to act for the client on a paying basis if the client gave his written assurance that he wanted the solicitor to deal with the matter. The only exception was in a case where the waiver was for a scheme operated by a local law society in a CAB or similar agency. But in the new code for waivers published in August 1977 the requirement of a written assurance from the client has been dropped.[90] (Unfair competition does, however, remain, rightly it is suggested,[91] as the test of the grant of a waiver for law centres or other salaried free legal services.) Unfair competition is inappropriate as the basis of rules regulating partnership or other working arrangements between private practitioners and members of other professions. It is not 'unfair' for an English and an American lawyer to offer their clients the benefit of a joint service, nor should it be treated as unfair for lawyers to take part in group practices provided by members of various different professions. Mixed practices no doubt require rules prescribing the code of conduct applicable to their members, but the concept of unfair competition has no legitimate place in the exercise of such controls.

In 1975, the Institute of Chartered Accountants amended its rules to allow its members to enter into partnerships with members of other professions subject to the consent of the Institute and to such conditions as it might impose. Several inquiries were received regarding the possibility of such arrangements between accountants and solicitors but inquirers were told that this was not possible because of the rules applicable to solicitors. The rule as regards solicitors should be relaxed to the same extent as that which applies to chartered accountants.[92]

7 Paying for Legal Services

The problem of paying for legal services raises three main kinds of question. First, are there adequate controls on the level of fees; second, are there enough ways to assist those who have difficulty in paying to get the legal services they need; and third, does the legal profession receive 'adequate' remuneration?

Controls on fees

The English legal profession, often the butt of gibes about its extortionate fees, has for a very long time been subject to a variety of formal controls over its charges. The two main forms of such control are external review or fixing of fees in individual cases and external fixing of fees for whole categories of work.

External review or fixing of fees on a case-by-case basis

Remuneration certificates from the Law Society From earliest days, solicitors' fees were charged on an item basis, and the items had to be stated in the bill. The earliest statute requiring solicitors to render itemised bills was passed in 1605. In 1883 scale charges were introduced for conveyancing, but until 1953 all other non-contentious (non-litigation) work and all contentious work continued on the item basis of charging. Item charges took no account of the difficulty of the matter. In 1953, the Solicitors' Remuneration Order introduced a new system of charging for non-contentious work other than conveyancing. It authorised such charges as may be 'fair and reasonable having regard to all the circumstances of the case', and in particular to seven factors – the complexity of the matter, the skill involved, the number and importance of the documents, the circumstances in which the work is done, the

time spent, the value of the money or property at stake, and
the importance of the matter to the client. The 1953 Order also
introduced the concept of the remuneration certificate. Since
scale charges for conveyancing were abolished in 1972[1] the
'fair and reasonable' test and the remuneration certificate procedure apply to all non-contentious work.

Under this procedure, in any piece of non-contentious work
the Law Society will give a certificate as to whether the charges
are reasonable. A client who is dissatisfied with the bill can ask
his solicitors to obtain such a certificate. The solicitor fills in an
application form and sends it with the file to the Law Society.
The client is asked for his comments and the file is then
considered by Council members of the Law Society or, in
some cases, practising solicitors on a panel maintained for the
purpose by the Law Society. Most files are seen by one solicitor but some are seen by two. The bill can be upheld or
reduced – but not increased. There is no charge to the client.
The certificate is binding on both parties unless challenged by
either through a court taxation of costs. The procedure is,
however, not available unless it is invoked within one month
of the payment of the bill or of the date on which the client was
told of his right to seek such a certificate. There were 1,021
certificates issued in 1974, 1,280 in 1975 and 2,010 in 1976. In
1,024 cases (24 per cent) the certificate ordered a reduction in
the charges.[2] Not unfairly the Law Society commented to the
Royal Commission that the figures showed that 'only a
minute proportion of non-contentious bills are referred for
remuneration certificates'.[3] (It thought that at least two million bills were delivered in conveyancing matters alone.) No
empirical study of this process has ever been made, nor is it
known to what extent clients are aware of the procedure.
There is no rule requiring solicitors to inform their clients of its
existence unless the solicitor wishes to sue to recover his
fees, in which case he must.[4]

Taxation by the court or other paying authority There are three
main types of circumstance where a bill is taxed by the court.
One, which has existed since 1729, is where a paying client
wants his own solicitor's bill to be reviewed. This applies to
any kind of matter, civil or criminal, contentious or non-
contentious. It can be invoked even if the client has signed an

actual agreement in advance as to the fees he will pay and even though he has actually paid.[5] The client issues a summons for which he must pay a court fee. If the taxation results in a reduction of the bill by one-fifth or more, the costs of the taxation are normally ordered to be paid by the solicitor; if not, the client must normally pay the costs. These include a court fee of 5 per cent of the taxed bill. Such taxations are very rare. In 1975, for instance, of a total of 7,740 taxations in the Queen's Bench and Chancery Divisions of the High Court, only 107 were of Solicitors' own clients bills. In 1976 it was 150.[6] There is no general duty on the part of solicitors to inform their clients of the possibility of such taxation unless they propose actually to sue for their fees. No action for the recovery of fees can be brought unless the client has been so informed. The Law Society's evidence to the Royal Commission again suggested that, in view of the probability that the total number of bills delivered annually by solicitors 'must be in excess of five million' the number of Solicitors Act taxations represented 'an infinitesimal proportion of the total'.[7]

A much more usual form of taxation is that ordered by the court. This happens under the English Indemnity Rule by which, unless the parties agree on costs, the loser in civil litigation is normally ordered to pay the taxed costs of the winner (in addition to his own full costs). The taxation is normally on a 'party and party' basis under which the loser has to pay all costs that were 'necessary or proper for the attainment of justice'. Less frequently it is on the more generous 'common fund' basis – which permits all costs 'reasonably incurred'. Even more infrequently it is on a 'solicitor and own client' basis, under which all costs are allowed 'except so far as they are of an unreasonable amount or have been unreasonably incurred'. In county court cases the level of fees is determined by the scale on which they are to be assessed. (Lower Scale applies to sums up to £50; Scale 2 to amounts of £50–£200; Scale 3 to £200–£500; and Scale 4 to over £500.) On a taxation of a solicitor and own client bill in a county court case the taxing officer may not allow more than would be allowed on a party and party taxation.[8] But this does not prevent a solicitor charging his client more if there is no taxation of the solicitor and own client bill. Taxations are not conducted by the judge who has heard the case. The file (together with the solicitor's bill and counsel's fee notes) is lodged with the court and the taxation is done by court officials – subject to a right of appeal ultimately to a judge. The principles and practice of such taxations are described in practitioners' works[9] and emerge from reported rulings in the rare appeals that reach the judges.

Compulsory taxation also occurs in certain classes of case for the solicitor and own client bill. Where the client is a minor or is under a mental disability, the court normally orders that there be a compulsory taxation. The same occurs when the solicitor acts for a trustee in bankruptcy or for liquidators in a compulsory liquidation. The taxation in such instances is normally on the common fund basis.

In a taxation between parties the effect of the process is that any reduction in charges results in a redistribution of the burden of costs. Thus, where the loser submits for taxation his opponent's bill of, say, £1,000 which is then reduced by £100,[10] the loser has to pay £900 of the opponent's bill, plus his own costs. The winner has to pay his own solicitors the £100 taxed off. In other words, the lawyers get paid in any event. Taxation simply determines how the burden is shared between the parties. By contrast, on a compulsory taxation the decision affects the amount finally received by the lawyers, who cannot charge more than has been allowed. Curiously, where a barrister's fees are reduced on a compulsory taxation, the solicitor remains technically liable to pay the barrister his full fees. Moreover, it was until recently a breach of etiquette for a barrister to waive any part of his agreed fee.[11] After the Law Society protested against this manifest injustice towards solicitors, the Bar changed its rule and *permitted* (but not required) barristers in this situation to reduce or waive their fees.[12]

A third form of taxation is in legal aid work. The taxing authority and, to some extent, the method of taxation differs according to the nature of the case.[13] For the work done in the higher courts and in the county court, taxation is in the hands of the taxing officials in the courts. For both civil and criminal cases dealt with in the magistrates' courts, and for work done under the Green Form scheme, the taxing authority is the Law Society's Area Committee. The Area Committee also has jurisdiction over High Court cases where the solicitor does not claim more than £200 in costs.

In the crown court the basis of taxation is a Guide laying down minima and maxima, which may, however, be exceeded if the case justifies it.[14] The Guide was produced by the Lord Chancellor's Office for the assistance of taxing officials and it is treated by them as their bible. There are different categories of fees depending principally on the length of the case and the number of pages of depositions (which is supposed to indicate the weight of the case).[15] When the clerk has found the appropriate section of the table of minimum and maximum fees he determines the *actual* fee by considering such less tangible factors as the seniority of counsel, the importance or complexity of the case, any special skill required and the extent of travel and hotel expenses incurred. If a case has been prepared on the basis that there will be a contest and the client pleads guilty at the last moment, the fee should reflect the extent of the actual preparation. The fees of QCs and of senior Treasury Counsel are stated to be 'at large' and not subject therefore to the table in the Guide.

There is also a power in the judges in crown courts to influence the levels of remuneration paid to legal aid lawyers. A Practice Direction in February 1977 stated that where the court thought that legal aid work had been unreasonably done (e.g. with a lack of 'reasonable competence and expedition') it could indicate this view which could (but need not) be taken into account by the taxing officials. Before making such observations, however, the judge ought to permit the solicitors and barristers to make representations to him in chambers. The lawyers would have a further opportunity to make representations to the taxing officials.[16]

In magistrates' court work the Law Society's Area Committee works primarily on the basis of an hourly rate (which differs somewhat from one part of the country to another). But consideration is also given to waiting time, to the amount of time that *should* have been spent and to the weight, complexity and importance of the case.[17] In civil legal aid work taxation is on the common fund basis, but in the High Court and above there is the statutory deduction of 10 per cent.

Fixed fees for classes of work

A much cruder approach to controls on fees is simply to fix the fees without regard to the differences between cases. This approach has been adopted in two different ways in the English system. One is the *ad valorem* scale fee; the other is the fixed fee for small matters.

Scale fees have been normal particularly in the field of property transactions. From 1883 to 1972, when scales were abolished, conveyancing was subject to scale fees that regulated the appropriate rate of remuneration by a sliding scale depending on the monetary value of the property involved. Separate scales for registered and unregistered land were laid down by a committee consisting of judges, solicitors, in the case of registered land the Chief Land Registrar, and, because he represented government by far the most important, the Lord Chancellor. A solicitor was permitted to agree in writing with his client for a fee in excess of the scale, but the Law Society ruled that it was normally unethical to undercut the scales.[18] In practice, the scale applied to virtually all cases.

Extra-statutory scale fees apply in certain categories of non-contentious business.[19] They have no binding force on the parties but they are in practice usually followed, though they are subject both to the remuneration certificate procedure and to a taxation under the Solicitors Act 1974. Such scales apply, for instance, in the field of mortgage work, to the range of fees agreed between the Law Society and the Building Societies Association ('the building society scale'), or to charges agreed between the Law Society and the Local Authorities Associations in cases of compulsory acquisition of unregistered land ('the local authority scale'). Fixed fees apply to hundreds of items in litigation such as the cost of making a telephone call, writing a letter, photocopying a document, serving a writ, etc. A standard fee is laid down primarily as a matter of convenience, in order to avoid the waste of time and money that would otherwise be involved in assessing an appropriate fee for large numbers of small or standard steps in liigation. A fixed fee normally precludes variation for exceptional cases.

Evaluation of methods of controlling fees

The right of a solicitor's client to test whether the bill was reasonable by asking the professional association for a remuneration certificate or by asking the court to tax the bill is a valuable right which ought to be available to clients of barristers too. If these mechanisms can work for the one branch they can work equally for the other. The view that the Bar is somehow 'different' is a form of special pleading.[20] Both procedures recognise that professional men do sometimes charge excessive fees and that it is right to give the client a remedy – even when he has previously agreed to the fee. Given the relationship between a professional man and his client, this seems an honourable and correct attitude.

But although both procedures should be extended to fees charged by barristers it would be wrong to believe that any system which relies on client initiative is likely to make much impact on the problem of controlling fees. In many cases the client will be ignorant of his right to ask for a remuneration certificate or to have a court taxation. It may be that solicitors should be required to state in small print at the bottom of the account the ways in which it can be challenged. Short of this it is inevitable that many will not realise that there is machinery available for such complaints. In particular, they will not appreciate that the Law Society offers a review process which is entirely free of charge. Even if the obstacle of the client's ignorance about the complaints machinery were met, there would still be the problem of ignorance of whether he has been charged an excessive fee. He may think the fee is high, but how is he to know that it is too high? (The ABA–ABF study found that it was the older, the least educated and the low-income respondents who were most likely to say that lawyers' fees were fair.[21]) The greatest difficulty of all, however, is that even if the client thought the fee *was* too high he would usually be reluctant to complain. To query a bill (especially that of a professional person) is likely to be seen by clients as unsporting, squalid and embarrassing. It is felt to reflect badly on the client himself, even possibly raising doubts as to his ability to pay.

The National Association of Citizens' Advice Bureaux proposed to the Royal Commission that, wherever possible, solicitors should give clients estimates of the likely costs. Where this was not feasible, clients should at the outset be given a leaflet describing the basis of charging. They should also be informed of their right to fix price ceilings beyond which the lawyer could not act without further express authority. (The legal aid authorities sometimes use this technique.) But although these suggestions deserve support they are unlikely to be of very great value. There will be too many instances where the estimate proves to be unrealistically low, or hedged about with so many qualifications as to be meaningless, or where the solicitor says that it is impossible to give any estimate at all. Leaflets describing the method of fixing fees are of little use unless the client knows how the system is likely to work out in his case – will he be charged on the basis of the time taken, the value of the amount in issue, the importance of the matter to him, the speed with which it must be completed, or the difficulty of the work? If, as would be normal, more than one of these factors is likely to be taken into account, what will be their respective significance? Since the solicitor is not likely to be able to give any concrete indication until the work is completed, the value of prior discussions of estimates or fee systems is somewhat limited. Fixing price ceilings may be useful as a means of permitting some minimum control by the client – but its main function is to keep the client informed rather than to limit fees.

The only real way of controlling fees is to regulate them from without, either on a case-by-case basis through taxation or some equivalent, or by prescribing fixed fees, or at least maxima. The strength of taxation is that it enables a reviewing authority (whether court official, Legal Aid Area Committee or other person) to exercise judgement in the light of the circumstances of a particular case. The process attempts to assign the individual case its correct position in the range of fees. Its weakness is that the process is in one sense bound to fail, there being no way of achieving uniformity of decisions as to where on the range of fees a case belongs. There would be some lack of uniformity even if all taxing officials were superbly trained for the task. Since this cannot reasonably be expected, it will be even greater. Lack of uniformity in assessment of fees is in fact a constant source of complaint of lawyers. Such a process also involves an immense cost in terms of time, money and effort expended in the offices of lawyers and of taxing officials. (Often the costs are increased through the employment by solicitors of specialised costs draftsmen who are masters of the art of preparing bills in litigation matters.) It is very unlikely that all these costs are justified by the results. In a survey of fees in crown courts I found that two courts assigned the same fee to all prosecution cases irrespective of the work involved. The Metropolitan Police receives a global amount for all its prosecution work for the entire year.[22] This broader brush approach could surely be applied usefully to much of the straightforward work.

A vast amount of taxation work might be avoided if, for instance, the authorities stated that a fixed fee would be paid for that class of work unless the lawyer could justify a higher fee by showing that the case was in some way unusual. This technique could be applied not only to most classes of work paid out of public funds but also to party and party taxations of privately financed work. It would, in fact, be applicable to any class of case where the work is fairly standard and where there is enough of it for the averaging of fees to give a reasonably fair result overall. Criminal work, debt collecting, divorce and personal injury cases might all be candidates. The fixed fees would have to differentiate between cases in the higher and the lower courts, between guilty pleas and not guilty pleas, and between cases depending on their length. Certainly the fixed fee would have to be reviewed regularly since, as it fell behind inflation, more and more practitioners would find it worth their while to claim a higher amount. It would also be desirable to specify the kind of work not included in the fixed fee for which an additional claim would have to be made. But subject to such detailed problems of establishing fixed fees on a sensible and fair basis, it may be possible to arrive at fixed fees for a considerable proportion of the work done in the courts. Provided that the lawyers retain the right to ask for a higher fee in appropriate cases, this might, on balance, be a useful reform.

How far should the same approach apply to non-contentious work, particularly conveyancing? Should scale fees be re-imposed? The problem of lack of uniformity of fees charged by different firms of private practitioners for similar work is less serious than it is when the fees are all paid by the same public purse. Nor is the time and effort argument very strong since most bills in conveyancing matters are relatively brief by comparison with the immensely prolix bills that have to be prepared for court work. But there are other arguments. The Prices and Incomes Board advanced two reasons in 1968 for wishing to see scale fees for conveyancing maintained. One was that it gave the client a measure of certainty. There was *some* force in this point though 'no more than is claimed for other forms of price maintenance'.[23] Its chief reason was that conveyancing was a monopoly and it was right that 'there should be some outside supervision over the charge'.[24] (This reasoning would still apply even if (as suggested above, p. 191) the monopoly were extended to include also licensed conveyancers.) In 1971 the PIB added that it was sceptical whether, if scales were abolished, price competition would in practice develop between solicitors. Even if it were permitted by the Law Society most solicitors would probably tend still to use the old scales out of habit and convenience and because most firms lacked the costing system to do otherwise. Price competition would involve 'far-reaching changes in the out-look of the profession and in the relationship between solicitor and client'.[25] Another reason for favouring scale fees is the rough justice in relating the size of the fee to the size of the property involved. Those who can afford to buy a larger house can usually afford to pay a higher legal fee.

The chief arguments for abolishing fixed scale fees are that it permits the fee to be related to the amount of work involved and may encourage price competition. On both, however, there is reason to doubt whether the argument reflects what is likely to happen. If the Prices and Incomes Board was right in believing that solicitors would tend to follow the old scales, in practice the value of the property rather than the work involved would continue to be the dominant element in the fee. (An extreme instance of this was the case in 1975 in which the court allowed a fee of £5,500 to solicitors who acted on a compulsory purchase of building land worth £2¼ million involving thirty hours of work and no unusual difficulties. The court said the weightiest element in the fee was the amount involved and applied a regressive scale.[26]) On the second argument, Lord Hailsham, the then Lord Chancellor, said he was abolishing scales in the hope that this would bring charges down,[27] but although in theory this might have occur-red, it does not appear to have done so yet. A survey by the Consumers' Association showed that, after abolition of scale fees, charges for unregistered conveyances had remained much the same as before but that those for registered properties had considerably increased.[28] The Law Society had suggested to the PIB that a relationship of 75:100 should exist between scales for registered and unregistered conveyances – which would have meant substantial increases in the scales for registered properties. The PIB explicitly stated that it 'saw no justification for this proposal which would lead to further major distortions in the relationship between costs and charges in conveyancing'.[29] The Consumers' Association survey showed, however, that when scales were abolished, the profession proceeded, in effect, to implement the Law Society's suggestion.

Whether fixed fees are higher or lower than fees in a free market obviously depends on the level at which they are fixed and the amount of competition generated when they are lifted. There is no reason why fixed fees cannot be combined with competition. The Prices and Incomes Board proposed that solicitors should be allowed to undercut scale fees. ('The standard externally fixed charge covers the normal case. Evidently there will on occasion be a need to exceed it. Equally obviously there will be cases where the standard charge is too high. Solicitors should then have freedom to ask for less from their clients and there should be no bar to a solicitor doing so.'[30]) The supervision required by a virtual monopoly should also be accompanied by competition.[31] The Monopolies Commission in November 1977 adopted the same view in relation to architects' scale fees.[32]

The balance of these arguments seems to favour scale fees, subject to the right to undercut – and to advertise the fact – without which the reform loses much of its value. But the scale fee must be fixed at a fair level. The same problem arises in the fixing of fees or of maxima in contentious matters or indeed in any class of work whether across-the-board or in individual taxations. When the statutory committee fixes the *ad valorem* scale fee for conveyancing, or the Lord Chancellor's Office produces a Guide to Taxation in the Crown Court or the taxing master allows a certain amount for the solicitors' 'care and conduct' of a personal injury claim, in each case there are at present no data to provide a rational basis for the figures that are allowed. The Royal Commission asked the Law Society, 'What detailed costings are normally available to those responsible for fixing scales or otherwise for regulating charges?' There was a one-sentence reply: 'So far as the Law Society is aware, no detailed costings are normally available to those responsible for fixing scales or otherwise for regulating charges, other than the evidence submitted to the Prices and Incomes Board some years ago.'[33] This was confirmed by Lord Gardiner when Lord Chancellor: 'The Statutory Committees did not seek to apply national economic policy and had no idea how lawyers' earnings are related to other peoples'; or to what extent there was a real case for an increase or not.'[34]

In order for these processes to become rational, there must be accurate, up-to-date information as to the pattern of work and the level of overheads incurred in doing that work. The fixing of appropriate fees for barristers in crown court work, for instance, depends on knowing the way in which 'average' barristers who do criminal work earn their living on a monthly or even annual basis. How much of their work consists of guilty pleas, not guilty pleas and not guilty pleas which become guilty pleas at the last moment? How much consists of Class III or Class IV cases as opposed to Class I or Class II cases? Fees (whether fixed or normal minima and maxima) ought to be based on some assessment of what the average barrister with the average case-load should be earning on a daily basis in the light of an average projection of annual earnings assessed on that basis.[35] Every barrister would not receive the average fee, but unless there is some information about averages, the process of fixing fees is necessarily a 'hit or miss' affair.

The Prices and Incomes Board analysed the relevant figures for solicitors. It concluded that the conveyancing scale fees should be revised upwards at the bottom and otherwise downward.[36] It found that conveyancing accounted for 55.6 per cent of solicitors' income but only 40.8 per cent of expenses, whereas in the field of contentious business a proportion of 28.8 per cent of total expense was incurred to earn 18.4 per cent of total income.[37] At most levels conveyancing, it found, was overly profitable and the fact that 'even with a charge determined from the outside, conveyancing should be so profitable' reinforced the view that the charge should be subject to supervision.[38] The Board rejected the argument that excess profits in one field were legitimate as a means of subsiding other less profitable work and it doubted whether this in fact happened to any very great extent.[39] County court work, it found, was unremunerative and accordingly fees in this field, it thought, should be increased by about 55 per cent. The increase should be such as 'to make it profitable for the specialist, continue to make it unprofitable for the non-specialist, and marginally profitable for the intermediate firm'.[40]

These principles should probably apply to any category of work where fees are fixed externally. In the legal aid field, for instance, it is vital that firms that do a fair amount of such work should be able to make some profit and that those who specialise in it should be able to make a good profit. There is evidence that the conscientious firm anxious to make a genuine contribution to providing quality legal services to the poor has in the past found it difficult to make a reasonable profit from legal aid work. One such London firm stated in 1976 that legal aid work accounted for 40 per cent of its time but only 25 per cent of the fees billed. Most of the privately financed work of the firm was relatively poorly paid. On a turnover of £102,000 the net profit in the year to 1976 to be shared between three partners was only £16,000. This gave a level of profit that was clearly lower than anything normal in private practice.[41] The study of legal services in Birmingham found that contentious legal-aid work could be highly profitable, provided there was a large turnover of cases and firms were 'geared up' by having sufficient junior staff and being specialised intensively through routinised procedures. But there was a distinct danger that such working methods might have costs in terms of lower-quality work.[42] The rates of remuneration paid by the state for this work should clearly not be fixed so low that the only way for a good firm to make a profit is to do the work in a hasty or superficial manner.

Recommendations for changes in fee structures of lawyers should always be based on detailed analysis of the relevant facts and figures including, in particular, the relation over a period of years of earnings, overheads and profits. The PIB proposed that it should itself be given a standing reference over solicitors' remuneration for this purpose in order to make possible the collection of statistics and information on a continuing basis. The Government in fact made such a reference. But the Prices and Incomes Board was abolished in 1971. The PIB had suggested that if it itself were not given the job, the

Government should undertake it. Statistics about professional earnings generally, it said, should be made available by the Government, either by the publication of existing material (as the Pilkington Royal Commission on Doctors' and Dentists' Remuneration had recommended in 1959) or by the collection on a sample basis of the kind of statistics included in its report.[43] Whether in fact the task is given to some agency specialising in the affairs of lawyers, or to a review body dealing with incomes of many groups, and whether the agency is part of or separate from government, there can be no doubt that the job *must* be given to someone.

Finance for those who lack the means to pay for legal services

A person's ability to pay the costs of legal services depends not only on the relation between the amount he is charged and his means but also on the relation between the cost and the antici-pated benefit to him. One may be able to afford £100 for a divorce but not for a consumer claim arising out of a defective washing machine. One may be willing to venture £250 in bringing an action for £2,000 damages but be unwilling to spend a quarter of that amount in trying to get bail whilst on remand on criminal charges. Absolute cost figures are there-fore only part of the story. Nevertheless they do provide some basis for assessing to what extent ordinary people will be able to afford legal services.

The costs of most civil litigation are prohibitively high. In 1973–4 the average costs in a random sample of High Court personal injury cases was over £1,000 in contested cases and almost £500 where the case settled.[44] Moreover, in civil liti-gation in England one always needs to calculate the risk of losing either at first instance, or, worse, in an appeal court, and then having to pay the costs of both sides at more than one level. The cost of an undefended divorce according to a Con-sumers' Association survey in 1977 was around £100. The same survey showed that for drawing up a straightforward will solicitors charged fees of only between £3 and £20 and for helping with a claim for faulty goods and services about half the clients were charged less than £25.[45] But there are always cases where the fees are much higher than the average. One person had to pay over £400 in a consumer claim and there were several divorce cases which cost over £400.[46] How is the potential litigant to know whether his case will turn out to be typical or unusual? It has already been seen (pp. 32–6 above) that one major form of help available to those of insufficient means is the legal aid scheme, which provides assistance (subject to a means test and a merits test) in both civil and criminal cases in any court and in any legal matter requiring advice or assistance short of litigation. For those whose means entitle them to legal aid on a nil or a small contribution the legal aid scheme offers a very desirable benefit. In work done under the Green Form scheme the contribution runs on a steep sliding scale. From November 1977 the range was from £3 for those whose take-home pay was between £23 and £26 to £36 for those whose take-home pay was between £46 and £48. In civil proceedings the contribution from income at the top rate could be more than £500 plus the whole of the difference between the free limit for capital (in November 1977, £340) and the assessed value of savings, up to a maximum of £1,600. The level of contribution may therefore be too high to make legal aid worth having.[47] Moreover, the means test limits for legal aid and for the Green Form scheme are very low. In fact the limit for the Green Form is lower than that for Supplementary Benefit! A further financial disincentive to legal aid is the 'statutory charge'. This is the requirement that any costs or damages recovered from the other side must first be paid into the fund which recoups itself in full for all costs incurred before paying out the balance to the assisted person.[48]

Legal aid in England today provides very substantial legal services. In 1976 there were 269,883 legal aid orders for proceedings in magistrates' courts and 91,184 for proceedings in crown courts, more than 200,000 legal aid certificates issued for civil proceedings and about 300,000 payments to lawyers in respect of advice and assistance under the Green Form scheme. Nevertheless, it remains true that the great bulk of the population is not eligible for legal aid. It may be, as the Law Society argued in February 1978,[48a] that it would cost relatively little to raise the means test limits and lower the contribution rate so as to bring many more people into the scheme. But it may still be hard to achieve it. (In Sweden, by contrast, virtually the whole population is within the means test limits.[49]) The chief question, therefore, is what other methods can be found to assist those who lack the means. Law centres are not the answer since these will tend to be established mainly in the very poor neighbourhoods where the majority of the local population would already qualify for legal aid. Moreover, insofar as they attract clients who are, or appear to be, outside the means test limits, law centres are likely in the future, as in the past, to operate an informal means test and send them to private practitioners. Those who belong to trade unions may receive assistance from them (see further, p. 305 below). Trade union help with litigation is, in one sense, an even better benefit than legal aid, since under legal aid the client may have to make some payment towards the other side's costs if he loses, whereas the trade union member will normally have the whole of such an order for costs met by the union that has supported his litigation. But for the most part such help is confined to matters arising out of the worker's employment and especially to accidents. Moreover, smaller unions do not have any extensive legal services assistance and about half the working population are not in unions anyway.

Proposed abolition of the Indemnity Rule

One suggestion that has been canvassed is to abolish the indemnity rule of costs so as to encourage the less affluent to undertake or to continue litigation who might otherwise shrink from doing so because of the effect of the 'double or quits' rule. It is bad enough to have to pay your own costs but it is worse to pay those of both sides if you lose. The inhibiting effect of the rule is clearly greatest for those with the least financial margin. If the rule were abolished, the argument runs, more well-founded actions would be brought. This approach has in fact been tried through the virtual abolition of the indemnity rule in small claims cases where the amount at stake is under £100. In such cases the winner cannot normally any longer look to the other side for payment of any of his costs other than a small nominal charge (in 1977, £3) for issue of the proceedings.[50] The number of small claims brought by individuals does appear to be rising, possibly because of the no-costs rule. But even if this were so, it would not follow that it would be desirable to abolish the indemnity rule generally.

In small cases the plaintiff may indeed be influenced by the difference if he loses between having to pay only his own lawyers (if he has any) and having to pay both his and his opponent's lawyers. But in more substantial cases this factor is not likely to make the difference between bringing or not bringing the proceedings. If the potential cost of losing a High Court case is in the region of £1,000 for one's own lawyers, that is sufficient disincentive for most people to discourage them from proceeding unless the prospects of success seem very clear. The fact that under the indemnity principle it might be £2,000 is then academic. In other words, abolition of the indemnity rule would not necessarily have any effect in promoting justified litigation which would not otherwise see the light of day. Possibly, it might even have the opposite effect. For the indemnity rule does at least have the great advantage that most of the winner's costs are paid by the loser. If the rule were abolished, there might be many cases in which the plaintiff would decide not to sue simply because a substantial part of his possible damages would be swallowed up in lawyers' fees. The game might then not seem worth the candle. On balance, except in very small cases, the less affluent probably derive more benefit from the indemnity rule than they would from its abolition.

One modification of the indemnity rule would, however, be beneficial as a means of relieving parties to litigation of an unfair burden of costs. This is where it takes two or even more attempts to get a 'correct' decision on fact or law. Where the decision at first instance is subsequently changed on appeal the ultimate losing party has to pay the costs of the whole process – including the first stage where he won. In 1969 Justice proposed that the ultimate loser ought only to have to pay for the costs at the first level. It was the fault of the system, not of the litigant, that the first court took a view of the law or the facts that was ultimately shown to be wrong. The litigant ought not to have to bear the costs incurred through the 'error' of the court. Under this proposal the ultimate winner would get his costs from the loser in the ordinary way but the loser would be able to claim from a Suitors' Fund the amount of the costs incurred attributable to the appeal. (The proposal also covered costs thrown away through no fault of anyone such as the illness or death of a judge.) The Suitors' Fund would be

created from a small extra amount added to the cost of issuing
a writ.[51]

Contingent fees

What, however, of contingent fees, an arrangement under
which the client typically agrees to pay his lawyers a percentage of the damages recovered if he wins but nothing or only
disbursements if he loses? This is the usual method for financing litigation in accident cases in the United States. Its great
virtue from the client's point of view is that he only pays his
lawyers their fees if he is first put in funds by winning the case.
The potential costs of the action should not therefore act as a
deterrent to litigation. The system obviously only applies to
cases involving claims for damages. Contingent fees would
normally give no financial advantage in the English system for
those now eligible for legal aid. A person who can get legal aid
without making any contribution or who pays only a small
contribution is obviously much better off than he could be on a
contingency arrangement. Those subject to a substantial contribution would possibly prefer a contingent fee if the chances
of success were uncertain, though if there were reasonable
chances of success, legal aid would be a better financial prospect than a contingent fee. Contingent arrangements might,
however, look more attractive for those ineligible for legal aid.
Under the present English rules such a person, if he loses, has
to pay his own lawyers in full and the opponents their taxed
party and party costs. If he wins, he pays his own lawyers the
difference between the party and party costs received from the
loser and their full solicitor and own client bill. If, instead, he
had a contingent fee arrangement, his liability to his own
lawyers would be greater if he won (because the solicitor and
own client bill would be higher to take account of the lawyer's
greater risk), but if he lost, he would pay his lawyers nothing.
This could save him a very substantial amount. His liability,
then, would extend only to meeting the winner's party and
party costs. A contingent fee arrangement might, therefore,
enable some to litigate who now decide that the potential costs
of losing are too great.

One common objection to contingent fees is that they permit lawyers to over-reach their clients by charging exorbitant
fees. This is relatively simple to avoid, however, by regulating

the permissible limits. Moreover, the regulated rates can be supplemented by a general rule of etiquette that fees not be excessive and by the normal machinery for taxation at the client's instance. The chief reason for contingent fees being barred in England[52] is that it might lead to unethical conduct by placing a premium on success. This belief is fervently held by the profession but it does not seem inherently probable. A profession whose members rightly pride themselves on their high standards of ethics is unlikely to be transformed by the possibility that in some cases the fee would be affected by the outcome. It would show singular lack of confidence in the probity of English lawyers to think otherwise. After all barristers are now allowed to make contingent fee arrangements in regard to their overseas work (see p. 167 above). In *Wallersteiner v Moir (No. 2)*[53] Lord Justice Buckley and Lord Justice Scarman both said they were opposed to contingent fees but Lord Denning, whilst accepting the general rule, thought an exception might be made for minority shareholders' actions. The Law Society have recommended that another be made for debt collection.[54]

As an alternative to contingent fees, Justice proposed in 1966 that there be a non-profit-making organisation to underwrite the costs of litigation for those who did not qualify for legal aid. The organisation (the 'Contingency Legal Aid Office') would accept cases that had a reasonable chance of success. The lawyers would then conduct the case in the ordinary way. If the plaintiff won, or the claim was settled, he would recover his costs from the defendant but a certain fixed proportion would be paid into the fund. If he lost, the fund would pay both his costs and those of his opponent.[55] The Bar, in its evidence to the Royal Commission, elaborated a very similar scheme, which they called a Suitor's Fund. The Bar thought, however, that the proposed scheme should be open to all except those who received legal aid subject to a nil contribution. Otherwise the litigant who had to pay a contribution on legal aid would be worse off than the richer litigant who could make use of the new scheme. Under the Bar's proposal the scheme would be run by the Law Society and the ordinary Legal Aid Area and Local Committees, thus avoiding the need for any separate administrative structure. A certificate would be issued on the same grounds as a legal aid certificate at present.[56] Justice estimated that the deduction from damages needed to finance the fund would be of the order of 20 per cent. The Bar considered that 15 per cent in county court work and 7½ per cent in High Court cases might be enough.

Like contingent fees, such a scheme would only help plaintiffs and would only apply to damages claims. From the plaintiff's point of view, the deduction of a proportion of any damages recovered would be less painful than the extra fees paid under the contingency arrangement, because the deduction should normally be considerably lower. The scheme should cost plaintiffs less. Also, since the lawyers would be paid in any event it would not create the ethical problems associated by many with the contingent fees. Presumably the scheme would have to be limited to individual plaintiffs – otherwise deductions, say, from a personal injury claim could swell the fund to the benefit of business concerns engaged in commercial litigation. But one major difficulty is that the plaintiff in a damages action usually succeeds and it is doubtful whether enough plaintiffs would participate in such a scheme to make it financially viable. Why should a plaintiff who believes he is likely to recover take part in a scheme that will cost him a part of his damages? The scheme would be mainly attractive to plaintiffs whose hopes of succeeding were not very good, but they would be ineligible since they would not succeed in getting a certificate.

The financial success of the idea would obviously depend on the participation of large numbers of successful plaintiffs. The Bar has proposed that the state should underwrite the scheme but it would presumably only be set up and continued if it succeeded in being more or less self-financing. If it worked, it would justify itself; if not, it would be wound up. In spite of the problems this idea therefore merits careful exploration. It would, of course, represent a different philosophy from that of legal aid which is based on the concept of a state subvention for the costs of those eligible that are not met by the litigant and his opponent. Here the underlying principle would be one of insurance. The litigant would agree to make a contribution to the fund, if successful, in return for the knowledge that, if unsuccessful, he would be relieved of the burden of costs. If enough litigants agreed to make it work this approach has advantages over the legal aid scheme. First the cost would be shared amongst litigants generally rather than being thrown on the state. Second, legal aid in England is in practice available only to a relatively small proportion of the population. Even if the means test limits were adjusted to bring in more of the population and even if the rate of contribution at the top end were lowered, the legal aid scheme would remain unattractive to the middle classes (as well as costly to the state). Many would still be outside the means test limits and those who were within the limits would find the contribution prohibitive, save in litigation involving very large claims. A fixed deduction from damages of something between 10 and 20 per cent in the event of success might be a way of making such actions accessible to the ordinary litigant.

Insurance and pre-payment for legal services

Another way of making legal services available to the ordinary citizen is through one of a variety of possible systems of insurance. Whereas contingency fees are paid by litigants, the principle of insurance spreads the cost much more broadly – and thereby makes it much less costly to each individual. The individual, for instance, pays a premium to an insurance company which then guarantees that in certain eventualities it will meet a stated range of costs arising out of legal problems. Such insurance is a familiar part of the ordinary motorist's policy which protects him against costs and damages arising out of an accident. A house-owner's policy likewise commonly includes protection against claims, including costs and expenses made against the house-owner in respect of personal injury.

But there are also policies which give protection not so much against narrowly defined kinds of risks or damage to property but against the costs of legal expenses more generally. Thus one English company, Strover & Co. Ltd, offers a Legal Costs and Expenses Policy through Lloyds which provides cover for the pursuit or defence of civil claims resulting from death or injury, physical loss to property, the purchase, hire or hire-purchase of goods or services founded on the defective nature of such goods or services or any contract of employment. It also gives cover against the costs of defending criminal charges and driving offences, excluding 'deliberate and criminal acts or omissions'. The policy covers the assured and his immediate family. He has to pay 10 per cent of all costs but initial advice for determining the viability of a legal action is entirely free. Cover includes costs of the opponent awarded against the assured in a civil action. Business matters are excluded. The same company, however, has a separate policy for employers providing cover against compensation awards made to employees, legal representation and other legal advisory services arising out of claims made by potential, present or former employees, and another giving cover against fees and expenses incurred through prosecutions under the Health and Safety at Work Act. Their competitors, DAS,[57] have an even larger number of policies. The family protection policy is divided into two sections – one for protection arising out of use of a car and the other for general and consumer protection including cover for damage to property, legal action arising out of employment, ownership or leasing of a home, claims against shops, manufacturers, repairers or those who have provided professional and other services. The two kinds of protection can be obtained together or separately. On the DAS policy there is no excess payable by the insured.

A variation on this theme is the membership organisation which provides legal services to those who pay regular dues. Many trade unions provide such services to their members, though usually only for problems arising out of their employment (see p. 305 below). The Automobile Association arranges and pays for the professional services of lawyers to defend its members in magistrates' courts against criminal charges arising out of motoring. The Medical Protection Society and the Medical Defence Union provide lawyers for their doctor members to assist in a variety of situations arising out of their professional work, including actions for negligence or disciplinary problems caused by patients' complaints.

The chief advantage of all such schemes is that they provide a method whereby those who cannot qualify for legal aid may nevertheless have the help of lawyers at a price they can afford. The individual gets the service at far less than its true cost, because the intermediary organisation collects payments from a large number of individuals only a proportion of whom will actually suffer the contemplated loss. ('Infrequent or unpredictable losses or expenses, too large and uncertain for the individual to budget for, can be made bearable if many similarly threatened individuals make small contributions so that the few unfortunates who suffer loss can be compensated.'[58]) A useful by-product of the system is that the group system may be able to obtain legal services at lower than normal costs simply through the bargaining power created by the volume of work it generates.

Where those who manage the scheme rather than the client employ, or at least nominate, the lawyer, the managers have the opportunity to influence not only the cost but also the quality of service. They can monitor the way an individual case is handled and may exercise a more subtle indirect influence through the lawyer's knowledge that badly handled work could result in the loss of a large number of clients to a competitor. They can lay down requirements as regards qualifications and experience for lawyers who participate. If the problems covered by the scheme fall into defined categories or types of work (motor accidents, accidents arising out of work, consumer claims, employment problems etc.) and the managers of the scheme use a list of lawyers, another advantage is that the lawyers will become expert in that particular field. Another benefit of all such schemes is that they help to encourage use of lawyers by lowering psychological as well as economic barriers to seeing a lawyer to solve a legal problem.

On the other hand, there are, of course, problems.[59] One is selection and control of the lawyers. Some schemes permit the client to pick his own lawyers,[60] in others the lawyers are selected by the scheme from a list which it keeps.[61] The profession naturally prefers open-panel schemes which preserve the right of all practitioners to compete for the work.[61a] It also prefers open panels because they make any form of effective control by the (possibly lay) managers of the scheme over the lawyers more difficult than where it operates through an identified list of lawyers. There is also less of a risk of a conflict of interest between the client and the scheme. The firm that constantly acts for members of a trade union, for instance, may find itself in a difficult situation if the member and the union disagree as to how his case should be handled. A firm that was not so dependent on the work from the union might be psychologically freer to represent the individual client according to his best interests. On the other hand, both the

managers of the scheme and the clients may derive genuine
benefits from the closed panel in terms of lower costs, greater
expertise and greater commitment to that class of client.

The Law Society has for many years had rules permitting
solicitors to act for members of associations which are their
clients.[62] These require that the association be one limited to
people concerned in a particular trade, occupation or activity
and that it be formed for the benefit of its members and not
primarily for the purpose of securing assistance with legal
proceedings. In litigation matters the fees must be paid by the
association; in non-litigation work, if the association does not
pay, the client must be told that he is free to consult any
solicitor and he must confirm in writing that he has no other
solicitor. In practice, however, the Law Society appears to
accept that firms that act for unions at least may take work for
members whether or not these rules have been strictly com-
plied with.

Another type of problem is how to control the amount of
work done under the scheme. Who is to decide whether the
case should be supported at all, and if so, to what extent and
with what commitment of staff, time, numbers of lawyers and
appeals? Here again there may be a conflict between the individual and those who manage the fund. In most schemes in
which the individual is not paying the direct cost of the service,
one of the conditions on which help is made available is that
the client foregoes his full control over the case. Those who
pay the bill normally require that for all but trivial expendi-
tures, approval be obtained for the case to be taken on and
continued. In this sense the position is similar to that under
legal aid. As in the legal aid scheme, in the event of a conflict
between the client and the lawyers as to whether the case
should be continued, the paying party, in the final analysis,
will tend to side with the lawyers. This is inevitable. Where the
lawyer and the client are agreed and are in conflict with the
paying intermediary, it is to be hoped that normally they
prevail. But this cannot be guaranteed.

There are other technical and organisational problems,[63]
but the most important difficulty that has so far emerged is
that it seems difficult to persuade the ordinary person (in
England at least) to take out insurance to meet the possibility
of having to incur legal costs. In 1977 in England a family

could obtain up to an aggregate of £10,000 a year worth of cover for legal costs and expenses for a premium of £15 with one company and £10,000 per case with the other company for a premium of £22. Considering the high costs of legal cases this is obviously good value, if one has the occasion to use it. But, so far at least, most individuals seem not to want to use their money in this way – probably because they do not regard the risk of needing a lawyer as sufficiently great to make it worth while. But although experience suggests that individual insurance policies are unlikely to become a major source of new funding for general legal services, there should be much greater scope for developing this concept through group schemes.

In Europe legal costs insurance has been established for decades. In Germany, particularly, it is an extremely flourishing business with twenty-four companies specialising in this form of insurance. In 1976 their total premium income was 1,051m DM of which DAS, the largest company had 45 per cent.[64] In the United States there has been a remarkable growth in pre-paid and group schemes in the past two or three years and it has been estimated that there may now be as many as 5,000 schemes in existence.[65] In Berkeley, for instance, 1,000 members of the Cooperative have joined Consumer's Group Legal Services where for a $25 membership fee they can call on a salaried lawyer for two office consultations per year and can get reduced rates for more complicated work from a panel of fifteen participating lawyers. The 10,000 members of the Laborers International Union in the Washington area have available the full-time services of six lawyers for help with personal problems. They pay nothing for the work done. The plan is financed by weekly deductions from their pay-packets. A scheme for 95,000 employees of the City of New York advertised for 50 lawyers to join its full-time staff. (1,500 applied!) The members contribute $26 a year and get a stated number of hours of legal help per year. The California State Employees' plan uses private firms on retainer but members pay no contribution. Instead their fees are 10–40 per cent lower than normal charges. Most schemes have been developed by unions or employers but some have been established by Bar Associations. In New York County, for instance, the local Bar have set up the Lawyers Legal Services Corporation. Some

250 lawyers have joined and each pays $25. The scheme is open to any resident of Manhattan with an income between $6,000 and $20,000 and assets not exceeding $25,000. The individual pays $100 to join plus additions for dependants. For his subscription he gets a 30 per cent reduction on fees up to $1,000 and thereafter a maximum charge of $30 an hour, which is well below current commercial rates. A similar scheme in Nassau County offers fringe benefits for the $100 subscription of up to two hours' free consultation plus free services for buying or selling property, eviction proceedings or the drawing up of a will. For other services the client pays agreed rates that are some 40–50 per cent lower than the normal rates. Consumer organisations, educational establishments and other groups are beginning to develop similar plans and there are also two insurance companies offering legal costs policies. The potential growth of the pre-paid movement in the United States was stimulated by the provision in the 1976 Tax Reform Act excluding from taxable income the value of benefits received through employer-funded plans. In August 1977 the U.S. Department of Labor had notice of 2,112 pre-payment schemes either financed wholly by employers or partly by employers and partly by employees. The numbers of persons covered by such schemes ranged from the very small (105 plans covered up to five employees), to the very large (there were 17 plans involving more than 50,000 employees). The largest plan to date is that of the Chrysler Company which in 1977 negotiated with the United Auto Workers to establish a Legal Services Plan to cover some 150,000 workers and retired workers. The plan was to be financed from a fund of some $22m which the company had previously held as an unemployment reserve fund.[65a] The work to be covered included divorce, wills, probate, bankruptcy, consumer complaints, landlord-tenant disputes, taking or defending tort actions and the defence of misdemeanor and juvenile court cases.

There is little doubt that these various types of schemes will increase and multiply and that, as a result, many Americans will receive legal services that they would otherwise not have had, at lower cost than their current market value and at a cost they can afford. At first blush this seems pure gain – not least for the lawyers who, presumably, would not participate in the schemes unless they could make useful profits from larger volume, lower price services. There is, however, one possible snag. This is the overall inflationary effect that such schemes may eventually have.[66] This has already occurred in American medical costs, partly it is thought as a result of massive increases in state and privately funded health insurance. People buy insurance to cover the costs of infrequent major expenses because to do so is cheap by comparison with the ordinary cost of such services. Insurance has the effect of bringing down the cost to the consumer and, naturally, consumers thereupon buy more of that good. The result is demand-pull inflation. If more people want legal services for which they pay through insurance schemes, the cost of those services will eventually rise. This has the effect of causing more people to buy insurance in order to protect themselves against the even greater cost of the services for those who are not insured. The process, as has been said, 'becomes a vicious cycle that feeds on self-fulfilling prophecy'.[67]

The risk of this happening in the legal field is no doubt less than in the medical, because of the much lower level of concern among the public about legal problems. But some such general inflationary effect would be likely to occur from any great increase in insurance schemes. The disadvantages of this have to be balanced against the benefits of achieving wider access to lawyers.

Funding for representation of the 'public interest'

The English system makes little provision for the financing of litigation in the name of the public interest. There are few examples of public officials charged with either the right or the duty to initiate or participate in legal proceedings in the name of the public interest,[68] nor are there many examples of ways in which public funds can be made available for the support of such litigation by private parties.

The only public official with important responsibilities in the field of litigation in the public interest is the Attorney-General. It is his duty to vet applications from private parties for permission to move by way of relator action to protect the public interest.[69] Such an action proceeds nominally in his name but, once leave is granted, it remains the action of the citizen who applies and it is the citizen who finances the case.[70]The Attorney-General has the right to intervene in litigation between private parties if he believes it raises a point of law of general public importance on which for some reason he wishes to express a view. Sometimes he is asked by a court to attend as *amicus curiae*. He also has an ancient general right to set the law in motion where a public right is infringed or where there is some abuse of statutory procedure or power by public authorities.[71] But this power is rarely used and then usually to enforce or uphold the law, rather than to change it.

There are virtually no English examples of public funds being available to assist private parties in litigation in the name of the public interest. The legal aid fund cannot be used for the purpose unless the applicant qualifies in the ordinary way by passing both the means test and the merits test. So where the House of Lords had given leave to appeal on a point of law of general public importance, legal aid was held to have been correctly refused because there was no sufficient prospect that the case would be won on the facts.[72]

Nor is legal aid likely to be available for a class or representative action, for the assets of the members of the class have to be aggregated for the purposes of the means test.[73] This would almost invariably make the class ineligible for legal aid – even though every one of its members was very poor. The Evershed Committee in 1953 recommended that parties to litigation involving points of law of exceptional public importance ought to be allowed to apply to the Attorney-General for a certificate which would then entitle them to be reimbursed for all their costs, irrespective of means.[74] The Law Society, ten years later, suggested a broader application of the same concept in the form of a committee appointed by the Lord Chancellor which would have the power to approve the use of public funds to defray the costs where litigation concerned a new or doubtful point of law. The law should be clarified at public rather than at private expense.[75] In 1977 Justice supported the Evershed Committee's recommendations but with the qualification that a certificate should be given by the High Court rather than the Attorney-General.[76]

Neither the Evershed Committee's proposal nor that of the Law Society has been implemented. The only moves in any such direction are provisions in the Sex Discrimination Act 1975 and the Race Relations Act 1976. These two Acts give the

Equal Opportunities Commission and the Commission for Racial Equality the power to assist individuals who are actual or potential aggrieved persons complaining of discrimination. Such assistance may be given either on the ground that the case raises a question of principle or because it is thought to be unreasonable to expect the complainant to proceed unaided – because of the complexity of the case, or because of the applicant's position in relation to that of the person against whom he is complaining, or for any other reason. Assistance can consist of advice, helping to secure a settlement, arranging for advice or assistance from a solicitor or barrister, arranging for representation in proceedings, or 'any other form of assistance which the Commission may consider appropriate'.[77] Such assistance can be given regardless of the means of the applicant.

There has as yet, however, been little in England to compare with the recent flowering in the United States of methods for using public moneys to promote legal representation of the public interest.[78] 'Public interest' law grew out of the experience of the 1960s when first the civil rights movement and then the legal services arm of the War on Poverty used the legal system and the courts to achieve many of their most spectacular gains. Foundations, in particular the Ford Foundation, had been mainly responsible for the funding of much of the most significant work in the race and poverty fields. The Ford Foundation again played a critical role in the promotion in the early 1970s of a new concept – law firms established in order to handle legal work in fields of public importance. It supported the Center for Law in the Public Interest, the Education Law Center, the Women's Rights Project, the Environmental Defense Fund, the Natural Resources Defense Council, Public Advocates Inc., the Sierra Club Legal Defense Fund and the Citizens' Advocate Center. Other public interest law firms, notably those associated with Ralph Nader, have been financed mainly through individual contributions from members of the public. Until 1969 there were only 15 non-profit public interest law centres with some 50 lawyers in the United States. By the end of 1975 the number of such centres had increased to 92 and there were some 600 lawyers working in them.[79] By 1975 the firms were litigating some hundreds of cases. It was said that public interest lawyers had contributed substantially to recognition of the rights of racial and ethnic minorities and women.

> They have had an important influence on the evolution of legal protection for the environment. They have virtually created new bodies of law to protect the rights of prisoners, the mentally ill, and the mentally retarded. They have been an innovative force in the administrative process, making governmental decision-making more open and accountable. They have explored new concepts of corporate responsibility.[80]

Wealthy foundations willing to support legal services experiments are, unfortunately, not common outside the United States. Moreover, institutions primarily funded by foundations are at risk since foundations like to support new concepts only until they are established and are usually reluctant to continue financial support indefinitely. Under the American costs rule, where each side bears its own lawyers' fees, it is difficult for public interest lawyers to recover their fees from their opponents in litigation.

The future of public interest law activities in the long run, both in the US and, even more, outside it, depends on the extent to which public funds can be found to support them. Public funding in this field in the United States has in fact been growing remarkably. Partly this has been directly through the Legal Services Corporation and its funding of the 'back-up' or law reform centres (see pp. 68, 83 above). But, increasingly, it has also been through a variety of other means. The Equal Employment Opportunity Commission has, for instance, made contracts with the NAACP's Legal Defense Fund for training lawyers in the handling of employment discrimination cases. Food Research and Action Center, a public interest law firm, is supported largely by the Department of Health Education and Welfare. Several law programmes to assist the elderly are financed by the Department of Health, Education and Welfare. The Department of Justice's Law Enforcement Assistance Programme finances representation for prisoners. The mentally handicapped and migrant farm workers are other groups receiving legal services through direct government funding.

In a 1975 Act, the Federal Trade Commission was authorised by Congress to pay for lawyers appearing for interests that 'would not otherwise be adequately represented in a rule-making proceeding and representation of which is necessary for a fair determination'. Half a million dollars was allowed for the first year. Groups that have received grants have included the Center for Auto Safety, the National Council of Senior Citizens and the Consumers' Union. The innovation appears to have been a success.[81] A bill sponsored by Senator Kennedy to authorise all federal agencies to fund public interest representation did not survive in 1977, but it was to be reintroduced. A related development has been the setting up in government itself of agencies to represent the public interest – of which the most novel is the New Jersey Department of the Public Advocate, established in 1974, with one division whose task it is to represent the public interest in both administrative proceedings and the courts. The Division has, for instance, brought a suit to challenge the constitutionality of the state's ban on prescription advertising, to establish some form of due process requirement before termination of public utility facilities and to require equal availability of municipally owned beaches to residents and non-residents alike.[82]

In America public interest law activities funded through the public purse are growing in scope and range. Could any comparable development occur in other countries? No doubt the legal-political culture in England is different and less responsive to lawyers as agents of change. But much of the work of the public interest lawyer is simply to provide representation for relevant interests that would otherwise be unrepresented. This is a familiar and indeed traditional role for lawyers to perform. Legal aid programmes all over the world testify to the willingness of governments to devote public moneys to provide representation in ordinary legal cases for the indigent. Public interest law is a natural development – a recognition that important interests go unrepresented not simply in criminal cases, divorces and personal injury claims. These, no doubt, are where one starts. But when these needs are beginning to be met, it is right to look further afield to identify new needs for legal services.

There are two possible approaches to the problem. One is to extend legal aid to cover proceedings brought by groups. This was proposed, for instance, by the Osler Committee in its

1974 Ontario Report. It found that there was general agreement that the existing restrictions on legal aid for class actions
and group proceedings should be changed. 'We think it right
and just that the Plan respond to the almost universal sense that
class actions and group proceedings should be, in appropriate
cases, funded by Legal Aid'.[83] It was impossible to prescribe
clear rules as to the kinds of case that should be within the
concept. Applications should be dealt with by the Area Committee which under the Committee's proposals, would
include laymen as well as lawyers. The kind of considerations
to be taken into account, however, would include the representative nature of the applicant; the purpose of the proceedings; whether the benefit would accrue to the public as well as
the members of the group; whether the effect of granting the
certificate might be to help to redress an apparent economic
imbalance; the availability of alternative sources of funding;
the competence of the group to represent its interest effectively; the financial resources of the group and of its members;
the prospects of success in the proposed action; the importance
of the issue; and the probable costs. This would 'involve a
significant departure from the traditional concept of Legal
Aid' but it would be responding 'to a legitimate and broadly
felt need' in the community.[84] The report also proposed that
for litigation by groups 'demonstrating a bona fide concern for
matters affecting the public interest' the ordinary indemnity
rule of costs following the event should be changed. In actions
by groups, whether or not they were legally aided, a successful
respondent should have the burden of satisfying the court that
no 'public issue of substance was involved in the litigation or
that the proceedings were frivolous or vexatious'.[85] The
Committee did not spell out the details of these proposals but
suggested instead that they should be examined by some
appropriate body. Clearly there would be considerable
difficulties in changes in the indemnity rule just for public
interest litigation and even greater difficulties if the change was
to benefit only plaintiffs. There would also be great problems
in distinguishing between actions that would deserve the support of legal aid 'in the public interest', and those that would
not. Inevitably the legal aid authorities would find themselves
involved in the, essentially social-political, problem of the
merits or otherwise of different kinds of campaign to get the

law changed through litigation. The merits test of being able to show that the case had some reasonable prospect of success would be relatively easy to apply. The means test would be much more difficult since most groups would be outside the ordinary limits and a special test would presumably have to be devised. But even if there were a special means test (or none at all), the main difficulty would remain the task of assessing the claim of any particular group to call on state funds from a policy point of view.

The second approach, one that is conceptually somewhat easier to operate, is to use public funds to support law firms, as in the USA, in specialist fields – housing law, consumer law, environmental law, the problems of mental patients, immigrants or prisoners. It has now been accepted in many countries that public moneys can legitimately be provided to support 'ordinary' law centres. The next step will be to use public funds to support lawyers working in a more focused way on the legal problems of particular groups whose problems are felt to deserve special attention. If, in the first instance, public money is not forthcoming, charitable funds may show the way in England and elsewhere, as has been the case in the United States.

Interest on solicitors' client accounts as a source of funding

Money for legal services, whether public or private, is never likely to be easy to find. One source which should therefore be tapped in England, as has already been done in other Commonwealth countries, is that of interest earned by solicitors on their clients' moneys. The present Rules require that a solicitor who holds client moneys, typically in a conveyancing transaction or probate matter, must place them in a separate account, which may be either a deposit or a current account. Most firms maintain both. If the client specifically asks for the interest to be paid to him, he has an absolute right to receive it. If, as is usual, he does not ask, the solicitor must nevertheless pay it to him where 'having regard to all the circumstances' including the amount and length of time for which the money is likely to be held, interest ought in fairness to the client to be earned for him.[86] The Rules state that interest ought in fairness to the client to be earned for him where more than £500 is held for two or more months. But they say nothing about the much more typical situation where thousands of pounds are held for a few days. The sums earned for the client in such cases are usually very small – interest on £10,000 at, say, 6½ per cent for seven days is £12.46, on which the client must pay tax at the rate for unearned income. But the aggregate amount for the firm and for the profession per year is very large. (In 1976, on the basis of very inadequate figures, I estimated that it could be of the order of £25m. a year, of which perhaps 70 per cent (or £17m.) was being retained by solicitors.[87] These estimates proved to be only slightly out – see p. 234).

In 1964, the House of Lords held that, in view of the fiduciary relationship that existed between solicitors and their clients, they had to account to their clients for every penny of interest earned on client account.[88] This caused consternation in the profession. A Solicitors Bill was, however, then before Parliament, and Lord Tangley, a former President of the Law Society, proposed an amendment to make interest payable only where it was fair to the client. His reason was not that he challenged the basic principle of the House of Lords decision. On the contrary. ('I want to make it abundantly plain that the solicitors' profession completely and absolutely accepts that decision'.[89] The sole reason for the amendment to the law, he said, was that it was a physical impossibility for solicitors to comply. Interest on client account was composed of large numbers of small amounts. It would be impossible for solicitors to work out how much was due to each client. ('It is really impracticable to do the arithmetic and to work it out.[90] As a statement of fact even in 1965, and certainly today, this seems unconvincing. It must be a simple matter for the solicitor to count the number of days for which the money has been on deposit, and then to calculate the interest due, with a ready reckoner. It would in reality be relatively easy to restore the full effect of the House of Lord's decision.

There is therefore a choice between three alternatives. Either the rules should remain as they now are and solicitors retain millions of pounds of clients' interest, or the money should be returned to the clients, or, thirdly, the money should be taken for public purposes. The third course has now been adopted in a number of Commonwealth jurisdictions including Alberta, British Columbia, Manitoba, New South Wales and Ontario. A similar scheme has been proposed by the Florida Bar Association.[91] The basic scheme in each case is to require solicitors to place client money (or part of it) on deposit and to pay the whole or a specified part of the resulting interest into a fund administered by trustees representing, typically, the profession, lawyer-appointees of the relevant Minister and a lay element. The objects of the fund are normally widely drawn and include such purposes as law reform, legal aid, education, law libraries, legal research, etc. There are no serious technical problems about the mechanics of such schemes. They work. The resulting funds could be used in England, for instance, to raise (or help to raise) the means test limits for legal aid and to reduce contributions, to finance the whole of the public sector in legal services including public interest law firms, to employ enough liaison officers for the whole country, to pay for the Law Society's advertising and its proposed institutional scheme of vocational training, to provide scholarships and loans for recruits to the profession, etc. The potential benefits are enormous; this is the legal version of the goose that lays (and will continue to lay) golden eggs. (According to the Law Society's remuneration survey, the solicitors' branch on 31 December 1976 held no less than £760m. in client accounts. During 1976 – a year of higher than usual interest rates – solicitors retained a total of £18.9m. interest earned on these accounts. Total gross receipts in 1976 were £685m. (or £106,600 on average per firm). Interest on client account retained by firms therefore represented 2.76 per cent of gross receipts.[91a]

In some jurisdictions lawyers have never been entitled to derive profit from their client accounts. Where this is the case the main opposition to the idea of using the moneys for public legal services purposes comes from the banks which are the chief beneficiaries of the status quo. Where, as in England, the profession derives a part of its gross income from this source it is obvious that the opposition will come from the lawyers. But the claim of the profession to the money must be a low one. The sole argument advanced by Lord Tangley was the minor problem of accounting difficulties. Even if this were valid it would not explain why solicitors should retain the money rather than have it devoted to public purposes. The profession today argues also that a loss in income would have to lead to a corresponding increase in fees. This suggestion must be based on the argument that solicitors' profit margin is so narrow that the loss of a few per cent of gross income would require an increase in fees. One way of avoiding or at least of reducing this danger would be to vary from year to year the proportion of interest earned that had to be paid over to the fund, depending on economic conditions. Even, however, if fees *were* increased it might still be worthwhile to create the fund. The raising of fees needed to make the difference to solicitors between a reasonable profit and none might be so slight as to be felt hardly, if at all, by the ordinary client. If this were so, the overall benefit of a princely annual sum available to be spent on public purposes might be thought to be worth the relatively insignificant raising in charges to some clients. This would be the more so if one appreciates that a high proportion of legal fees are paid by bodies or individuals that can afford them – the business community, the rich, insurance companies, and those transferring or inheriting property.

But even if, as between the solicitor and public purposes, the latter have the stronger case, it does not follow that the public purposes have a higher claim than the client. Should not the law simply attempt to enforce the House of Lords decision? Certainly the client ought always to get the money if he asks for it. But if he does not know about it should he be told, or should he simply be given the money whether he asks for it or not? If the amount due to the client were large I would favour an automatic accounting to the client. But in the case of the great majority of very small sums (say, under £50) the benefit to the client would be so small compared with the scale of potential benefit from the fund that I believe it could properly be used for the greater public good.

Does the legal profession receive fair remuneration?

Members of most professions and certainly lawyers are like most of the rest of mankind in wanting their share of material blessings. They may not be money-grubbing, but they want enough to be able to enjoy the standard of living and status to which they think themselves entitled. (The middle classes regard it as axiomatic that higher educational training and intellectual capacities carry the right to jobs that are not only more satisfying and agreeable than those available to others

but also that pay more.) But how much should lawyers earn?
There is unlikely to be general agreement even as to how to
set about answering the question. Should lawyers earn more
(or less) than doctors, surveyors, accountants, teachers,
architects? Should lawyers in private practice earn more (or
less) than those in salaried employment in commerce or industry? Should barristers earn more than solicitors or vice versa?
There are no agreed criteria or standards to answer such questions.[92]

Numbers coming into the profession

There are, however, some questions that can be posed that do
have meaning. One is whether the rate of new entrants to the
profession is sufficient. There is presumably some connection
between the economic situation of a profession and its capacity
to recruit enough new entrants of appropriate quality. On
quality there appears never to have been much serious complaint, irrespective of whether times were good or not. But
economic conditions have plainly had a great effect on numbers. In the 1950s, when economic conditions at the Bar were
notoriously poor, the annual rate of entry was lower than the
exodus through retirement and withdrawal from practice.
There was a net loss in numbers in every year from 1954 to
1959.[93] From 1960 onwards, with the growth in legal aid, the
trend was reversed and there has been a net gain ever since. In
the period 1960 to 1970 the net annual increase averaged 78;
from 1971 to 1976 it was 233.[94] According to the Bar's own
evidence to the Royal Commission, it can now 'probably
absorb no more than a net annual increase of about 200'.[95]
During the 1960s, it said, there was probably some shortage of
barristers. According to all the Bar's information, the shortage
was over and there was now a surplus which could become
substantial if the rate of growth between 1971 and 1976 were to
continue.[96] (In 1976–7 the net increase in fact went down to
109 compared with 235 and 278 in the two previous years.) It
was desirable that there should always be a small surplus, 'to
cover fluctuations of demand and to provide a reservoir upon
which solicitors can draw when they are under pressure, to
avoid clashes and to provide sufficient competition to ensure
reasonably high standards'.[97] But there was a danger that the
surplus might become excessive. The Bar said that there was

also a slight shortage of senior juniors in all fields which should, however, clear itself when those under 10 years Call joined the band of those between 10 and 20 years Call.[98]

On the solicitors' side of the profession, the position has been broadly similar. The average annual intake of students in the period 1950 to 1960 was 711, from 1961 to 1970 it was 2,027 and from 1971 to 1976 it was 3,302. In 1976, new students numbered 3,950.[99] In the 1960s, the Law Society, like the Bar, had been concerned about recruitment and had launched a campaign to get more entrants from schools. It told the Prices and Incomes Board in 1968 that although numbers were rising the profession was short of manpower. It referred to a shortage of some 5,000 solicitors.[100] The PIB concluded, however, that if there was any shortage, it was not as great as the profession contended and that neither the trend nor the level of remuneration constituted any obstacle to recruitment.[101] Ten years later the Law Society told the Royal Commission that 'the rate of recruitment to the profession is higher, probably much higher than the existing prospects justify'.[102] The current position was that there was 'no appreciable shortage or surplus generally of newly enrolled or experienced solicitors'.[103] Equilibrium was maintained only because solicitors worked long hours[104] and had to do so because they could not afford to take on additional staff. In the previous five years there had been a very large rise in solicitors' overhead costs, forcing many firms to employ fewer staff than they would have employed if they could have afforded to. But no local law society had reported any evidence of serious current imbalance between supply and demand. If these economic factors continued, there was likely to be 'an appreciable surplus of newly enrolled solicitors'.[105]

Market forces, albeit in a rough and ready way, do therefore exert a considerable impact on the rate of supply and demand. If, as seems possible, the rate of increase in the past few years has been too steep, it will presumably slow down as law students at universities are advised that prospects of getting a seat in chambers or a position in a solicitor's firm are less bright than in the early 1970s. But the evidence of the past ten years has been that, to judge from numbers alone, both sides of the legal profession have been in an uncommonly healthy state.

Earnings

A second question that can be posed is, what is the range of net earnings in the profession and how does it compare with those in other fields? The Pilkington Royal Commission on Doctors' Remuneration found that in 1955–6 solicitors ranked fourth and barristers sixth in average earnings of a number of different professions. (The first three professions were medical consultants, actuaries and dentists, with general medical practitioners fifth.)[106] When the Pilkington Royal Commission looked at average earnings over a working life from age 30 to 65, barristers ranked third (after medical consultants and actuaries) and solicitors fourth.[107] The Prices and Incomes Board in its report in 1968 concluded that 'compared to what is known of changes in other incomes, solicitors have fared reasonably well over the whole period of comparison'.[108] Their average increases approximated to those of all wage earners and salary earners. They were lower than those of doctors but higher than those of dentists and architects.

The Bar Both the Bar and the Law Society conducted remuneration surveys for the Royal Commission. On the basis of the Bar's survey, its total gross receipts in 1974–5, excluding VAT, were £37.9m. – £9.7m. for QCs and £28.2m. for juniors.[108a] Table 7.1 shows the net earnings (after deduction of expenses, but before tax) of the Bar in 1974–5. The distribution of net incomes appears in Table 7.2. The overall average income for the Bar as a whole was £7,279.[109] (The recommendations of the Review Body for doctors' pay in 1974–5 were designed to give general medical practitioners an income of £6,147 p.a.[110] The salary scale for consultants as at 1 January, 1975 was from £5,433 to £7,947 plus merit awards.[111] The Bar Association for Commerce, Finance and Industry remuneration survey showed that in 1974 the median figure was in the £7,000 to £8,000 band.)[112]

The general picture that emerges is that many very young barristers do worse than beginners in other fields, though some do well even at that stage. (The upper quartile of those of under 3 years' seniority in London specialist chambers earned an average of £3,690 net. In London common law practice the figure was £3,046 and on circuit £4,404.) At all levels there are great variations in income, but broadly there was a rapid rise in

Table 7.1
Average net earnings before tax of barristers, 1974–5

	£	% at the Bar (October 1974)
QCs appointed in or after 1972	18,690	4
QCs appointed before 1972	19,405	7
Juniors of over 15 years' seniority	8,612	18
Juniors of 9–15 years' seniority	8,607	18
Juniors of 4–8 years' seniority	5,675	28
Juniors of 0–3 years' seniority	2,753	25
		100

Source: Bar Council, *Evidence, Survey of Income at the Bar* 1974–5, calculated from Table 14A and, in the case of juniors, Bar, *A Commentary on the Survey of Income, Addendum to Submission No. 8*, Table A, p. 1, and Table G, p.6.

Table 7.2
Distribution of barristers' average net earnings, before tax, 1974–5

	Upper decile	Upper quartile	Median	Lower quartile	Lower decile	Average	Total (October 1974)
	£	£	£	£	£	£	
QCs	29,592	21,944	16,284	11,447	8,053	18,018	(345)
Juniors	11,234	7,602	4,778	2,305	782	6,069*	(3,025)

* Adjusted as in Table G.

Source: Bar, *Evidence, A Commentary on the Survey of Incomes 1974–5, Addendum to Submission No. 8*, Table F, p. 5.

earnings for those in the period of 4 to 8 years' seniority. (The median net income for London specialists, London common law practitioners and circuiteers in the first three years of seniority were respectively: £1,931, £1,572 and £2,717. The comparable figures for those between 4 and 8 years' seniority were £6,485, £4,811 and £5,956.[113]) The rise continued for those in London common law work and for circuiteers and continued at an even greater rate for London specialists. (The median income of those of from 9 to 15 years' seniority in the two former categories were £7,766 and £7,683 and for London specialists was £11,335). Thereafter earnings levelled off, save for those who became QCs (usually in their late thirties or early to mid forties). As appears from Table 7.1, the average earnings of the 10 per cent of the Bar who become QCs are dramatically higher than those for juniors – though the lower quartile of QCs was earning virtually the same as the upper decile of junior barristers (£11,447 as against £11,234). But Table 6.1, p. 175 above, showed that the median net incomes of even newly appointed QCs were roughly double those of both juniors at 9–15 years' seniority and juniors of over 15 years' seniority.

The Bar's evidence to the Royal Commission said that a member of the Bar starts with no guarantee of high earnings in later life. His existence was 'precarious' and his security was 'minimal'.[114] This is undoubtedly true for some. The lowest quartile of juniors of over 15 years' seniority were earning only just over £5,000 net in 1974–5 and the equivalent for those with between 9 and 15 years' seniority was only slightly more. On the other hand, the prizes for the high fliers were very great. The upper quartile of London specialist QCs were earning around £30,000 net and in common law work some £20,000. Moreover, a not insignificant proportion of barristers eventually go onto the bench where they receive both high salaries and inflation-proofed pensions. (In 1976 there were 682 pensionable judicial and quasi-judicial posts of which 495 (72 per cent) were held by barristers and the rest by solicitors.[115] The number of barristers appointed to such posts was 27 in 1973, 30 in 1974, 43 in 1975 and 38 in 1976.[116]) In addition, some barristers leave the Bar to go into financially attractive employment in business, industry and the City.

Solicitors Prior to the Bar's remuneration survey in 1977 there were no reliable data about the earnings of barristers. In the case of the solicitors' branch there was some such information – chiefly in the form of the elaborate studies conducted by the Prices and Incomes Board based on data for the year ending

October 1966 and the year ending October 1968. In 1966, the net income of principals in private practice averaged £4,870. The median was £4,180. Sole practitioners earned slightly more than partners in a two-man practice, but apart from that, the larger the firm the higher the income. The lowest quartile of solicitors earned less than £2,640 and the upper quartile more than £6,135.[117] The Board said that the spread of earnings in a profession was bound to be fairly wide. The very young and the very old (who continued to practice long after retiring age) would have limited earning power. Some deliberately restricted the work they would do and there were some who were unsuccessful. But although there were some parts of the country where earnings were especially low (particularly the West and Wales) there was no need to increase the income of the profession generally in order to benefit those categories.[118] Solicitors in private practice were found to be earning roughly £1,000 more than those in commerce and industry after allowing for fringe benefits. The private practitioner had more financial and other risks, and worked somewhat longer hours, but he had personal and professional independence not enjoyed by the employed solicitor. The Board thought the difference of about £1,000 a year adequately reflected these different factors.[119] It concluded that there was no case for increasing the profession's total income either on the grounds of recruitment or on the basis of earnings.[120]

The Board's second report in 1969 broadly confirmed the findings of the first. The median income of principals had risen from £4,180 in 1966 to £4,514 in 1968. One-man practices had continued to lose ground.[121] The trend of incomes in the profession over recent years as disclosed by the Board's surveys had 'not been out of keeping with the incomes policy',[122] and from the prices point of view, the profit earned by the profession appeared adequate to secure the investment of the necessary resources by way of manpower.[123]

After the Board's reports came the sudden dramatic rise in inflation. This had two effects. One was a great rise in the cost of overheads. The other was an unprecedented boom in property prices. The rise in the value of houses, in the words of a former member of the Council of the Law Society, 'meant for most solicitors a golden harvest'.[124] In its first report in 1968 the PIB said that the increase of income of the solicitors' profession was due mainly to the rise in the prices of houses and an increase in the number of conveyances. In the previous ten years 'solicitors' income from conveyancing of private houses [had] increased by 2½ to 3 times'.[125] The profession had therefore been able to benefit from the inflation in property values. This inflation has increased even more in the period since the PIB's last report. The average price of houses in England and Wales increased between 1965 and 1970 from £3,768 to £4,975 – an increase of 33 per cent. The equivalent increase between 1970 and 1976 (from £5,632 to £11,800) was 109 per cent. In spite of this gigantic leap in house prices the profession complained bitterly that its profit margins were eaten away by rising overheads and that inflation caused severe cash-flow and capital investment problems. Certainly the pattern of conveyancing transactions was uneven. The Inland Revenue estimated the total value of sales of land and buildings in England and Wales in 1973 to be about £12,000m., falling to £10,000m. in 1974, rising to about £12,000m. again in 1975 and to £13,500m. in 1976, falling again to an annual rate of £12,500m. in the first half of 1977.[126] But most of this fluctuation was due to significant falls in the level of non-residential sales. According to the PIB's 1968 estimates, conveyancing of residential properties forms some 50 per cent of total solicitors' income compared with 5 per cent attributed to non-residential conveyancing.[127] According to the Inland Revenue's figures for October 1973 and 1974 and November 1975 and 1976, the values per month of sales of residential property went from £760m. to £786m. to £879m. to £1,021m. whilst the figures for non-residential sales were £365m., £180m., £156m. and £194m.[128] But the significance of these figures and their impact on overall earnings was difficult to evaluate in the absence of the Law Society's Remuneration Survey undertaken for the Royal Commission. Unfortunately, owing to unexpected delays, the results of the survey were not available in time to be included in the book.

8 The Management of Legal Services

The proposition that legal services involve the public interest would not, today, be challenged by anyone. It is implicit even in the way that the profession defines its own role. The Law Society's evidence to the Royal Commission stated:

> When a profession is fully developed it may be defined as a body of men and women (a) identifiable by reference to some register or record; (b) recognised as having learning in some field of activity in which *the public needs protection* against incompetence, the standards of skill and learning being prescribed by the profession itself; (c) *holding themselves out* as being *willing to serve the public*; (d) voluntarily submitting themselves to *standards of ethical conduct* beyond those required of the ordinary citizen by law; and (e) undertaking to *accept personal responsibility to those whom they serve for their actions* and to their profession for maintaining *public confidence*.[1]

The italicised phrases show strikingly the extent to which lawyers conceive of their role in terms of service to the public. At the same time, the statement makes clear the profession's belief that its discipline is self-imposed. The standards of skill and learning are those 'prescribed by the profession itself', the lawyers 'hold themselves out' to serve the public, they 'voluntarily submit' to their specially high standards, they undertake personal responsibility to their clients and the profession. The Bar's evidence to the Royal Commission claimed that self-regulation was one of the essential ingredients of the independence of the profession, which in turn was vital to the administration of justice and freedom itself.[2] The first ingredients of independence, it said, were independent professional organisations or bodies 'responsible for determining standards and content of education and training for the profession' and 'responsible for maintaining standards of conduct'.[3] It is part of the basic credo of the professions that they can be trusted to recognise the public interest and to give it effect.

This claim, unavoidably, is self-serving. It fails, as soon as professions can be shown to be falling short of their own high standards. Since human institutions that live up to their ideals are rare, there have inevitably been instances when the profession has found its rules and practices strongly criticised from outside. Sometimes it has itself recognised the justice of such criticisms by altering former rules and practices – though, it must be said, usually only after protracted resistance.

Occasionally governments and the legislature have taken an interest in the affairs of the profession. Thus, early in the nineteenth century, there was a flurry of Select Committee Reports – in 1821, on the admission of attorneys and solicitors,[4] in 1834 on the Inns of Court[5] and in 1846, on legal education.[6] Eight years later, in 1854, there was a report of commissioners on legal education in the Inns of Court.[7] There have also been a whole series of statutes going back centuries regulating and controlling solicitors.[8] But for about a hundred years, from 1850 to the mid-twentieth century, the legal profession was, if anything, becoming less and less subject to external control. With the exception of the imposition in 1883 of scale fees for conveyancing, the legislature passed effective power over its affairs to the profession. The 1922 Solicitors Act provided that attendance for one year of lectures at the Law Society's school of law was compulsory for all except those with approved degrees and experienced managing clerks. The 1933 Solicitors Act gave the Council of the Law Society power (though subject to the approval of the Master of the Rolls) to make rules about the keeping of separate clients' accounts and for regulating any other matter of professional practice, conduct and discipline of solicitors. The 1949 Legal Aid and Advice Act entrusted the full responsibility for running the legal aid scheme to the legal profession. The leading historians of this development have said:

> The extent of self-government which Parliament granted to solicitors was exceptional. While the legislature had insisted on introducing non-professional members on the bodies responsible for the education and discipline of doctors, nurses, midwives, dentists, pharmacists and architects, no non-lawyer could interfere with the affairs of solicitors. The junior branch of the legal profession had obtained by legislation almost the same measure of self-government as the senior branch had always had without.[9]

In recent years, however, there have been two new trends – one the partial democratisation of the internal management structure of the legal profession, the other a growth in the involvement of outsiders.

Growing democratisation of government of the profession

The Bar

The Bar was traditionally run by the Inns of Court through the benchers, a self-perpetuating body of senior members. Halsbury's *Laws of England* in 1973 stated:

> The benchers are the governing body who alone have power to fill vacancies in or add to their number, to admit persons as students, to call students to the Bar and to exercise a disciplinary jurisdiction over members of the Inn ... They can refuse to admit a person as a student, or to call a student to the Bar. They can expel any member, and can disbar a barrister or suspend him from practice for a period, and can disbench one of their own number. The benchers alone decide on the amount of the fees which the members of the Inn have to pay, and on the application of the moneys so raised. In all these matters they are entirely outside the jurisdiction of the ordinary courts, but their decisions are subject to an appeal to the Lord Chancellor and the judges of the High Court of Justice sitting as a domestic tribunal.[10]

In the seventeenth and eighteenth centuries there were sporadic attempts by individual barristers to achieve some measure of participation in the government of the Inns, but these were unsuccessful. After disturbances in 1730 the bench established the rule that it would henceforth entail expulsion 'ipso facto for any man at any time hereafter to take upon him, to exercise or claim any power, liberty or authority to govern within the House, otherwise than as subordinate and subject to the orders and government of the Masters of the Bench'.[11]

The benchers for centuries were practitioners. Those that became sergeants[12] or judges left the Inn. But the sergeant's order went into decline in the mid-nineteenth century and the last sergeant was appointed in 1875. In the same year the Inns decided that sergeants and judges could remain members of their Inns and from that date the control of the Inns effectively passed to the judges and elderly or retired barristers. The judges dominated the Inns in their dual capacity – as benchers and as the appeal body from decisions by the benchers. Not only were ordinary members of the Inns entirely excluded from the government of the Inns, but their affairs were mainly in the hands of non-practitioners.

Challenge to the power of the benchers came very slowly. In 1883, young barristers formed a Bar Committee whose members were elected by the whole Bar. In 1895, this became the Bar Council, which, throughout the first half of the twentieth century performed the trade union and management function for the practising bar, without, however, making much impact on the powers of the Inns. In 1966 a new body, the Senate of the Four Inns, was set up in an attempt to provide a co-ordinating body for the Inns and the Bar Council. The Senate consisted of the Treasurer plus six benchers from each of the four Inns of Court and six representatives of the Bar Council. The decisions of the Senate only bound the Inns insofar as they did not involve them in expense. In other words, the Inns still retained effective control. Dissatisfaction with this position led, in 1970, to a suggestion from the Lord Chancellor, Lord Hailsham, that the Bar would do well to put its own house in order. The result was the setting up, in 1971, of a committee under Lord Pearce. After a protracted period of gestation, the Committee's work led in turn to the present Senate of the Inns of Court and the Bar, which represented the first genuine shift of power toward practitioners.[13]

The governing body, the Senate, consists of some 90 members. Of these, 36 are from the Inns, 39 are elected by the Bar, 3 are circuit judges and 1 represents the holders of minor judicial office. There is power to appoint a further 12 members. At first sight, therefore, it appears as though the powers of the Inns and the practising Bar are roughly equal. But the important new element is that the representatives of the Inns consist of 24 benchers plus 12 barristers *elected* by non-bencher members of the Inns. Practitioners should always, therefore, have a clear majority on the Senate. Moreover, the Bar's 39 representatives must include 18 practising junior barristers, including at least 6 under seven years' Call and 6 representing approved associations of employed barristers.

The Senate 'lays down general policy on all matters affecting the profession, other than matters within the exclusive jurisdiction of the Inns or the Bar Council'.[14] It meets four times a year and acts through a number of committees. The Bar Council consists of the 39 Bar representatives elected to the Senate, together with the Attorney-General, the Solicitor-General and the leaders of the circuits. It operates notionally as a committee of the Senate, but it is an 'autonomous body for the purposes of its own separate powers and functions, in the performance of which it is not subject to any directions from the Senate'.[15] It meets once a year in general meeting in London.

Government of the Inns, however, remains wholly dominated by the Benchers, and therefore undemocratic and in the true sense irresponsible. The Pearce Committee said: 'Usually only very senior members of the profession, many of them already judges when elected, become Benchers and thereafter take part in the government of their Inns'.[16] It has been calculated that in 1975 there were 471 benchers of whom only 112 (24 per cent) were in practice. The junior bar, with over 90 per cent of those in practice, had only 17 representatives on the benches of the four Inns. Judges made up 45 per cent of the benches and judges and retired barristers between them were over 70 per cent of the total.[17] There is no annual report of the Inns through which the benchers could explain policy to their members, nor any annual meeting at which issues of common concern could be discussed. (The Pearce Committee actually proposed annual meetings,[18] but none of the Inns has yet followed the suggestion.) The Inns retain considerable powers over vast properties and large revenues. Little is known, even by members, of the way in which these powers are exercised – in spite of the fact that the benchers hold their properties as trustees and are therefore liable to account to the beneficiaries (students and barristers). (Halsbury's *Laws of England* states categorically that 'the property of each Inn is vested in trustees . . . and is held on a charitable trust for the furtherance of the study and practice of law'.[19]) If this is right, the Inns should long ago have registered with the Charity Commissioners and thereby made their books open to public inspection. The Inns always resisted any such suggestion until 1974 when they did in fact apply for recognition as charities in order to save a massive amount in corporation tax.[20] The suggestion has recently been made (repeating a proposal made nearly a hundred years ago) that the benchers ought to be *elected* by members of the Inns, that judges should not be eligible to be benchers, save in an honorary, non-voting capacity, and that the Inns should be brought under the same kind of statutory control as applies to Oxford and Cambridge colleges.[21] Implementation of such proposals would at least make the Inns accountable to their members.

The solicitors' branch

On the solicitors' side of the profession, the first attempt at organisation and management, the Society of Gentlemen Practisers in the Courts of Law, founded in 1739, 'began and remained a London Society for a select few chosen on the club principle'.[22] The Society had an elected committee of twenty, and general meetings were held twice yearly. But its numbers were very small – possibly never more than 150.[23] In the 1820s a rival group issued a prospectus for a new Law Institution to provide an establishment for attorneys close to the courts and the Inns of Court. It sought its members from the whole profession, but the prospectus made it clear that they were to be 'only of the most respectable and leading men in the Profession (it being intended carefully to exclude all disreputable characters)'.[24] This, it was thought, would 'serve to impress the Public with a higher opinion than it at present entertains of the weight and respectability of the profession at large'.[25] By 1825, 334 subscribers had agreed to buy shares and on 29 March of that year a meeting of subscribers was held in Serle's coffee house and a committee was appointed.

What was at first intended to be a useful amenity rapidly became something more ambitious – a body to represent the profession at large. In 1831 it received its Royal Charter with the somewhat awkward name of 'The Society of Attorneys, Solicitors, Proctors and others not being Barristers practising in the Courts of Law and Equity in the United Kingdom'. In 1833 the management committee informally renamed the body the 'Incorporated Law Society of the United Kingdom', but the long title remained technically the correct style until it was changed to 'The Law Society' in the Royal Charter of 1903.

Any solicitor could become a member of the Society on simply paying the entrance fee and subscription. In 1845 a new

Royal Charter transformed the former management commit-tee into the Council consisting of not more than 30 nor less than 20 members. These numbers have been increased from time to time – in 1872 to 50 plus 10 extraordinary members drawn from presidents of local law societies, in 1954 to 65 (extraordinary members to be abolished), and most recently in 1969 to 70. For many years convention dictated that the President was the longest-serving member of the Council, but this unwritten rule was broken in 1953,[26] since when the Council has selected whomever it thought most suitable, provided he has served for not less than 10 years as a Council member. In 1977 the first woman was elected to the Council.

Although in theory anyone could join and anyone could be elected a Council member, in practice the Society, in elections to the Council and in appointment to the offices of Vice President and President, was heavily biased toward London members. The first non-London solicitor to become President was Mr C. T. Saunders in 1884.[27] At that time there were also few local law societies and probably as many as half of the profession did not belong to any law society. But this gradu-ally changed. By the turn of the century, the Law Society itself claimed about half those with practising certificates as mem-bers and the proportion increased decade by decade until today it is well over 90 per cent.[28]

There are now 120 independent local law societies, 9 grouped law societies and the Worshipful Company of Sol-icitors of the City of London, through which the Law Society informs itself of opinion in the profession. The Law Society has an annual conference outside London and an annual gen-eral meeting in London. There are regular meetings for presi-dents and secretaries of local law societies to meet with the Law Society's Council and staff. The *Law Society's Gazette*, published weekly, is also an important vehicle for views in the profession. Elections to the Council are today held on the basis of constituencies each of which elects a number of members proportionate to the number of members practising there. Official nominees of the Council or the local law societies have a distinct advantage in such elections, but occasionally a candi-date who has not been officially sponsored does get elected. The power of the profession to resist decision-making from the Council was felt in 1974 in the rejection of the Council's policy of replacing articles with a practical skills course.[29] More recently, pressure generated by country and City solicitors forced the Council to abandon its policy of making entry into the profession virtually all-graduate to the exclusion of direct entry from school. The views of the profession have also been exhaustively canvassed in the course of the preparation of the Law Society's evidence to the Royal Commission through extensive consultation between the Law Society's committee and local law societies. Inevitably, there are always voices to complain of the excessive power of Chancery Lane in handling the affairs of the profession, but the formal structure and its operation in modern times do give anyone interested in the affairs of the profession the opportunity to express views at meetings, to vote on candidates for election and to raise issues for discussion in the legal press.

Growing involvement of outsiders

The other development of the past few years, and a much more significant one, has been the growth of the involvement of outsiders in the affairs of the profession. A generation ago the idea that lay persons could have any useful role in the running of the legal profession would have seemed outlandish. Today the question is not whether, but how much?

Various forms of lay participation have already been noted. Lay persons have been involved in the disciplinary process since 1967. In its evidence to the Royal Commission in 1977, the Bar even said, that 'the lay representatives [in the disciplinary process] have played a most valuable part in the affairs of the profession', and 'There may be a case for extending lay representation in connection with professional conduct and disciplinary matters still further, and for increasing their influence, e.g. by asking the lay representatives to furnish an annual report on their activities'.[30] But, inconsistently and with no explanation, the Bar went on: 'We do not think that lay representatives in any other aspect of the organisation or regulation of the profession is [sic] necessary or desirable, although some committees (for instance the Social Welfare Working Party) might sometimes benefit from the co-option of lay members'.[31] If lay participation has proved valuable in the field of discipline, it is not apparent why it should not be valuable in other fields.

The role of the Lay Observer has already been noted. There is no doubt that, so far as it goes, this has been a successful innovation and one that is likely to be extended – in particular, by increasing his jurisdiction to cover complaints against barristers. Another apparently successful development has been the largely lay management committees of law centres. According to a survey of the first fifteen law centres, all but two had such committees.[32] In most it was said by those working in the law centres to be either 'important', 'quite important' or 'increasingly important'.[33] The committee normally met monthly (7 cases), every 6–8 weeks (3 cases), or quarterly (3 cases).[34] In their evidence to the Royal Commission the Law Centres Working Group stated that an effective Management Committee acted 'as a constant check that the Law Centre is remaining responsive to local need'. It also fulfilled the additional function 'of preventing the lawyer from drifting back into a professional distance from the community and hiding in the shadows of professional or technical language or ideas'.[35] Membership of the committee, typically, consists of a mixture of local citizens and representatives of relevant community organisations. In the Adamsdown centre in Wales, for instance, the committee included a local shopkeeper, a steelworker, an ambulance attendant, a bricklayer, a motor mechanic and two housewives – all elected at a public meeting. In Balham, the committee consisted of three elected members of the local council, two from the local Law Society, one from the CAB, one from the Council for Community Relations and representatives of a tenants' group, an old age pensioners' group, and an organisation of coloured people.[36]

It might have been expected that the Law Society would object to such committees as potential sources of interference in the work of lawyers and thereby a threat to the independence of the profession. But in fact it appears never to have taken this general point. The only times when the Law Society raised such difficulties were over proposed centres (notably at Hackney, Haringey and Coventry) where there appeared to be a danger that the local council which was funding the centre would demand an undue share of power on the committee. In the lengthy negotiations from 1974 to 1977 between the Law

Society and the Law Centres Working Group and other relevant agencies over waivers, there was little controversy on
this point. In its final form the relevant clause and its accom-
panying note read:

> In the case of salaried solicitors, the Law Society's policy is as
> follows: (a) To insist that there be a management committee
> which is independent of the funding agency and of centres and
> local government none of whose representatives should be *ex
> officio* chairman, vice chairman or secretary of the management
> committee;
>
> Note: Although not a condition for the grant of a waiver, it is considered
> that a majority of the voting members of the management committee of a
> salaried service should normally be able to represent the interests of the
> recipients of the service. It is appropriate for the management committee
> to include representatives of other agencies providing advisory or allied
> services.[37]

The formula did not attempt to define the phrase 'able to
represent the interests of the recipients of the service', but it
was not intended that this should be thought to require any
form of election or other formal process.[38] So far, at least, lay
participation on these committees does not seem to have given
rise to any real problems.

Another form of lay involvement in the affairs of the profession is that of the *ad hoc* official committee. An outstandingly
successful example of this genre was the Beeching Royal
Commission on Assizes and Quarter Sessions set up in 1966 by
Lord Gardiner, the then Labour Lord Chancellor. The Commission had a formidable lay chairman and three other laymen
out of nine members. Lord Beeching played a dominant role in
the work of the Commission. The report recommending the
substantial reform of the higher courts system[39] was well
received and was implemented without delay and with little
change by the incoming Conservative Government in the
Courts Act 1971.

The history of the three reports of the Prices and Incomes
Board on solicitors' remuneration was less smooth. In 1967,
the Labour Government asked the Board to examine 'all relevant factors affecting the professional earnings of solicitors'. In
its report in 1968, the Board made recommendations for alter-
ations of the scale fees for conveyancing and of charges in
county court cases, and recommended relaxation of the rules

inhibiting competition between members f the profession.[40] In March 1969 the Board was asked by the Government to keep the remuneration of solicitors under continuous review and it produced two further reports, in November 1969 and March 1971,[41] before being disbanded by the Conservative Government in 1971. The second and third reports broadly confirmed the findings and recommendations of the first. The Board recommended some increases in fees, but the tone of its reports was, in many respects, critical of the profession. Thus, the Board rejected the profession's claim that its earnings had fallen behind inflation.[42] It thought the profession had only itself to blame for losing much lucrative tax work to accountants.[43] It disagreed with the profession's contention that competition must lead to a loss in quality of the work done.[44] It recommended the abolition of the restrictive rule that a solicitor could not engage another solicitor in a different area as his agent for advocacy, but had to employ a barrister instead.[45] It thought an independent inquiry was needed into the division between barristers and solicitors.[46] It recommended that solicitors should be permitted to undercut scale fees.[47]

The Board's philosophy of fostering greater competitiveness was completely rejected by the profession. The profession was, moreover, remarkably successful in the succeeding years in resisting implementation of the Board's recommendations. In fact the only important proposals made by the Board that were implemented were those for *increases* in fees. The Board found that solicitors overall were making substantial 'excess profits' out of conveyancing. It recommended increases at the bottom end of the scale but decreases for the rest. The Government accepted the report in July 1968. But the following March it asked the Board to review its earlier recommendations. In November 1969 in its second report the Board confirmed its proposals,[48] and within twenty-four hours the Government again accepted the report. Lord Gardiner, the Lord Chancellor, in April 1970 produced draft Remuneration Orders giving effect to the Board's proposals, but before they could be put into force the General Election intervened and the Conservatives formed the new government. Lord Hailsham proved more receptive than his predecessor to pressure from the Law Society. His Remuneration Orders, which came into force in February 1971, increased fees up to £3,000 (instead of £2,000 as recommended by the PIB) and eliminated the recommended decreases.[49] The proposal in the Gardiner draft Order that scale fees be maxima and subject to undercutting was dropped. In its final report, in March 1971, the Board said the value of the increases was about £5m. a year. It recommended various changes designed in aggregate to reduce annual revenue by some £6m.[50] These were never made. Instead, in 1972 scale fees were abolished altogether.[51]

The Monopolies Commission, likewise, has had only moderate success in its brushes with the lawyers. In 1967 the Commission was asked by the then Board of Trade to report on the general effect on the public interest of restrictive practices in the supply of professional services. The Commission investigated the restrictive practices of some 130 bodies. But its report did not make detailed criticisms of the rules or practices of any of the professions under review. It was of a more general nature and proceeded mainly by stating broad principles rather than by applying them to the circumstances of any particular profession. The Commission said that its report 'should not lead to judgment being pronounced on the practices of an individual profession until that profession has had an opportunity to answer, in the light of its own circumstances, any specific criticisms which may appear to arise from our general conclusions'.[52] Having reviewed the pros and cons of different forms of restriction, the Commission said there was no reason to suppose that all the restrictive practices currently maintained were justifiable.[53] The probability that restrictive practices contrary to the public interest existed in the professions could not be regarded with indifference. The first step should be to invite the professions to examine their restrictive practices 'in the light of the general guidance' in the report 'with a view to abolishing or amending them, as necessary'.[54] But this would not in itself be enough. The report did not give clear enough guidance to the profession, 'however detached their judgment and however determined they might be to apply the considerations to their own practices'. But the Commission doubted 'whether this detachment and determination could in fact be counted on'.[55]

Professional bodies are, on the whole, sincerely convinced of the desirability of their practices and some of their views on this subject appear to us to be based on an idealised view of their functions. To this extent, and also because an element of self-interest is inescapable in all these matters, we cannot regard them as entirely reliable or impartial judges of the public interest.[56]

The Commission recognised that both the Privy Council and the Board of Trade had certain supervisory functions with regard to registered professions and to certain professional bodies in other professions, but it doubted whether either body was equipped to undertake the functions of independent supervision of, or participation in the control of, the professions. One possibility was that each profession would set up its own body, possibly with a lay chairman, to consider and adjudicate upon complaints and abuses. Another was that conditions of entry and of practice in each profession should be governed by a body equivalent to the existing registration councils, where members would be appointed both by the professional bodies and, directly or indirectly, by the state. Another possibility was that there should be a permanent commissioner or body of commissioners (similar to the Professions Board in Quebec) for all the professions, with the duty of applying the considerations set out in the report to each individual profession, with the necessary judicial and executive enforcement powers for the purpose. The Commission rejected all these ideas. It thought it would be preferable for the Government to refer back to it individual practices for detailed investigation. If, on scrutiny, any were found to be contrary to the public interest, the Government would have power to deal with them by Order in Council.[57]

This last suggestion was accepted. The Secretary of State in November 1970 first asked each profession to consider the implications of the report. Each profession informed him that it had nothing to add to its earlier views. The Law Society, for instance, said that, having, as requested, reviewed again all its restrictive practices, it had concluded that 'all solicitors' restrictive practices have justified themselves over the years as being in the public interest'.[52] The Bar said that certain changes had been made in its restrictive rules but that it did not accept the need for further changes.[59] In July 1974, the Monopolies Commission was asked by the Director of Fair Trading to look at two kinds of restrictive practices as they affected lawyers – restrictions on advertising by barristers and solicitors, and the Two Counsel rule requiring a client also to pay for a junior barrister if he wished to employ a Queen's Counsel. The Commission, as has been seen, reported in July 1976 that the Two Counsel rule and the restrictions on advertising by solicitors were both against the public interest but that the restrictions on advertising by barristers were justifiable. The Report on the Two Counsel rule was accepted and implemented. That on advertising was rejected.[60]

The latest *ad hoc* inquiry into the legal profession is that of the Royal Commission itself. Plainly, this is much more significant than that of either the PIB or the Monopolies Commission. This is partly because of the authority of a Royal Commission as compared with that of any other form of official investigation. Partly it is a function of the all-embracing terms of reference given to the Royal Commission, compared with the relatively limited scope of the earlier inquiries. But perhaps the main reason is the broader composition of the Commission and the fact that it includes individuals who, in a sense, represent the profession. Both the PIB and the Monopolies Commission were felt by the profession to be basically hostile to lawyers. To some extent this was due to what the profession felt to be their undue predilection for criteria of judgment appropriate to the world of commerce and trade. But very largely it was because the profession distrusted the membership. (Mr David Napley, in his 1976 Presidential address to the National Conference of the Law Society, expressed this feeling with characteristic vigour in speaking of the sub-committee of the Monopolies Commission that prepared the report on advertising: 'This group comprised a merchant banker, a professor, two lecturers in economics, an expert in economics and an academic lawyer. All exceedingly able and thoroughly worthy persons, but, it would seem, not one of them with a moment's experience of the dangers and trials of daily practice as a solicitor.'[61])

Of the fifteen members of the Royal Commission, the chairman and eight members are laymen,[62] two are critics from within the profession[63] and four are 'orthodox' lawyers.[64] At least six members of the Commission were, therefore, expert in the problems of the profession before they started. Moreover, a Royal Commission takes so much time to collect its evidence and receives so much of it,[65] that by the time it finishes even the lay members must know an immense amount about the profession. It will be hard for the critics of its report to claim that the members did not sufficiently under-stand the profession and its ethos[66] – especially, of course, if the orthodox lawyer members concur in its conclusions and recommendations.

The right kind of balance between laymen and experts from within the profession has been struck in the Lord Chancellor's Legal Aid Advisory Committee. This committee was estab-lished at the suggestion of the Rushcliffe Committee on legal aid. The Rushcliffe Report stated that, although some witnes-ses had urged a state scheme of legal aid and others had urged that local authorities should control it, 'nearly all agreed, eventually, that a scheme administered by the lawyers would be best'.[67] Attempts were made during the passage of the legislation to secure lay participation in the committees to run the scheme. But the profession protested that this would make them subject to possible political domination and the Law Society was reported to have told the Lord Chancellor 'that if the Plan were amended in this manner, the members of the Law Society would not participate in the Plan's supervision or serve on the [certifying] panels'.[68] A section was actually inserted into the Act forbidding any lay participation in the committees.[69]

But the Rushcliffe Committee did recommend that the responsible minister – the Lord Chancellor – should have an advisory committee of persons knowledgeable in the work of the courts and in social conditions. The function of the com-mittee would be to consider the interests of the citizens and to advise on matters of general organisation. It was also to com-ment on the annual report made by the Law Society on the working of the scheme.[70]

The committee's composition has, of course, changed from time to time since it was established in 1950. But the essential features have remained constant. The chairman and a large number of the members have always been laymen, whilst the secretary has been from the Lord Chancellor's Department. The Committee's reports fall into three main periods. For the first ten years or so it was mainly concerned to spur the Government on to bring the whole of the scheme envisaged in the 1949 Act into effect. The first reports repeated, again and again, complaints as to the slow progress in achieving this objective. By 1960, the whole scheme was fully in force and for the next few years the Advisory Committee expressed itself as fairly satisfied – subject to anxiety that the means test limits were too low and that the legal advice scheme was used too little. From about the sixteenth report, for 1966–7, the Committee became increasingly concerned at the weaknesses in the scheme. In 1967 it invited the Law Society to consider how it could be improved and this initiative led, in due course, to the proposals for the £25 scheme and the Advisory Liaison scheme. Its annual reports showed growing sensitivity to, and concern over, the problem of the unmet need for legal services.[71] In the 1950s and early 1960s the annual reports were terse and hardly discussed issues of policy. From the late 1960s the Committee increasingly became involved, and indeed took a leading part, in the debate over the best means to develop legal services. (The average length of reports in the early 1960s was some 4–5 pages; between 1974 and 1977 it has been 14–16 pages.) It evaluated the various proposals of the Law Society, the Labour and the Conservative Lawyers, and others. It held special conferences in different parts of the country with a wide range of experts on legal services problems. Successive Lord Chancellors have naturally relied on the Committee for guidance, but it has also established itself more broadly as the most authoritative body in the field of civil legal aid. There is no way of evaluating the balance of contribution from lay and from lawyer members, but there is no doubt that the laymen have, over the years, played an important part in the Committee's work.

In June 1976, the Lord Chancellor, Lord Elwyn-Jones, said that, although the administration of legal aid should be left with the Law Society, 'the present legal aid administration is criticised as being too much in the hands of the lawyers and I think there is indeed room for the injection of a strong lay element into it'.[72] This concept was elaborated by the Law Society in its evidence to the Royal Commission. The nucleus of its proposal was the creation of a sub-committee of each of the fourteen area legal aid committees (to be called the Area Legal Services Committee). This committee would include 'a balance of representatives drawn from the Area Committee itself and from other local organisations involved in the provision of legal services including, for example, Citizens' Advice Bureaux, local authority Social Services, Probation Service, courts administration, advisory centres, legal advice and law centres and perhaps the local University'.[73] The size of the committee should be around twenty. Its job would be to have 'primary responsibility for the co-ordination and provision of adequate legal services in its area'. It would be 'in an ideal position to decide where legal services needed supplementing, and by what means'. It could help to establish new solicitors' firms and legal aid law centres in suitable areas. 'It would initiate and encourage the setting up of Duty Solicitor Schemes, CAB Rota Schemes, arrangements for referral of clients from advice centres, the training of voluntary workers, and the extension of arrangements for advice and representation in tribunals.'[74] The Law Society's national legal aid committee would, similarly, be broadened to include laymen. In May 1977, the Law Society, anticipating legislation, invited an experienced CAB worker and the director of social services in the London borough of Brent to join its Legal Aid Committee as participant observers. Also in 1977 it announced the formation of a Legal Services Committee for the Manchester area with lawyers and lay members 'in almost equal proportions'.[75]

There is no doubt that these proposals have considerable value. The establishment at both national and local level of committees of those concerned with the provision of legal services seems obvious sense. The mere fact that the different individuals and organisations in the field of legal services sit around the same table on a regular basis is bound to lead to improved working relationships and the smoothing out of problems that would otherwise go unresolved or even unrecognised. But should such committees be committees or sub-committees of the Law Society? The involvement of laymen in decision-making by the Law Society's bodies does give them a measure of influence. On the other hand, the national legal aid committee and, even more, the sub-committees of local area legal aid committees would be organs of the Law Society, subject to its overall policy direction and control. It would be difficult, probably impossible, for the legal services committees to adopt policies at variance with those of the Law Society. This could be a problem, for instance, in the relationship between the public and the private sector.

According to the Law Society's evidence to the Royal Commission, the tasks for the proposed committees would include not merely 'co-ordination' but also 'provision' of legal services. They would 'help' to establish new firms of private practitioners and law centres. Inevitably, at this stage, the concept lacks the clarity of detailed elaboration. How could the committees 'help', and in particular, would they have control of funds to establish law centres? Who would select the lay and other outside experts – the Law Society or the responsible Minister, or would they be selected by some other method? The history of the relationship between public and private sectors in England suggests that differences of approach are inevitable. How would such conflicts be resolved? In a committee of the Law Society it would be remarkable if they were not normally resolved in line with the policies of the Law Society, which in the past at least has tended to favour its main component element, the private sector. It is unrealistic to expect any organisation to adjudicate even-handedly between two interests one of which is consistent with its main philosophy while the other is not.

The laymen and other experts working on such committees could, therefore, play a valuable role, but in cases of difficulty and conflict they would, in the final resort, be powerless. If there was a problem on which the policy of the Law Society diverged from that of the outside experts, they would either be outvoted in the sub-committee or, at best, the sub-committee would be overruled by some higher Law Society committee. The addition of laymen to national and local legal aid committees might, therefore, be a way of improving their effectiveness and of strengthening their work. It would not be a way of ensuring decisions that reflected the needs of the public interest.

This point was grasped, but not fully met, by the Lord Chancellor's Legal Aid Advisory Committee in its evidence to the Royal Commission. It agreed with the plan that the Law Society should run the legal aid scheme through new legal services committees, consisting of lawyers and laymen, at both the local and the national level. The laymen, it thought, should be not less than one-third of the members.[76] But the

Advisory Committee made no reference to the critical question as to who would appoint the lay members of such committees. The legal services committees, it thought, should make annual reports not only to their parent body in the Law Society, but also to the Lord Chancellor direct and through him to the Advisory Committee.[77] The constitutional relationship between the National Legal Services Committee and the Council of the Law Society would 'need to be worked out in detail'. The guiding principle 'must be that in matters outside the statutory legal aid scheme the Committee is answerable not to the Council, but direct to the Lord Chancellor'.[78] Even without the statutory scheme, however, 'it should be open to any member of the Legal Aid Committee to bring his views to the attention of the Lord Chancellor direct'.[79]

This model is no doubt an improvement on the scheme proposed by the Law Society, but it would be unlikely to work well. If the legal services committees are committees of the Law Society, the attempt to make them at the same time answerable to the Lord Chancellor is bound to create tensions and difficulties. For instance, would the annual reports from the local and national legal services committees be published? If not, much of the benefit of having them would be lost. But if they were published and if they differed in their approach from that of the Law Society itself, it would create an awkward situation, both for the Law Society members on such committees and the Law Society itself and for the lay members. A system based on divided loyalties and responsibilities is never desirable, if it can be avoided. (For an alternative model, see p. 266 below.)

The Labour Party and the Society of Labour Lawyers proposed to the Royal Commission that laymen should be added to the Senate of the Inns of Court and the Bar, and to the Council of the Law Society, as has been done in several Canadian provinces.[80] If these bodies exercised mainly trade union functions such an idea might be inappropriate. But in fact both exercise powers and functions that go beyond a trade union role. In the case of the Bar there is an actual separation between the Senate, which has the general policy-making function, and the Bar Council which carries out the trade union function. On the solicitors' side of the profession the functions of the Senate and the Bar Council are combined in the Council of

the Law Society. It is because both the Bar and the Law Society have duties that must be performed in the public interest
that it is legitimate to suggest that the public interest must be
appropriately represented. The point was made more than a
hundred years ago by the Common Law Commissioners in
the context of the question whether the Inns of Court ought
to be in sole control of the question of admission of members:
'the ordinary immunities of a voluntary society ought not to
be allowed to any body of persons claiming to be the medium
of admission into one of the learned professions. If the Body
is to enjoy this privilege, it is no longer a private association,
but one in which the public has a deep interest, and the proceedings of which, if not adapted to the purposes of general
utility, ought to be made so by the interposition of Law'.[81]
What was true in 1834 in relation to admission to the Bar is
even more true in the latter part of the twentieth century in
relation to the great range of issues in the field of legal services
dealt with by the two branches of the profession.

It appears that this principle is in a sense accepted by the Law
Society – though its full implications have not been seen. In its
evidence to the Royal Commission the Law Society said that it
took the view that 'where matters of broad policy are in issue,
and where decisions on such policy can have an effect upon the
public interest, it may well be appropriate to have lay representation'.[82] On the other hand, the Law Society said it was
'wholly opposed' to lay representation in matters of detail. For
one thing, the laymen would often have difficulty in understanding technical matters. Also, there were problems of
confidentiality and client privilege. There would, for instance,
'clearly' be no part for a layman to play on the Law Reform
Committee of the Council or 'any of the other Committees
which deal with the technical and complicated problems
which arise within the profession'.[83]

These passages show the Law Society struggling unsuccess-
fully to arrive at some acceptable formulation of views on this
currently vexed issue. It is trite that matters of broad policy
lurk in issues of seeming detail. No doubt some items on a
committee's agenda raise greater public policy issues than
others. But the distinction is unlikely to be happily drawn if it
is based on an attempt to segregate matters of detail from the
rest. Only lawyers would think to say that there could clearly

be no role for laymen in the Law Reform Committee. (Apparently the Council of the Law Society forgets that most MPs, who, after all, make the laws, are laymen.) Nor does mention of the problems of confidentiality and client privilege advance matters. If members of the profession can be entrusted with these problems, so, too, can responsible laymen – as is clear from the fact that they are already entrusted with functions in the sensitive field of discipline. The fact is that the performance of most of the main committees of all professions would be assisted by the addition of some sensible laymen.

Clearly there must be limits to this principle. One could not in good conscience ask people to devote their time to helping members of a profession sort out trivial problems. But, provided some balance is kept, the concept could be very valuable – or, at the very least, worth trying out. The reasonable starting-point would seem to be the main committees of the two branches – the Executive Committee of the Senate and the Council of the Law Society. There are fully active retired people in their late sixties or early seventies whose abilities and energies are at present grossly under-utilised. Former Permanent Under-Secretaries, university administrators, leading industrialists, journalists, trade unionists, and others still active in the field such as CAB workers, might be willing to serve without remuneration on a regular basis in the inner councils of a leading profession. These, after all, are just the kind of individuals who are appointed to serve as members of Royal Commissions and similar inquiries. Their function would be to hold up the 'public interest' mirror to the members of the profession. Both branches of the profession have, from time to time, lent themselves to policies, rules and practices that they were later persuaded to abandon as being against the public interest. The chief purpose of having laymen involved in the internal decision-making processes is to reduce this danger. Obviously, the lay element would need to be sufficiently large to be effective. One or two laymen in a body of 70 or 90 would be useless. But six or eight or ten might make an impact, provided that they serve for long enough to master the problems with which they have to deal, and that they have the right to call for the assistance of the staff of the professional body on matters where they want fuller information. They would be on the same basis as to confidentiality as other members of the bodies on which they served. In order to make their independence a reality, they should, of course, be appointed by the Minister rather than by the profession. It is difficult to see any valid objection to the idea. What kind of business would any profession desire to conduct that could not be discussed before responsible laymen, subject to the usual canons of confidentiality?

But however beneficent the effect of lay participation in helping the professions to avoid some of the more egregious errors of judgment that occasionally mar their good name, their power would, of course, be circumscribed. They would be a small minority on the bodies on which they sat. Their struggles would be conducted behind closed doors. No one could know to what extent, if at all, they exerted any real influence. In theory the laymen could be asked to publish a separate annual report. The Bar even suggested that this would be valuable for the laymen involved in the disciplinary process.[84] But, in practice, this would be unlikely to pay dividends. If they agreed with the way the profession conducted itself it would add little to say so. This would be implicit in their participation in the committees to which they had been appointed and their failure to resign. If they disagreed, it would be difficult for them to say so without breaking the code of confidentiality and thus destroying the relationship of trust upon which their role would be based. The more the laymen had fought to uphold the public interest against the arguments of a self-centred profession, the less their annual report could expose the true situation. An annual report in this context would, therefore, be of little value.

A committee of a profession even with laymen members can never be an adequate 'public interest watchdog'. There must therefore be some higher body charged with this responsibility. This is precisely the function performed by the Lord Chancellor's Legal Aid Advisory Committee in the more limited sphere of civil legal aid. This committee costs little to run. It brings together the lawyer and the lay experts. It permits the problems of the day to be analysed and discussed with the relevant vested interests. Being an official body, the Advisory Committee can invite anyone to appear before it. It can hire consultants and could mobilise the research capabilities of the government service. Through its annual report it educates the profession, the minister and his officials, the press, MPs and the public at large, on current issues and problems. As an emanation of the Lord Chancellor's Office, it is serviced by civil servants from that department and through them it can be kept abreast of governmental policy-making, and of the problems faced by the executive. On the other hand, it is independent of both government and the profession. The Minister must often have found his hand with the Treasury strengthened by a report of the Advisory Committee calling for more public expenditure. The advice of the Committee is the more weighty and influential by virtue of the fact that it is not *parti pris* in the battle between the different elements in the legal services field.

In its evidence to the Royal Commission the Lord Chancellor's Legal Aid Advisory Committee suggested that this function should continue to be performed by itself – with terms of reference expanded to include criminal legal aid and all other-publicly financed legal services.[85] It agreed that there was also a case for the Advisory Committee to be given responsibility for reviewing the private sector in legal services, but decided against it for pragmatic reasons of economy of effort. ('On balance, and bearing in mind that the resources available for this work are not limitless, we think that it would be wiser to restrict the jurisdiction of the advisory body to publicly-financed legal services'.[86]) Both Justice and the Society of Labour Lawyers, however, as well as the National Association of Citizens' Advice Bureaux, proposed that a purely advisory committee, with no executive functions should have a remit to cover the whole field of legal services.

It would be most unfortunate if the jurisdiction of the Advisory Committee were expanded to include only publicly financed legal services. The Advisory Committee was surely wrong to say, as it did in its Evidence, that these 'are the services in which the public has the most direct interest' and in which accordingly 'there is the greatest need for public scrutiny'.[87] The overwhelming bulk of legal services are provided to private paying clients, all of whom are members of the public. The inquiries of the Prices and Incomes Board and of the Monopolies Commission, as well as that of the Royal Commission itself, were all focused on private sector work of the profession. If the public is not to have the protection of such external scrutiny in the field of private sector legal services, problems in the field must either be left wholly to the profession itself, which, in the latter part of the twentieth century, is plainly unacceptable, or *ad hoc* inquiries must be set up from time to time, as in the past. A standing review body to take stock of legal services generally on a continuing basis would be infinitely preferable. The members of *ad hoc* inquiries disperse when their report is completed. The expertise they have laboriously built up is lost. A standing body can build on its accumulated knowledge, experience, and reputation.

Nor need the extra burden of work be so formidable. The Advisory Committee would have the benefit of the report of the Royal Commission which would have explored most of the relevant problems. It will take years for the Royal Commission's report to be fully digested, implemented and absorbed into the system. An Advisory Committee with the same broad terms of reference as the Royal Commission itself would be able to act as midwife to the Report – evaluating reactions, considering objections, proposing variations on the recommendations of the Report in the light of later events or further deliberations. The government (as well as the profession) will be greatly assisted by having an expert independent body to advise it on all matters arising from the Royal Commission's Report both in the short and in the long term.

The Legal Services Committees proposed by both the Law Society and the Lord Chancellor's Committee should then be attached to the Advisory Committee as its sub-committees. Their members would be appointed by the Lord Chancellor. Their functions would be those proposed by the Law Society – to identify local needs, to co-ordinate local resources, to initiate or encourage the initiation of new methods of providing legal services and generally to monitor the state of legal services in the area. The Law Society and its Legal Aid Committee (with or without laymen) would perform the executive functions; the legal services committees would report not to the Law Society but to the Lord Chancellor's Advisory Committee, which would receive reports also from those responsible for the publicly funded salaried sector of legal services. Such a structure would avoid the conflicts of interest and divided responsibilities implicit in the schemes proposed by both the Law Society and the Lord Chancellor's Advisory Committee. With part-time members and a small Secretariat it should also be very inexpensive.

Membership of the Advisory Committee would obviously be important. The present Advisory Committee consists of individuals none of whom represent any of the main vested interests in the field of legal services. The Royal Commission, by contrast, has several members who are closely associated with some of the leading protagonists in the debates inside the profession, notably the Bar, the Law Society, the Law Centres Working Party, and the Legal Action Group; as well as others associated with outside groups such as the TUC and the Consumers' Association, and individuals who belong to no recognisable group. Both models have strengths and weaknesses. The two chief objectives are that the Advisory Committee be able to speak for the public interest (for which purpose it must be, and be seen to be, independent of the contending factions), and that it be capable of being both persuasive and effective (for which purpose it must not be so independent of the contending factions as to be unaware of their real concerns or, on the other hand, incapable of getting their agreement to new ideas). The two objectives are, to an extent, contradictory and require delicate handling. The members of an overall advisory committee must, at the least, have the confidence of the different organisations concerned. If not, they will find ways of undermining the committee's authority. On the other hand, the Advisory Committee should be more than a meeting-place for the vested interests. It should be above the struggle. Even members drawn from organisations with vested interests in the field should feel their highest loyalty to the committee rather than to their constituency. The National Association of Citizens' Advice Bureaux (NACAB), which supported this idea in its evidence to the Royal Commission, said that 'it would bring together those most concerned with legal services at both the national and the local level and would permit them to work in cooperation for the improvement of services provided to the public'.[88] The concept of such a broadly-based Advisory Committee is the best hope that proposed solutions to problems will be consistent with the changing needs of the community.

A related question is what, if any, external agency or body should have the duty of approving professional rules of practice, conduct and discipline? The function is an extremely important one. In England, the Master of the Rolls was given the task of approving such rules for solicitors in 1933. There is no way of knowing how successive holders of his office have discharged this responsibility, but even on the improbable assumption that they were unusually sceptical about suggestions made by the Law Society, the Master of the Rolls is unlikely to be an adequate custodian of the public interest in this field. This is because, irrespective of his individual merits, the Master of the Rolls is not involved in legal services debates and is, therefore, likely to be ignorant of many of the relevant considerations.

The Master of the Rolls sees the Law Society, but he sees no one else connected with this important field of public policy. Thus, in the past ten years, during which there has been furious debate over legal services, the present incumbent, Lord Denning, appears not once to have asked to meet with any other group involved in the field. He has, not for instance, had a single meeting on these issues with representatives of the leading organisations in the field – The Legal Action Group, the Law Centres Working Party, the citizens' advice bureaux, or even with the Lord Chancellor's Legal Aid Advisory Committee. He does not subscribe to the *Legal Action Group Bulletin*, the only specialist journal in the legal services field. (The Law Society takes 64 copies and the Lord Chancellor's Office takes 35 copies.) When in 1976 the Monopolies Commission reported on advertising by solicitors, he apparently did not receive a copy of its report (and six months later had not seen it).[89] In other words the Master of the Rolls is outside the mainstream of public discussions in the field. Even if the Master of the Rolls *did* try to see all the relevant groups before approving any proposals put to him by the Law Society, he would not be a suitable person to exercise this function. The authority and dignity of his office does not lend itself to the process of lobbying appropriate to hammering out public policy in this area.

A committee comprising experts in the legal services field is likely to be a much more knowledgeable body for assessing the merits or otherwise of the existing or proposed new rules of practice for the profession. If the task of approving such rules were given to the proposed Advisory Committee, this would compromise its impartiality in its advisory capacity. It would be difficult for such a committee to criticise existing rules if it were also in the position of having to approve new ones. Equally it would be awkward if the committee in its 'advisory' capacity wished to suggest new rules which it would then later have to consider, wearing its 'approving' hat.

Since therefore both the Master of the Rolls and the Advisory Committee are unsuited to the task, a new body should be constituted for the purpose. This might be a small committee consisting, say, of the Master of the Rolls, the Chairman of the Advisory Committee, the Chairman for the time being of the National Consumer Council or the Monopolies Commission, and perhaps two others. Neither the profession nor its critics should have members on the committee, but both should have the opportunity to make representations to it. Thus, there would have to be a procedure for the public announcement of any proposed changes in the rules of professional practice, and a period of time for written observations to be made to the committee. If the committee saw the professional body, there would have to be some formal or informal rule that it would also hear other sides of the argument. Any change in the rules would have to secure the consent of the committee.

The procedure, whatever it is, should obviously apply to the Bar as much as to the solicitors' branch. There is not the slightest justification for subjecting solicitors to external scrutiny in this area whilst leaving the Bar free of it. If external supervision is appropriate for one, it is appropriate for both. The only reason why the solicitors have in the past been subject to such controls and the Bar has not, is the historical tradition that the Bar has some special entitlement to regulate its own affairs. If this belief ever had any justification it certainly has none today.

Developments in lay participation in the running of legal services have occurred in recent years in other countries too. In Sweden, legal aid is run by Public Legal Aid Boards consisting of a lawyer chairman and four other members, of whom two must be laymen.[90] In Manitoba, in April 1977, there were five lawyers and five laymen on the board of the Legal Aid Services Society (with one vacancy).[91] In British Columbia, the Legal

Services Commission in May 1977 had four lawyers and one layman. The fourteen lawyer directors of the Legal Aid Society appoint six laymen to sit with them. The boards of the community law offices (the equivalent of English law centres) were composed mainly of laymen, generally with one or two lawyers out of eight members. An active debate was in progress as to whether laymen should be appointed as benchers of the Law Society.[92] In Quebec, the Commission des Services Juridiques, which consists of twelve members, in May 1977 had, apart from the chairman and vice-chairman, three private practitioners, one law professor, one notary in private practice, two housewives, one teacher and one trade unionist. The Commission appoints twelve-man boards of the eleven regional corporations – at least one-third of whom must be lawyers while at least one-third must be 'persons residing in the region served by the regional corporation'. It has been the practice so far not to appoint more than four lawyers to such regional boards.[93] The Quebec Bar Act of 1966–7 provides that the General Council of the Bar shall include four members appointed by the Quebec Professions Board, two of whom must not be members of any professional corporation. (In May 1977, none of the four were members of any profession.[94])

In Saskatechewan, the Community Legal Services Commission has nine members, of whom one represents the Law Society, and one represents the Federal Attorney General, and one is the Provincial Director of the Commission. Three members are appointed by the Government and three are elected by the chairmen of the local Area Boards. In May 1977, the three Government nominees were, respectively, a psychologist who was also chairman of the Commission, a Queen's Counsel, and a community worker; the three elected chairmen from the Area Boards were two community workers and one minister of religion. The Area Boards have responsibility for ensuring the availability of quality legal services to the local residents. They have an even higher lay content – one, said to be typical in May 1977, had a farmer, two housewives, a community native worker, a member of the National Alcoholics Commission, a corporal in the police, a retired farmer and two persons on social assistance.[95] In Alberta, the governing and policy-setting body of the Legal Aid Society has fifteen members, three of whom are lay – in May 1977, respectively a former court reporter, a professor of business administration and a native Director of Native Counselling Services of Alberta.[96]

In Ontario there is substantial lay membership of the Law Society's Legal Aid Plan In 1974 the Osler Report on Legal Aid proposed that the scheme be run, instead, by an independent corporation with a twenty-man board of whom nine should be appointed by the Law Society and the remainder by the Lieutenant Governor. The Report rejected the Law Society's view that the administration of legal aid should be left exclusively to lawyers. 'The appropriate institutions to govern the Legal Aid Plan ... should resemble a partnership between the Law Society and the public ...'[97] Members of the public 'should have a prominent and significant role'. To this end the nine members of the Board to be appointed by the Lieutenant Governor should 'come from the lay public'.[98] The Osler Committee recommended that the area committees which would decide both on individual grants of legal aid and on policy for their own districts should consist, as to half, of laymen.[99] In Australia, as has been seen,[100] the principle of a mixed body of lawyers and laymen to run legal aid has been accepted even by the Law Society. The recent debate thus has been only as to whether such a commission should be national or state based. The 1978 legal aid report in the Republic of Ireland also proposed that an independent agency consisting of lawyers and laymen should run the legal aid system.[101]

The Law Society Act 1970 in Ontario required that regulations by the benchers required the approval of the provincial cabinet, insofar as they affected matters such as admission, conduct and discipline of lawyers, the publication of a code of professional code and ethics, legal education and the operation of local law associations. The Attorney-General was stated to be 'the guardian of the public interest' on all matters to do with the legal profession.[102] A Law Society council was established to oversee the way the members of the Law Society were discharging 'their obligations to the public and generally matters affecting the legal profession as a whole'.[103] There were to be representatives from the professional body, the law schools, law students and young lawyers and not less than nine lay members appointed by the government. The Council, for

various reasons,[104] was not a success, and two years later it
was set aside. The legislation was amended to provide instead
for the appointment of four lay benchers to the Law Society.
Four lay benchers have been appointed in Manitoba[105] and in
California there are now six lay governors of the State Bar out
of a total of 21.[106]

Concentration on the advantages of lay participation in the
affairs of the profession should not, however, lead to the
assumption that it is any kind of panacea. It may be no more
than window-dressing. Whether it is effective depends on the
quality of the individuals brought in, the extent to which they
are willing to work at learning the problems of the profession,
sympathetically and at the same time critically, and whether
they are willing to express their views. There is always the
danger that they will be bamboozled by the skilful arguments
of lawyers, though this can be countered to some extent by
ensuring that members of the committees in question include
not only laymen but also lawyers who are critical of the
Establishment view. Without such lawyer-critics the lay
members, however strong-minded and independent, are
likely to lack the necessary detailed information to make their
full contribution. Much may also depend on the arrangements
for the servicing of such committees and whether the laymen
have enough briefing to understand the issues when they come
to meetings. From this point of view there is an advantage if at
least some of the lay members come from organisations that
have experience or views on the relevant issues.

There is also the problem that 'familiarity breeds affection,
understanding and ultimately acquiescence'.[107] There is no
guarantee that the watchdog will necessarily bark at the right
time. There are various techniques for helping to keep such
bodies up to the mark. The periodic appointment of new
members, the requirement of annual reports, continuing
debates in the legal and in the lay press, all help. The effectiveness of such bodies is a function partly of their membership
and partly of the climate of opinion in which they work. If well
constituted, the combination of representatives of the profession together with some lawyer-critics of the profession and
intelligent layman should be better than the 'straight' members of the profession on their own.

9 The Need for Legal Services

Problems of definition

There is today widespread agreement that, in spite of the recent proliferation of new techniques for bringing legal services to the community, there remains a considerable 'unmet need for legal services'. The Lord Chancellor's Legal Aid Advisory Committee stated in 1974, for instance, that, while the position varied from one area to another, it had little doubt that 'there are many people whose legal rights are, for a variety of reasons, at present going wholly by default'. Some were unaware that they possessed such rights, others realised it but did not know how to obtain help in enforcing their rights or lacked the money or the ability to do so. The geographical distribution of solicitors was 'very ill-suited to serve many of the poorer and more disadvantaged sections of the community'. Moreover, there were areas of the law, 'notably those relating to housing, landlord and tenant matters and welfare benefits', where expert advice and assistance were urgently needed but 'often hard to come by'.[1] Evidence to the Royal Commission repeated this theme over and over again.

But when one comes to attempt a definition of concepts such as 'the need for legal services', or 'an unmet need for legal services', or even 'a legal problem', formidable and indeed insoluble difficulties appear.[2] A legal problem may be defined to include any difficulty which can be solved by reference to law. Alternatively, it might be defined much more restrictively to mean problems that are in fact taken to lawyers. By this standard a social security problem would not qualify as a legal problem. Again, it may mean those matters that lawyers, or at least some lawyers, at any given time think *ought* to be taken to them for solution. Some lawyers would identify the social security problem as 'legal', others might not.

The 'need' for legal services will depend on many variables.

The need of the rich man to redress a legal wrong may be less than that of the poor man afflicted by the same problem. Perception of need will be influenced by the availability of resources. Thus, in an affluent society willing to make relatively lavish provision for legal services to the poor, the need may be for lawyers in the lowest courts, whereas, in a country with a less developed legal aid system, the lower courts may be regarded as unimportant by comparison with the greater need for lawyers in the higher courts which normally deal with more important cases. Ingenious lawyers will find new concepts and new rights in existing law and thereby create new needs. The more legal services are provided, the more the community may perceive the need for lawyers. (It has been found that if the number of hospital beds is increased, the average length of stay in hospital increases too.)[3] Moreover, the concept of need presumably ought to include some sense of a hierarchy of values. The need for a lawyer of a man who faces a charge carrying the death penalty is different from that of another whose kettle proves to be defective. Both can validly be said to need a lawyer, but the disparity between the extent of their needs is so gross as to require some stratification of levels of need. At the extremes this can be done without difficulty. But how is one to reach agreement as to the relative need of one man for reinstatement in his job, against another's claim for compensation for loss of the sense of smell, or a third man's protection against eviction?

One tenant faced with a notice to quit may throw it into the fire, believing (rightly) that he is fully protected by the Rent Acts. Another does so because he believes (wrongly) that he is legally protected, but he comes to no harm because the landlord fails to follow through with proceedings for possession when the tenant sits tight. Did either have a 'need' for legal services? Or what of the tenant who leaves on receipt of the notice to quit because he believes (rightly) that he is not protected and he prefers to take the opportunity of reasonable alternative accommodation which has just presented itself rather than stay to fight a costly, losing battle? Should he first have seen a lawyer? From a certain point of view it would, of course, be reasonable to say that in any of these situations the tenant would have benefited from the additional peace of mind of having legal advice. Yet, there is room for differing views as to whether there was or was not a need for legal advice. The answer may be influenced both by one's capacity for empathy and by the value one places on the intervention of lawyers.

It cannot be assumed that a person with a legal problem has any need for legal services if by that is meant the services of lawyers. He may be best advised to take his problem, at no cost, to the local citizens' advice bureau, his trade union official, or a well-informed friend or relative. He may indeed be best served by doing nothing at all and allowing the problem to go unresolved, or to solve it by quite different means. A study of the behaviour of businessmen in Wisconsin has shown, for instance, that they seldom used legal sanctions to settle their disputes.

> Disputes are frequently settled without reference to the contract or potential or actual legal sanctions. There is a hesitancy to speak of legal rights or to threaten to sue in these negotiations. Even where the parties have a detailed and carefully planned agreement which indicates what is to happen if, say, the seller fails to deliver on time, often they will never refer to the agreement but will negotiate a solution when the problem arises apparently as if there never had been any original contract.[4]

Even a lawyer faced with a legal problem in his own family may decide that the time, trouble and emotional energy required to take up the cudgels on his own behalf are simply not worth while.[5] (How many lawyers have not even made a will?) Life is short. Most people have more agreeable ways to spend their time than in pursuit of legal remedies. It would be a sorry society where the citizen who suffered a legal wrong reached instinctively for his lawyer, like a gunfighter for his six-shooter in the Wild West. As has been said, it may be better for society that a tenant whose roof is leaking fetches a ladder rather than a lawyer.[6]

Whether needs for legal services are 'unmet' poses yet further problems. Are such needs met regardless of the skill of the particular lawyer, or the cost or the delays? What of the need implicit in the fact that in many legal confrontations one side is wholly inexperienced while the other is a 'regular' who knows the ropes? Marc Galanter has explored the relative advantages of the 'repeat player' as against the 'one shotter'.[7] This form of need occurs typically in personal injuries litigation with the private individual up against an insurance company. It is not only that the insurance company understands the process better than its opponent. This disadvantage can, to an extent, be redressed by ensuring adequate legal services. But the outcome of the case is less critical for the repeat player who can take the long view and thus take risks which the individual who only has his one case cannot afford.[8] This form of need or pressure is endemic in the situation, as are other discrepancies between the parties, such as differences in wealth, power and resources. A sensitive measure of unmet need might take some account of the actual scope of a lawyer for influencing the situation. Thus, a client's need for a lawyer to help him meet a criminal charge might be said to be greater where he is innocent and the evidence against him is relatively thin, than where he is guilty and the police have a cast-iron case.

Studies of the problem of unmet need

Because of all these difficulties it is impossible to measure the exact extent of the need for legal services or of the unmet need for such services. There is no way in which such an attempt could be made intellectually respectable. As the Lord Chancellor's Legal Aid Advisory Committee said in evidence to the Royal Commission, 'We do not believe that there is a precise degree of unmet need which can be established by scientific enquiry. It must to a considerable extent be a matter of impression and opinion, varying with the view taken of such matters as the proper function of lawyers, the legal system, other social services etc.'[9] But there are nevertheless many ways in which the problem of the need for legal services can be investigated. Such research is a very recent development. Although there were a few earlier studies of the subject in the United States,[10] the literature of the subject effectively dates from about 1965.[11] The main work has been done in the United States, the United Kingdom, Australia and Holland.[12]

One form of such studies has been to investigate whether those who appear in the courts are legally represented. In any system of trial the unrepresented person may be handicapped by not having someone to speak for him and the more so in an adversary system where the burden of making one's own case lies on the parties. Obviously, the effect of such disadvantage is likely to be especially serious in criminal cases. A number of studies in England in the late 1960s and early 1970s showed, for instance, that, contrary to popular belief, the majority of those sent to prison by magistrates were unrepresented.[13] Empirical study showed that defendants in criminal cases pleaded guilty more often when they were unrepresented than when they were represented[14] and that those who were represented were twice as likely to be acquitted.[15] Three surveys in national insurance and supplementary benefit tribunals showed that there was a dramatically higher success rate for those who were represented than for those who were not.[16] It is, of course, true that all these studies were conducted without a control group and, in theory, the results might therefore have been due to differences between the cases rather than to the presence or absence of representation. But, rightly or wrongly, it was generally accepted that they did demonstrate one kind of 'unmet need'.

Another approach has been to go into the community to ask citizens about their legal problems. The most common technique of such studies is to take a check-list of 'legal problems' and ask members of the community which, if any, they have experienced, and, if so, what they did about them. It is obviously important in conducting such research not to alert the respondent to the fact that he is being asked about his response to legal problems. If he knew this it might slant his replies. He is, therefore, asked simply whether he has had, say, an accident, or has divorced his spouse, or has ever been threatened with eviction. It is then possible to evaluate the extent to which different members of the community do have problems that by one or another definition may be said to be 'legal'.

The main study in the United Kingdom was carried out in three poor London boroughs by the writer with two colleagues. We asked our 1,651 respondents whether, in the period from 1960 to 1967 (when the interviews were carried out), they or a member of their family had had any of sixteen different types of legal problem ranging from matters that are commonly taken to lawyers such as accidents, buying or selling a house, making a will, or matrimonial problems, to others less commonly perceived as requiring the help of lawyers, such as social security problems, having a landlord

who did not do the repairs, unsatisfactory consumer transactions or being in arrears with instalment payments.[17]

The most common problems reported were repairs not
done by the landlord (310 of the sample, or 19 per cent, had
had one or more cases of this in the seven-year period covered
by the survey); purchases of defective goods (270 or 16 per
cent); accidents (243 or 15 per cent); making a will (183 or 11
per cent); and a debtor who would not pay (124 or 7 per cent).
Only 74 (4 per cent) reported having bought a house in the
seven-year period, but it must be remembered that the sample
was expressly drawn from the three poorest boroughs in
London. Even granted, however, that the sample was not
fully representative of the whole population, it does appear
that legal problems are not *all that* common. This is confirmed
by the recent joint American Bar Association and American
Bar Foundation study which was based on a fully representative national random sample. Although no less than 67 per
cent of the sample had at some time consulted a lawyer, the
average number of legal problems reported by the sample was
only 4.8 over a lifetime.[18] No doubt this was an underestimate
– as a result of failures of memory and the fact that the respondents were being questioned from a long check-list of 'legal
problems' which would nevertheless have omitted some. But
these figures are helpful in giving some, albeit vague, con-
creteness to the quantification of legal problems.

But do the poor have fewer legal problems than the rest of
the population? In the study of the three London boroughs we
found that those eligible for legal aid and those outside the
legal aid limits reported about the same proportionate number
of problems in six out of the sixteen problem categories:
taking a written lease, having a landlord who failed to do the
repairs, being threatened with eviction, being behind on
instalment payments, receiving less than one's right amount of
social security and 'other court proceedings'. In matrimonial
problems and juvenile court cases those eligible for legal aid
reported distinctly more problems. In the remaining
categories of problem those ineligible for legal aid had more
problems. The greatest differences between the two groups
were on house buying, purchasing defective goods and having
a debtor who would not pay. (See Table 9.1, below, for actual
figures.) The striking fact about these results, however, was

not that there were differences between the income groups but that in most problem categories they were not all that great and that the poor reported a large number of legal problems of all types. These results are the same as those of other studies in Holland[19] and the United States.

Thus in the ABA–ABF study it was found that there were considerable variations amongst respondents as to the incidence of legal problems – 8 per cent had none at all, while, at the other extreme, 1 per cent had more than twenty problems each. Males had slightly more than females (5.2 on average compared with 4.5), whites reported four problems for every three reported by blacks/latinos. The higher the education, the more the legal problems – possibly because they had more problems but possibly because they were more likely to notice them. Also, the higher the income, the more problems were reported. Thus the 40 per cent of the population with the highest income accounted for the same number of problems as did the lowest 60 per cent. But a great part of the difference was due to the relatively much smaller number of problems relating to the acquisition of property and estate planning reported by the poor. These were overwhelmingly the most common reasons for seeing a lawyer and they were disproportionately problems reported by the richer respondents. There was no difference as between rich and poor in regard to the incidence of reports of marital problems, employment problems in regard to collecting wages or job discrimination, consumer problems, personal injuries or violations of constitutional rights.[20] The study showed, therefore, that there were some differences between respondents in number and kind of legal problems reported, but that these differences for the most part were not all that great, and, moreover, that the poor had a substantial range of legal problems just as did those who were less poor. The fact that there were some differences between young and old, black and white, rich and poor, educated and less well educated, male and female, is hardly surprising. But it is much less significant than the fact that all types and conditions of people do have legal problems.

Information about the existence of a type of problem does not in itself, however, reveal the extent of 'needs' for legal or other advisory services. In most instances it is necessary to go on to discover something more about the problem before one can say that there was, or probably was, or at least may have been, a 'need for advice'. Thus, in our London study we tried to formulate standards for assessing need. In the case of those who reported accidents, for instance, we took as having been in need of advice only those who thought that someone else was at least partly responsible for the injury. (We therefore excluded for this purpose those who wrongly thought that they were wholly to blame, all of whom certainly ought to have had legal advice, but who could not usefully be asked what they had done to get advice since, by definition, they had almost certainly done nothing.) In the case of those whose landlords had failed to do repairs we took as in need of advice those who had reported what we regarded as 'serious repairs left undone or done badly or done unreasonably slowly'. For 'taking a lease' we regarded as in need of advice only those who said they had been presented with a written lease for signature. In buying a house we treated everyone as automatically in need of advice; but for 'purchase of defective goods' we categorised as in need of advice only those who reported a serious fault, noticed within one month of purchase and where complaint to the vendor had brought unsatisfactory results. Obviously these decisions as to what constituted a need for advice in the sixteen problem categories were not only conservative but also highly artificial, suitable, if at all, only for research purposes.

In the study in three London boroughs, having determined, by our necessarily crude and inadequate measure, who was 'in need of advice' we then looked to see how many had taken advice and from whom. We tried also to ascertain the pattern of referrals – though in many instances respondents appeared not to have any clear recollection of how they had reached their ultimate 'main adviser'. In 270 out of 450 cases (60 per cent) the main adviser had been a solicitor; in 48 it was one or other arm of the council, in 30 cases it was a citizens' advice bureau and in the remaining 98 cases it was one of a large number of 'other' advisers – MPs, relatives, friends, the police, bank manager, accountant, surveyor, trade union official, court clerk, doctor, marriage guidance service, probation officer, hospital almoner, etc. (In 4 cases the identity of the main adviser was not known.)[21]

Table 9.1 (published here for the first time) shows the

proportion in each problem area who took advice from a solicitor or other adviser and the proportion who took no advice. The table is, in effect, a summary of the whole story of 'unmet need'. The definition of 'need for advice' was very conservative,[22] yet the table shows that in every problem category except that of buying a house less than half of those who had such a need saw a solicitor and that in most categories the majority saw no-one. Making every necessary allowance

Table 9.1

Percentage of respondents defined to have a 'need for advice' who took advice

	Took advice from solicitor	Took advice from some other source	Took no advice	Total
Buying a house	96	4	–	100 (74)★
Making a will	48	12	40	100 (175)
Other court proceedings	43	9	48	100 (46)
Accidents	41	17	42	100 (181)
Matrimonial	40	10	50	100 (52)
Taking a lease	30	3	67	100 (54)
Taking debtor to court	28	29	43	100 (21)
Attempted eviction	25	43	32	100 (60)
Debtor would not pay	19	9	72	100 (47)
Attempt to evict	17	33	50	100 (18)
Instalment arrears	7	4	89	100 (28)
Employment	4	34	62	100 (80)
Social security problems	3	16	81	100 (74)
Repairs undone	1	32	67	100 (123)
Defective goods	–	8	92	100 (27)

★ Actual numbers of respondents shown in brackets.

Source: B. Abel-Smith, M. Zander and R. Brooke, *Legal Problems and the Citizen*, 1973 (Heinemann, London); figures based on re-working of data in Table 32, p. 154, and Table 35, p. 158.

for margins of error, the table surely demonstrates as clearly as anything could that the problem of unmet needs for legal services (or other advisory services in the legal field) is very extensive.

This evidence is supported by an important new study (unpublished at the time of writing) by the Oxford Centre for Socio-Legal Studies which investigated a national sample of 1,177 cases of injury sufficiently serious that the victim was unable to carry on with his normal daily activities for two or more weeks.[23] Most lawyers would probably agree that such a person is 'in need of advice'. Accidents are, of course, a field in which lawyers are very active. Even though there are some firms that are great specialists, there cannot be many firms of solicitors that do not have some work in the personal injury field. Even if they do not handle it themselves, they would certainly know where to send someone who came in with such a problem. Table 9.2 shows that no less than 767 (65 per cent) of the entire sample did not even think of the possibility of claiming compensation. A further 10 per cent who thought of the possibility took no positive action of any kind. It was not always the case that because a victim failed to think in terms of compensation he did not perceive an element of fault on the part of another in causing the accident. Many of the victims were, for instance, passengers in traffic accidents who were unwilling to take any steps because the driver was a friend or relative. Although they stated that the accident was completely the fault of the driver of their car, they excused their failure to think of claiming by saying, 'Well, my injuries weren't really that serious' – even when on the face of it the injuries were quite substantial. There seemed to be an implicit assumption that injuries must be very serious to warrant invoking the law – an alien and aggressive force – against a friend or relation. This constraint was not, however, felt so much in relation to an unknown driver or an impersonal employer. On the whole, however, those with the serious injuries were more likely to seek advice than those with the less serious.

Those who failed to take advice gave a familiar catalogue of reasons – the trouble involved, fear of the cost, doubts about the likelihood of success, ignorance of the possibility of making a claim and the like.[24] Of those who took their cases to a

Table 9.2

Fate of injury cases causing two or more weeks of interruption
of activities (Total in sample: 1,177 cases)

	No	%
Did not consider possibility of a claim	767	65
Thought of possibility but did nothing about it	148	12
Took positive action of some kind	262	22
Contacted a solicitor personally or by proxy	237	20
Solicitor began proceedings	200	17
Settled out of court	151	13
Settled in court	5	0.4
Still undecided	58	5

Source: Paper read by Hazell Genn of the Oxford Centre for Socio-
Legal Studies at Legal Action Group Seminar, 20 May 1977.

lawyer, no less than 92 per cent had discussed the possibility of
making a claim with someone else beforehand, and of those,
no less than 73 per cent stated that the idea of obtaining
compensation first came from another person. More than
two-thirds of those who contacted a lawyer said that the first
impetus to get in touch with a lawyer had come from another
person, often a trade union official. The role of the trade union
officials was not confined to helping with cases of industrial
injury. Often they gave advice to members injured outside of
the work situation. The police, workmates, and local medical
practitioners also played a definite role in influencing an individual's decision to claim, or indeed in planting the original
idea. These are all people with whom the victim of the accident
has contact in the ordinary course of events after an accident.
They do not have to be sought out. Moreover, to judge by
events, the pre-sifting by the lay adviser prior to consultation
with a lawyer was remarkably accurate. Of the 237 cases in
which someone contacted a solicitor, the solicitor started formal legal proceedings in as many as 200, or 84 per cent. This
suggests that a solicitor is only approached when it seems
clear, from other advice, that a claim is desirable. In a survey in
Scotland, more than half of the 651 respondents thought that
solicitors spent at least half a day or more in court on an

average day. Only about one person in 200 thought a solicitor spent no time at all in court on an average day.[25] This might help to explain why so many people appear reluctant to use a lawyer. They associate the solicitor primarily with litigation and they do not want to get involved in so drastic an activity. In a study of the handling of consumer problems by eighty householders in South London the researchers found that most respondents thought that one went to a solicitor in order for him to go to court. Few realised that solicitors undertook negotiations.[26]

The Oxford researchers found that of those who actually contacted a solicitor, only a quarter knew at the outset of the legal advice scheme and less than a half knew of the legal aid scheme. Fear of the cost may have been, as they indicated, an important factor in the decision of those who did not see a solicitor, but the majority of those who saw a solicitor did so in spite of ignorance of the availability of the legal aid scheme. The Oxford study, therefore, confirms that in an area in which the legal profession has a substantial number of clients, the great majority of those who suffer fairly serious injuries do not take – or even consider taking – advice.

The proportion of the whole population who have used lawyers at one time or another is not, in fact, small. In the Scottish survey it was 44 per cent, in the American ABA–ABF study it was 66 per cent, in a study in three poor areas in Sydney, Australia it was 64 per cent.[27] In the first English study to be conducted with a national random sample, 19 per cent of the total (22 per cent of the men and 16 per cent of the women) had seen a solicitor within the previous twelve months.[28]

Most empirical studies prove that the lower economic and social groups use lawyers less than the more affluent.[29] Thus the study in England of use of solicitors based on a national random sample showed that 30 per cent of social classes A and B had dealings with a solicitor in the previous twelve months, compared with 26 per cent of Class C1, 17 per cent of Class C2 and 12 per cent of Classes D and E.[30] The same was found in the survey in Scotland. ('The higher the social class the greater the extent of contact with a solicitor. The average household income of users of solicitors is considerably higher than the average for non-users'.[31]) This was the case, too, in the study

THE NEED FOR LEGAL SERVICES   285

conducted in the three London boroughs. As Table 9.3 shows,
we found that those proportionately most likely to use a
solicitor were the more affluent, those in the higher social
classes, and the better educated. Those in work used solicitors
more than those not in work; men more than women; those
under 65 more than those over 65; and the married more than
those who were single, divorced or widowed. In each of these
seven breakdowns the differences were statistically highly
significant. It is interesting that the greatest differences of all
emerged not on social class or income, but on educational
background. The joint ABA–ABF study showed precisely the
same. Overall, lawyers where consulted 'for slightly less than
one third of all the problems encountered that reasonably

Table 9.3
Percentage who saw a solicitor in seven year period by
personal characteristics

	Income			Sex		Age	
Not entitled to legal aid	Entitled to contributory legal aid	Entitled to free legal aid		Male	Female	Under 65	Over 65
29	19	13		23	18	23	15

Marital status				Employment		Social Class					
Married	Single	Divorced	Widow	In work	Not in work	I	II	III1	III2	IV	V
24	19	18	15	23	18	53	44	28	17	20	16

Education		
Higher qualification	'O' or 'A' level	No qualification
76	36	20

Source: B. Abel-Smith, M. Zander and R. Brooke, *Legal Problems and the Citizen*, 1973, Table 36, p. 159.

could be called legal problems'.[31a] It found that those with higher incomes, and those who were white and male, used lawyers more than those with lower incomes and those who were black.[32] But the greatest contrast in use of lawyers emerged through comparing groups of different educational background. The authors said: 'The increase in mean use by education is not only consistent over all educational levels, but intensifies dramatically as education increases beyond high school and especially after college.' (All these differences were, however, less marked for those under 35.[32a])

But the fact that overall the middle classes use lawyers more than the poor does not establish that the poor do not use them. The London study showed that those eligible for legal aid use lawyers relatively about as much as do those outside the legal aid limits. (These figures were not included in the book because of the small numbers – they are published here for the first time.) But, in spite of the small numbers, they make the point. Those eligible for legal aid were 60 per cent of the sample. Table 9.4 shows a total of 301 visits to lawyers – of which 158 (or 52 per cent) were by respondents eligible for legal aid. Inspection of the details discloses that in most problem categories the poorer respondents saw lawyers in proportion to the numbers in that income group who reported having had the problem. It is true that this was not a random sample of the national population, and possibly such a study would show different results. (Considering that the sample was drawn from the three poorest boroughs in London its composition was not in fact as different from that of the whole population as might have been expected – the figures, with those for the sample given first, were: Social Class I, 3 per cent (3 per cent); Class II, 9 per cent (15 per cent); Class III, 50 per cent (48 per cent); Class IV, 21 per cent (23 per cent); and Class V, 13 per cent (8 per cent).) But, the ABA–ABF study which *was* a national random sample shows much the same. Real property and estate planning were easily the most common problems taken to lawyers, and the mean income of those users of lawyers was high ($12,000 to $13,000).[33] But in all other problem categories the mean income of users was significantly lower – in employment problems, for instance, it was half that in real property matters (below $6,000) and in marital problems and crime it was well below (under $9,000 in

Table 9.4

Numbers seeing solicitors as main adviser by income
(The percentages show the proportion in that income group
who reported having had the problem)

	Those whose income made them eligible for legal aid %	Those whose income put them outside the legal aid limits %
Taking a lease	7 (2.9)	8 (3.2)
Landlord did not do repairs	1 (20.5)	0 (18.7)
Threatened with eviction	8 (3.6)	5 (4.1)
Attempt to evict	2 (0.9)	1 (1.9)
Buying a house	17 (2.0)	40 (8.6)
Purchase of defective goods	1 (14.6)	2 (22.1)
Own instalments in arrears	1 (4.5)	1 (5.2)
Debtor would not pay	3 (5.6)	4 (10.1)
Taken to court for debt	1 (1.6)	5 (3.0)
Death in the family	18 (*)	15 (*)
Making a will	33 (9.0)	24 (13.3)
Accidents	40 (13.4)	23 (17.8)
Social security benefits	0 (5.8)	1 (5.8)
Employment problems	2 (4.8)	1 (7.9)
Matrimonial problems	14 (3.7)	5 (1.9)
Other court proceedings	9 (2.9)	8 (2.7)
Juvenile court proceedings	1 (2.6)	0 (1.9)

* figures not available.

Source: B. Abel-Smith, M. Zander, R. Brooke, research conducted for *Legal Problems and the Citizen*, 1973.

both cases).[34] In the study in Sydney, Australia, respondents who had consulted a lawyer did not tend to be markedly more affluent than those who had not.[35] We know, too, that in England the poor do use the legal profession massively in at least three problem areas – crime, where virtually all those who appear in the crown courts are represented on legal aid;

divorce, where most petitioners qualify on the more rigorous civil legal aid eligibility screening; and personal injury cases, about half of which are supported by legal aid. In 1976–7, legally aided plaintiffs recovered some £44m. in damages – mainly in personal injury cases.[36]

Attempts to explain the causes of unmet need

What is it, then, that explains why some who need professional or equivalent advice seek it, whilst others do not? Many have said that it is primarily a matter of poverty. One reason for this conclusion is that studies have focused on the problems of the poor rather than investigating the problem in the whole population. (Our own London study, even called the London Law and Poverty Study, is a good example.[37]) Having made the assumption that unmet need for legal services primarily afflicted the poor, the researchers found their theory confirmed when they discovered that in some respects the poor used lawyers less than the middle classes. They then jumped to the conclusion that the fact of poverty was the prime cause of the disadvantages suffered in the legal system by the poor. (The analogy with research into the causes of crime is, perhaps, relevant. It was common at one time to draw from the fact that most criminals were poor the conclusion that poverty was the cause of criminality.) The theory that poverty is the chief cause of the unmet need collapses in the face of the empirical evidence that those who need advice and do not seek it include many who are not poor and those who do seek it include many who are poor.

A more sophisticated theory is that it is not so much a matter of poverty in the strict sense but rather of poverty in the more general, socio-psychological sense. Thus, Jerome Carlin and Jan Howard, in their major 1965 article 'Legal Representation and Class Justice',[38] argued that the unmet need for legal services was something that affected primarily the poor because they lacked 'legal competence'. They were less likely than the more affluent to recognise their problem as legal, they were less likely to have the psychic and physical energy to take up the cudgels on their own behalf, they were less likely to know how to find a lawyer and, if they did get to a lawyer, they were more likely to have their case refused. Moreover, lower-class persons were handicapped by not normally having organised groups to help them and to alert them to their rights. This approach is obviously a considerable advance on the crude equation of unmet need with the simple fact of poverty. But, as an explanation of unmet need for legal services it is equally unsatisfactory. The facts on which the Carlin–Howard thesis was based are probably more or less true in most Western countries. But, they do not justify the conclusion, for the conclusion leaves out of account two other sets of relevant facts. One is that in some fields many poor persons do get the help of lawyers, whilst in others, many who are not poor lack such help. The second is that use of lawyers varies enormously as between different kinds of problem. In other words, the kind of problem seems to cause much greater differences in lawyer use than the kind of potential client. In the London poverty study it was found that lawyers were used to a greater or lesser extent for house purchase, court proceedings, accidents, matrimonial problems, vetting of leases, making a will and attempted evictions. They were hardly ever used for instalment arrears, employment problems, juvenile court proceedings, social security problems, landlord's repairs undone or defective goods.[39] The ABA–ABF study reported very much the same. Lawyers were used mainly for purchase of property, settlement of estates and matrimonial problems, but hardly at all for the great majority of problem categories.[40] The Australian study found the same.[41] There is also the Wisconsin study of the behaviour of businessmen (above, p. 275) to suggest that non-use of lawyers to solve 'legal problems' is not necessarily evidence either of poverty or of 'legal incompetence'. The theory of legal incompetence must, therefore, be discarded as inadequate.

A third approach is that of Leon Mayhew and Albert Reiss in their 1969 study based on a random sample of the Detroit population in which they put forward what has come to be called the 'social organisation' theory.[42] They recognised that wealth, social class, race, sex, age and other similar factors might all play a role in determining whether someone sought the help of a lawyer to solve a legal problem, but none of these, either singly or in aggregate, was the real explanation. The heart of the matter, they thought, was that 'attorney client relations occur in the context of a complicated network of social organisation'.[43] It was important to know something about 'the character of routine, organised activity within the legal agency, the social organisation of the institutional arena subject to legal regulation'. Out of the social links between these spheres flowed a routine pattern of contact between the legal agency and the public. Legal practice was both specialised and stratified. The stratification of access to resources in the population paralleled this differentiation and stratification of legal practice. The demand for legal services in certain areas (e.g. estate, tax, criminal and contract problems) produced a response from competitive lawyers who moved in to fill vacant niches so that distinctive patterns of practice emerged in various problem areas. There were also distinctive patterns of use of legal services which reflected variations in the patterns of problems experienced in various structural locations (such as by communities or by race or ethnic groups), and corresponding differences in the social organisation of legally relevant activity.

Thus, Mayhew and Reiss argued, property was the social institution most likely to require the intervention of a lawyer. 'Property as an institution is socially organised so as to bring its participants into contact with attorneys. . . . The purchase of legal services is often necessary to acquire, maintain, and increase property.'[44] The legal profession was organised to service business and property interests; the social organisation of business and property were highly legalised. 'Out of this convergence emerges a pattern of citizen contact with attorneys that is heavily orientated to property.'[45] The data supported the proposition that 'a substantial portion of the income differential in contact with attorneys is accounted for by the greater participation of high income persons in the institution of property'.[46] Thus, 77 per cent of white respondents and 51 per cent of black respondents were home owners. Home ownership had brought blacks into contact with the legal profession – 36 per cent of blacks had seen a lawyer about buying a home, a figure virtually the same as the 37 per cent of whites who had seen a lawyer for this purpose. But the passing on of property was less embedded in the black than in the white culture, which explained why 20 per cent of whites but only 5 per cent of blacks had seen a lawyer about settling an estate. On the other hand, family structure in the black community was more fluid (and therefore more prone to the creation of 'legal problems'). This could explain why, among blacks, problems of divorce, alimony and child support were the second most common reason for seeking the services of a lawyer, whereas amongst whites they were only the seventh most common reason.[47]

The 'social organisation' theory[48] is a much richer and more fruitful approach than that of either the 'poverty' or the 'legal competence' theory. It focuses attention on a wider range of detail of relevant human action. But it, too, fails to explain important relevant facts that must somehow be accommodated if the theory is to be acceptable. (A theory which conflicts with valid empirical data has to be discarded. Exceptions do not prove rules, they disprove them.) The main problem with the 'social organisation' theory is that it does not comport with the fact that, even in fields in which there is a strongly developed pattern of contacts between lawyers and clients, considerable numbers of those affected by that problem do not use lawyers. Our London study showed that those who 'needed advice' and did not seek it from any source in traditional areas of legal practice amounted to very high proportions of those who were in that situation of need: suing for debt, 72 per cent of the sample; making a will, 71 per cent; taking a written lease, 66 per cent; evicting a tenant, 50 per cent; matrimonial problems, 50 per cent; court proceedings other than any mentioned separately in the questionnaire, 48 per cent; accidents, 42 per cent.[49] Indeed, the only problem area in which the proportion of those in need not seeking advice was lower than 31 per cent was that of buying a house, where everyone had advice and in virtually all cases from solicitors. The results of the London study are now amply supported by the findings of the Oxford inquiry into a national random sample of accident victims with fairly serious injuries. Only a small proportion of those who suffered the injuries even considered making a claim. Similarly, in the ABA–ABF study in many problem categories a considerable proportion of respondents who reported problems took no advice.[50] Why?

The two main facts that have to be explained are: first, that there are some problem areas in which the legal profession functions effectively and on a considerable scale, but in which substantial numbers of those affected by the problem do not seek the help of lawyers; and, second, that in many more areas there is no effective pattern of contact between lawyers and clients. Both these facts have been solidly documented. The best approach is to focus on each problem area separately since each has its own special circumstances. The ABA–ABF studies showed that some very common legal problems had a high incidence of lawyer use, others did not.[50a] Conversely, some infrequent legal problems had a high frequency of lawyer use. Thus, in the field of house buying, in England at least, almost everyone has until now used a lawyer, probably because of the widespread belief that the job is well-nigh impossible or at least extremely irksome and dangerous for a layman to undertake.[51] Lawyers are used to a substantial extent in criminal cases because it has over the past few years become the policy of the judges, the Lord Chancellor and the Home Office and has been generally accepted in the legal and political culture, that those charged in magistrates' courts of the more serious offences, and those appearing in higher courts, whether or not the case is serious, should get legal aid. If they do not think of applying, it will be suggested by the duty solicitor, or the defence lawyer, or by the court clerk or a police or prison officer, by a fellow prisoner, or, failing all the above, by a friend or relative. The more legal aid is granted, the more the word appears to get around. In the matrimonial field a vast number of impecunious abandoned wives have managed to get legal aid, probably because they wanted to take the very serious step of seeking a divorce sufficiently strongly to find out about the possibility of getting help with the costs. Again, it would probably be known by social workers, marriage guidance workers, local authority officials, and housing managers that legal aid can normally be obtained by a deserted wife.

Such facts help to explain why, in some fields, there is a pattern of contacts between lawyers and laymen. They do not explain why lawyers are not used by large numbers of those affected by the problem. A vital clue here may prove to be three findings of the Oxford study (p. 283 above): first, that of those who took their accident cases to lawyers, as many as 92 per cent had discussed the possibility of making a claim with someone else beforehand; second, that of those, no less than 73 per cent said that the idea of making a claim came first from that person; and third, the fact that the solicitors initiated a claim in 84 per cent of the cases brought to them. The hypothesis suggested by these findings is that the most significant difference between those who take advice and those who do not, at least in many problem categories, may turn out to be the fact that one group has contact with a knowledgeable lay person whilst the other does not.

If so, the hypothesis has the merit of according with common sense. Going to a solicitor is probably regarded by most of those who contemplate it as being about equal in attraction to seeing the dentist – it may be necessary, but it is hardly likely to be a pleasant experience. (If anything, visiting a dentist may be seen as less disagreeable since the pain is usually short-lived and predictable, and the cost, under the National Health Service at least, is usually slight). Many people will need help in diagnosing that their situation is 'a legal problem' on which the help of a lawyer could be valuable. But even those who appreciate this may still require a good deal of persuasion before they decide to take the step of actually seeing a lawyer.

The Oxford findings on the importance of lay intermediaries is supported by other empirical evidence. In a study of no-fee or low-fee cases in New York, Philip Lochner found that a crucial role in bridging the gap between clients and lawyers was played by intermediaries of many different kinds – doctors, employers, union officials, city councillor, neighbours, friends, fellow members of organisations such as the Elks, or just a brother-in-law.[52] In a study of personal injury suits, again in New York, it was found that the presence of an authority figure substantially increased the chances that a person would make a personal injury claim.[53] But much more research is needed on how people come to use lawyers or other advisers for legal problems and to what extent attitudes to lawyers, knowledge of the law, age, sex, educational level and other personal characteristics affect the tendency to seek help for legal problems.[54]

It seems likely that formal means of facilitating access to appropriate advisers will prove to be less important than informal systems. Thus research suggests that friends, relatives and neighbours are much more frequently used sources of referral to lawyers than advertising, official referral lists or even lay advisory agencies. In the study of the three London boroughs, for instance, those who knew of a firm of solicitors within an hour's travel distance of home or work were asked how they had got to hear of them. Of 815 respondents, 261 (32 per cent) said they saw the name-plate as they passed by; 252 (31 per cent) said they were given the name by a friend, relative or neighbour; and in 92 cases (11 per cent) the solicitor had acted for the respondent or his family before. Three-quarters of the total, therefore, had used informal means of knowledge. Only 107 said they had the name from a formal source – employer (39 cases), trade union (31), citizens' advice bureau (24), free legal advice service (8), or the police (5). (There were 103 cases in which the respondent said he did not know or in which he specified miscellaneous other sources of advice.)[55] In the Australian Law and Poverty survey, 78 per cent of those who had been to a solicitor found him through informal contacts – friends or relatives, or because he had acted for the respondent or a member of his family before.[56] In Mayhew and Reiss' Detroit study a similar pattern emerged. Friends, relatives and neighbours (including in some cases lawyers) were the actual or anticipated source of referral in 73 per cent of cases, compared with 'formal organisation referral' in 17 per cent and 'mass society information' in 10 per cent.[57] In the Oxford accidents study, friends and relatives were the source of advice to see a solicitor in 75 cases, trade union officials in 72 cases and miscellaneous others in 26 cases. In the ABA–ABF study too relatives or friends were 'the primary source for the information on which lawyer selection was based'.[57a]

If lay intermediaries are as important as these findings suggest in steering clients to legal advisers, a number of conclusions (some hopeful, others less so), would seem to follow. First, various suggested strategies for improving access to legal services need to be further tested. Advertising (both institutional and by individual firms), education about legal matters in schools[58], placing lawyers in areas where at present there are few, and community education (lectures, leaflets, posters, notices on summonses and other court documents, discussion programmes on radio and television, use of 'legal problem' situations in popular radio or television series, etc.) may all help. Thus people might be alerted by such means to the fact of the legal aid scheme and the local availability of lawyers and other advisers, and they might be given some elementary grasp of some useful 'rules of thumb'. Thus it would be helpful if victims of accidents realised that one can get damages even if one is receiving pay from an employer, that a claim is not barred merely because one was partly to blame for the accident, and that the law may in any event take a less severe view of fault or blame than that of the layman. Victims of serious accidents may normally get advice, but there must be very large numbers of people who do not realise that even for relatively minor injuries the law gives them the right to claim a few hundred pounds in damages. Similar misconceptions no doubt exist in many other fields.

But the problem is not simply to reduce ignorance but even more how to make people conscious of the fact that, in the given situation, advice from a lawyer (or some other appropriate near equivalent) would be worth having. Leon Mayhew has said that the critical question is 'the public sense of the relevance and effectiveness of legal advice and representation'.[59] Those who feel the need to see a lawyer normally manage to find one – irrespective of social class or income. But in a high proportion of legal problem areas the ordinary citizen has no awareness that lawyers might be able to help. (In Mayhew's Detroit study he found that over a third of the sample reported problems with government agencies. Of those who thought this was among the two most serious problems they had ever experienced, only 13 per cent had consulted a lawyer. Even though this was an area which respondents described as being one of 'vindication of lawful rights', 'only a minuscule proportion regarded lawyers as a fruitful source of help or redress'.[60] Mayhew concludes that programmes designed merely to help people find lawyers, e.g. through referral lists and the like, are of limited potential.

More is needed, therefore, than general advice, information, or improved education. In many cases reluctance to go to a lawyer is only likely to be countered effectively by verbal advice, or even persuasion, from a trusted source. How, then, can one improve the capacity of lay intermediaries to help potential clients to take the crucial first step of taking competent advice?

Insofar as most lay intermediaries are, and will likely remain, friends, relatives or neighbours, the problem does not admit of any easy answer. But there may nevertheless be benefits to be obtained from improving the capacity of official or formal agencies to recognise legal problems and to direct potential clients to suitable advisers. The precise method for achieving this will depend on the problem area and the potential resources of lay advisers, who might, with some modest further training, be mobilised to provide the crucial advice and counselling. England is in a fortunate position in having a large number of lay agencies that either do already, or could, provide such advice on a substantial scale. (Chapter 10 is devoted to the subject.) In the matrimonial field, social workers, marriage guidance counsellors and citizens' advice bureau workers, if properly trained, are probably best placed to give the necessary guidance. In the field of landlord–tenant disputes, the counter clerks in the housing department of the local authority and rent officers are the obvious sign-posts to lawyers. In employment, trade union officials can play this role; in cases that come to court it could be the court clerk or even the judge. In the accidents field, police officers, doctors, hospital almoners and even nurses might be used to communicate basic information about the desirability of taking legal advice for anyone who has suffered personal injuries. Experimentation and research would presumably show what are the most cost-effective methods of tackling the problem.

In some fields progress will be very difficult – especially those where the citizen does not in the ordinary course come into contact with any official agency or lay adviser. Moreover, even the knowledge that he might benefit from advice will not always persuade the 'victim' to seek such advice. Research in London has shown, for instance, that many tenants in very run-down premises who were often paying too much rent were ignorant of the existence of the rent officer for unfurnished premises and of the rent tribunal for furnished premises – both of whose chief role is to fix rents. At the end of the interview respondents were asked whether, in the light of the information gained, they would now try to get their rent reduced. They were also given the address to which to go. A significant number (91 out of 402) said they would. Yet only 5 actually went.[61] In other words, even people who are in need of a service, and who get so far as to say they will go (where the service could bring benefits out of all proportion to the minor trouble involved and, moreover, costs nothing), may, in the end, find any number of reasons for not going. If research shows this to be true of a large proportion of those affected by the problem, it may because the system is not well adapted to their needs. (If one is concerned to have fair rents fixed it may be better to send the rent officer round to every home rather than to wait for tenants (or landlords) to apply.) But if the system is the best that can be devised and if those affected are aware of the different ways of getting appropriate advice and nevertheless choose not to take such advice, it has to be accepted that they are exercising their right to decide for themselves what is in their own best interests.

In a celebrated article in 1963, Professor Charles Reich of Yale suggested that such interests as rights to welfare benefits, job and retirement rights, and civil rights would only be adequately protected when lawyers came to see them as property rights.[62] It may prove truer to say that before lawyers can see them as property rights, clients or at least their lay advisers must. When the clients come in, the lawyers will soon enough master the relevant law and make themselves available – subject, obviously, to appropriate arrangements by legal aid, pre-paid schemes, etc., for paying for such services. The search in each case must be to find a way to promote the role of the informed intermediary, the person who can discuss with the potential client the desirability of making a claim, and who can help him to the starting line. In the fields where the ordinary citizen does use lawyers – other than for buying and selling of houses – the differences in the degree of use of lawyers between income groups are relatively slight. In most areas of legal problems neither the poor, nor the middle classes, nor the rich use lawyers to any great extent. This is as true in the United States as in the United Kingdom. If one thinks that lawyers can make a difference to the solution of the large number of legal problems on which they are not now consulted, there is here a great unmet need for legal services and a little-tapped source of work for the lawyers and those who help them.

10 Alternatives to Lawyers

The effective handling of legal problems does not necessarily require the use of lawyers. The English legal profession, unlike its counterparts in some countries, enjoys no monopoly over the giving of legal advice and there are many different kinds of non-lawyers who handle matters that require legal expertise or knowledge. Accountants, for instance, have for years competed with solicitors in the tax field, and banks in the probate field. In fact, in recent years, the use of non-lawyers has developed as a major new source of assistance and advice. A study of the phenomenon by the National Consumer Council (NCC) has described the recent explosion of lay advisory agencies as forming, in effect, a new social service.[1] In the 1960s, the main sources of such advice were citizens' advice bureaux, trade unions and newspapers, plus unadmitted staff in solicitors' offices.[2] With the exception of the last, these have all expanded and there are now, in addition, consumer advice centres, housing aid centres, specialist centres in such fields as money matters or planning problems and a large and constantly changing number of 'neighbourhood advice centres'.

The main reason for this great growth in advisory services, as the NCC Report said, is of course the growing complexity of the modern welfare state. ('Society has become so complex that the collective experience and advice of friends and neighbours is no longer enough to draw on. Specialist knowledge and skills are needed to cope with an increasingly forbidding bureaucractic apparatus.'[3]) Thus, the NCC's 1977 report, *Means Test Benefits*, listed forty-five separate means-tested schemes ranging from supplementary benefits to rent allowances, from school meals to spectacles. Each scheme was encrusted with its own rules and regulations. A layman could not know whether he was entitled to one or other of these benefits. 'He clearly has to rely on advice from someone who does know, and unless the nature of government suffers a remarkable change, the same need will become more, rather than less, marked in the future.'[4] This does not, however, explain why from the mid–1960s the importance of this need was increasingly recognised. The need had, after all, been there throughout the twentieth century. For whatever complex of reasons this period of modern history found in many countries significant movements aimed at improving the citizen's access to information to enable him to 'get his rights'. In England there is a rich mix of organisations and institutions that express this trend.

Unqualified lawyers in solicitors' offices

For more than a century solicitors have used non-solicitor staff to perform lawyers' tasks on a massive scale. Unadmitted clerks, formerly known as managing clerks and today as legal executives, today provide something around a quarter of the profession's total man-power for work on legal matters.[5] This represents a decline over the past fifteen years from something over half[6] but it still represents an enormous dependence on staff who lack the full training of lawyers. According to the Prices and Incomes Board, in 1967 the average firm of solicitors had 2.2 partners, 0.5 assistant solicitors, 0.8 articled clerks, 2.6 unadmitted members and 7.8 clerical staff.[7] In 1977 the comparable figures were 3 partners, 1 assistant solicitor, 2 unadmitted members (legal executives or other equivalent), and 1 articled clerk, plus 1 other fee earner, and 13 clerical staff (10 full-time and 3 part-time). Unadmitted persons were therefore just over 40 per cent of the fee earners in 1967 and some 25 per cent in 1977.[8]

The work done by legal executives obviously depends on the skills and training of the individuals concerned and the needs of firms. Much of it is in the fields of conveyancing, probate work and litigation. In theory, legal executives work on relatively routine tasks under the supervision of qualified solicitors. In practice, many legal executives take substantial responsibility for their work and much of this work goes well beyond routine functions. They commonly take the initial instructions from clients, undertake interviewing of witnesses, instruct counsel, handle ordinary transactions unaided and draft bills of costs. As has been seen (p. 190 above), advertisements asking for legal executives commonly indicate that the applicant should be able to work with little or no supervision. Legal executives have, until recently, not had a right of audience in open court though they could appear in chambers before Masters and High Court judges, registrars and county court registrars. They can, therefore, appear in county court small claims arbitrations (see p. 324 below). But, as a result of a long process of negotiation with the Law Society and the Lord Chancellor's Office, the Administration of Justice Act 1977 gave the Lord Chancellor power to grant persons in 'relevant legal employment', including legal executives, rights of audience in county courts. The first directions under the power envisaged rights of audience for the very limited category of unopposed applications for adjournment and applications for judgment by consent. But although this is a modest step, it is obviously the thin end of the wedge. In its evidence to the Royal Commission, the Institute of Legal Executives urged that they should have greater rights of audience in county courts and magistrates' courts and proposed that legal executives be recognised as 'legal representatives' in tribunals. It also proposed that its Fellows be allowed to administer oaths and affirmations and to take statutory declarations, that solicitors should be allowed to form profit-sharing arrangements with legal executives and to place the names of Fellows on their note-paper. (It has already been seen (p. 191 above) that the Institute did not, however, ask that the solicitors' monopoly over conveyancing be broken.)

These growing ambitions reflect the obvious hope of legal executives to be recognised as, in effect, the third branch of the legal profession. (If this happened, the Bar might be said to be the upper-middle-class element, solicitors the middle-middle-class branch and legal executives the lower-middle-class section of the profession.) This is a relatively rapid recent development. In 1949, examinations were started for Solicitors' Managing Clerks. In 1963 the old style 'managing clerk' gave way to the new title Legal Executive and a new system of examination and qualification came into effect with the founding of the Institute of Legal Executives. There were three classes of members – Fellows, Associates and students.[9] In 1977 the entry requirement for students was raised from one 'O' level in English Language to four 'O' level passes at Grade C or three 'A' level passes. In 1977, too, the Institute applied to the Privy Council for a Royal Charter (though the Law Society opposed the application).[10]

Considering the thrust of these developments, it is not surprising that there should be some tension between legal executives as a group and the solicitors' branch. (The Chairman of the British Legal Association, a right-wing ginger group in the profession, warned in December 1976 of the 'thrusting ambitions' of the legal executives. The Institute, he suggested, had 'grown too big for its boots'. The standard of education demanded for legal executives was 'deplorably low'. If the claims for extended rights for legal executives were granted, 'it must serve to damage (the) profession and the public and will ultimately lead to a profession so debased in its standards of education ... as to make it, on the one hand, not worth entering and on the other, no longer a shield for the true freedom of the peoples of these islands'.[11] A century ago the tone of the Bar towards the ambitions of solicitors was not dissimilar. In 1847 a legal writer said that barristers, who 'acquired greater learning, greater intellectual acumen and a higher and more thoughtful tone of mind' then was to be found in the solicitor class should not be expected to entertain the possibility of being in one profession with persons whose 'mental activity is spent in the transaction of a multiplicity of trivialities'.[12]

Whatever role for legal executives is envisaged by the Royal Commission, it seems both likely and desirable that it will continue to be an important one. The fact that lawyers have used unadmitted personnel to conduct a great part of their work obviously reflects the fact that much of it is within the competence of less than fully qualified practitioners. The public ought to benefit from their use in two ways. First, charges should be lower than if the work were done by fully qualified, and presumably higher paid, persons. Second, insofar as less qualified persons handle work that lies within their competence, the time of the more skilled members of firms ought to be reserved for the more demanding or exacting tasks. Efficiency demands that tasks should be matched so far as possible to the abilities of those available to perform them. To use a qualified solicitor on work that can be handled adequately by someone with lesser qualifications is a waste of abilities. A contributor to the recent debate in the *Solicitors'*

Journal on the aspirations of legal executives suggested that this happened on a considerable scale. ('The real problem is that many solicitors themselves are content to abuse their training and abilities by spending much of their time dealing with run-of-the-mill matters which any competent Fellow or even able Associate of the Institute of Legal Executives could manage to do as well.'[13]) It is obviously difficult to determine by rule what should be done by solicitors and what by unadmitted personnel (including articled clerks). The fewer the restrictions, the easier it is for firms to use unadmitted persons to the fullest extent of their capacities.

Citizens' advice bureaux

Citizens' advice bureaux (CABs) were started at the outset of the Second World War. They were planned when it became clear in 1938 that there was a real risk of war and that, if it happened, ordinary people would require help and guidance. Within months of the outbreak of the war there were some 1,000 bureaux in existence. Funds came from central government. At the end of the war central funds ceased, but to some extent they were continued by local authorities. The number of bureaux gradually declined in the 1950s to around 400. In 1960, however, central funding started again when the Ministry of Housing and Local Government resumed payment of a grant to the central office, and in 1963 this was supplemented by a grant from the Board of Trade in response to a recommendation of the Molony Committee on Consumer Protection. This grant has continued ever since. (The Department of Prices and Consumer Protection is today the chief funding department.) In December 1973, the Minister for Consumer Affairs announced a grant of nearly £1.5m. spread over five years (1974–9) in addition to the normal grant. With increases for inflation the actual sum paid is about £2½m. In December 1966 there were 473 bureaux. By April 1976 it was 674. In March 1977 this number had increased to 710. In the late 1960s a target was established of having a bureau in every town with a population of over 30,000. This has now virtually been achieved.[14] Inevitably, urban areas are best provided for, but experiments are now being tried in rural communities with mobile bureaux, telephone links, and trained workers holding sessions in different identified places. In very scattered communities local citizens with some limited information are mobilised to act as 'signposts' to help people with queries to contact the nearest bureau.

All bureaux are registered as members of the National Association of Citizens' Advice Bureaux (NACAB). Registration requirements specify minimum standards regarding organisation, staffing, training, opening-hours and premises. The country is divided into nineteen areas each served by a team headed by an area officer. Local bureaux in each area send representatives to the area committee and delegates from the area committee make up the National Council which is the chief policy-making body. Bureaux meeting collectively in the annual meeting are the ultimate authority for the service.

Funding is mainly from local moneys. Central funds go chiefly to the headquarters organisation, NACAB, though part of the recent special development grant has been used for improvement and expansion of local bureaux. Apart from this grant, NACAB in 1975–6 had an income of only £330,000, more than four-fifths of which came from central funds. Local bureaux are financed by local authorities. This, in theory, threatens the independence of the bureaux, but in practice it has not seemed to have this effect. One reason may be that, until recently, CABs have tended to provide information in a neutral way without 'taking up the cudgels' for their clients. As this changes (see p. 318 below), the problem of independence may become a more difficult one.

There are more than 9,000 workers who staff the CABs, of whom more than 95 per cent are voluntary workers. CAB workers, therefore, provide an enormous unpaid man-power resource who have to commit themselves to do at least one session per week. Training is by a combination of basic introductory courses, on-the-job training and formal courses organised at area level. A variety of courses are run – for organisers, for experienced workers, for less experienced workers, on new legislation or on particular problems. Most bureaux organisers are paid and full-time, as are also the staff of NACAB.

In addition to general advice, bureaux increasingly offer specialist advice facilities – on consumer, financial, housing, welfare rights, planning or architectural problems. Some have salaried lawyers (see p. 81 above). Some have tribunal advocacy services (see pp. 318–20 below).

The central office provides an information service for all bureaux. There is a monthly issue of information on new legislation, regulations, CAB procedures and organisation. New official leaflets are sent out with background material together with amendments and additions to existing material. The loose-leaf service (Citizens Advice Notes or CANS) can be purchased by other agencies. Individual bureaux can also ring or write for help with individual queries. The NACAB department is staffed by trained officers with a wide range of contacts and knowledge.

CABs handle a vast range of problems free of charge and without regard to means. The number of inquiries in 1976–7 was an estimated 2.9m. of which some 20 per cent were categorised as Family and Personal, 17 per cent related to Housing, Property and Land, and 17 per cent to Consumer matters, Trade or Business.[15] The special survey conducted in 1977 for the Royal Commission on Legal Services showed that about a third had some legal component.[16] This was a more or less consistent pattern in all bureaux, irrespective of the area they served. (The percentage of 'legal problems' reported by bureaux varied from a low of about a quarter to a high of about a half. Since they were diagnosed as 'legal' by the mainly lay workers rather than by lawyers the estimate is likely to be distinctly on the low side). This means that CABs could be receiving a million or more inquiries a year with a legal component. Of these, bureaux themselves dealt with 5.3 out of 10, referred 3.6 out of 10 to lawyers of one kind or another, and sent the remaining 1.1 out of 10 to other specialists.[17]

There is general agreement that the citizens' advice bureaux are a crucial element in the whole legal services picture. There is also empirical evidence that the ordinary citizen not only uses them on a massive scale but has confidence in them as a source of advice on legal problems. The National Consumer Council conducted a national survey in 1976 involving a random sample of 1,021 people. They were asked whether they had ever been in touch with any advice agency and if so, which. One in three had been to some form of agency for advice and of these, half had been to a CAB, far more than to any other agency.[18] In the survey of the three poor London boroughs, of the 1,651 respondents there were 361 who at one time or another had visited a solicitor[19] and 266 who at one time or another had visited a CAB.[20] When all 1,651 respondents were asked what was the best place for the ordinary citizen to go to with a legal problem, the CAB was mentioned more frequently than any other place or type of person. (34 per cent mentioned the CAB, compared with 26 per cent who said a solicitor in private practice or at a legal advice centre, 11 per cent who said the Town Hall and 17 per cent who said they did not know.)[21] In view of the general popularity of the CAB service it is not surprising that witness after witness in evidence to the Royal Commission suggested that CABs be regarded as of central importance in the provision of legal services and that they be supported by appropriate additional funding to enable them to play an even more significant role in the future.

Trade unions

The unions have for many years provided very considerable legal services to their members. The bulk of such services relate to problems arising out of employment – accidents at work, breaches of the contract of employment, dismissal, entitlement to social security benefits and the like. Many unions also cover claims arising out of accidents caused whilst members are travelling to and from work, and some help with criminal prosecutions connected with employment. The TUC's evidence to the Royal Commission drew on the results of a survey of all affiliated unions conducted in 1977 (half, representing about 77 per cent of all union members, replied to the questionnaire). The survey showed that 14 of the 55 unions that replied covered accidents not arising in connection with employment and 8 unions had a general advice service which offered at least one advice session free of charge or for a nominal fee. One union ran a service available twenty-four hours a day.

Unions vary greatly in the way in which they use lawyers. The initial processing of problems and potential claims is invariably handled by union officials – branch secretaries, shop stewards, divisional or regional officials, or headquarters staff, depending on the nature of the problem, the size of the union and the system used. Of the 55 unions that replied to the

TUC's 1977 questionnaire, less than half had either a separate legal department (17 unions) or a full-time officer with special responsibility for administering legal services (4 unions). Many of the smaller unions left this entirely to the General Secretary or the Assistant General Secretary (18 unions) and in other unions (15 in the sample) the administration of legal services was carried out by other full-time officers either at head office or at regional level, as part of their general duties.

Where legal departments existed, their size varied. Ten had staffs of less than 5, five had a staff of between 5 and 10, and two had departments of between 15 and 20. The overwhelming majority of the staff had no legal qualifications: only 5 union legal departments of the 55 had any qualified lawyers – though one union with 280,000 members (the National Union of Teachers) had seven qualified legal staff. (The majority of those with legal qualifications had only law degrees and were not either barristers or solicitors.) The precise functions of legal departments vary from union to union. In some they perform only administrative tasks – examining applications for legal assistance and referring all but the obviously hopeless to outside solicitors. In some unions they continue to take an active part in assisting the solicitors in the subsequent negotiations; in others they leave it to the solicitors to handle the entire matter. In some unions, by contrast, the legal department itself investigates and negotiates settlements in accident claims, gives advice and information on employment and social security law and undertakes representation in tribunals. In unions that have no legal department, the tendency is for the officials responsible to pass cases on to solicitors, but some also give advice. Full-time officials play a particularly important role in the field of tribunal cases.

Most unions (29) stated that they provided some training for full-time staff on their role in the field of legal services. Twelve ran their own courses, eight said they used courses run by the TUC and a further five used both their own and courses run by the TUC. Most unions provided information about the law and changes through circulars, bulletins, TUC materials and subscriptions to appropriate journals. Some unions had produced their own detailed guides to certain areas of the law.

Solicitors were used mainly in the field of accident cases. The decision as to whether to use a solicitor was normally left to the discretion of the full-time official handling the case. Most unions negotiate some claims directly, but one disadvantage of this is that the union cannot recover its own costs, whereas the costs of solicitors can be claimed on a settlement. The Winn Committee on Personal Injuries Litigation doubted whether it was wise for unions to rely on their own non-lawyer staff for the handling of common law claims for damages. ('We are sure it is wise to expedite the placing of a claim in the hands of a solicitor, because we are convinced that expertise of a high order is required for the proper conduct of negotiations or litigation about personal injury. We believe more sophistication is called for than is likely to be possessed by Union representatives.'[22]) The validity of this view as an overall assessment has, however, been challenged by the two authors of a 1977 survey of trade union legal services who commented that their evidence did 'not bear out this assertion in relation to several unions'.[23] The greater use of solicitors was made by smaller unions with least resources of their own.

The majority of unions (40) used no more than three different firms of solicitors, but the firms they used might instruct agents for cases distant from their own offices. Some unions, however, preferred to use a large number of firms of solicitors: nine used between 5 and 20 firms, one union used 30 firms and three unions said they used a different solicitor in every major town. In general, a large part of the unions' legal work was handled by a small number of firms which provided a special expertise in the relevant fields of law.[24]

There is no breakdown of the volume of work handled respectively by non-lawyers and by lawyers working for the unions. A survey conducted in 1966 showed that the unions collected over £10m. in damages for their members in personal injuries cases. The LSE survey in 1971, based on 49 unions covering 96 per cent of all members of unions affiliated with the TUC, suggested that trade unions at that time processed about 100,000 accident forms as potential claims, negotiated some 50,000 of these as claims and collected damages amounting to some £20m. More than 95 per cent of the claims were settled before action.[25] The TUC's survey for the Royal Commission showed that in 1974 the 37 unions which replied to this part of the questionnaire (representing 35 per cent of all union members) handled 50,000 accident forms and recovered some £33m. in damages. The figures for *all* the unions must, therefore, now be well in excess of £50m.

There are no recent figures for the number of cases in which unions provide representation in tribunals. The LSE survey based on 1971 figures estimated the number as some 10,000 a year.[26] Since then the importance of tribunal work has considerably increased, particularly as a result of the coming into force of the Equal Pay Act 1970, the Sex Discrimination Act 1975 and the Employment Protection Act 1975. In national insurance tribunals and industrial tribunals, trade unions provide the bulk of all representation. Professor Kathleen Bell has estimated that in national insurance local tribunals, of the small proportion of appellants who were represented (four-fifths were not), three-quarters were represented by trade union officials.[27] Solicitors are used for the most complex cases, but the overwhelming bulk of representation by unions in tribunals is through their own officials. The tendency to prefer union officials is no doubt strengthened by the fact that, unlike cases in court, the costs of the successful party in tribunals cannot be recovered from the loser. The unions therefore have to pay the lawyers even when they win the case.

Legal services for their members are seen by trade unions as an important service. It is thought to aid in recruitment and retention of members and generally to reinforce union consciousness. The 1971 LSE survey estimated that the costs of providing union legal services was in the region of £½m. in direct administration costs to the unions plus legal fees of £1.35m.[28] The TUC 1977 survey showed that the estimated administrative costs of just 13 unions were some £211,000 and that fees paid to solicitors by a total of 30 unions were £1.1m. (The administrative costs in both the LSE and the TUC surveys did not take account of the proportion of wages and other expenses of full-time officers and their staffs attributable to the time spent on legal work.) The TUC evidence to the Royal Commission said that the cost of providing legal services now represented a considerable element of total union expenditure. In several unions it was in the range of 4 to 6 per cent of the total budget and in some instances it was even higher. The general expansion of union legal services was said to be 'in line with the generally increased concern about greater need for legal services'.

Consumer advice centres[29]

In October 1969, the Consumers' Association opened the first consumer advice centre in shop-front premises shared with a local CAB in Kentish Town in London. The CAB handled consumer complaints in the ordinary way; the consumer advice service dealt with pre-shopping advice and information. The centre was used by some 40,000 people in the two years it was open. The Consumers' Association then campaigned to get local authorities to set up comparable facilities. The first local authority centre was established in July 1972 in Greenwich. Several other London boroughs quickly followed suit and from 1974 authorities outside London joined in this development. At the end of 1975 there were 74 local authority consumer advice centres (CACs), including 10 mobile units. By the end of 1976 there were between 100 and 120, following the provision of an exchequer grant of £1.4m. in December 1975. In July 1977 the Minister of State announced that some £3.5m. was being made available to cover the costs of the 120 consumer advice centres and over 250 local price surveys.[30]

Most centres are run in shop-front premises by consumer protection departments of local authorities – otherwise known as trading standards offices (formerly the 'weights and measures inspectorate'). In some areas the local authority relies on the CAB to provide front-line consumer advice services. The service often provides pre-purchase information and handles post-shopping complaints. In some areas pre-shopping advice includes detailed consideration of the shopper's individual circumstances. According to the 1977 report of the National Consumer Council, 'Some advice centres confine themselves to giving aggrieved consumers an explanation of their rights and information about how to exercise them. Others are prepared to act as conciliators, seeking to resolve disputes by bringing trader and consumer together to negotiate a mutually acceptable settlement.'[31] Where this cannot be achieved 'most centres will then give the consumer information on how to take the complaint to the county court'. Some centres limited the help they gave to providing information about procedure and form-filling; others went further and actively assisted the complainant to process complaints in court.[32] A survey of fifty-one such centres in 1975 showed an average annual intake of more than 8,000 queries per year. On this basis it was estimated that the centres as a whole were handling some 500,000 cases a year.[33]

Housing advice centres[34]

The first specialist service directed at the housing field appears to have been the Catholic Housing Aid Society, founded in 1956 with the intention of helping working-class families to buy houses. The Seebohm report on Social Services[35] in 1968 suggested that topics on which the public needed more advice included landlord–tenant law, rent fixing, public health requirements and building society facilities. It proposed that local authorities should 'provide a centre for housing advice and guidance to which the public as well as workers in statutory and voluntary agencies can turn'.[36] In 1970, the first housing advice centres were opened in London – by Lambeth local authority and by the Catholic Housing Aid Society and Shelter which jointly opened the Shelter Housing Aid Society (SHAC) in South Kensington. In 1971, the Minister of Housing wrote to twenty-nine local authorities known to have special housing difficulties recommending that they set up housing advice centres. Various authorities responded to this call. In a Circular on homelessness in 1974 the Department of the Environment said that housing aid centres should be an integral part of any housing authority's homelessness service, and if authorities had not already got a housing aid service, they should go about establishing one. In June 1976 it was estimated that there were some 160 such centres, two-thirds of which were run by local authorities and one-third of which were independent.[37] The independent centres were financed mainly by voluntary organisations such as Shelter. The National Housing Aid Association, founded in October 1976, has more than 300 members. Its objectives are to promote a comprehensive service of aid, advice and information directly accessible to the general public on housing matters, the expansion and improvement of the housing stock and housing policies and procedures, that would 'ensure for everyone adequate and secure accommodation at a price they could afford'.

The function of the centres is to provide assistance to individuals with housing problems, to collect more general information on housing problems and to work on policy problems in the housing field. SHAC had some 8,000 clients in

its first year. Leeds Housing Information Centre, established
in 1970 with three advisers, handled 11,000 inquiries in the
first year. In 1976 the number of inquiries had risen to 19,000,
though the staff was still only three. Lambeth HAC received
26,000 inquiries in the first year; Hammersmith dealt with
14,500 callers in the first year.[38]

Specialist 'lay' advice centres

A significant development in recent years has been the proliferation of specialist organisations devoted to producing
advice. Examples include: the Claimants' Union for recipients
of supplementary benefits,[39] MIND in the mental health field,
the Public Health Advisory Service (PHAS) in the public
health field,[40] Chiswick Women's Aid for battered wives,
Money Advice centres, the Child Poverty Action Group
(CPAG), and Release. The Child Poverty Action Group, for
instance, with a national office in London and some sixty
branches throughout the country, has provided an expert
service in the field, principally, of social security benefits. It
was started in 1965. In 1977 it had an office staff of ten including one lawyer. It publishes pamphlets, leaflets and guides,
organises courses and lobbies MPs, Ministers and the media.
But in addition to activities devoted to improvement of the
law and its procedures, CPAG also has a service of advice to
individuals. To handle individual inquiries it established the
Citizens' Rights Office (CRO) as a separate part of its own
function. The CRO handles phone enquiries on individual
problems from any part of the country from individuals or
from those who advise them – social workers, community
workers and the like. It has some 10,000 such calls a year.

Release was started in 1967 as a national advice service in
response to the great rise in the numbers of young people
charged with drug offences. It receives upwards of 400 queries
a week, or more than 20,000 per year. It has a staff of full–time
counsellors plus voluntary workers. Drugs cases have always
been the main focus of the service but advice is given also on
immigration problems, on difficulties faced by tenants, squat-
ters or welfare claimants. The organisation has a mass of
information on the courts, the police, social services and medical and psychiatric facilities. It provides introductions to sympathetic lawyers with special expertise in the fields covered by

the organisation. The lawyers used by Release are chosen not only for competence but also for their willingness to turn out in the middle of the night to see a client in the police station and to give advice on the telephone at night as well as by day. It has a comprehensive index of sister organisations and contacts throughout the country.

MIND (the National Association for Mental Health) has in the past few years developed a significant Legal and Welfare Rights Service. It advises patients, relatives, friends, MPs, lawyers, social workers, psychiatrists and bodies such as Community Health Councils, trade unions and voluntary bodies. It has been actively involved in cases before the courts and has represented claimants before the European Commission on Human Rights. It frequently represents (or arranges representation) at Mental Health Review Tribunals and Industrial Tribunals. The legal adviser, Mr Larry Gostin, an American, has written extensively in the field and is regarded as one of the leading specialists on mental health legal matters. In 1977 the Department of Health and Social Services made a grant of some £6,000 to enable MIND to develop its service by improving its capacity to provide or arrange for representation in tribunal cases and to undertake research.

Neighbourhood advice centres

In the past decade there has been a great increase in the number of advice facilities as part of a variety of local initiatives. Settlement houses, community work projects, tenants' groups and a variety of other information and advice services have mushroomed. Many social service departments have established family advice centres. Housing Departments have set up centres to cater for the needs of people in general improvement and housing action areas. Planning departments have done the same before undertaking major redevelopments. The Home Office's Community Development Project established several neighbourhood advice centres. Some of these developments are funded by public moneys (typically Urban Aid or local authority moneys). A report in September 1973 showed that 168 Urban Aid grants had been made for advice services of which 27 were described as neighbourhood and generalist and another 33 were family advice centres.[41] Urban Aid grants are normally only for a limited period, usually three to five years. When this funding ceases, the continuation of the operation depends on finding some alternative source of support. Many have slender resources and manage simply on the efforts of volunteers. The NCC's 1977 report said: 'The predominant professional discipline of full-time staff of neighbourhood advice centres is community work rather than advice as such.'[42] The emphasis within centres 'is on developing the confidence and skills of local people to enable them to solve their own problems, rather than on the development of what they see as client dependency'. As a result, according to the National Consumer Council, some tended to be somewhat dismissive of the need for training'.[43] But in this respect they varied. Many volunteers as well as full-time workers were taking advantage of courses, on subjects such as housing rights and welfare rights, organised by specialist bodies like Shelter, the Child Poverty Action Group and the Legal Action Group.

Social workers

If social workers could be trained to identify a legal problem when they saw one, and to know how to handle it, their clients would benefit greatly. The value of social workers as identifiers of legal problems is the greater because their clients tend to be those with acute difficulties, often of a complex and interrelated kind, who are unable to help themselves. They are the submerged part of the population about whom so much concern is expressed – those who, above all, fail to get their rights. Unfortunately, social workers on the whole are not well trained in this sense. This belief was confirmed by a recent study of two social services departments.[44] The researcher, Andrew Phillips, spent some four months observing more than 100 members of 12 area teams in both urban and rural settings and their handling of legal problems. He had full access to all files.

He found that legal problems occurred much more frequently than was appreciated by the social workers. He instanced as examples: illegal evictions, property that was unfit, disputes with landlords over rent and repairs, nuisance disputes between neighbours, personal injury cases, worries over the handling of a deceased relative's estate, problems arising out of mental illness, matrimonial problems over maintenance, separation, division of property, custody over and access to children, adoption, unemployment benefit and other social security claims. Analysis of the referral sheets of one area team over a full year showed (on a conservative estimate) that such problems arose in about one-third of all cases – many more than most social workers expected or realised. In all the offices visited by the researcher, the first reaction was to suggest that the visit would be unproductive. A typical opening remark was: 'I haven't many cases of interest to you – a few matrimonial'. There was widespread ignorance of the legal aid scheme in general and even of the Green Form scheme. This, he said, led to complete unreality about the likely cost of legal help, and the availability of legal aid; 'there was extreme reluctance to refer the very poor to solicitors, yet these are the very people who qualify for legal aid'. With a very few exceptions, social workers had no knowledge of which solicitors did which sort of work. It was unknown in the groups studied for any social worker to have a relationship with a solicitor so as to be able to use him as an instant informal source of legal advice. None of the teams studied had any member, either formally or informally, recognised as being 'the legal expert'. Library facilities were limited. ('Each area office had books and leaflets, often out of date, in no particular order. To find, for example, a legal aid leaflet was troublesome, even if such a leaflet was there . . . in no office was there a consistent method of keeping information comprehensive and up to date.') Many cases were closed after only one contact – which made accurate information from the outset especially important.

Another author has said of social workers in the Wolverhampton area that they lacked training and information in the area of welfare rights, that departments were ambivalent about this area and gave no lead to their workers who, as a result, tended to hesitate before becoming involved in something so time-consuming as representation. Some authorities, however, had recognised the problem and had appointed Welfare Rights Officers.[45]

The Central Council for Education and Training in Social Work (CCETSW) set up a Working Party in 1972 to inquire into the subject of legal training for social workers. The Report of the Working Party[46] drew a distinction between 'professional law' which has to be mastered by social workers in order to enable them to perform their ordinary duties (e.g. the Probation Rules, provisions regarding child care or detention on grounds of mental incapacity) and other additional aspects of law. Thus it was desirable for social workers to have some knowledge of the role of law in society, of the administration of justice (the basic structure of the courts, the legal profession and the legal aid system), and of 'general law' (the law that affects the day-to-day life of the client as a citizen, e.g. as a tenant, a victim of an accident, a defendant in a criminal or debt case, a purchaser of defective goods, etc.). The Council criticised the meagre content of social work training courses on legal matters. Even professional law was not always adequately taught and this was the more true of 'the administration of law' and 'general law'. Not that it was either possible or desirable to try to turn social workers into mini-lawyers. The Report recognised that there were obvious risks when a worker was called on to give information and advice on matters about which he has not been properly trained. But practice had to be related to reality. There were areas of law on which lawyers themselves had insufficient knowledge – supplementary benefits was an example.

> Moreover, in some situations the hope that a client will go to a lawyer is unrealistic. In practice the choice is often between getting advice from a social worker or getting no advice at all.[47]

Notwithstanding growing involvement of lawyers with social welfare law, the Report said that 'there will continue to be many cases where someone else, and perhaps particularly the social worker, must adopt a quasi-legal role for want of any better alternative'.[48] Social workers ought to be trained to recognise the existence of legal problems, to give such information and advice as they are able and then to refer the problem to a lawyer or other appropriate adviser. The Report made recommendations for the improvement of social-work training courses to achieve these objectives.

The writer was a member of the Working Party and subscribes both to its diagnosis of the problem and to the prescription offered. It will be some years before one will be able to begin to measure the effect of the Report even in crude terms, such as the number of new lecture courses started in response to its suggestions. Reactions to the Report in journals, at special conferences held to discuss it and in informal discussions suggest, however, that its recommendations were broadly acceptable. The main problem is that of including yet another important topic in training courses, and of teaching the subject sufficiently well to give social workers a basic minimum of information with an understanding of how to master more 'in post'. The Working Party accepted the severe limitation that 'general law' and 'the administration of justice' would in practice not be able to claim more than about ten to twelve lectures in a two-year course. But a smattering, if well-taught and backed by continuation training and up-to-date information, may just make the difference between a social worker who can make the legal system work for the client and one who cannot.

Such training may even help to break down some of the barrier of hostility that undoubtedly infects the attitude of social workers towards lawyers. The study by Andrew Phillips of the handling of legal problems by social workers reported that such hostility was an important factor in the reluctance of social workers to use lawyers. They were seen, to varying degrees, as promoters of discord and tension, as too slow, as lacking insight, sympathy or understanding for their client's problems. There was resentment of the fact that they made a profit out of people's troubles, and even out of social workers by using their reports. Some solicitors were seen as arrogant. There was an overall view that solicitors were unhelpful, that law was an alien world with an alien language.

Partly, this tension was caused by genuine differences of approach between lawyers and social workers. Where lawyers emphasised clients' rights, the social worker tried to help him to adjust to his situation, say, as victim of an accident or a bereavement. The researcher came across a case in which the social worker actually recognised a serious legal problem where a client knew that he was dying of cancer and had been living with a woman who was not his wife. On his death without having made a will, his property would pass to his wife whom he had not seen for years. From the lawyer's point of view the urgent need for legal advice would be obvious. The social worker dealing with the case consciously decided not to raise the problem, on the grounds that it would be an unpleasant and distressing intervention at odds with the social worker's function of easing a stressful situation. Similarly, an injured worker was more likely to be put in touch with an occupational therapist than a lawyer. One was seen almost to exclude the other.

Granted that there are real differences of approach between lawyers and social workers in terms of their methods and even objectives, clearer understanding of the nature of the conflict of values may help to resolve them and to avoid their more harmful effects. Hostility based on ignorance and fear can be diminished by better knowledge; hostility based on perceived clashes of values can at least be somewhat diminished by defining the issues and seeking accommodations designed to respond to the client's best interests.

Lay advocates

The Bar devotes most of its time to advocacy and some solicitors do a great deal of advocacy in the lower courts. But qualified lawyers are far from having a total monopoly over the field. Advocacy is also done by persons who have some legal training but are not qualified lawyers. Legal executives in solicitors' offices, as has been seen, have rights of audience in proceedings in chambers and, from 1978, in some formal uncontested matters in open court. Bar students have, since 1972, run the Free Representation Unit, providing representation in tribunal cases in London and the surrounding area. In 1975–6, the unit handled nearly 1,000 cases. The service is now supported financially by the Bar and, as has been seen, special rules of ethics have been adopted to permit barristers to participate (see p. 168 above). University law students are beginning to take up tribunal advocacy on a voluntary basis and may soon do so as part of the curriculum of their courses.[49] (In the United States, university law students now undertake a significant volume of representation *in courts*, as part of clinical education programmes. Even Chief Justice Burger, who in other contexts has expressed concern over the level of competence of advocates in the US, has approved this development.[50]

A great deal of advocacy, however, is done by persons who are outside the legal profession altogether. One familiar, long-standing example is the massive involvement in advocacy in the magistrates' courts of police officers who present the prosecution case. In tribunals, where, so far, there has been no legal aid, most advocacy has always been by laymen. Two studies by Professor Kathleen Bell showed how small a role lawyers play in national insurance and supplementary benefit cases. In 80 per cent of national insurance cases, the appellant had no representation at all. When there was a representative in tribunals it was usually a trade union official (16 per cent). Relatives and friends represented some 4 per cent and lawyers only 1 per cent.[51] In supplementary benefit appeal tribunals the bulk of representation (13 per cent) was by friends and relatives. The others who did advocacy were claimants' unions (2 per cent), social workers (1 per cent), trade unions (0.5 per cent) and lawyers (0.2 per cent).[52]

The present tide is running strongly in favour of more and better lay advocacy. The Institute of Legal Executives proposed to the Royal Commission that rights of audience for Fellows be enlarged. Trade Unions are expanding their advocacy services, especially in Industrial Tribunals. Citizens' advice bureaux used to take the view that advocacy went beyond their proper neutral or impartial stance. They confined their role in tribunals to attending with the client to provide moral support and assistance by way of explanation and guidance. But in the past few years this has changed. In March 1974, CABs were told by their head office that 'CAB policy is now to encourage Bureaux to undertake an extension of their existing work by providing lay assistance before tribunals, and to offer the CAB service as a principal participant, provided funds are made available for recruiting, training, certification and expenses'. A detailed examination of their impartiality had revealed that it was not prejudiced by this extension of CAB activity to any tribunal available to the individual contesting a decision with a state welfare benefit or other system. Such assistance was also possible when individuals were in conflict with each other, as in rent tribunals, though it was said not normally to be desirable to represent both parties in such cases.[53]

A number of different schemes have been started. In October 1975, a CAB tribunal assistance scheme was begun in Newcastle upon Tyne; in 1976, a Tribunal Assistance Unit was established in the Chapeltown CAB in Leeds and in 1977, a representation project financed by the EEC's Anti-Poverty programme was started in the Wolverhampton area to serve nine CABs. The project in Chapeltown, for instance, consisted of one worker and a part-time secretary. The worker was also deputy organiser of the bureau and devoted only part of his time to tribunal work. The first report, for the six months ending February 1977, stressed that the combination of tribunal work with ordinary bureau work had proved valuable, as tribunal problems were not always visible or easily identifiable. The client with such a problem did not always recognise it and bureau workers needed special training to spot them. Before the project began the number of tribunal inquiries per month was negligible (0.3 per cent in the month before it began). By the end of one month they had increased to 13 per cent and at the end of six months they constituted 20 per cent of the total number of inquiries at the bureau![54] The report states that as many as half would probably not have come to light had it not been for the existence of the project.[55] Moreover, counting only cases which had by then ended in some result, nine out of ten of these 'invisible' tribunal cases had been resolved in the appellant's favour. Only about one-sixth of all the tribunal cases, however, actually went to a hearing.[56] This was said to be 'one of the most significant features' of the project's experience. Even the successes had mainly been achieved prior to the hearing – through the application of ordinary CAB skills of mediation and negotiation. On the basis of this experience the report suggested that if enough CAB workers could be trained to recognise the problems it would make a great impact on the problems of their clients ('Today a CAB worker without some tribunal know-how is like a boxer without gloves or a golfer without a putter.'[57])

The National Council of NACAB decided at its meeting on September 1977 that tribunal advocacy by CABs should be expanded. Several witnesses who gave evidence to the Royal Commission strongly supported the idea that lay advisory agencies and other similar agencies should conduct more advocacy. The National Consumer Council argued that 'Less articulate people cannot be left to their own devices armed with nothing but a leaflet. They need the guidance and sympathy of an adviser and a helping hand throughout the various

stages of getting their problems solved.'[58] People should be
left to help themselves so far as they were able, 'but for the
diffident, the inarticulate, the apprehensive and unsure, the
prospect of confronting a shop manager or an official, let alone
appearing in court or before a tribunal, is a daunting one'. Too
often they would not do such things, however crucial they
might be, unless they could rely on practical support from
somebody whose knowledge and experience they could trust.
'Advice centres need, therefore, to be prepared to undertake
advocacy as well as advice.'[59] A similar view was put, too,
from a more surprising source, the Bar. It proposed that 'first
tier' advice agencies such as citizens' advice bureaux, consumer advice centres or housing aid centres, should have staff
'trained to assist clients in tribunal cases which do not need the
services of a lawyer or other professional adviser such as an
accountant or surveyor'.[60]

There is plainly a need for some method to fund out of
public moneys, and to develop, a national system of tribunal
advocates. If the state is prepared to support representation in
courts to the tune of tens of millions of pounds a year it should
be willing to spend much smaller sums on representation in
tribunals. Tribunals, for all their vaunted informality, are
mini-courts. Appellants who are represented have a dramatically higher success rate than those who are not.[61] The statistics clearly show that *the type of representation makes far less
difference to the outcome of the case than the mere fact of representation*. Friends and relatives have almost as high a success rate as
other kinds of, presumably, more qualified types of representative such as a trade union official, a social worker or a
lawyer.[62] For the cases that require it, legal aid in some form
should no doubt be available, but the majority of tribunal cases
do not demand such expensive advocacy.

The Legal Action Group has proposed that there should be a
national network of tribunal representation services, provided
by lawyers and licensed lay advocates. Solicitors should be
able to provide representation under the Green Form Scheme.
Local tribunal agencies with tribunal officers should be established to provide advice and representation, to recruit and train
representatives and to monitor the state of local tribunal services. There would be a national body to license local tribunal
agencies and to supervise training programmes.[63] This

scheme was rejected as too cumbersome and costly by the Lord Chancellor's Legal Aid Advisory Committee, which, in 1974, proposed instead that legal aid be extended to all tribunals (through use of the Green Form scheme) and that financial assistance be given to lay agencies providing tribunal services, such as CABs. [64] In its evidence to the Royal Commission, the Advisory Committee repeated this recommendation, though it suggested that, in view of financial constraints, legal aid might be given for some tribunals before others. (It thought that Industrial Tribunals were the most pressing candidate for legal aid.) [65] The Labour Party and the Trades Union Congress proposed that legal aid should not be extended to tribunals but that instead block grants should be given by the state to the agencies that provide tribunal representation. [66] Whether legal aid is now extended to tribunals or not, the even greater need is for the provision of lay advocates in substantial numbers. CABs, trade unions and specialist bodies that undertake work in tribunals should receive ear-marked funds to develop advocacy services. The citizens' advice bureaux would be an especially suitable body for this purpose since it provides a generalist service, has over 700 bureaux, has the means to provide training and enjoys the confidence of both the government and the public. It has already taken the first steps in this field and should now be made the main focus of a national network of lay advocacy services for tribunal work.

The scope for lay advocates to appear in tribunals is clear. It is not yet certain whether there is any equivalent prospect in regard to courts. In 1970, in *McKenzie v. McKenzie*,[67] the Court of Appeal ruled unanimously that 'any person whether he be a professional man or not, may attend as a friend of either party, may take notes, may quietly make suggestions and give advice'. The decision became the basis of a movement of 'McKenzie men' whose role it was to assist otherwise unrepresented persons. But the McKenzie man concept has not yet flourished. It was taken up principally by disaffected or underground organisations. The best known – Up Against the Law – was founded in March 1973 in order to fight the legal system in much the same way that Claimants' Unions contested social security cases. (The manual produced by the organisation said that 'lawyers are so buried in all this legal bullshit that they have a fine record of selling our interests down the river and conning the innocent into pleading guilty'.) But Up Against the Law ceased to exist in 1976 and there is now no organisation that uses the McKenzie concept to any significant extent. Moreover, in 1974 Lord Denning doubted whether it really extended to advocacy,[68] and although courts retain a complete discretion to admit anyone as a spokesman in a particular case, not much use seems now to be made of the device.

But it would appear to have some potential for development. Social workers are an obvious group who could receive training on how to assist clients in courts. If CAB workers can be successfully trained to represent clients in tribunals, some of them could also become court advocates. No doubt courts are more formal institutions than tribunals. No doubt, also, a trained lawyer, other things being equal, should be a better advocate than a less fully trained para-legal worker. But this is not the issue. The problem is that in the lower courts there are innumerable cases in which parties are unrepresented. Even if there were enough lawyers to conduct all the court cases in which representation was 'needed', it might not be reasonable to place the burden of such costs on the state if a cheaper and adequate response were available in the form of trained laymen. In many court cases, what the unrepresented person needs most is someone to help him with a combination of suggestion, prompting and, here and there, a word spoken on his behalf. Knowledge of the facts of the case with a minimal grasp of the elements of court procedure and of the rules of evidence would probably suffice to place the trained lay advocate in a position to do a reasonably good job in a considerable number of cases. Certainly this hypothesis deserves to be tested. Opposition from the legal profession would have little weight unless careful experimentation had shown the concept to be unworkable. Tribunals may be somewhat different from courts, but in many respects they are similar – in both, decisions are made by an impartial adjudicator after a process of argument on issues of fact and law. Lay advocates with appropriate training are likely to be able to fill some of the gaps in the system of representation provided by lawyers.[69]

The do-it-yourself movement

A different way to reduce the need for lawyers is to simplify legal procedures or to provide official assistance so as to make it easier for the ordinary person to handle his own case. One example is the work of the Personal Applications Department in the probate field which is available to persons who need guidance as to how to handle a deceased person's estate. The clerks in the department are not permitted to give legal advice, but they can and do assist tens of thousands of persons each year on how to fill in the forms necessary to obtain letters of administration or grants of probate. A free pamphlet is sent out which explains the procedure and further inquiries are handled over the telephone, in writing or over the counter. Outside London there is no personal application department as such, but district probate registrars are available by appointment to assist persons with such guidance.

Two areas in which there have recently been important procedural simplifications are those of small claims and divorce. Small claims are mostly processed in the county court, but the plaintiff is normally a company or creditor institution, rarely a private citizen. Serious agitation for reforms to make it easier for the individual to bring a small case began as a result of the Consumer Council's 1970 pamphlet *Justice out of Reach*. This showed that more than 90 per cent of a random sample of county court cases were brought by firms or a public utility board. The individual was the plaintiff in only 9 per cent. One reason was 'the bewildering maze of rules and practices' which surrounded the county courts. Solicitors who had been interviewed 'were unanimous in saying that it was a rare person who could successfully fight a case of any complexity unrepresented'. The forms for starting or defending actions were too complex, lay litigants were liable to be bemused by a variety of pre-trial notices, they had little idea what evidence was needed to establish a case and the procedure at a court hearing was 'quite beyond the capabilities of the average person'.

The Consumer Council's suggestion was that a new procedure be designed under which the registrar of the county court would run an informal court for small claims brought by individuals. Companies and other legal entities would be barred from using the court as plaintiffs. Representation by lawyers would be prohibited. The main burden of handling the claim would be taken over by the court. The individual would come to tell his story to the court office. A court officer would 'interpret his story, write out a claim for him, and send a summons to the other party'. The court officer would tell the plaintiff what evidence was needed. A senior court officer would be available to sort out the main issues in complex cases. The registrar would hold the hearing in his own office rather than in a court room, and it should be possible to have the hearing in the evening rather than in working hours. He would allow the parties to tell the story in their own way and there should be no rules of evidence or procedure. The registrar, instead of adopting the traditional approach of an English judge of just sitting to listen to the evidence, would himself have the task of finding out as many of the facts as possible. His aim should be to reach an amicable settlement. If this proved impossible, he would give judgment. Costs should be limited to a small filing fee.

The detailed proposals in this pamphlet were not implemented, but they had a considerable impact and were eventually the basis for a number of important changes. First, there were privately financed experiments in Manchester and London with informal systems for arbitration of small claims, an important factor of which was that representation by lawyers was wholly prohibited.[70] The chief weakness of these was that they depended on voluntary agreement to arbitrate and could not, therefore, work unless both parties agreed to participate. It appears that these experiments will not survive for lack of continuing finance.[71] It is also clear that it would be much too costly to set up a complete system of small claims courts separate from the county courts. But although the Lord Chancellor's Office was not persuaded to adopt this approach, it did introduce its own new system. In August 1973, compulsory arbitration was introduced for small claims in the county court. If the sum in issue is less than £200 or if both parties agree, the registrar has power to order that the dispute should be dealt with by an arbitration heard in private without formal rules of evidence. Either side can ask for arbitration. If the other side objects, the registrar must decide if arbitration will take place. The arbitrator, normally the registrar himself, sits without robes. An inquisitorial method of procedure is supposed to be adopted so that the court can help each party to bring out his case. If the plaintiff loses in a claim for less than £100, he normally gets no costs from the loser.[72]

This system, so far as it goes, appears to have proved a modest success. In the first year, ending December 1974, the number of cases referred for arbitration was 4,932. In the second year it was 8,095 and in the third it was 12,003. The numbers involved are not large but they are not insignificant. The plaintiff is an individual in about half the cases – a much higher proportion than in the ordinary county court case. He is a defendant in about three-quarters. But, perhaps surprisingly, the no-costs rule has not had the effect of inhibiting the use of legal representation. In about half the cases neither side is represented, in about a third only the plaintiff is represented, in less than 10 per cent only the defendant is legally represented and in about the same proportion both sides are represented.[73] The plaintiff usually wins – in 1975 the proportion overall was 85 per cent of cases in which there was a decision. Individuals were represented in 38 per cent of cases, compared with firms which were represented in 59 per cent. Representation, or the lack of it, made some but not a great difference to the outcome of cases. Whether the plaintiff was an individual or a firm made virtually none. In 1975 in cases ending with a result where the plaintiff only was represented, the plaintiff succeeded in 93 per cent of cases where he was an individual and 89 per cent where it was a firm; when only the defendant was represented, the plaintiff's success rate was reduced to 74 per cent for individuals and 79 per cent for firms; when both sides were represented, the figures were 84 per cent for individuals and 82 per cent for firms; and when neither side was represented the success rate was 89 per cent for individuals and 86 per cent for plaintiff firms.[74]

The handling of small claims cases by private individuals has been further promoted by a number of additional steps. The Lord Chancellor's Department produced a free, plain man's guide to county court procedure, *How to sue and defend actions without a Solicitor*, hundreds of thousands of which have been distributed through county courts and citizens' advice bureaux. There was also a simple leaflet, *Suing on your own*. At every county court there are a set of draft particulars of claims in question and answer form which are now used by seven out of ten litigants in person. New and simpler basic forms of request, summons and enforcement have also been introduced.

The Lord Chancellor's Office has also made considerable efforts to improve the training of citizens' advice bureau workers and those in consumer advice centres. Staff of the Lord Chancellor's Office now participate in this training. The objectives of this new programme are to get workers in the lay advisory agencies to know where the local court is situated and the range of work it handles, and to meet the court staff so that personal links are established. They sit in actual court cases to see how things are done. They are trained to fill in all the necessary forms required for the making, defending or enforcing of a small claim. The training scheme is based on liaison between CAB area officers and courts administrators. Training courses with collaboration between the officials of the Department and of the Consumers' Association have also now been instituted for the staffs of consumer advice centres. One-day courses run regionally are financed by the Department of Prices and Consumer Protection. The aim is that all advisers in the centres master the intricacies of small claims procedures.

In two large county courts a specific officer was designated, in 1977, to look after litigants in person and to liaise with all local agencies that might help a litigant in person. In another two courts the CAB started an office in the actual court building so that people could approach the CAB worker for guidance on procedure and procedural difficulties. Judges, registrars and clerks all referred people to the CAB worker for help.

In the field of divorce the Lord Chancellor, as has been seen, announced in June 1976 that legal aid was being withdrawn from undefended cases. This announcement was greeted with much alarm from lawyers, not only because they were understandably concerned about the loss of an estimated £6m. of income, but on behalf of clients who, it was feared, might be cast adrift without adequate professional assistance at a moment of considerable personal anxiety. But the change was based on the observation that the actual hearing in the typical undefended divorce case was more or less a formality, lasting, on average, a matter of five to ten minutes. In 1969, a new special procedure had been introduced whereby in some types of case[75] a divorce could be obtained without any hearing at all. This special procedure was extended to all uncontested cases in 1977. If the proceedings are uncontested (as is normally the case), and if the registrar certifies that the papers are in order, the judge can grant a divorce decree nisi without either party being present. This is in fact now the almost invariable rule for uncontested cases. If there are small children, the petitioner is asked to come to tell the judge about the arrangements for them in a hearing in his chambers. (The respondent may also come if he or she wishes.) If the case is uncontested, it is thought that there is no need for a lawyer and legal aid is not now normally available for this stage. But the hearing is usually brief, the judge normally accepts the proposals made by the petitioner (often without over-much enquiry[76]) and the withdrawal of legal aid in this category of case appears to be justified as a means of effecting useful economies. Legal advice and help continue to be available under the Green Form scheme before the hearing to handle the earlier stages of a divorce and after the hearing to process contests over custody of children or division of property. Full legal aid is available where there is a contest or the hearing is in open court or where the applicant cannot manage his own case because of some physical or mental handicap.

To coincide with the publication of the new rules in April 1977, the Lord Chancellor's Office published *Undefended Divorce*, a free, plain man's guide to procedure in this field, too. The initial print order for this page booklet was for 1 million copies. As in the small claims field, there is also a shorter leaflet to explain the gist of the procedure. Both the leaflet and the booklet are available from CABs and county courts. The system for handling cases conducted by litigants in person is designed with the aim that, whenever he is required to do anything, a notice is sent to him by the court, giving information about the next step. It is hoped that the proportion of those conducting their own divorces entirely without the help of lawyers will increase substantially. In 1976 the proportion of do-it-yourself divorces was already one-sixth. By autumn 1977 in London it had risen to one-third, and outside London it was as high as two-thirds. It is not known what proportion of petitioners in these cases had legal advice under the Green Form scheme.

In April 1976 new legislation was brought into force to permit successful litigants in person to recover some of their costs from the losing defendant. Previously, litigants in person (unless they were lawyers) could only recover in costs out-of-pocket expenses and nothing for their own work or loss of time.[77] The Litigants in Persons Act 1975, sponsored by the Consumers' Association, provides that the litigant in person can recover costs and disbursements necessarily and properly incurred where a represented party would have been entitled to make such a claim. The scales of fees allowed under the Rules are not over-generous,[78] but again this is a small step in the direction of making the courts more available to the ordinary citizen.

It is certain that there will be further developments in the same general direction. There is great official interest in the topic, partly in order to save the cost of legal aid payments to lawyers and partly to respond to the growing strength of the 'do-it-yourself' movement in the field of legal services. There is, for instance, a new attitude to the role of court clerks in assisting litigants in person. A new official notice displayed in all county court offices specifically states that although the staff should not give legal aid advice, they should, wherever possible, give procedural advice. Training courses for those entering the court service now include a section on helping the litigant in person. The Lord Chancellor's Office is in regular contact with organisations such as the citizens' advice bureaux to get feedback as to how the present system is working and how it might be improved. (The Lord Chancellor's Office is, for instance, a member of the NACAB's Legal Services Group.) Other official developments pending in mid-1977 included a draft pamphlet explaining enforcement of judgment debts to be published by the Lord Chancellor's Department when finances permitted, proposals for the simplification of procedure in possession cases, a Working Party set up by the Lord Chancellor to make proposals on procedure in civil cases, and another committee, under a High Court judge, on simplification of personal injuries litigation – quite apart from the work of the Royal Commission on Legal Services and that of the new Royal Commission on Criminal Procedure, both of which are likely to make proposals designed to improve the position of the ordinary person in the toils of the legal system. There are, similarly, proposals to cheapen legal proceedings by reform of both the law and practice – for instance, in the field of conveyancing.[79]

The relationship between legal, para-legal and lay advisers

Advice and other help with legal problems is given by a great range of advisers. At one end of the spectrum there is the legal profession consisting of a mix of fully qualified personnel (barristers and solicitors) and semi-qualified members (legal executives and articled clerks). There are a considerable number of specialist advisers with varying degrees of qualifications and expertise in handling legal problems (including advocacy) in trade unions, consumer advice and housing aid centres, claimants' unions, and organisations such as Release, the Child Poverty Action Group, MIND and the National Council for Civil Liberties. To varying extents, these bodies also deal with advice on matters not raising legal problems. Finally, there are an even larger number of advisers who offer generalist services – notably citizens' advice bureaux, newspapers with an advisory service,[80] and neighbourhood advice centres, plus others for whom the giving of legal advice is peripheral to their main activity, but who nevertheless find themselves being asked for such help – social workers, the police, 'the town hall', the clergy and other authority figures in the community.

Many of these systems depend wholly, substantially, or to some extent on funds drawn from the public purse. Civil legal aid is paid for via the Lord Chancellor's Department, criminal legal aid through the Home Office; law centres are financed by a combination of funds drawn from Urban Aid (the Home Office until June 1977 and now the Department of the Environment, plus local authorities), local authority direct grants and the Lord Chancellor's special law centres fund. The National Association of Citizens' Advice Bureaux (NACAB) derives most of its moneys from the Department of Prices and Consumer Protection (DPCP), whilst local bureaux are financed by their own local authorities plus the special five-year development grant made available from the DPCP for the years 1974–9. Consumer advice centres are financed by the DPCP, housing aid centres are funded by local authorities or private bodies such as Shelter, neighbourhood advice centres are financed variously by housing departments, social services departments and other parts of local authorities. Although much of the work of handling legal problems is supported by public funds (in 1977–8 some £91m.[81]), much is also based on voluntary activities – for instance, of lawyers in free legal advice sessions, and of the majority of CAB workers.

One question posed by this hodge-podge is whether it is satisfactory to have advice and services in the field of legal problems provided by so many disparate agencies with little co-ordination and with a great variety of funding sources. One obvious disadvantage of the present situation is that it is no one's responsibility to consider the balance of advisory services needed and available in each area. Organisations each go their own way. Their activities overlap. Some areas are over-provided where others suffer from a scarcity of services. There is no attempt to plan the best use of resources by an evaluation of the relative performance and cost of different systems for providing help to the public. The disadvantages of this situation were pointed out in the recent report of the National Consumer Council.

> Almost any central or local government (sic) can and does provide money, but none is required to do so. The overall effect is chaotic. In some areas no public money is available to support advice services. In other areas local authority departments appear to vie with one another to set up their own specialist service, for example consumer advice side by side with housing advice and so on ... With so many discretionary points of funding, co-operation and co-ordination of the various services to further the consumer's best interests are at the best difficult and at the worst downright discouraged. It has directly contributed to overlapping and duplication of effort for certain groups in certain areas and at the same time failed to ensure the provision of any services whatsoever for some of those in greatest need. The result is only too apparent – there is no coherent national policy towards advice services in the UK.[82]

Similar concern has been voiced by the Lord Chancellor's Legal Aid Advisory Committee in regard to the variety of sources of funding in the field of work done by lawyers at public expense.[83] The plan of the Lord Chancellor's Committee would be to have legal services committees of lawyers (two-thirds) and laymen (one-third) at both the local and the national levels sorting out the problems and making policy. They would be answerable both to the Law Society and to the

Lord Chancellor. The Lord Chancellor would have political responsibility for legal services provided by lawyers in private practice, by lawyers in law centres and by citizens' advice bureaux. CABs were now probably 'the largest suppliers of legal services after the legal profession' and if there was to be proper planning and allocation of legal services as a whole, they ought to be brought within the same system.[84] But other forms of advisory services such as those of consumer advice centres would remain under their present ministerial direction.

The solution offered by the National Consumer Council is that the Department of Prices and Consumer Protection should be given the responsibility of bringing together those in Whitehall involved in the provision of advice services to work out a national policy and subsequently to be responsible for both its implementation and funding. The policy would be based on the use of both statutory and voluntary services. The model for funding should be that of Urban Aid – a mixture of central government and local government money. The DPCP would produce guidelines about the desirable balance between statutory and voluntary services, about training and other support services. At the local level each local authority should be asked to prepare strategic plans identifying the nature, extent and location of the services required. Plans should be prepared and then executed by a committee including, also, representatives of the local voluntary bodies active in the field. After a transitional stage the production of a satisfactory plan should be a condition for receiving central government funds. The NCC Report did not discuss how, if at all, these new arrangements should affect the system for providing or managing services provided by lawyers, but it seems that there was no intention that these should be included.[85]

Although both these schemes address themselves to the problem of co-ordination of services, neither really solves it. Under the Advisory Committee's scheme, the Lord Chancellor would be in charge of 'legal services' provided by lawyers and by CABs but not by others such as housing aid centres, consumer advice centres and the social services, nor by the army of neighbourhood advice centres. Under the NCC's plan, the Department of Prices and Consumer Protection takes primary responsibility for services provided by non-lawyers (including CABs) but has no concern with services provided by lawyers. In either case the danger of a lack of co-ordination would continue.

In terms of achieving a single source of ministerial responsibility the problem is probably insoluble. No minister other than the Lord Chancellor (or some future equivalent in the House of Commons) is likely to be placed in charge of the services provided by lawyers. But even if he also took over the CABs it seems improbable that this minister would also be made responsible for all the other lay advice agencies. Similarly, the Minister for Prices and Consumer Protection might be made *primus inter pares* for services provided by non-lawyers (with or without CABs) but he is unlikely to be put in charge of the legal profession. The best that can be hoped in this situation, probably, is that there be some form of co-ordinating committee between *all* the government departments involved in financing and providing advisory services.

But even if such a committee existed, it would inevitably operate at the macro level and could hardly descend to much detail. Certainly, something more is needed at the national and, even more, at the local level. The solution propounded by the Law Society and the Lord Chancellor's Advisory Committee (pp. 258–61 above), is to have legal services committees consisting of both lawyers and laymen with the laymen being at least one-third of the membership and representing a variety of interests including that of CABs, local authority social services departments, probation services, courts administration, etc. The solution offered by the NCC for advice services generally is to have committees established by the local authority with wide membership drawn from voluntary bodies and (presumably) lawyers.

These proposals appear to be in conflict, but they need not be. Even if the scheme propounded by the NCC were to come into being, there would still be a need for an appropriate network of committees of lawyers and laymen to deal with the special problem of legal services provided by lawyers. Lawyers should play a part in the local committees set up to deal with advice generally, just as laymen from a variety of agencies and backgrounds should serve on the committees established to deal more specifically with 'legal services'. The

best hope for coordination at the local level is to ensure that
there is considerable overlap between the membership of both
kinds of committee and that each is kept informed of what the
other is doing.

All this is at the level of monitoring, planning and management. But what of the relationship between lawyers and
laymen when it comes to service to the client? At present, the
lay public may go direct to solicitors and to lay advisory
agencies, and both the legal profession and the lay agencies
may also act on referral as second tier advisers. In the view of
the National Consumer Council and of the Bar, the first
burden of advice ought to be borne by the first tier service and
the more expert, second tier level of adviser ought to be called
in only where needed. According to the NCC, there should be
a 'basic local general practitioner service that would be the
foundation tier of a properly integrated local advice structure'.[86] Surveys (as has been seen, p. 304 above) had shown
that the ordinary citizen's first choice of advisory agency even
for legal problems tends to be the citizens' advice bureau. The
NCC Report proposed that the first tier would be provided
primarily by CABs, but also by community-oriented neighbourhood advice centres. The GP service should be available
at a very local level – 'people need an advice centre in their own
neighbourhood and not miles away'.[87] There should, in
future, therefore, be more provision for small CAB centres at
a very decentralised level, staffed, as now, mainly by volunteers. But to function properly GP advice centres would need
to have a close and properly organised working relationship
with the specialist services, such as those of housing or consumer experts and lawyers. The Bar Council, in its evidence to
the Royal Commission, envisaged a similar division between
first tier advisers (citizens' advice bureaux, consumer advice
and housing aid centres) and second tier facilities (lawyers in
private practice, law centres and legal resource centres) which
would be used on referral from first tier centres.[88]

But apparently neither the National Consumer Council nor
the Bar intended to suggest that lawyers should necessarily be
confined to clients who were passed on to them from other
agencies. In the case of private practitioners this must be
obvious. There could be no question of any restriction by
government or other fiat limiting clients of solicitors to those

who had first been processed by CABs or other first tier advisers.

Law centres might be in a different situation. There are, in fact, law centres (e.g. Paddington and Hackney) where, apart from emergency cases, the centre normally sees only clients who have been referred from the CAB in the same building. Where the two operate in the same building or very close to one another, this policy is easy to operate. The advantage of making law centres second tier advisers is that it would ensure that their time was used on problems that had already been sifted. To that extent it would maximise the use of scarce resources. The danger would be that law centres might get cut off from the communities they were set up to serve. The more they engaged in community or group work the more this would be unfortunate. Also, insofar as they were performing a casework function it might be inconvenient for lay clients to have to go to the lawyers via a first tier adviser – especially since it is a known fact that some clients who are referred fall through the net and never arrive at the other end. If law centres were to become wholly or mainly second tier advisers it would be vital to ensure that they maintained open lines of communi- cation and referral with all local agencies. There should be no question of referrals having to come through a single agency such as the CAB. But if the law centre and its management committee are content that it be used as a second rather than a first tier advisory service, there is no reason why this should not be allowed or perhaps even encouraged. It would, in any event, be right to test the idea by experiment.

This would, however, be only a very small application of the concept of second tier advisers. Solicitors and all other advisory agencies would have to remain first tier advisers who would also on occasion be used as the second tier. Administra- tively this may appear regrettable but in practice it should give rise to few problems. It is much more important that there be flexible lines of referral and the maximum number of access points for the public than that there be organisational tidiness. The public seem reasonably good at selecting the appropriate adviser for a problem. The overwhelming majority of cases brought to solicitors or to law centres *are* legal problems. The great majority of matters brought to CABs are in fact handled by the CAB even when they are 'legal problems'. There is no way in which overlap between advisers can be eliminated. In the medical field, patients can be organised so that they go first to a GP and only to a specialist if referred by a GP. But this is because doctors have a virtual monopoly of providing medical services. The field of legal services is more multi-faceted and is not therefore subject to the same marshalling of clients and advisers. Lawyers, CABs, consumer advice centres, housing aid centres, neighbourhood centres, officials in the town hall, rent officers, police officers, newspapers, court clerks, probation officers, local councillors, MPs and others will all continue to be involved in providing legal services. This is not merely inevitable but also most desirable. It recognises the fact that there are many places where the citizen can get tolerably competent advice on legal matters. It accepts and builds on the desire of advisers to join different agencies and to serve the public in different capacities. Each agency and profession has its own values, skills and traditions. Communication and the ease of referral of clients from one to another should of course be improved. Appropriate committees should be responsible for ensuring that there is the right balance between generalist and specialist services in an area and that enough is done to train advisers to the appropriate level of competence. But a diversity of types of adviser should be regarded as a great benefit to the community.

11   The Future

Certain future developments seem inevitable. There will be increasing pressure on governments to spend more money in the field of legal services and more money *will* be spent. The ideal of equality of all citizens before the law requires that those 'in need' of lawyers who lack financial resources be helped by the state and, as society develops, the concept of 'need' expands. Most legal aid systems will be based on a mixed system of private practitioners and state salaried lawyers. In countries such as England where legal aid has been channelled via private practitioners, the chief structural expansion in the next decade or two will be in the building-up of the public sector to complement the role of the private profession. In countries such as the United States, where legal aid is currently being dispensed mainly through salaried Legal Services Corporation lawyers and salaried Public Defender Offices, the development may be rather in the opposite direction of enabling private practitioners to play more of a role in the provision of state-funded services. (There is a certain irony in the fact that the welfare state in England has so far produced a legal aid system based mainly on private practice, whereas America's more capitalist society has concentrated its legal aid efforts so largely in a separate public sector of legal services.)

The relationship between the private and public sectors in each country will depend on a variety of factors. In very poor countries with a tiny legal profession, the government may reasonably decide that the best way to secure legal services for the population is to employ many of the small number of lawyers on government salaries. Their services can then be made available either free to all, or free to those who qualify on a means test, or partly free and partly subject to a contribution. In countries with larger legal professions, most lawyers are likely to be in private practice. The choice is then either to confine state-funded legal services to the salaried public sector

or to encourage private practitioners also to play some role. If
the objective is to spread legal services as widely as possible
through the community, at the lowest cost, it would, in most
countries, be sensible to capitalise on existing firms of private
practitioners. In England, private practitioners outnumber
public sector lawyers by more than 340 to 1 and in the United
States by over 80 to 1.[1] It will clearly be impossible, even in the
richest countries, to set up salaried law firms in every area
where there are substantial numbers of potential clients poor
enough to qualify for their services. Even if law centres can be
put in the worst slums, the poor do not all huddle conveniently
in ghettoes. In most industrialised countries they are spread
over substantial areas – in rural as well as urban communities.
If clients cannot afford to use private practitioners and there are
no law centres in their areas, they are effectively deprived of
the services of lawyers. The only solution to this dilemma is to
permit poor clients to use the services of private practitioners
and by one means or another to subsidise such work. It may be
that private practitioners are not likely to undertake the kind of
'law reform' or group legal service undertaken by salaried
lawyers in at least some countries but to limit legal aid work to
salaried lawyers is drastically to restrict the scope of legal
services to the poor.

The development of the public sector is still in its earliest
stages and it would be premature to think that we could yet
discern its likely ultimate shape or dimensions. On one or
other side of the Atlantic or both there has now been some
experience with: (1) law centres/neighbourhood law firms
handling 'ordinary' legal problems such as divorce and other
matters commonly dealt with by private practitioners; (2) law
centres/neighbourhood law firms handling problems such as
landlord–tenant matters, immigration, tribunal cases, social
security and other problems that do not commonly reach
private practitioners; (3) salaried lawyers specialising in community or group work as opposed to casework for individuals;
(4) salaried lawyers working in specialist law reform or
'back-up' centres and public interest law firms; (5) salaried
lawyers working as additional aides in generalist bodies such
as the CAB and in specialist bodies, in England, such as
NCCL, Release, MIND or CPAG or, in the United States,
organisations concerned to assist women, prisoners, ethnic or

racial groups, consumers, environmentalists, civil liberties organisations and the like. All of these are legitimate and valuable ways of using lawyers. Experiment and local conditions will show how to provide the most appropriate mix in any given country.

If the role of the salaried sector should be to fill the gaps, which of many possible gaps should be made priority targets? For some, the most useful function of the state-salaried lawyers is to do individual cases of much the same kind as are done by private practitioners in areas where private firms have not set up; others prefer them to handle mainly individual cases that are not taken to private firms; others again will see the role of the public sector lawyer as chiefly to handle cases on a broader canvas than for the individual client.

These objectives are to some extent incompatible. If the salaried lawyers concentrate on providing traditional private practitioners' services, they will be inundated with the usual matrimonial, personal injury and criminal work. If they mainly work for individuals in fields where private practitioners do little – landlord–tenant, social security, immigration, consumer problems and the like – where are local citizens in their areas to get services in the traditional fields? The same problem will exist to an even greater extent if the public sector lawyers concentrate on work for groups rather than for individuals.

There are no 'correct' answers to these questions. It is a matter of choice of emphasis which will vary from one country to another and even to some extent from one locality to another. The writer's preference, at least for England, is to use public sector lawyers primarily for work that is not being done by private practitioners and to place primary emphasis on legal services on the macro rather than on the micro level. Servicing of groups and of the local community as a whole is likely to provide greater value for money than action taken simply on behalf of individuals. Let private practitioners and case-work advice agencies serve the personal needs of the individual client; let law centres, on the whole, work more for tenants' associations, consumer, environmental or youth groups, the local trades council, claimants' unions, and the like. The law centre should service them in much the same way as the private practitioner serves his clients – forming organisations,

negotiating contracts, settling disputes, handling litigation
and 'lobbying' the legislature. The publicly salaried lawyer
should have no less broad an approach but should exercise his
skills on behalf of the largest potential number of clients.
Wherever appropriate, his work should be integrated with
that of other experts (say in housing, social problems, public
health or taxation), and with community workers and community representatives. In 1974 the Adamsdown Community
and Advice (Law) Centre, for instance, used the Green Form
scheme to get expert consultants' reports costing £1,800 to
contest the local council's plan to clear and rebuild the area.
The report substantiated the contention of local residents that
rehabilitation of housing was a better overall policy than slum
clearance. Brent law centre reported in February 1978 that it
had got the local council to agree to give its tenants the same
rights as regards security of tenure as were available under the
Rent Acts to private tenants. These are typical group-oriented
legal services. In addition to the public sector lawyer in law
centres there should be others in public interest law firms, in
CABs, attached to specialist bodies such as the Child Poverty
Action Group and in a variety of other placements where they
can make a contribution to solving legal difficulties of disadvantaged groups. Legal aid should also be extended to
permit representation of groups by private practitioners as
well as by salaried lawyers.[2]

The lawyer's role is to help the client to improve his situation. In the case of the publicly salaried lawyers who sees his
client to be the local community (or, even more broadly, the
general community of similarly placed individuals) this is
likely to lead the lawyer into activities that may be both visible
and controversial. He may be accused of engaging in politics,
of abusing his position as a lawyer, of leading rather than of
following his clients. There are, of course, important ethical
problems in such relatively open-ended situations. (The existence of a management committee including lawyers and
non-lawyers will often help both to protect the lawyers from
unjustified attacks of this kind and, where the criticisms are
justified, to control the zeal of the lawyers.) But there is
nothing reprehensible in the publicly salaried lawyer from
devoting energies to 'reform' – whether in the classic form of
test-case litigation, or in other less traditional ways – lobbying

the council for a more consistent policy in allocation of public housing, managing a campaign to get tenants to apply to the rent officer to have their rents reduced, or researching and then publicising defects in the existing law. The lawyer is not merely entitled but in duty bound to deploy his best energies and skills in the service of his clients. The American Bar Association has even laid on the lawyer the obligation that if he believes 'that the existence of a rule of law, substantive or procedural, causes or contributes to an unjust result, he should endeavour by lawful means to obtain appropriate changes in the law'.[3] Most lawyers pay only lip-service to the idea, a few undertake law reform work in their spare time. But the publicly salaried sector has made it an important element in its daily working life.

The effect is far from negligible. In the hundred years to 1967 during which legal aid in the US was dominated by the outlook of the ordinary private practitioner, no legally aided case was brought to the United States Supreme Court. In the five years between 1967 and 1972, lawyers working with a law reform orientation in the OEO legal services programme brought no less than 200 cases to the Supreme Court. Of these, 136 were decided on the merits and 73 were won.[4] Lawyers working for the poor have won major victories on behalf of tenants, consumers, welfare recipients, prisoners, ethnic minorities, and a variety of other disadvantaged groups.[5] In America procedural law permits fuller use of class or representative actions than, for instance, the English.[6] It allows argument to be addressed to the court on the social and economic implications of legal rules.[7] Written briefs may be submitted by expert third parties on important pending problems of law.[8] American judges may also be more creative than others in their development of the law and the written constitution offers opportunities for test-case litigation that are not so readily available by other means. But, whatever the precise local situation, even a small group of expert lawyers committed to improving the lot of the disadvantaged could in most countries make a distinct impact.

Naturally, the more successful they are, the more they will run into opposition. Lawyers for the poor who provide representation in ciminal cases, divorces or personal injury claims are one thing; but lawyers who seek changes with significant economic or social impact are bound to meet countervailing forces. If, for instance, a judicial decision creates too many costs or other problems for public authorities, legislation may be introduced to reverse it.[9] But this is only to say that lawyers who work in the public sector are as much prone to the pressures of the real world as anyone else. It is often a difficult question whether, on balance, it is better to make a frontal assault on some aspect of the status quo and thereby risk provoking a strong counter-reaction or whether a more indirect approach may not, in the longer run, be more effective. Each situation must be judged on its merits.[10]

Whatever the role of lawyers in the private or the public sector, it is certain that part of the public's need for legal services will increasingly be met by further strengthening of advisory services provided by non-lawyers or para-professionals. In England this movement is already well-developed and is likely to grow even stronger in coming years. From the government's and the client's point of view it has the attraction of making advisory services available at a lower cost than that of fully-trained lawyers. It is, of course, crucial to the success of non-lawyers participating in the handling of legal problems that they receive adequate training to equip them for the work. In this regard there is considerable room for improvement. But, provided training can bring para-professionals to a reasonable minimum level of competence, the advantages in using them greatly outweigh the dangers. The tendency to compare them unfavourably as advisers and lay advocates with qualified lawyers is to make the best the enemy of the good. The question is not whether they are the equal of lawyers but whether they are good enough to cope reasonably well with their ordinary clients, either by handling their problems or by referring them to more expert facilities. There is ample evidence that some of the tasks performed by lawyers can also be performed by others. Moreover, the general public is aware of the fact. In the national random sample study conducted by the American Bar Association and the American Bar Foundation, no less than 75 per cent of respondents agreed with the statement that 'There are many things that lawyers handle that can be done as well and less expensively by non-lawyers'.[11]

The growing proliferation of lay advisers and lay advocates

must be supplemented by improved information for those faced by legal problems as to how to deal with them. Institutional advertising by the profession, advertising by individual lawyers through referral lists, legal directories and, in the future, through the local press, will all help. But probably much more crucial is relevant information for 'lay intermediaries' who see citizens with legal problems and could push them to seek appropriate advice. Hospital workers, doctors, social workers, local authority officials who see the public, court clerks, police and probation officers, trade union officials, and public health inspectors are all in a position to influence those whom they see in the course of their ordinary work. It is not their primary function to give advice on legal problems. Yet they ought to have a basic minimum of knowledge about the legal aid and assistance schemes and of the new scheme under which solicitors give an initial interview for a fixed fee, plus a smattering of knowledge to enable them to recognise the existence of some of the most common forms of legal problem. It would be possible to assemble a 'kit' of information that could be communicated in one lecture to trainees in various fields on Recognising a Legal Problem and What to Do About It. Such an approach might, at little or no cost, do more to reduce the unmet need for legal services than any amount of expensive advertising.

The legal profession is gradually coming to accept that, although it may be the largest single purveyor of legal services, it is by no means the sole provider of such services. In fact the non-lawyers (CABs, unions, newspapers and a host of other specialist and non-specialist advisory facilities) between them probably give more legal advice than the legal profession. The growing realisation that the lawyers are only *primus inter partes* helps to create the atmosphere which leads to the establishment of *ad hoc* or standing committees on which different advising professions and agencies are represented. Over the past years, especially in the 1970s, in England there has in fact begun to be a sense of community amongst those involved from different vantage-points in the field of legal services. The Law Society, the Law Centres Working Group, the Legal Action Group, the National Association of Citizens' Advice Bureaux, the Lord Chancellor's Legal Aid Advisory Committee and the officials in the Lord Chancellor's Office know one another well. There are frequent occasions for both formal and informal meetings. The fact that most of those involved know and respect each other helps in the ironing out of the inevitable differences of view. Occasionally these prove too great for compromise but, much more frequently, decisions are agreed or at least influenced by the course of prior discussions. The formulation of policy is also greatly assisted by the fact that there are two weekly journals[12] (the *Law Society's Gazette*, and the *New Law Journal*) and two monthlies (the *Guardian Gazette* and the *Legal Action Group Bulletin*) which regularly carry articles and comment on current problems in the field and are widely read in the profession.

The legal profession, albeit slowly and somewhat grudgingly, is now also beginning to come to terms with the new era in which more than lip-service has to be paid to the principle of accountability to the public interest. In England it has accepted lay members in the profession's disciplinary processes, a Lay Observer to review the Law Society's complaints machinery, and lay members of the Law Society's Legal Aid Committee and of its new unofficial Legal Services Committee in Manchester. The majority of most management committees of law centres are laymen, as are about half the members of the Lord Chancellor's Legal Aid Advisory Committee and more than half of the Royal Commission. The next stages in this development may be lay members on the central committees of the profession and an advisory committee with substantial lay membership to report annually on any aspect of legal services whether in the private or the public sector. At least as important will be some mechanism for conducting authoritative research on current problems in the field of legal services. Detailed study of anonymous random samples of cases may not be a perfect technique, but it is likely to be the best available instrument for evaluating and, therefore, of raising the quality of work done by the profession. Either the Lay Observer or the Lord Chancellor's Legal Services Advisory Committee might be appropriate offices from which to operate a Legal Services Research Unit. There must also, clearly, be some permanent reputable method for assessing the level of incomes and of overheads of lawyers so as to permit fees paid out of the public purse to be fixed on a rational and fair basis. The machinery for approving the rules of ethics will also have to be broadened so as to get informed representation of the public interest.

There is bound to be further movement in the direction of abolishing restrictive practices and reducing the scope of monopolies. The climate of the times is no longer in sympathy with the philosophy that gave the profession special economic protection at the expense of clients. In recent years the Bar has found itself constrained by outside criticism to abolish the rule requiring special fees on circuit, the Two-Counsel Rule and the Two-Thirds Rule, and both sides of the profession have liberalised their rules on advertising and on working free of charge for the poor. In each of these cases dire consequences for the public well-being were predicted by the forces of conservatism; in every case they failed to materialise. The next candidates for reform in England are likely to be rules that regulate unfair competition, that restrict rights of audience, that prevent direct access of clients (especially professional clients) to barristers, and monopolies over conveyancing and probate transactions. In countries where the legal profession enjoys a monopoly over the giving of legal advice, this must be a prime target for removal.

All of the changes and improvements so far mentioned can be, and very likely will be, achieved. They are simply the logical development of principles already broadly agreed and established. There are others, however, which are much more difficult to realise. One is the problem of cost. Lawyers in all countries are an expensive resource. Experience suggests that, no matter what efforts are made to reduce the cost of legal services, they will always remain effectively beyond the purse of most of the population. This is so even when the potential client actually has the money to pay the fees that lawyers must charge in order to make a reasonable profit. The problem is not so much lack of the money as an unwillingness to use it for such services. The purchaser of a house is prepared (though he is not delighted) to spend a substantial sum of money on legal fees in order to get the house. Someone who wants a divorce may likewise regard it as sufficiently a priority to spend what it costs. But large numbers of people who have money to spend on a car, holidays, entertainment, clothes, furniture, the home and the (quite expensive) services of such as builders, decorators, electricians or even doctors, are not prepared to

spend money on the services of lawyers, unless they feel they
have to. The state, through the legal aid scheme, makes provision for those at the bottom of the economic scale, but, given
the competing claims on public moneys, in most countries
there will be limits to the amount of money the state is likely to
be willing to spend to provide legal services for the ordinary
working population. Sweden appears to be the only country in
the world at present where legal aid covers most of the population.[13] Moreover, even the legal aid scheme cannot cope
with the problem of small claims where the cost of pursuing a
remedy with the help of lawyers is always likely to be out of all
proportion to the amount at stake.[14]

Apart from ampler provision for free or subsidised services
paid for out of general taxation, there are no complete answers
to the problem. Contingent fee arrangements may provide a
partial solution for damages actions, especially perhaps under
the scheme proposed by Justice (p. 218 above). The other chief
hope is insurance, either through policies taken out by individuals or through group schemes of one kind or another.
Individual policies seem unlikely to become sufficiently popular to make any great impact on the problem. Even if they
were added as an optional extra to some form of ordinary
insurance package – houseowners, house contents or motor-
ists' policy – the probability is that relatively few people would
select it. Group policies are more likely to afford cover for
large numbers, particularly as fringe benefits offered by
unions and employers. But even if these increase greatly, the
bulk of the population will probably remain outside such
schemes. For them, the cost of going to law will remain an
almost insuperable hurdle.

It must also be admitted that even those who do use lawyers
will not always get the service their cases deserve. Though
little research has yet been done on the quality of legal services
it is obvious that time, money and skill are not available in
unlimited quantities. The large corporate client or the rich
individual can afford to have armies of top-class lawyers. A
law centre may also be in a position to provide unusually
extensive services for the occasional very important case. A
case that is argued in the Court of Appeal is likely to be
prepared twice as well as when it was heard at first instance
and, when it goes on to the House of Lords, even greater

efforts are usually rewarded by a hearing that is twice again as careful and searching. By comparison with the quality of the presentation in the House of Lords, the argument in the High Court comes to look almost second-rate. Yet few cases ever go beyond the High Court and most are disposed of at lower levels. The amount of preparation and the quality of advocacy in the ordinary run-of-the-mill case in the magistrates' courts, the county courts and even the crown courts is far from ideal. Private practitioners are driven to cut corners by the need to make a profit; law centre lawyers are overwhelmed by their case-load. Few lawyers are in the fortunate position of having just the right number and the right kind of clients to enable them both to earn what they consider to be a reasonable profit and also to give the best service of which they are capable. Moreover, given the shortcomings at all levels of legal education (in the universities, in the polytechnics, in the professional schools, under articles and in pupillage), it is not to be expected that all lawyers are adequately trained for their work. In England, post-qualification training courses are becoming more popular in the solicitors' branch and this will no doubt grow – but those most in need of such help are those least likely to seek it.

The problem of the unmet need for legal services is therefore a permanent condition. There will always be large numbers of people who need or could benefit from advice and assistance with legal problems who, for a variety of reasons, will not get such help. Equally, there will always be a need for legal services that is only partially met – because of work that is done less well than it should be. On the other hand, there is also some reason for optimism. Lawyers in most countries are as intelligent, as hard-working, and as devoted to the interests of their clients as any other group in society. They care a great deal about their work and their profession. Not only do they commonly find a great deal of satisfaction in their work, but most of what they do is highly regarded by their clients.

It is unlikely that even the most reform-oriented lawyers will transform society.[15] The early rhetoric of the OEO legal services movement suggested that lawyers for the poor might succeed in working miracles. The first director of the OEO Legal Services Programme in 1966 said 'Our responsibility is to marshal the forces of law and the strength of lawyers to combat the causes and effects of poverty. Lawyers must uncover the legal causes of poverty, remodel the systems which generate the cycle of poverty and design new social, legal and political tools and vehicles to move poor people from deprivation, depression and despair to opportunity, hope and ambition ...'[16] Sober appraisal more than ten years later shows that, on the whole, the poor remain disadvantaged, discriminated against – and poor.[17] Legal services have brought substantial and worthwhile gains; they have not ushered in the millennium.

The scope and the limits of the role of lawyers will vary from country to country – depending, amongst other things, on the traditions of different societies. In the United States, lawyers dominate every aspect of public life – not only are they deeply involved in the affairs of their clients, but lawyers run business, the state and the federal legislatures, and the higher reaches of the civil service. In most other countries they are less pervasive. The impact that lawyers can make in achieving change will, of course, depend not only on the traditional role of the profession in each country, but as much on their energy and creativity and on the extent to which new initiatives find either a positive or a hostile response in the reaction of the judges, the legislature and the public.

But most practitioners, whether in the public or the private sector (even in the United States), do not spend their time testing the limits of the law, nor in expanding the class of work done by the profession. They devote themselves rather to helping the clients who come to them in more or less traditional ways, on a broadly familiar range of problems. As society and the law become increasingly complex, the need for the skills of lawyers and others with knowledge of the law becomes more and more important. The role of lawyers and of para-legal workers in the future is, therefore, bound to be even more important than in the past. There are large numbers of people of every social class, income group, age, sex, racial and ethnic background with a great range of unmet needs for competent advice and assistance on legal problems. Lord Elwyn-Jones, speaking as Lord Chancellor in the House of Lords of the unmet need for legal services, said: 'We confront, my Lords, not a pool but an ocean'.[18] There is little hope that this will ever change; but the size of the ocean *can* be reduced.

Notes

Evidence = *Memorandum of Evidence to the Royal Commission on Legal Services 1977*

Preface

1 House of Commons, *Hansard*, 12 February 1976, vol. 905, col. 617.

Introduction

1 *The Times*, 7 November 1950.
2 *The Times*, 20 March 1951.
3 Timothy Daniell, *Inns of Court*, 1971 (Wildy and Sons), Foreword.
4 See p. 37 below.
5 M. Cappelletti and J. Gordley, 'Legal Aid: Modern Themes and Variations', 24 *Stanford Law Review*, 1972, p. 347. Professor Cappelletti was author of the first, historical section.
6 Ibid., p. 350.
7 Ibid., p. 351, n. 22.
8 Ibid.
9 Ibid., p. 351.
10 Ibid.
11 Ibid., p. 352.
12 Ibid.
13 Ibid., p. 354.
14 Ibid., p. 357.
15 Ibid., pp. 359–60.
16 Lord Chancellor's Legal Aid Advisory Committee, *Evidence*, p. 28, para. 25.3.
17 M. Zander, 'Costs in Crown Courts – A study of lawyers' fees paid out of public funds', *Criminal Law Review* [1976], p. 5. This led within days to the call by Mr Jack Ashley MP for a Royal Commission, see *The Times*, 7 January 1976.
18 *New Society* 15 January 1974, *The Sunday Times*, 25 January; *The Times*, 26 January; the *Daily Mirror*, 28 January; *The Guardian*, 9

February; *The Observer*, 15 February; *The Economist*, 21 February.

19 The Legal Action Group was founded in 1971. Its members are barristers, solicitors, academic lawyers, social workers and other lay advisers. Its concern is to promote improved legal services for the community and especially for those in deprived areas. It publishes an influential monthly journal – the *LAG Bulletin*. In January 1978 it had over 3,800 subscribers. Its address is 28A, Highgate Road, London NW5.

20 *The Times*, 29 February 1976.

21 Royal Commission on Legal Services, *Report on Progress*, April 1977, Cmnd. 6770.

22 One was, however, set up almost immediately in New South Wales.

23 The terms of reference were stated to be: 'To inquire into the law and practice relating to the provision of legal services in England and Wales and to consider whether any, and if so what, changes are desirable in the public interest in the structure, organisation, training, regulation of and entry to the legal profession, including the arrangements for determining its remuneration, whether from private sources or public funds, and in the rules which prevent persons who are neither barristers nor solicitors from undertaking conveyancing and other legal business on behalf of other persons' (905 House of Commons, *Hansard*, 12 February 1976, col. 618).

1   The Private Profession

1 *Law Society's Gazette*, 21 February 1973, p. 1445.

2 C. M. Campbell and R. J. Wilson, 'Public Attitudes to the Legal Profession in Scotland', summary of report published by Law Society of Scotland, 1973, pp. 9–10. See *Law Society's Gazette*, 18 July 1973, p. 2082.

3 Consumers' Association, *Which?*, May 1977, pp. 297–301. See to same effect M. Murch, 'The Role of Solicitors in Divorce Proceedings', *Modern Law Review*, 1978, pp. 28–30.

4 B. Abel-Smith, M. Zander and R. Brooke, *Legal Problems and the Citizen*, 1973 (Heinemann, London), p. 249.

5 Barbara Curran, *The Legal Needs of the Public, Final Report* (American Bar Foundation, 1977), Fig. 5.21, p. 206; Table 5.15 p. 210. The survey was based on interviews with a national random sample of 2,064 adults in thirty-three States and the District of Columbia.

6 Ibid., p. 214.

7 See, for instance, the Declaration of Bath resulting from a meeting of representatives of the Bar Council and the Council of the Law Society which stated 'that the interests of the public are best served by a legal profession divided into two branches: barristers and solicitors, of equal status but with different and complementary functions'. (Bar Council, *Annual Statement*, 1975 6, p. 39; *Law Society's Gazette*, 17 December 1975, p. 1246.)

8 The Bar Council recently ruled that 'where there is no heating in chambers (as a result of the energy crisis) it would not be improper for a member of the Bar, as a last resort, to attend a conference at a solicitor's office, but it would be preferable, if possible, to find a neutral venue' (*Annual Statement*, 1973–4, p. 29). In the same issue of the *Annual Statement* it was stated (p. 41) that the Bar Courts Committee in considering luncheon facilities for counsel in new courts thought that as a general principle whenever reasonably possible, counsel 'should not be asked to share a room for luncheon' with solicitors.

9 These figures include grants of legal aid for trials in magistrates' courts, trials in juvenile courts and committal proceedings. The total number of proceedings in magistrates' courts in the two years were: 1,044,835 and 2,173,939.

10 Figures supplied by the Building Societies Association.

11 The evidence of one set of chambers to the Royal Commission stated, however, that they did in fact have a profit-sharing scheme in defiance of the rules. (*Evidence*, Wellington Street Chambers, para. 3.)

12 PIB, *Standing Reference on the Remuneration of Solicitors, First Report*, 1969, Cmnd. 4217, p. 28 – calculated from Table 1.

13 Ibid., p. 37 – calculated from Table 10.

14 Ibid., p. 29 – calculated from Table 2.

15 PIB, *Solicitors' Remuneration*, 1968, Cmnd. 3529, p. 11, para. 32.

16 L. Bridges, B. Sufrin, J. Whetton and R. White, *Legal Services in Birmingham*, 1975 (University of Birmingham), pp. 40–3.

17 Figures supplied by the British Medical Association.

18 K. Foster, 'The Location of Solicitors', *Modern Law Review*, 1973, p. 153.

19 A. P. Blaustein and C. O. Porter, *The American Lawyer*, 1964, (University of Chicago Press), p. 13; New South Wales Bureau of Crime Statistics and Research, *Territorial Justice in Australia*, 1974, cited in J. Disney *et al*, *Lawyers*, 1977 (Law Book Co. Ltd, Sydney) pp. 175–6.

20 Bridges *et al.*, op. cit. (note 16 above), p. 18.

21 Ibid., Table 1.3, p. 17.

22 Research in Wolverhampton has shown that an advice centre on

a housing estate was greatly used. In a six-month period almost
half the local inhabitants consulted the centre and about a third
of the inquiries were in regard to social security matters.
(NACAB Occasional Paper, 'Welfare Advice and Advocacy',
by Roger Lawrence, 1977, p. 25.)

23 Curran, op. cit. (note 5 above). Information originally in type-
    script. Now to be used in separate forthcoming article.
24 Abel-Smith et al., op. cit. (note 4 above), p. 192.
25 See Legal Action Group Bulletin, April 1975, p. 88.
26 There is provision for special allowances to practices in desig-
    nated areas consisting of flat rate additions to basic practice
    allowances (in 1977, £750 p.a. or £1,150 p.a.), plus four types of
    initial practice allowances payable for four years as a way of
    encouraging doctors to work in designated areas. (National
    Health Service, 'How the Family Doctor is Paid', NHS Note
    2A, DHSS Information Division, April 1976, para. 2A and 17.)
27 This was first proposed by the Society of Conservative Lawyers
    in Rough Justice, 1968 (Conservative Political Centre).
28 Law Society, Evidence, Memorandum No. 3, Part 1, p. 233.
29 Quoted in House of Commons, Hansard, 5th Series, Vol. 231, 8
    November 1929, col. 1416.
30 Poor Prisoners' Defence Act 1930, s.2.
31 Legal Aid Act 1974, s.29 (1).
32 Criminal Statistics, 1976, Cmnd. 6909, p. 355, Table 24 (c).
33 These criteria were first articulated by the Report of the
    Widgery Committee, Legal Aid in Criminal Proceedings, 1966,
    Cmnd. 2934, para. 180, p. 48.
34 See M. Zander, 'Legal Aid Contribution Orders', New Law
    Journal, 1 January 1976, p. 4.
35 See generally E. J. T. Matthews and A. D. M. Oulton, Legal Aid
    and Advice, 1971 (Butterworths, London).
36 Report of the Committee on Legal Aid and Legal Advice in England
    and Wales, 1945, Cmnd. 6641.
37 Legal Aid Act 1974, s.7(5). See Matthews and Oulton, op. cit.
    (note 35 above), pp. 122–37, and A. F. Seton Pollock, Legal
    Action Group Bulletin, December 1973, p. 264; and 'Legal Aid:
    The Factor of Reasonableness', Solicitors' Journal, 1 March 1974,
    p. 123. See also R. White, 'Being Reasonable about Legal Aid',
    Solicitors' Journal, 1973, pp. 883, 885.
38 See R. v. Legal Aid Committee No. 1 (London) Legal Aid Area, ex
    parte Rondel [1967] 2 Q. B. 482.
39 For a table of recent changes see 26th Annual Report on Legal Aid,
    1975–6, p. 59. For the latest figures at time of writing see Law
    Society's Gazette, 9 November 1977, p. 962.
40 26th Annual Report on Legal Aid, 1975–6, pp. 79–80.

41 Ibid., p. 61.
42 He cannot be required to pay more than is reasonable, which is usually given this interpretation. (Legal Aid Act 1974, s.8(1)(e).) The resulting hardship to a successful unassisted party is alleviated by the provisions of the Legal Aid Act 1974, s.13, which permits the court to order that the whole or part of his costs may be paid out of the fund.
43 *26th Annual Report on Legal Aid*, 1975–6, calculated from Appendix 1 and 2, pp. 13–14.
44 Ibid., Appendix 21, p. 40.
45 The Law Society, 'Legal Advice and Assistance', 1968; and see further the Law Society's second memorandum under the same title July, 1969.
46 Law Society, *Evidence, Memorandum No. 3, Part 2*, p. 172, para. XIX. 16.9.
47 See 'In Praise of the Green Form Scheme – Sort of', *Legal Action Group Bulletin*, February 1975, p. 35.
48 *25th Annual Report on Legal Aid*, 1974–5, Appendix D, p. 55–62.
49 *24th Annual Report on Legal Aid*, 1973–4, p. 49.
50 The Trades Union Council and the Labour Party, however, urged instead that public funds be given to the lay agencies that do or could provide a tribunal advocacy service (e.g. trades unions, citizens' advice bureaux and specialist bodies such as the Child Poverty Action Group or MIND) to enable them to strengthen their work in this field. (The Labour Party, *The Citizen and the Law*, 1977, para. 7, pp. 7–10.) The trade unions oppose the extension of legal aid to tribunals mainly because they are reluctant to see their members (or potential members) use lawyers rather than trade union services. Their opposition has applied equally, however, to tribunals where trade unions play little or no role, such as those in the rent or supplementary benefit fields.
51 *Criminal Statistics*, 1976, Cmnd. 6909, Table 24 (c), p. 355.
52 National Council for Civil Liberties, *Rights*, Vol. 1, No. 2, November 1976, p. 11. The refusal rate is roughly 10 per cent of applications for legal aid in the magistrates' courts. (See *Criminal Statistics*, 1976, pp. 337–49.) There are still however considerable variations as between courts – see H. Levenson, 'Criminal Legal Aid in 1976', *New Law Journal*, 19 January 1978, pp. 52, 53–54.
53 M. Zander, 'Costs of Litigation – A Study in the Queen's Bench Division', *Law Society's Gazette*, 25 June 1975, p. 680.
54 According to one study on divorce county courts, representation there was about equally divided between barristers and solicitors; see E. Elston, J. Fuller and M. Murch, 'Judicial Hear-

ings of Undefended Divorce Petitions', *Modern Law Review*, 1975, p. 613.

55 Bar, *Evidence, Addendum to Submission No. 8*, p. 3, Table C.

56 Ibid., Table K, p. 9.

57 PIB, *Solicitors' Remuneration*, 1968, Cmnd. 3529, Table 15, p. 49. The dominance of property matters in the work of the profession was confirmed in a survey of matters taken to solicitors by a random sample of the population: 'Who Goes to Solicitors?', 66 *Law Society's Gazette*, 1969, p. 174. But the higher social classes had distinctly more property problems. Property accounted for 55 per cent of the problems reported by the AB social class compared with 37 per cent of the DE class.

58 *26th Annual Report on Legal Aid*, 1975–6, Appendix 13, p. 27. Some firms have more than one office.

59 Ibid.

60 Bridges *et al.*, op. cit. (note 16 above), Table 1.9, p. 34.

61 Ibid., p. 36.

62 Ibid., p. 37.

63 Ibid.

64 Ibid.

65 Ibid.

66 See for instance Lord Chancellor's Legal Aid Advisory Committee in *20th Annual Report on Legal Aid*, 1969–70, para. 15, p. 38.

67 See *26th Annual Report on Legal Aid*, 1975–6, Appendix 5, p. 18.

67a See, for instance, F. R. Marks, K. Leswing, B. A. Fortinsky, *The Lawyer, The Public and Professional Responsibility*, 1972 (American Bar Foundation).

67b See *Balancing the Scales of Justice: Financing Public Interest Law*, 1976, a report of the Council for Public Interest Law, 1250 Connecticut Avenue, Washington DC 20036, especially pp. 281–311; and M. Zander 'Pro Bono Publico', *Law Society's Gazette*, 27 September 1972.

68 Joel F. Handler, Ellen Jane Hollingsworth and Howard S. Erlanger, 'The Public Interest Activities of Private Practice Lawyers', *American Bar Association Journal*, November 1975, p. 1388. The study is to be published in book form as *Lawyers and the Pursuit of Legal Rights*, (Academic Press) in 1978.

69 *American Bar Association Journal*, May 1977, p. 678.

70 The number of divorces (to the nearest hundred) in 1961, 1966, 1971 and 1976 respectively was: 25,400; 39,100; 74,400 and 126,700.

71 See Gerald Sanctuary, 'Should the Profession Advertise?', *Law Society's Gazette*, 10 November 1976, p. 933; and Law Society, *Evidence, Memorandum No. 3, Part 2*, pp. 68–70.

72 *Law Society's Gazette*, 4 October 1972, p. 902; Law Society, *Evidence, Memorandum No. 3, Part 2*, p. 78. Positive results were also obtained by a two-week campaign conducted at the cost of £10 per solicitor in the Bolton area – *Law Society's Gazette*, 19 June 1974, p. 598.

73 The campaign is described by the Lord Chancellor's Legal Aid Advisory Committee in the *23rd Annual Report on Legal Aid, 1972–3*, p. 35, para. 18.

74 *Law Society's Gazette*, 14 September 1977, p. 749; *Law Society's Gazette*, 19 October, p. 883.

75 Law Society, *Evidence, Memorandum No. 3, Part 2*, p. 80.

76 *Law Society's Gazette*, 4 October 1974, p. 902.

77 *Law Society's Gazette*, 12 May 1976, p. 404.

78 M. Arnott and E. Rodnight, 'Public Policy and Measuring the Open-ended Situation', 1974 (ESOMAR Hamburg Conference Publication), p. 468.

79 Ibid.

80 Schlackman Research Organisation, 'An Investigation into Current Awareness and Knowledge of the Legal Advice and Assistance Scheme Among Recommenders and Potential Clients', April 1975, unpublished, Table 1.

81 Arnott and Rodnight, op. cit. (note 78 above), p. 478.

82 Schlackman Research Organisation, op. cit. (note 80 above), Table 29, p. 47.

83 Ibid., p. 41.

84 The Lord Chancellor's Legal Aid Advisory Committee in its evidence to the Royal Commission said: 'Experience has taught that mass publicity for the legal aid scheme, beyond the minimum necessary to explain the scheme to users by leaflets, etc. is not good value for money. The number of times that most people are likely to need the help of a lawyer, and therefore the proportion of people who need such help at any one time, is too small for such publicity to be very cost-effective ... better results are obtained by concentrating on providing information at the point of immediate need. This is why it seems to us particularly important to ensure that full information about the scope and availability of legal services is given to the advisory workers who come into direct contact with so many people who need help on legal matters'. (Para. 3.4, p. 7.)

85 *In Re a Solicitor* [1945] 1 All E. R., 445.

86 Law Society, *Evidence, Memorandum No. 3, Part 2*, p. 77, para. VIII. 2.8.

87 Law Society, *A guide to the professional conduct of solicitors*, 1974, p. 84, para. 2.2

88 Ibid.

89 The Citizens' Advice Bureaux Evidence to the Royal Com-
    mission stated (p. 57) that 31 per cent of bureaux were able to
    refer clients to solicitors' offices for initial interviews at a fixed
    fee which varied from nothing to £6 for half an hour. The
    thirteen Local Law Societies in Greater London agreed a £5 fixed
    fee system in early 1976 – *Solicitors' Journal*, 22 July 1977, p. 488
    – but no solicitor was obliged to take part in the scheme.
90 *Law Society's Gazette*, 22 June 1977, p. 529.
91 See especially, *Legal Action Group Bulletin*, June 1977, p. 122.
92 Monopolies Commission, *Services of Solicitors in England and
    Wales in relation to Advertising*, 1976, p. 41, para. 136(3).
93 Ibid., p. 40, para. 135.
94 Ibid., p. 33, para. 108.
95 Ibid., p. 33, para. 109.
96 Ibid.
97 Campbell and Wilson, op. cit. (note 2 above), p. 17.
98 Law Society, *Evidence, Memorandum 3, Part 2*, p. 176, para. XX.
    17.3.
99 53 L. Ed. 2d 810(1977).
100 The majority consisted of Blackmun, Brennan, White,
    Marshall and Stevens JJ. Chief Justice Burger, Powell, Stewart
    and Rehnquist JJ dissenting thought that advertising of legal
    services would be injurious to the public interest.
101 The court said it found 'the postulated connection between
    advertising and the erosion of true professionalism to be
    severely strained' (p. 826). It presumed that lawyers much
    conceal 'the real-life fact that lawyers earn their livelihood at the
    bar' (ibid.). Lawyers charged fees – and were even normally
    required to do so by their rules of ethical conduct. 'If the
    commercial basis of the relationship is to be promptly disclosed
    on ethical grounds, once the client is in the office, it seems
    inconsistent to condemn the candid revelation of the same
    information before he arrives at that office' (ibid.). Far from
    advertising lowering the profession in the eyes of the com-
    munity it was the profession's failure to make itself known to
    the community that created public disillusionment with the
    profession. The ban on advertising originated as a rule of eti-
    quette and not as a rule of ethics. 'Early lawyers in Britain
    viewed the law as a form of public service rather than as a means
    of earning a living, and they looked down on "trade" as
    unseemly' (p. 828). Since the belief that lawyers are somehow
    above trade has become an anachronism 'the historical founda-
    tion for the advertising restraint had crumbled' (ibid.).
102 No doubt advertising of prices did not convey information
    about quality of service but this did not mean it was misleading;

'it seems peculiar to deny the consumer, on the ground that the information is incomplete, at least some of the relevant information needed to reach an informed decision' (p. 830). Prohibition of advertising restricted the flow of information to consumers. The public was able to appreciate the limitation of advertising.

103 Although advertising might increase the use of the legal system this was not necessarily a bad thing. 'We cannot accept the notion that it is always better for a person to suffer a wrong silently than to redress it by legal action' (p. 831). Fear of the cost was an important factor in a large section of the population not being served by lawyers. A rule allowing restrained advertising would be in accord with the bar's obligation to 'facilitate the process of intelligent selection of lawyers, and to assist in making legal services fully available' (ibid.).

104 Where consumers of other products had access to price advertising, prices were often dramatically lower than they would be without advertising. It was entirely possible that the effect of advertising would reduce rather than increase costs (p. 832).

105 Lawyers inclined to cut quality would do so regardless of the rule on advertising. Moreover, clinics with standardised procedure for routine problems might improve service (p. 832).

106 Most lawyers, the court said, would no doubt continue to uphold the integrity of the profession and of the legal system (p. 833).

107 p. 1058. See also *American B. A. Journal*, Jan. 1978, pp. 23, 36–8.

108 *American Bar Association Journal*, September 1977, p. 1234.

109 The writer attended a Law Society press conference on 19 July 1977 at which its then President, Mr David Napley, said he hoped that the Supreme Court's decision would have no impact in England.

110 Law Society, *Evidence, Memorandum, No. 3, Part 2*, p. 75, para. VIII. 1.2(a).

111 Lord Chancellor's Legal Aid Advisory Committee, *Evidence*, para. 12, p. 15.

112 Law Society, *A guide to the professional conduct of solicitors*, 1974, pp. 85–6.

113 Ibid.

114 *26th Annual Report on Legal Aid*, 1975–6, p. 6, para. 20.

115 Justice, *The Unrepresented Defendant in Magistrates' Courts*, 1971 (Stevens, London).

116 Law Society, *Evidence, Memorandum; No. 3, Part 1*, p. 224, para. XXI. 5. The Law Society published a Guide to Duty Solicitor Schemes in the *Law Society's Gazette*, 2 June 1975, p. 577. See also P. A. Thomas and Geoff. Mungham, *A Report on the Duty*

    Solicitor Scheme operating in the Cardiff Magistrates' Courts: 1973–4; 'Duty Solicitor Schemes: A LAG Report', *Legal Action Group Bulletin*, September 1974, p. 207; Michael King, *The effects of a duty solicitor scheme*, Cobden Trust, 1976.

117 The importance of providing proper legal services in prisons was strongly emphasised in the Evidence of the Howard League for Penal Reform to the Royal Commission.

118 In November 1977 if the client had take-home pay of between £23 and £48 he had to pay a contribution on a sliding scale from £3 to £33. The average gross weekly wage of all men over 21 in full-time work as at April 1977 was £78.60. For men and women over 18 it was £69.30p. (Dept of Employment, *Gazette*, October 1977, p. 1053, Table 1; p. 1170, Table 126.)

119 The Lord Chancellor's Legal Aid Advisory Committee said in evidence to the Royal Commission that the new fixed fee scheme 'may do more than any other single recent measure to conquer the reluctance of members of the public to seek the help of a lawyer'. Looking further ahead, there was a case for building this voluntary arrangement into the statutory Green Form scheme. However, that needed further examination than it had yet given the idea (p. 14, para. 11.4).

120 *American Bar Association Journal*, September 1976, p. 1124.

121 This point is made by Barlow Christenson in *Lawyers for People of Moderate Means*, 1970 (American Bar Foundation), pp. 211–13, in commenting on an experiment with low-cost cheap services provided in Neighbourhood Law Offices in Philadelphia. The scheme there was established in 1964 by the Philadelphia Bar Association. The scheme had served quite large numbers of clients but in spite of much commendation in the lay and legal press it had not in 1970 been copied anywhere else in the country. Christenson speculates that an important reason might be the lawyer's disinclination to offer that form of service. It appears that this may be changing.

122 *American Bar Association Journal*, October 1977, pp. 1361, 1374.

123 *Legal Action Group Bulletin*, November 1977, p. 251.

2   The Public Sector in Legal Services: A New Concept Established

1 Lee Silverstein, *Defence of the Poor*, Vol. 1, 1965, p. 41.

2 Ibid.

3 Letter to the writer from Laurence Benner, National Director for Defender Services, 29 July 1977.

4 Ronald Sackville, *Legal Aid in Australia*, 1975 (Commission of Inquiry into Poverty), p. 93, s. 3.55.

5 Ibid., p. 89, s. 3.38.
6 Ibid., p. 98, s. 3.74–5.
7 Ibid., p. 78, s. 3.1.
8 B. Abel-Smith and R. Stevens, *Lawyers and the Courts*, 1967 (Heinemann, London), p. 317.
9 Seton Pollock, 'Legal Aid as a Social Service', *Law Society's Gazette*, June 1970, p. 399.
10 *24th Report on Legal Aid and Advice*, 1973–4, p. 37.
11 The stages are set out in E. J. T. Matthews and A. D. M. Oulton, *Legal Aid and Advice*, 1971 (Butterworths, London), pp. 17–18.
12 Pollock, op. cit. (note 9 above), p. 399.
13 Earl Johnson Jr., *Justice and Reform*, 1974 (Russell Sage, New York), p. 9.
14 J. Carlin and J. Howard, 'Legal Representation and Class Justice', 12 *University of California Law Review*, 1965, pp. 381, 410.
15 Reginald Heber Smith, *Justice and the Poor*, 1919 (Carnegie Foundation, New York), pp. 257, 261.
16 See generally Johnson, op. cit. (note 13 above), pp. 21–35.
17 Ibid., pp. 22–3, 25–7.
18 Ibid., pp. 23–5.
19 Ibid., pp. 27–32.
20 73 *Yale Law Journal* 1964, p. 1317.
21 Ibid., p. 1352.
22 Johnson, op. cit. (note 13 above), p. 188.
23 Ibid., p. 167.
24 *Proceedings of the Harvard Conference on Law and Poverty*, 1967, pp. 3–4.
25 See Johnson, op. cit. (note 13 above), pp. 176–82.
26 Law reform centres included: the Center for Social Welfare Policy at Columbia University; a housing law centre at the University of California, Berkeley; a consumer law centre at Boston University Law School; a juvenile law centre in St Louis University; an employment law centre in New York; an education law centre at Harvard Law School; a health law centre at UCLA Law School; and an elderly law centre at the University of Southern California. For the friends and supporters of OEO legal services, the back-up centres were its chief ornament and success; for the programme's enemies, such as Governor Reagan, they were its most objectionable feature.
27 'Poverty and the Law', *Socialist Commentary*, September 1966, p. 15. See also M. Zander, 'Lawyers on the Doorstep', *The Guardian*, 19 January 1967.
28 Meeting of 15 February 1967.
29 *16th Annual Report on Legal Aid*, 1965–6, p. 51, para. 9.

30 *17th Annual Report on Legal Aid*, 1966–7, pp. 57–8.
31 Ibid., p. 58, para. 34.
32 Society of Labour Lawyers, *Justice for All*, Fabian Research Series, 1968, p. 1.
33 Law Society, 'Legal Advice and Assistance', February 1968, para. 23.
34 Ibid., para. 22.
35 The Labour Party had said: 'There are obvious objections to the state itself establishing and maintaining legal advice bureaux. Not the least of these objections is that the State itself is directly or indirectly affected by many of the claims upon which such bureaux would have to advise. Nor, in the opinion of the Labour Party, is it desirable that local authorities should be entrusted with the duty of establishing and maintaining legal advice bureaux ... Differences, political or otherwise, might well arise were a local authority to be held responsible directly or indirectly for the advice given in any particular matter. Moreover, it has to be borne in mind that many local authorities, particularly those concerned with passenger transport undertakings, are themselves frequently parties to litigation ... ' (*Report of the [Rushcliffe] Committee on Legal Aid and Legal Advice*, 1945, Cmnd. 6641, para. 129.)
36 The writer was present throughout.
37 Law Society, *Legal Advice and Assistance*, February 1968, para. 19.
38 Ibid., para. 20.
39 Ibid.
40 As has been seen (p. 60 above), the Law Society's original scheme based on salaried advisers was abandoned in favour of private practitioners giving advice in their offices.
41 *17th Annual Report* (note 30 above), para. 21.
42 *Justice for All* (note 32 above), pp. 50–4.
43 See especially Seton Pollock, *Legal Aid – The First 25 Years*, 1975 (Oyez, London).
44 Unpublished, speech of Mr Seton Pollock, Oxford, 3 August 1968, p. 6. I am indebted to Mr Pollock for making the text available to me..
45 Ibid., p. 7. As has been seen (p. 28 above), in fact the distribution of solicitors is far from even.
46 Ibid.
47 But, as has been seen (pp. 39–40), the great majority of the profession do very little legal aid work.
48 Pollock, op. cit. (note 44 above), p. 10.
49 Ibid., pp. 14–16.
50 Pollock, op. cit. (note 43 above), p. 92. The use by Mr Pollock

of the word 'propaganda' to describe the Labour Lawyers' draft was, no doubt, to distinguish it from the Law Society's paper.

51 Ibid.
52 Ibid., p. 94.
53 I invited Mr Pollock to show me any *unpublished* Law Society document supporting his assertion that the Law Society favoured the idea in 1968. None was forthcoming.
54 *Law Society's Gazette*, November 1968, p. 655.
55 Ibid.
56 Ibid.
57 For a 'blow-by-blow' description of the process leading to this vote see Johnson, op. cit. (note 13 above), pp. 49–64.
58 Marna S. Tucker 'Pro Bono ABA?', in R. Nader and M. Green (eds), *Verdicts on Lawyers*, 1976 (Crowell, New York), p. 25.
59 *Justice for All*, op. cit. (note 32 above).
60 Cf. doctors, p. 31, n. 26 above.
61 Society of Conservative Lawyers, *Rough Justice*, 1968, p. 20.
62 Seton Pollock, 'The Future of Legal Aid in England', *Law Society's Gazette*, March 1969, p. 174.
63 Ibid.
64 Law Society, 'Legal Advice and Assistance', July 1969, p. 9 – both (d) and (e) were new.
65 *Report of the Advisory Committee on the better provision of Legal Advice and Assistance*, 1970, Cmnd. 4249.
66 Ibid., para. 19, p. 7.
67 Ibid.
68 Ibid.
69 Now to be found in Legal Aid Act 1974, s. 16.
70 *23rd Annual Report on Legal Aid*, 1972–3, p. 35, para. 19.
71 *24th Annual Report on Legal Aid*, 1973–4, p. 56, para. 54.
72 *25th Annual Report on Legal Aid*, 1974–5, p. 50, para. 51.
73 *26th Annual Report on Legal Aid*, 1975–6, p. 72, para. 50.
74 Law Society, *Evidence, Memorandum No. 3, Part 1*, p. 205, para. XX. 2.2.
75 Ibid., p. 217, para. XX. 18.6.
76 Ibid., p. 208, para. XX. 5.4(ii); p. 214, XX. 14.3; p. 217, XX. 18.3; p. 224, XXI. 5.3; *Memorandum No. 3, Part 2*, p. 178, XXII. 2.1. The main functions of the liaison officers would include setting up rota schemes in CABs and duty solicitor schemes in magistrates' courts, dealing with special referral problems, setting up tribunal representation schemes, educational work with CABs, social workers, school children etc. and also consultation with area legal services committees and identifying where law centres are needed. (Letter to the writer from Mr S. Hillyard, 18 May 1977.)

77 Law Society, 'Legal Advice and Assistance', 1969, para. 41.
78 Ibid.
79 Ibid., para. 42.
80 For a survey of the first centres see M. Zander and P. Russell, 'Law Centres Survey', *Law Society's Gazette*, 10 March 1976, p. 210. See also A. Byles and P. Morris, *Unmet Need: The case of the neighbourhood law centre*, 1977 (Routledge & Kegan Paul), and Adamsdown Community Trust 'Community Need and Law Centre Practice', 1978.
81 Newham Rights Centre.
82 See, for instance, House of Lords *Hansard*, vol. 350, cols. 381–2; vol. 351, cols. 1079–81; vol. 353, cols. 2294–5; vol. 362, cols. 771–2; vol. 371, cols. 12–16.
83 Zander and Russell, op. cit. (note 80 above), p. 213, Q. 32.
84 See Law Centres Working Group, *Evidence*, para. 3.24, p. 34.
85 House of Lords *Hansard*, vol. 350, cols. 381–2.
86 House of Lords *Hansard*, vol. 351, cols. 1079–89.
87 Ibid., col. 1081.
88 This section is largely based on information in the evidence of the Greater London Citizens' Advice Bureaux Lawyers' Group to the Royal Commission on Legal Services.
89 Ibid., para. 4.46, p. 28.
90 See Martin Partington, *Recent Developments in Legal Services for the Poor: Some Reflections on Experience in Coventry*, CDP Occasional Paper, No. 13, 1975.
91 Ibid., p. 38.
92 NACAB, *Evidence*, para. 199, p. 94.
93 Ibid., para. 248, p. 119.
94 Ibid., para. 191, p. 91.
95 Ibid., para. 171, p. 83.
96 *Legal Services Corporation Annual Report*, 1976, pp. 7–8.
97 Thomas Ehrlich, 'A Progress Report from the Legal Services Corporation', *American Bar Association Journal*, September 1976, p. 1140. The word 'equivalent' was used advisedly to indicate that some of those thrown into the battle would be para-legal workers (ibid.).
98 Reported in a paper presented by Mr J. P. Harkins, Director of ALAO, at the International Colloquium on Legal Aid and Legal Services, London, October 1976, para. 3.4. (Published by the Common Law Exchange Society, 5 Palo Alto Square, Suite 283, Palo Alto, California 94304.)
99 Ibid., para. 3.12–13.
100 Ibid., para. 4.18.
101 J. Disney *et al.*, *Lawyers*, 1977 (Law Book Co. Ltd, Sydney), p. 395.

102 Australian *Hansard*, 9 October 1975, pp. 1979–80: 'I believe we need a rationalised system of legal aid . . . operating through the States but with Federal involvement and Federal support financially and, if necessary, legislatively. For instance, we could have in each State a legal aid commission which would have within it the necessary salaried service to the extent to which that was thought prudent.' (Cited by Harkins, op. cit. (note 98 above), para. 8.6.)
103 J. Disney *et al.*, op. cit. (note 101 above), pp. 393–6, for details of the various extant forms of salaried services in Australia.
104 Harkins, op. cit. (note 98 above), para. 9.2.
105 Ibid., para. 9.6.
106 Legal Aid Commission Act 1976.
107 M. Cappelletti, J. Gordley and E. Johnson, *Toward Equal Justice: A Comparative Study of Legal Aid in Modern Societies*, 1975, pp. 645–6.
108 Report of André Saint-Cyr, Secretary to the Provincial Legal Aid Directors of Canada, at International Colloquium on Legal Aid and Legal Services, London, October 1976, published by the International Common Law Exchange Society, p. 20. (See also Rosalind Brooke, 'Legal Services in Canada', *Modern Law Review*, September 1977, p. 583.)
109 Saint-Cyr, op. cit. (note 108 above), p. 27.
110 Ibid., p. 7.
111 Ibid.
112 Ibid., note (8).
113 *23rd Annual Report on Legal Aid* 1972–3, p. 37, para. 25; *24th Annual Report on Legal Aid* 1973–4, p. 55, para. 53; *25th Annual Report on Legal Aid* 1974–5, p. 50, para. 50.
114 *26th Annual Report on Legal Aid* 1975–6, p. 70, para. 44.
115 Ibid., p. 71, para. 48.

3 The Public Sector: Its Scope, Role and Management

1 Law Society, *Evidence, Memorandum No. 3, Part 1*, p. 216, para. XX. 16.1.
2 Ibid., para. XX. 16.3.
3 Ibid.
4 See M. Zander and P. Russell, 'Law Centres Survey', *Law Society's Gazette*, 10 March 1976, p. 210, Q. 31.
5 For a full account see M. Zander, 'Waivers – the end of a long story?', *New Law Journal*, 22 December 1977, p. 1236.
6 T. Lund, *The Professional Conduct and Etiquette of Solicitors,* (The Law Society 1960), pp. 22–3.
7 Unpublished memorandum of May 1974.

8 House of Lords *Hansard*, vol. 353, 30 July 1974, col. 2294–5.
9 It was debated at the instance of Mr Jack Ashley MP in the House of Commons – see House of Commons *Hansard*, 5 April 1976, vol. 909, col. 193. *The Guardian* commented 13 April 1976. The *New Law Journal* had two strong editorials on 25 March and 15 April 1976.
10 *Law Society's Gazette*, 31 August 1977, p. 698.
11 Law Society, *Evidence, Memorandum No. 3, Part 1*, p. 187, para. XIX. 7.2.
12 See B. Cooke, 'A View of the Contribution Aspect of the Criminal Legal Aid Scheme', [*1970*] *Criminal Law Review*. p. 485. In 1976 contributions ordered to be paid amounted to £1.1m. as against £32.8m. expended in criminal legal aid (*Criminal Statistics*, 1976, p. 357). There are no figures for the sums recovered.
13 As has been seen, p. 36 above, in 1976 only 2.9 per cent of defendants were privately represented.
14 A. Bruzelius and P. O. Bolding, 'An Introduction to the Swedish Public Legal Aid Reform', in M. Cappelletti, J. Gordley and E. Johnson Jnr. (eds.), *Toward Equal Justice: A Comparative Study of Legal Aid in Modern Societies*, 1975 (Oceana Publications), p. 568. For Quebec see Legal Aid Act 1972, ch. 14, set out in *Toward Equal Justice*, pp. 584–614.
15 See p. 51 above.
16 House of Lords *Hansard*, vol. 371, 15 June 1976, col. 1214.
17 Ibid., col. 1215.
18 NACAB, *Evidence*, p. 92.
19 Zander and Russell, op. cit. (note 4 above), Q. 12A, p. 209.
20 J. Handler, E. Hollingsworth, H. Erlanger and J. Ladinsky, *Lawyers and the Pursuit of Legal Rights* (forthcoming); page references not available at time of writing. I am indebted to Professor Handler and his colleagues for making the manuscript available to me prior to publication.
21 For an expression of concern on this score see *Legal Action Group Bulletin*, October 1976, p. 224.
22 Handler *et al.*, op. cit. (note 20 above).
23 Ibid.
24 Ibid.
25 See, for instance Pat Carlen, *Magistrates' Justice*, 1976 (Martin Robertson, London), p. 91; J. Baldwin and M. McConville, *Negotiated Justice*, 1977 (Martin Robertson, London), chapter 3.
26 For an attempt to separate sense from nonsense on this issue see M. Zander, 'Independence of the Legal Profession – what does it mean?' *Law Society's Gazette*, 22 September 1977, p. 758.
27 Legal Services Commission Act, S.B.C. 1975, ch. 36.

28 The Legal Aid Services Society Act of Manitoba Act, S.M. 1971, ch. L 105.

29 The Legal Aid Act, S.N. 1975, ch. 42.

30 The Legal Aid Act 1977.

31 The Legal Aid Act, S.Q. 1972, ch. 14.

32 The Community Legal Services (Saskatchewan) Act, S.S. 1973–4, ch. 11.

33 Legal Services Corporation Act 1974.

34 Report by J. P. Harkins, op. cit. (note 98, Chapter 2 above).

35 *Report of the (Osler) Task Force on Legal Aid*, 1974.

36 Legal Action Group, *Legal Services: A Blue-print for the Future*, 1978, p. 19, para. 69.

37 Ibid., p. 20, para. 70.

38 *Report*, op. cit. (note 35 above), p. 37.

39 *Report of the Committee on Civil Legal Aid and Advice*, 1978 (Ministry of Justice, Republic of Ireland).

40 It said that 'A strong case would have to be made out for the drastic step of divesting the Law Society of this important responsibility, especially in view of the heavy costs, both financial and in terms of morale and efficiency, which have to be paid for institutional upheaval and re-organisation' (*Evidence*, p. 36, para. 25.17).

41 House of Lords *Hansard*, 15 June 1974, vol. 371, col. 1215–18.

42 The rates stated in 'The Survey of Law Centres', *Law Society's Gazette*, 10 March 1976, p. 209, Q. 15 were significantly lower than those available at that time in private practice.

43 See for an interim report, *Legal Services Corporation Delivery Systems Study*, July 1977.

44 *26th Annual Report on Legal Aid*, 1975–6, p. 27, Appendix 13.

45 See in particular Earl Johnson Jnr., in *Toward Equal Justice: A Comparative Study of Legal Aid in Modern Societies*, pp. 133–80; and a rejoinder by Samuel J. Brakel, 'Styles of Delivery of Legal Services to the Poor: A Review Article', *American Bar Foundation Research Journal*, 1977, p. 219; and a reply by Johnson, ibid., p. 943.

46 J. Casper, *American Criminal Justice: The Defendant's Perspective'*, 1972, p. 100; Samuel J. Brakel, *Judicare: Public Funds, Private Lawyers and Poor People* (American Bar Foundation, Chicago), Table 7.1, p. 92; and discussion by Brakel, op. cit. (note 45 above), pp. 243–8.

47 *25th Annual Report on Legal Aid*, 1974–5, p. 50, para. 50. See to same effect NACAB, *Evidence*, p. 97.

48 *26th Annual Report on Legal Aid*, 1975–6, p. 8, para. 35.

4   The Quality of Legal Services: Discipline and Complaints

1 B. Abel-Smith and R. Stevens, *Lawyers and the Courts*, 1967 (Heinemann, London), p. 218.
2 For a description of the whole procedure see Bar, *Evidence, Submission No. 7*, p. VIII, 1–7.
3 In *Re S. (A Barrister)* [1970] 1 Q.B. 160 the Visitors to Gray's Inn set out the history and practice of such appeals.
4 Bar, *Evidence, Submission No. 7*, p. VIII. 6, Table 2.
5 *Law Society's Gazette*, 26 May 1976, p. 451.
6 Bar, *Annual Statement*, 1972–3, pp. 23–4.
7 *Law Society's Gazette*, 25 May 1976, p. 476.
8 Harry Kirk, *Portrait of a Profession*, 1976, (Oyez, London), pp. 72–3. Harry Kirk was a member of the Council of the Law Society for nineteen years.
9 *Re Weare a Solicitor* (1893) 2 QB 439.
10 Solicitors Act 1974, Part II.
11 See *New Law Journal*, 6 April 1972, p. 297; 20 April 1972, p. 343; 11 January 1973, p. 27; 8 March 1973, p. 213; 26 April 1973, p. 381; 15 November 1973, p. 1030; 31 January 1974, p. 89; 18 April 1974, p. 354.
12 The retired headmaster of Repton was asked to perform this function first for six months and then for a second period of six months but the appointment was not renewed a second time.
13 For a detailed description of the process see Law Society, *Evidence, Memorandum No. 2, Part 1*, pp. 41–8.
14 Information supplied to the writer by the Law Society.
15 Bar, *Evidence, Submission No. 7*, p. VIII. 6, Table 2.
16 *First Report of the Lay Observer*, 1976, p. 2, para. 11–12; *Second Annual Report of the Lay Observer*, 1976–7, para. 8.
17 *Second Report*, op. cit. (note 16 above), para. 8.
18 Ibid.
19 *First Report*, op. cit. (note 16 above), p. 4, para. 24.
20 Law Society, *Evidence, Memorandum No. 3, Part 1*, p. 57, para. 45 (4)(iv).
21 *First Report*, op. cit. (note 16 above), p. 5, para. 27.
22 F. Raymond Marks and Darlene Cathcart, 'Discipline with the Legal Profession: Is it Self-Regulation?', *Law Forum*, 1974, p. 193.
23 *First Report*, op. cit. (note 16 above), p. 7, para. 37.
24 *Law Society's Gazette*, 25 May 1977, p. 476.
25 *Law Society's Gazette*, 19 April 1972, p. 332.
26 *Second Report*, op. cit. (note 16 above), p. 3, para. 12.
27 Ibid., para. 11.
28 Ibid.

29 Law Society, *Evidence, Memorandum No. 3, Part 1*, p. 76.
30 Ibid.
31 Ibid.
32 ABA Special Committee on Evaluation of Disciplinary Enforcement, *Problems and Recommendations in Disciplinary Enforcement*, 1970, p. 93.
33 Ibid., pp. 93–4.
34 Ibid., p. 94.
35 Ibid.
36 Ibid., p. 95.
37 *Evidence*, para. 38. The Young Solicitors' Group of the Law Society in its evidence to the Royal Commission proposed (p. 20) that a client who was advised by a second solicitor that he had no claim in negligence against a former solicitor should be able to ask for an informal opinion from the local Circuit judge. If the judge thought the solicitor was wrong he would record the fact in writing and, subject to means, this should be sufficient ground for the issue of a legal aid certificate. One imagines, however, that the judges are likely to be even less willing to embark on such a task than the Law Society or the Lay Observer.
38 [1969] A.C. 191.
39 *Ali v Sydney Mitchell and Co* [1977] 3 All E.R. 744. In December 1977, the case was on appeal to the House of Lords.
40 [1967] 1 Q.B. 471. The Court of Appeal held that although solicitors were wholly liable, barristers were wholly immune from liability.
41 *The Times*, 22 October 1966; *The Sunday Telegraph*, 23 October 1966; *The Financial Times*, 24 October 1966; *The Economist*, 29 October 1966; the *New Statesman*, 11 November 1966.
42 *New Law Journal*, 27 October 1966, p. 1445.
43 *Solicitors' Journal*, 28 October 1966, p. 797.
44 *Law Society's Gazette*, November 1966, p. 425.
45 *Journal of the Law Society of Scotland*, November 1966, p. 206.
46 The prestigious all–party British Section of the International Commission of Jurists.
47 See *Law Society's Gazette*, 15 October 1975, p. 1021, and 17 December 1975, p. 1260. For details of the experience see *Law Society's Gazette*, 30 November 1977, p. 1041. In the year to 31 August 1977 there were 646 claims notified in respect of 6,850 firms.
48 E. H. Steele and R. T. Nimmer, 'Lawyers and Professional Regulation', *American Bar Foundation Research Journal*, 1976, p. 957.
49 For a summary see M. Zander, 'The State of Knowledge about

the Legal Profession', *New Law Journal*, 23 September 1976, p. 959. See also Consumers' Association, *Which?*, May 1977, p. 297.

50 So, in the writer's 'Legal Advice and Criminal Appeals', [1972] *Criminal Law Review*, p. 150 there were pages of comment, both favourable and unfavourable, about the conduct of cases by the lawyers (see pp. 154–64). See to same effect A. E. Bottoms and J. D. McClean, *Defendants in the Criminal Process*, 1976, (Routledge and Kegan Paul, London) pp. 154–60. In J. Baldwin and M. McConville, *Negotiated Justice*, 1977 (Martin Robertson, London), some defendants were reported as believing that they had been induced to plead guilty by undue pressure from their barristers or by some form of improper plea bargaining. It may or may not have occurred, but any attempt to understand the problems surrounding guilty pleas must plainly include the dimension of the defendant's perspective.

51 *The Guardian* 9 June 1977 (Letters).

52 The survey of CAB workers for the Royal Commission showed that on the whole there was 'clearly a high degree of satisfaction among bureau organisers with their local legal services' (NACAB, *Evidence*, p. 47, para. 99).

53 Leona Vogt and others, 'Field Test Results of Peer Review Quality Assessment of Legal Services' 1976 (Urban Institute, 2100 M Street, N.W. Washington D.C. 20037). The assessments were based on interviews with the lawyers on a sample of cases drawn by the lawyers. This is obviously not the best way to draw a sample, but it seems adequate to test the ability of independent assessors to agree on their assessments.

54 Ibid., Fig. 1, p. 18.

55 D. Rosenthal, *Lawyer and Client: Who's in Charge?*, 1974 (Russell Sage Foundation, New York), p. 59.

56 Steele and Nimmer, op. cit. (note 48 above), p. 963.

57 For a successful use of this technique see M. Zander 'Legal Advice and Criminal Appeals', [1972] *Criminal Law Review*, p. 1260 which revealed failings in the system of providing advice on appeals to defendants in criminal cases. It led in due course to a new system – see M. Zander, 'Legal Advice on Criminal Appeals: The New Machinery', [1975] *Criminal Law Review*, p. 364.

58 A classic instance was the attempt by the Bar Council to persuade the Home Office not to permit publication of the book *Negotiated Justice*, op. cit., note 50 above which criticised barristers for the way they handled plea bargaining. See editorial comment in the *New Law Journal*, 22 September 1977, p. 926 and *The Times*, 24 September 1977. The intense public con-

troversy over the book may be seen in *The Sunday Times*, 18 September 1977; *The Observer*, 18 September 1977; *Law Society's Gazette*, 28 September 1977, p. 793; 6 October 1977, p. 830; 19 October 1977, p. 877; *New Law Journal*, 22 September 1977, p. 926; 6 October 1977, p. 989; 13 October 1977, p. 1014; and letters in *The Times*, 12 May 1977; 17 May 1977; 29 September 1977; 1 October 1977; 5 October 1977; 7 October 1977; 11 October 1977; 14 October 1977; 15 October 1977; 17 October 1977; 18 October 1977; and 19 October 1977. See also M. Zander, 'The Legal Profession and Academic Researchers – a Plea for a Better Relationship', *Law Society's Gazette*, 21 December 1978, p. 1121.

5 The Quality of Legal Services: Education and Training

1 Bar, *Evidence, Submission No. 3*, p. 8, para. 22.
2 Law Society, *Evidence, Memorandum, No. 3 Part I*, p. 85, para. X.2.2.
3 For a succinct account of the history of English legal education see the *Report of the (Ormrod) Committee on Legal Education*, 1971, Cmnd. 4595, pp. 3–20. The full history remains to be written.
4 *Report of the Select Committee on Legal Education*, 1846, Vol. X, British Parliamentary Papers, p. lvi, para. 3.
5 Ibid., para. 2.
6 Ibid.
7 J. F. Wilson and S. B. Marsh, 'A Second Survey of Legal Education in the United Kingdom', *Journal of the Society of Public Teachers of Law*, July 1975, Table 1, p. 249.
8 Ibid., pp. 241–2.
9 *Ormrod Report*, op. cit., (note 3 above), p. 54.
10 'Survey of legal education', op. cit. (note 7 above), Table 6, p. 252, and Table 10, p. 256.
11 The Society of Public Teachers of Law, *Evidence*, para. 11.
12 'Survey of legal education', op. cit. (note 7 above), Tables 27 and 28, pp. 280–1.
13 See M. Zander, 'Law Students and Community Action', in *Education and Social Action*, 1975, ed. Goodlad (George Allen & Unwin, London); and Martin Partington, 'Putting Law into Perspective', *The Times Higher Education Supplement*, 25 February 1977. In the United States in the past few years law students have started to play a considerable role in the field of legal services – see M. Zander, 'Clinical Legal Education', *New Law Journal*, 22 February 1973, p. 181. A survey for the academic year 1976–7 showed that 90 per cent of American law schools had some form of clinical education – 139 schools reported 494

clinical programmes in 57 fields of law (see *American Bar Association Journal*, September 1977, p. 1277).

14 The six core subjects for both branches of the profession are Constitutional and Administrative Law, Contract, Torts, Criminal Law, Land Law and Trusts. The Ormrod Committee had recommended that the CPE consist of the first five of these subjects as 'core subjects' plus at least three optional subjects (op. cit., note 3 above, para. 113).

15 *Law Society's Gazette*, 14 May 1975, p. 505–6.

16 Law Society's *Evidence, Memorandum No. 3, Part I*, p. 93. Geoffrey Woodroffe, 'Whatever Happened to Ormrod?' *Legal Action Group Bulletin*, November 1977, p. 256.

17 *Law Society's Gazette*, 14 December 1977, p. 1087.

18 The Bar's *Evidence, Submission No. 3*, p. 8, para. 22, stated that in 1975, 87 per cent of intending practitioners called to the Bar were graduates of British universities and that 81 per cent of these were law graduates. On these figures, 71 per cent were law graduates, 16 per cent were non-law graduates and 13 per cent were not graduates of British universities. The Law Society's *Evidence, Memorandum No. 3, Part I*, p. 85 stated that, of those admitted in the year to July 1976, 60 per cent were law graduates, 17 per cent were non-law graduates, 17 per cent were school leavers, 4 per cent were former barristers, overseas solicitors or foreign graduates and 2 per cent were 'Others equated to graduates'.

19 See for instance, Q. Johnstone and D. Hopson, *Lawyers and their Work*, 1967 (Bobbs-Merrill Co. Inc., New York); Society of Labour Lawyers, *Legal Education*, 1969 (Fabian Research Series); M. Zander, *Lawyers and the Public Interest*, 1968 (Weidenfeld & Nicolson, London).

20 *Law Society's Gazette*, 27 July 1977, p. 648.

21 Law Society, 'The Ormrod Report: A consultative document'; 1974; printed in the Ormrod Report itself, op. cit. (note 3 above), Appendix F.

22 See *Law Society's Gazette*, 5 June 1974, p. 517; G. Woodroffe, op. cit. (note 16 above).

23 Law Society, *Evidence, Memorandum No. 3, Part I*, p. 92, para. X.3/5/7.10.

24 *Ormrod Report*, op. cit., (note 3 above), para. 161.

25 *Accountancy*, September 1977, p. 76.

26 Bar, *Evidence, Submission No. 7*, p. XI.23, para. A.23.1.

27 Ibid., para. A.23.2.

28 Law Society, *Evidence, Memorandum No. 3, Part 1*, pp. 108–18.

29 *Law Society's Gazette*, 19 October 1977, p. 869.

30 *Ormrod Report*, op. cit., (note 3 above) para. 170.

31 A proposal for the training of English judges was made in 1976 in a Consultative Working Paper by a Committee under Lord Justice Bridges set up by the Home Office and the Lord Chancellor's Office. ('Judicial Training and Information', August 1976.) The committee proposed courses for judges, for instance, on sentencing, penal theory and criminology. The final report was due in 1978. (*Legal Action Group Bulletin*, September 1976, p. 199).

32 From 1977, the Law List gives numbered signs indicating the specialities of barristers. A questionnaire was distributed by the Bar Council to which between 30 and 40 per cent of the Bar responded as to their special fields. (See Bar, *Annual Statement*, 1976–7, p. 21 and *Law Society's Gazette*, 28 July 1976, p. 631.)

33 Law Society, *Evidence, Memorandum No. 3, Part 3*, p. 45, para. 29(ii).

34 The entire set of rules are set out in *California State Bar Journal*, Jan./Feb. 1973, vol. 48, No. 1; See in ABA, *Specialisation*, 1974.

35 Gordon M. Weber, 'Why Formal Legal Specialisation?', *American Bar Association Journal*, July 1977, p. 952.

36 ABA, *Specialisation*, 1974, pp. 35, 39–42; D. Fromson, 'Let's Be Realistic About Specialisation', *American Bar Association Journal*, January 1977, p. 76.

37 ABA, op. cit., (note 36 above), pp. 36, 47; *American Bar Association Journal*, January 1977, p. 76; *Florida Bar Journal*, March 1974 issue.

38 Monopolies Commission, *A report on the supply of Services of Solicitors in relation to advertising*, 1976 (HMSO) para. 117.

39 Pat Carlen in *Magistrates' Justice*, 1976 (Martin Robertson, London) reports that over half of a group of probation officers she interviewed said that at first appearance defendants in the magistrates' court 'understand nothing at all'. One third thought they understood 'very little' (at p. 83). The main theme of the book is that all the participants are playing a game of which they know the rules; the defendant's role is to play dummy.

40 NACAB, *Evidence*, para. 243, p. 11).

41 See for instance, W. H. Marston, 'Studies in Testimony, 15 *Journal of Criminal Law and Criminology*, pp. 5–32; and A. Anastasi, *Fields of Applied Psychology*, 1964 (McGraw-Hill Book Co. New York), p. 548.

42 K. W. Wedderburn, *Actes du Sixième Congrès International de Droit de Travail et de Sécurité Sociale*, 1966, Vol. III, Rapport national, Grande Bretagne, pp. 15–16.

43 The College of Law, *Evidence*, p. 5.

44 Consumers' Association, *Which?*, 1977, p. 297.

45 D. Rosenthal, *Lawyer and Client: Who's in Charge?*, 1974 (Russell

Sage, New York).
46 Ibid., p. 68.
47 Ibid., p. 152.
48 Ibid., p. 56.
49 K. Bell *et al.*, 'National Insurance Local Tribunals', 4 *Journal of Social Policy*, 19 pt.1, p. 21 and *Research Study in Supplementary Benefit Appeal Tribunals*, 1975 (HMSO) p. 16.
50 Peter Webster, 'Lawyers Social Welfare Law', *Law Society's Gazette*, 31 March 1976, p. 278.

6 Monopolies and Restrictive Practices

1 This has for long been the English rule – first enunciated by Lord Macclesfield in *Mitchel v Reynolds* (1711) 1 P. Wms. 181. In 1894 Lord Macnaghten said: 'All interferences with individual liberty of action in trading and all restraints of trade of themselves if there is nothing more, are contrary to public policy and therefore void. That is the general rule. But there are exceptions. . . . It is a sufficient justification, and indeed it is the only justification, if a restriction is reasonable in reference to the interests of the parties concerned and reasonable in reference to the interests of the public. . . . (*Nordenfelt v Maxim Nordenfelt Guns and Ammunition Co.* [1894] A.C. 535, at 565).
2 Thus the Restrictive Trade Practices Act 1956 included a presumption that every registered restrictive agreement was against the public interest. The presumption could only be set aside if the court was satisfied that the agreement met one of the 'gateway' criteria – e.g. that it yielded specific or substantial benefits to consumers, that it increased exports or that it maintained employment in a particular area – *and*, second, that such advantages outweighed 'any detriment to the public or to persons not parties to the agreement' (s.21).
3 Monopolies Commission, *Report on restrictive practices in relation to the supply of professional services*, 1970, Cmnd. 4463, para. 281.
4 Ibid., para. 283.
5 Ibid., para. 284.
6 *The Pharmaceutical Society of Great Britain v Dickson* [1968] 2 All E.R. 686. See also to similar effect *Goldfarb v Virgina State Bar*, 421 US 77 (1975).
7 At p. 703 A.
8 Ibid., at D.
9 The restrictions were designed to stop chemists from selling 'non-traditional' pharmaceutical goods. They were challenged by Boots Ltd.

10 See Dennis Lees, *Economic Consequences of the Professions*, 1966 (Institute of Economic Affairs), pp. 5–6. See also M. Zander, *Lawyers and the Public Interest*, 1968 (Weidenfeld & Nicolson, London) which is devoted to the problems of monopolies and restrictive practices in the English legal profession.

11 Law Society, *Evidence, Memorandum, No 3, Part 2*, p. 77, para. VIII.2.7.

12 The point was made by Lord Justice Sachs in the Court of Appeal in the case brought by Boots Ltd against the Pharmaceutical Society (note 6 above). Whether raising standards was a valid justification of a restrictive practice, he said, depended on whether the standard in question was necessary. ('Subject to one rather important consideration, the higher the standard, the better for the public. That consideration may arise thus: the higher you raise the standard of qualification and ethics, the higher will be the remuneration they may reasonably expect, irrespective of whether the standard is strictly necessary for the tasks in hand. . . .' ([1967] 2 All E.R.558, 570 at F). The greater the restrictions on the ways in which pharmacists could earn their living, the greater the difficulty in making the business economically attractive, so the fewer the pharmacies available to the public and the higher the charges payable by the public and the National Health Service (ibid.).

13 Bar, *Annual Statement*, 1973–4, p. 33; *Law Society's Gazette*, 25 January 1976, p. 70.

14 The new approach was adopted by the Bar in December 1974 – see Bar, *Annual Statement*, 1974–5, pp. 41–2. The latest version of these rules appears in *Law Society's Gazette*, 29 June 1977, p. 148.

15 See Bar Council, *Annual Statement*, 1973–4, pp. 30–1.

16 See Bar, *Annual Statement*, 1971–2, pp. 18, 25–6, 41–3.

17 The rule was abolished in 1964 after the report of the Gardiner Committee set up by the Bar Council recommended its abolition.

18 In 1966, the Two-thirds Rule was abolished and replaced by a new rule – that the junior should receive the fee he would have earned if he had done the case on his own. The Law Society publicly criticised this new rule on the day it was adopted as offending the principle that 'counsel is properly paid for the work that he does' and that the public should not be asked to 'pay for work not done or for services not rendered' (Law Society press release, 22 June 1966). In 1971 the Bar adopted a new rule – that the junior instructed with a QC be paid 'a proper fee' (Bar Council, *Annual Statement*, 1971–2, pp. 61–2, Part 1, 4).

19 For details see B. Abel–Smith and R. Stevens, *Lawyers and the Courts*, 1967 (Heinemann, London), pp. 33, 34, 36, 48, 83, 92, 104, 233, 234, 249.

20 Avner Offer, 'The Origins of the Law of Property Acts 1910–25', *Modern Law Review*, 1977, pp. 505, 522.

21 Abel–Smith and Stevens, op. cit. (note 19 above), p. 204.

22 For an account of the restrictions before their recent liberalisation see M. Zander, *Lawyers and the Public Interest*, 1968, Chapter 10.

23 Monopolies Commission, op. cit. (note 3 above), para. 297, p. 72.

24 This point emerges especially from the researches of J. R. Forbes, now of the University of Queensland, Brisbane. See especially his 'The Divided Legal Profession in Australia: History, Rationalisation and Rationale – The English Background', *Queensland Lawyer*, 1977, supplement to Vol. 4, Part 1, and for a summary of this theme his 'Division of the Profession: Ancient or Scientific', *Law Society's Gazette*, 26 January 1977, p. 67.

25 Michael Birks, *Gentlemen of the Law*, 1960 (Stevens, London) p. 105.

26 The arguments for the divided profession are rehearsed especially in G. Gardiner, 'Two Lawyers or One', 23 *Current Legal Problems*, 1970, p. 1, and evidence to the Royal Commission submitted by the Judges of the High Court, the Bar (*Submission No. 7, s.IV*), and the Law Society *Memorandum No. 3, Part 2*, pp. 43–62. See also F. A. Mann, 'Fusion of the Legal Profession', *Law Quarterly Review*, July 1977, p. 367. The case against the divided profession is made, for instance, in M. Zander, *Lawyers and the Public Interest*, 1968, pp. 271–332, and M. Zander, *Evidence to the Royal Commission*, pp. 75–88. See also the writer's, 'Why the Royal Commission is likely to recommend reform of the divided profession', *Law Society's Gazette*, 27 October 1976, p. 882.

27 Monopolies and Mergers Commission, *Report on the supply by Her Majesty's Counsel alone of their services*, 1976; for details of the new rule see *New Law Journal*, 6 October 1977, p. 983, *Law Society's Gazette*, 28 September 1977, p. 802 and 25 January 1978, p. 70.

28 Bar, *Evidence, Submission No. 8*; calculated from Table 14.

29 Ibid., calculated from Table 15.

30 See Consolidated Regulations of the Honourable Societies of Lincoln's Inn, Inner Temple, Middle Temple and Gray's Inn.

31 In the case of the English student at an English university these are likely to be: Admission to the Inn (£82–85); tuition at School of Law for Part II (in 1976–7, £320); Bar Examination (£20); Call

to the Bar (£75). See Bar, *Evidence, Submission No. 7*, p. XI.16.

32 Dining in one's Inn a certain number of times per term for twelve terms is part of the process of qualification. On application it can be done in the year of the vocational course and the year after Call. Dining costs in all between £25 and £40 depend ing on the Inn – plus the cost of travel and overnight accommodation for those who come from out of London.

33 See Law Society's Training Regulations.

34 *Law Society's Gazette*, 27 July 1977, p. 660.

35 Two years for the law graduate; two and a half years for the non-law graduate; four years for the non-graduate.

36 See *Konigsberg v State Bar*, 353 US 252, 262 (1957); *Ex parte Tziniolis, Re The Medical Practitioners Act* (1967) 84 W. N. (Pt.2) NSW 275, 300.

37 *Report of the Committee on Legal Education*, 1971, Cmnd. 4595, p. 72, para. 149.

38 Ibid.

39 Ibid.

40 Bar, *Evidence, Submission No. 7*, p. XI. 50–51.

41 *Law Society's Gazette*, 29 June 1977, p. 552.

42 Law Society, *Evidence, Memorandum No. 3, Part 1*, p. 101.

43 *Low Pay Bulletin*, December 1976, p. 2.

44 Associate Members of the Law Society, *Evidence*, p. 6.

45 Bar, *Evidence, Submission No. 5*, pp. 16–17.

46 See *O'Toole v Scott*, [1965] A.C. 939; confirmed in *Simms v Moore*, [1970] 3 All E.R. 1.

47 Bar, *Evidence, Submission No. 7*, p. I.18, para. A.29.10.

48 Ibid., para. A.29.11.

49 Ibid., p. I.19, para. A.29.13.

50 Ibid.

51 Ibid., p. I.20, para. A.29.25.

52 Ibid., p. I.22, para. A.29.29.

53 'The Courts Bill', Memorandum published informally by the Law Society, 1970, para. 6.

54 Law Society briefing paper for MPs on the Courts Bill.

55 Law Society, *Evidence, Memorandum No. 3, Part 2*, p. 23; para. 1.21.2.

56 Ibid., p. 25; para. 1.21.10.

57 The James Committee stated that in 1974, magistrates' courts dealt with 87 per cent of those proceeded against for indictable offences, all of whom could have elected trial at the higher level (*Report on Distribution of Criminal Business*, 1975, Cmnd. 6323, para. 20). Conversely, a private survey (unpublished) prepared for the Committee found that 60 per cent of those dealt with by crown courts could have been tried summarily. In civil cases,

the maximum jurisdiction of county courts – now £2,000 – covers the overwhelming majority of both debt and personal injury cases brought in the High Court.

58 A. E. Bottoms and J. D. McClean, *Defendants in the Criminal Process*, 1976 (Routledge & Kegan Paul, London), p. 158.

59 Bar, *Evidence, Submission No. 7*, pp. VI.1–4; Law Society, *Evidence, Memorandum No. 3, Part 2*, pp. 65–7.

60 Bar, *Evidence, Submission No. 7*, pp. VI.2–3; para. A.6/7.6(b).

61 Ibid., A.6/7.6(d).

62 Law Society, *Evidence, Memorandum No. 3, Part 2*, p. 67.

63 *Alfred Crompton Amusement Machines Ltd v Cmnrs of Customs and Excise (No 2)* [1972]2 All E.R.353, 376.

64 See *Law Society's Gazette*, 30 April 1975, p. 470, for a statement that the Lord Chancellor had agreed to extend rights of audience for Fellows of the Institute of Legal Executives in certain uncontested or formal proceedings in both magistrates' courts and county courts. But this took an unconscionably long time to implement. The Administration of Justice Act 1977 made provision for new County Court Rules but by the end of 1977 no such rules had been published. (See also House of Lords *Hansard*, vol. 382. col. 840; vol. 383, cols. 468–71.)

65 Law Society, *Evidence, Memorandum No. 3, Part 1*, pp. 121–52; *Memorandum No. 3, Part 2*, pp. 98–126.

66 Ibid., Part 2, p. 110; 9.2.

67 The Institute of Legal Executives in its Evidence to the Royal Commission prepared a long list of such advertisements taken from issues of the *Guardian Gazette* for the period from January 1975 to April 1977.

68 Michael Joseph, *The Conveyancing Fraud*, 1976, especially pp. 60–78 ('The Solicitor Leaves Everything to Chance').

69 Law Society, *Memorandum No. 3, Part 2*, p. 114, para. 9.25.

70 Institute of Legal Executives, *Evidence*, p. 130, para. 26 and 27.

71 Ibid., para. 28.

72 The Solicitors Act 1974 restates the previous position that the prohibition on conveyancing by unqualified persons does not apply to barristers or notaries public (s.22(2)).

73 Bar, *Evidence, Submission, No. 13*, p. XIV.7; para. A.10.4.

74 Solicitors Act 1974, s.23. The monopoly dates from 1877.

75 Law Society, *Evidence, Memorandum No. 3, Part 2*, p. 129, para. 23.

76 The Law Society's attempt to drive them out of business for infringing the probate monopoly failed in 1883 in the House of Lords – see *Law Society v Waterlow Bros* (1883) L.R. 8 A.C. 407.

77 Law Society, *Evidence, Memorandum No. 3, Part 2*, p. 131, paras. 38–40.

78 Justice, *Home-Made Wills*, 1971 (Charles Knight and Co., London), p. 1, para. 2.
79 Ibid., p. 7, para. 12.
80 Solicitor's Act 1974, ss.20, 22.
81 *O'Toole v Scott* [1965] A.C. 939.
82 Law Society, *Evidence, Memorandum No. 3, Part 2*, p. 137.
83 *Report of the Committee on Personal Injuries Litigation*, 1968, Cmnd. 369, para. 53.
84 Ibid.
85 Law Society 'Claims Assessors and Contingency Fees', 1970.
86 *The Guardian*, 28 January 1978.
87 Law Society, *A guide to the professional conduct of solicitors*, 1974, p. 85, para. 3.3.
88 Ibid., pp. 90–1, para. 3.16.
89 Ibid., pp. 115–17.
90 *Law Society's Gazette*, 31 August 1977, p. 698.
91 See p. 94 above.
92 See further Law Society, *Evidence, Memorandum No. 3, Part 3*, pp. 3–7.

7 Paying for Legal Services

1 The Solicitors' Remuneration Order 1972. See *Law Society's Gazette* 19 August 1972, pp. 721–2.
2 Law Society, *Evidence, Memorandum No. 3 Part 1*, p. 165. Nothing is known of the basis on which such reviews proceed.
3 Ibid., para. XVI. 16/17/18.6.
4 This requirement was introduced in the Solicitors' Remuneration Order 1953, Schedule II, Proviso (b). It is contained now in the Solicitors' Remuneration Order 1972, s.3(2) (i). The client must also be told of his right to a court taxation.
5 Solicitors' Act 1974, ss.57(5), 60(2), 61(2) (b).
6 *Judicial Statistics*, 1975, Cmnd. 6634, p. 97; 1976, Cmnd. 6875, p. 92.
7 Law Society, *Evidence, Memorandum No. 3, Part 1*, p. 168, para. XVI.21.4.
8 Solicitors Act 1974, s.74 (3).
9 Notably *Butterworths Costs*, 4th ed., 1971. See also Michael Cook, 'The Cost of Legal Services – The Adrenalin Factor', *Law Society's Gazette*, 25 January 1978, p. 76.
10 A study by the writer showed that in Queen's Bench Division taxations the average amounts taxed off were relatively small. In 59 per cent of cases the amount taxed off was under 10 per cent of the bill and in 78 per cent it was under 15 per cent. (M. Zander, 'Costs of Litigation', *Law Society's Gazette*, 25 June 1975, p. 683.)

11 *W. W. Boulton, Conduct and Etiquette at the Bar*, 1965, 4th ed. (Butterworths, London) p. 45, para. (13). 'Counsel ought not, save in exceptional circumstances, to allow alteration or elimination of the agreed fee after the case has been heard or settled and the mere fact that the fee has been reduced on taxation is not such an exceptional circumstance.'

12 Ibid., 1975, 6th ed., p. 49, para. 13. The new rule states that, although a reduction of an agreed fee on taxation is not an exceptional circumstance, 'counsel may treat as exceptional circumstances' cases where there is a compulsory taxation which results in fees being disallowed that cannot be recovered from the lay client. It seems quite remarkable that the Bar should still condone the barrister's insisting on his full pound of flesh in such cases at the expense of his solicitor. For details of the Law Society's (unpublished) protest see M. Zander, *Lawyers and the Public Interest*, 1968 (Weidenfeld & Nicolson, London) p. 109.

13 See generally Law Society's *Evidence, Memorandum No. 3, Part 1*, p. 195.

14 In crown court cases the maximum remained unchanged from 1960 to 1977. Not surprisingly, considering inflation, the escape clause became used in normal rather than exceptional circumstances (see M. Zander, 'Costs in Crown Courts' [1976] *Criminal Law Review*, Table 10A, p. 22). In January 1977 the Bar and the Law Society, in an unprecedented step, brought legal proceedings against the Home Office to have the Regulations declared void. (*Law Society's Gazette*, 26 January 1977, p. 49.) As a result of ensuing discussions, the action was withdrawn and new Regulations came into force in June 1977. The old Regulations allowed higher fees than the maxima only in exceptional circumstances; the new Regulations refer instead to 'the nature, importance, complexity or difficulty of the work or the time involved' (Legal Aid in Criminal Proceedings (Fees and Expenses) (Amendment) Regulations 1977).

15 Lord Chancellor's Office, 'Guide to Taxation', 1972, unpublished, states (p. 4) that the taxing officer's first task is to decide into which class a case falls. 'In most cases this will be determined by the number of pages of depositions/statements.' A summary of the Guide was published in *Law Society's Gazette*, 26 July 1972, p. 676.

16 *Practice Direction* [1977] 1 All E.R. 542.

17 See *Law Society's Gazette*, June 1969, p. 339.

18 The rule against undercutting of scale fees dates from the 1930s. In 1934 it was made clear that touting included undercutting and 'the acceptance by a solicitor of remuneration at less than the

statutory or customary rate with the object of attracting
...business' (Law Society, *Annual Report*, 1934, p. 57).

19 For a full statement of these see *Law Society's Gazette*, 28 February 1973, p. 1474. The Law Society announced in 1977 that the scale for unregistered land sales to local authorities was being abolished. (*Law Society's Gazette*, 26 October, 1977, p. 909).

20 For a choice example see the reasoning of the Evershed Committee as to why it would be wrong to impose external controls over fees on barristers. It said it was not satisfied 'that members of the Bar should in respect of their fees be subject to this form of control, which in some hands might be used very harshly and which we fear in some circumstances might seriously impair the tradition and standing of the Bar' (*Final Report of the Committee on Supreme Court Practice and Procedure*, 1953, Cmd. 8878. para. 801).

21 Barbara Curran, 'The Legal Needs of the Public' (American Bar Foundation, 1977), p. 247.

22 M. Zander, 'Costs in Crown Courts' [1976] *Criminal Law Review*, p. 7.

23 PIB, *Remuneration of Solicitors*, 1968, Cmnd. 3529, para. 46.

24 Ibid.

25 PIB, *Standing Reference on the Remuneration of Solicitors, Second Report, 1971*, Cmnd. 4624, pp. 22–3, para. 62.

26 *Property and Reversionary Investment Corpn. Ltd. v Secretary of State for the Environment* [1975] 2 All E.R. 436. For a caustic comment on the discrepancy between fair and reasonable remuneration for heavy conveyancing (£183 per hour) compared with that for a solicitor in a legal aid murder case (£20 per day), see *LAG Bulletin*, May 1975, p. 115. For a different view see Cook, op. cit. (note 9 above). See also Roger Bowles and Jennifer Phillips, 'Solicitors' Remuneration: A Critique of Recent Developments in Conveyancing', *Modern Law Review*, November 1977, p. 639.

27 *The Times* and *The Guardian*, 2 May 1972.

28 See Consumers' Association, *Which?*, June 1975.

29 PIB, *Standing Reference on the Remuneration of Solicitors, Second Report*, 1971, Cmnd. 4624, p. 31, para. 86.

30 PIB, op. cit. (note 23 above), para. 49.

31 Ibid.

32 Monopolies and Mergers Commission, *Architects' Services with reference to scale fees*, 1977.

33 Law Society, *Evidence, Memorandum No. 3, Part 1*, p. 162.

34 Interview in *New Law Journal*, 1 January 1970, p. 3.

35 The Law Society seems to accept this proposition. The Royal Commission asked whether it was possible or appropriate to

have regard to a notional annual salary when fixing fees for individual cases. The Law Society replied that 'notional and actual salaries are taken into account' in these circumstances (Law Society, *Evidence, Memorandum No. 3, Part 2*, p. 162). The Bar, by contrast, was hostile to the idea. (*Bar, Evidence, Submission No. 13*, p. XVI. 18–19).

36 PIB, op. cit. (note 23 above), p. 23, para. 69.

37 Ibid., p. 16, para. 48.

38 Ibid., p. 16, para. 49.

39 About half the firms in its sample gave no free advice to casual (as opposed to regular) clients: more than a third refused certain unprofitable forms of work and many others limited such work to established clients (ibid., para. 60). Moreover it is not obvious why clients in one category of work should subsidise other clients. Nor do those firms that earn the greatest 'excess profits' necessarily provide the bulk of unprofitable legal services.

40 PIB, op. cit. (note 23 above), p. 21, para. 65.

41 'The Economics of a Legal Aid Practice', *Legal Action Group Bulletin*, December 1976, p. 269. The author said, 'There is little doubt that legal aid can be made more profitable if it is handled exclusively by junior staff' but his firm resisted this (p. 270). Legal aid work, far from being easier than non-legal-aid work, was often more difficult, because, so often, the client lacked the education or resources to help himself.

42 Bridges, Sufrin, Whetton and White, *Legal Services in Birmingham*, 1975 (University of Birmingham), pp. 40–4.

43 PIB, op. cit. (note 23 above), pp. 25–6. The Monopolies Commission in 1977 suggested that an independent committee to fix recommended scale fees for architects and surveyors should be appointed by the government (op. cit., note 32 above), para. 283, p. 84).

44 M. Zander, 'Costs of Litigation', *Law Society's Gazette*, 25 June 1975, p. 680. (NB. There are serious printing errors in the two right-hand columns of p. 680. Apply to the writer for correct text.)

45 Consumers' Association, *Which?*, May 1977, p. 300.

46 Ibid., p. 299–300.

47 The Law Society told the Royal Commission that 'There is a good deal of evidence that many people refuse an offer of a legal aid certificate because they feel they cannot afford the contribution demanded'. (*Evidence, Memorandum No. 3, Part 1*, p. 188, para. XIX.8.5.)

48 For recommendations on this of the Lord Chancellor's Working Party and Advisory Committee see *25th Annual Report on*

Legal Aid, 1974–5, pp. 46, para. 35 and pp. 62–5.

48a See Law Society, *Evidence, Mem. No. 3, Part 3*, pp. 39–41, 48 and 50. See also *27th Annual Report on Legal Aid*, 1976–7, pp. 71–2, 117–25.

49 Those eligible are individuals who earn less than eight times 'the basic amount' of social insurance which in October 1977 was 11,800Kr. The limit for 1977–8 therefore was 94,400Kr. According to official Swedish statistics in 1977, some 95 per cent of the population earned less than 80,000Kr.

50 See N. E. Hickman, 'Small Claims and County Court Costs', *New Law Journal*, 1 September 1977, p. 856.

51 Justice, 'A Proposal for a Suitor's Fund', 1969.

52 Both the Bar and the Law Society reaffirmed their opposition to contingent fee arrangements in their evidence to the Royal Commission – *Bar, Evidence, Submission No. 13*, pp. XVI. 22–3; Law Society, *Evidence, Memorandum No. 3, Part 2*, pp. 155–9. On the subject generally see F. B. MacKinnon, *Contingent Fees for Legal Services*, 1964 (Aldine, Chicago).

53 [1975] 1 All E. R. 849.

54 Law Society, 'Claims, Assessors and Contingency Fees', 1970.

55 Justice, *Trial of Motor Accident Cases*, 1966 (Stevens, London) p. 4 and *Evidence*, pp. 48–9. The scheme was endorsed by the President of the Law Society in October 1977 – *Law Society Gazette*, 6 October 1977, p. 822.

56 Bar, *Evidence, Submission No. 13*, pp. XVI. 23–4.

57 Jointly owned by Phoenix Assurance Co. Ltd. a British company and the German company DAS (Deutscher Automobil Schutz) which has the largest share of this market in the world. See generally W. Pfenningsdorf, *Legal Expense Insurance*, 1975, (American Bar Foundation); and Barlow Christenson, *Lawyers for People of Moderate Means*, 1970 (American Bar Foundation) Ch. VII.

58 Pfenningsdorf, op. cit. (note 57 above), p. 3.

59 For discussion see especially Pfenningsdorf, op. cit., (note 57 above) and Preble Stolz, 'Insurance for Legal Services: A Preliminary Study of Feasibility'. 35 *University of Chicago Law Review*, 1968, p. 417.

60 This is the case with the two English insurance policies offering Legal Fees and Expenses Insurance – subject, however, to the approval of the insurance company. It is understood that this proviso is inserted principally to permit the insurers to veto the employment of solicitors who have previously shown themselves to be incompetent. It is said to be virtually never used.

61 This is the position with the unions, the Automobile Association, the Medical Protection Society and the Medical Defence Union.

61a The battle over open and closed panel plans has been a major political issue in the legal profession in the United States. See Sandy Dement, 'Prepaid Legal Services: Now In the Middle Phase', *Employee Relations Law Journal*, Spring 1975, pp. 620–35.

62 The first general waiver was granted in 1962. See now *Law Society's Gazette*, 24 January 1973, p. 1338, and Law Society, *A Guide to the professional conduct of solicitors*, 1974, pp. 89–90.

63 See especially Pfenningsdorf and Stolz (op. cit. notes 57 and 59 above), and W. Pfenningsdorf and S. K. Kimball, 'Regulation of Legal Services Plans', *American Bar Foundation Research Journal*, 1977, pp. 359–454 and by same authors, 'Legal Services Plans: A Typology', *American Bar Foundation Research Journal*, 1976, pp. 411–509.

64 West Germany in 1976 had 60 per cent of the premium income of specialist legal costs insurers in Western Europe. The next largest shares were Switzerland (9.8 per cent), France (9.76 per cent), Spain (8.88 per cent). Belgium had 3.84 per cent, Holland 3.56 per cent and no other country had more than 1 per cent. The UK's share was 0.04 per cent.

65 See, for instance, Philip J. Murphy, 'The Prepaid Legal Services Picture', *American Bar Association Journal*, December 1976, p. 1569; Philip J. Murphy, 'Prepaid Taking Root', *Trial*, published by the Association of Trial Lawyers of America, June 1976, p. 14.

65a Information supplied by Sandy Dement, Executive Director of the National Consumer Center for Legal Services, Washington D.C.

66 This point is made by Jeffrey C. Bauer, 'Health Insurance: A Precedent for Legal Services Insurance', *American Bar Association Journal*, August 1976, p. 1007.

67 Ibid., p. 1008.

68 But see also the Fair Trading Act 1973 s. 35 which gives the Director of Fair Trading the power to bring proceedings in the Restrictive Practices Court where anyone is pursuing a course of conduct that is 'detrimental to the interests of consumers' and peaceful persuasion has failed.

69 See J. L. J. Edwards, *The Law Officers of the Crown*, 1964 (Sweet & Maxwell, London) pp. 286–95.

70 The Attorney-General's discretion in such decisions cannot be challenged in the courts – *Gouriet v Union of Post Office Workers* [1977] 3 All E. R. 70 (H.L.).

71 For examples see S. A. de Smith, *Judicial Review of Administrative Action*, 2nd ed., 1968 (Stevens, London), pp. 466–81.
72 *R v Legal Aid Committee No. 1 (London) Legal Aid Area, Ex Parte Rondel* [1967] 2 QB 482 (at p. 492). The Lord Chief Justice said 'If one looks at it from the point of view of the use of public money or from the point of view of the unfortunate defendant ... it would be quite wrong if the committee were not entitled to take into consideration what I call the merits of the action itself'. See also *United Dominions Trust Ltd. v Bycroft* [1954] 3 All E. R. 455 in which Lord Evershed in the Court of Appeal said: 'The Legal Aid Act was devised to assist those whom it finances in the course of litigation and not indirectly to assist other parties, or even the general public, in determining points of interest' (at p. 459).
73 See E. J. T. Matthews and A. D. M. Oulton, *Legal Aid and Advice*, 1971, (Butterworths, London), pp. 129–31.
74 *Final Report of the Committee on Supreme Court Practice and Procedure*, 1953, Cmnd. 8878 para. 640 et. seq.
75 Law Society, 'The Indemnity Rule', *Annual Report*, 1963–4, p. 77, para. 19.
76 Justice, *Lawyers and the Legal System*, 1977, p. 11, para. 36.
77 Sex Discrimination Act 1975, s.75; Race Relations Act 1976, s.66.
78 See generally *Financing Public Interest Law in America*, a Report of the Council for Public Interest Law, 1976, 1250 Connecticut Avenue, N.W., Washington D.C. 20086. See also Sanford M. Jaffe, 'Public Interest Law – Five Years Later', *American Bar Association Journal*, August 1976, p. 982 and Mitchell Rogovin, 'Public Interest Law: The Next Horizon', *American Bar Association Journal*, March 1977, p. 335; and M. Cappelletti, 'Governmental and Private Advocates for the Public Interest in Civil Litigation: A Comparative Study', *Michigan L. R.*, 1975, p. 794.
79 *Financing Public Interest Law*, op. cit. (note 78 above), p. 79.
80 Ibid., p. 4.
81 Under the Magnuson-Moss Warranty and FTC Improvement Act of 1975. See *Financing Public Interest Law*, op. cit. (note 78 above), p. 272.
82 Ibid., p. 149.
83 *Report of the (Osler) Task Force on Legal Aid*, Ontario, 1974, p. 98. See also Law Society *Evidence, Memorandum No. 3, Part 3*, p. 43, para. xix.17.19.
84 Report, op. cit. (note 83 above).
85 Ibid., p. 100.
86 Solicitors' Accounts (Deposit Interest) Rules 1965, r.2; see *Law Society's Gazette*, 1965, p. 504.

87 See M. Zander, 'Should Lawyers Profit from their Client Accounts?' *New Law Journal*, 6 May 1976, p. 456.

88 *Brown v C.I.R.* [1964] 3 All E. R. 119.

89 House of Lords *Hansard*, vol. 264, 11 March 1965, col. 253.

90 Ibid., col. 255.

91 *American Bar Association Journal*, June 1977, p. 780.

91a Data communicated by Sir Henry Benson, Chairman of the Royal Commission on Legal Services, during the writer's oral evidence 1st February 1978.

92 See Pay Board, *Report on Problems of Pay Relativities*, 1973, Cmnd. 5535; Review Body on Top Salaries, *Report on Top Salaries*, No. 6, 1974, Cmnd. 5846; A. Fels, *The British Prices and Incomes Board*, 1972 (Cambridge University Press); Joan Mitchell, *The National Board for Prices and Incomes*, 1972 (Secker & Warburg, London); and A. Rees, *Economics of Work and Play*, 1973 (Harper & Row, New York).

93 The Bar only started to collect statistics on the numbers in practice in February 1953.

94 Calculated from Bar, *Annual Statements*.

95 Bar, *Evidence, Submission No. 7*, p. I.5, para. A.6.10.

96 Ibid., para. A.6.15.

97 Ibid., p.I.6, para. A.6.17.

98 Ibid., para. A.6.18.

99 Calculated from Law Society's *Annual Reports*

100 PIB, *Standing Reference on the Remuneration of Solicitors, First Report*, 1969, Cmnd. 4217, para. 17, p.6.

101 Ibid., para. 26, p.9.

102 Law Society, *Evidence, Memorandum No. 3, Part 2*, p. 15, para. I.5.1.

103 Ibid., para. I.5.2.

104 The Prices and Incomes Board rejected the suggestion that solicitors worked longer hours than others: '. . . the numerous solicitors covered by our inquiry do not claim to be working markedly different hours from those worked by people in other professions and in comparable senior ranks of business, commerce and public administration' (PIB, *Remuneration of Solicitors*, 1968, Cmnd. 3529, para. 19).

105 Law Society, *Evidence, Memorandum No. 3, Part 2*, p. 15, para. I.5.3.

106 *Royal Commission Report on Doctors' and Dentists' Remuneration*, 1960, Cmnd. 939, Table 12, p. 44.

107 Ibid., Table 9, p. 40.

108 PIB, op. cit. (note 104 above), para. 17.

108a Bar, *Evidence, Submission No. 8, Survey of Income 1974–5*, calculated from Tables 7 and 8 on the basis of the number of prac-

titioners shown in Table 1.
109 Calculated from the average figures for QCs and juniors in Table 7.2.
110 *Review Body of Doctors' and Dentists' Remuneration*, 1975, Cmnd. 6032, para. 53.
111 Some 43 per cent of all hospital consultants are full-time, the rest are part-time, but nearly all of these are paid 9/11ths of their Health Service salary. In 1977 there were approximately 24,000 GPs and some 12,000 consultants. About one third of the consultants receive merit awards on one of four grades. From April 1975 these amounted to: C awards (obtained by some 61 per cent), £2,025; B awards (obtained by 27 per cent), £4,761; A awards (obtained by 9 per cent), £8,169; and A+ awards (obtained by 2 per cent), £10,689. (Source: British Medical Association).
112 Bar, *Evidence, Addendum to Submission No. 8, 1974–5)*, Appendix 2 to Annex, p. 19.
113 Bar, *Evidence, Submission No. 8, Survey of Income 1974–5*, Table 15A, p. 24.
114 Bar, *Evidence, Addendum to Submission No. 8*, p. 15, para. 43.
115 House of Commons, *Hansard*, vol. 911, 20 May 1976, col. 658.
116 House of Commons, *Hansard* vol. 910, 3 May 1976, col. 227–8. Figures for 1976 kindly supplied by the Lord Chancellor's Office.
117 PIB, *Remuneration of Solicitors*, 1968, Cmnd. 3529, para. 27, p. 10.
118 Ibid., para. 21, p. 8.
119 Ibid., para. 22, p. 9.
120 Ibid., para. 24.
121 PIB, *Standing Reference on the Remuneration of Solicitors, First Report*, 1969, Cmnd. 4217, para. 8, p. 3.
122 Ibid., para. 15, p. 5.
123 Ibid., para. 26, p. 9.
124 Harry Kirk, *Portrait of a Profession*, 1976 (Oyez, London), p. 96.
125 PIB, op. cit. (note 117 above), para. 20.
126 A. T. Dunn and A. Ganguly, 'Recent Trends in Sales of Land and Buildings', forthcoming – a follow-up of A. T. Dunn and J. Astin, 'Surveys of Conveyancing', *Economic Trends*, May 1974, and A. T. Dunn, 'Conveyancing since 1973', *Economic Trends*, September 1976. I am greatly indebted to Mr Dunn and Mr Ganguly for permitting me to see their 1978 article in draft. See also R. Bowles and J. Phillips, op. cit. (note 26 above), pp. 640–2.
127 PIB, op. cit. (note 117 above), Table 15, p. 49.
128 A. T. Dunn and A. Ganguly, op. cit. (note 126 above), Table A.

8   The Management of Legal Services

1   Law Society, *Evidence, Memorandum No. 3, Part 2*, p. 26, para. I.29 (my italics). See also ibid., p. 76, para. VIII.2.4.
2   Bar, *Evidence, Submission No. 7*, p. I.24, para. A.34.1.
3   Ibid., p. I.26, para. A.35.1–2.
4   *Report from Select Committee on Admission of Attornies and Solicitors*, 1821, British Parliamentary Papers, 1821, vol. IV, p. 325.
5   *Second Report from the Select Committee on the Inns of Court*, 1834, British Parliamentary Papers, 1834, vol. XVIII, p. 331.
6   *Report from the Select Committee on Legal Education*, 1846, British Parliamentary Papers, 1846, vol. X, p. 1.
7   *Report of the Commissioners appointed to inquire into Arrangements in the Inns of Court*, 1855, British Parliamentary Papers, 1854–5, vol. XVIII, p. 349.
8   The first piece of legislation was the Act of 1402 (4 Hen 4.) c.18, which required that attorneys must be examined by the justices and have their names put on the roll. Subsequent Acts were passed in vast numbers. The solicitors Act of 1843 repealed no less than 60. Since then there have been a further 25 – in 1860, 1870, 1874, 1877, 1881, 1888, 1894, 1899, 1906, 1918, 1919, 1922, 1928, 1932, 1933, 1936, 1940, 1941, 1949, 1956, 1957, 1959, 1965 and 1974.
9   B. Abel-Smith and R. Stevens, *Lawyers and the Courts*, 1967 (Heinemann, London), p. 192.
10 *Halsbury's Laws of England*, 1973, vol. 3 (4th ed.), para. 1106.
11 A. R. Ingpen, Master Worsley's Book, 1910, p. 124, cited in *The Bar on Trial*, Robert Hazell, forthcoming, (Quartet Books), chapter 3, n. 67. I am indebted to Robert Hazell for allowing me to read his manuscript prior to publication.
12 Sergeants were the first class of advocates to emerge. At first they acquired a monopoly of advocacy in the Court of Common Pleas in the thirteenth century. In time the tradition developed that all common law judges were appointed from the ranks of sergeants. They later came to share the right of audience with barristers.
13 The history is set out in the Bar's *Annual Statement*, 1973–4, pp. 20–4.
14 Bar, *Evidence, Submission No. 1*, p. 8, para. 34.
15 Ibid., para. 36.
16 Pearce Committee, *First Interim Report*, 1972, para. 42.
17 *The Bar on Trial*, op. cit. (note 11 above), chapter 3 (page reference not available at time of going to press).
18 Pearce Committee, *First Interim Report*, 1972, para. 67.
19 See 117 *New Law Journal*, 15 June 1967, p. 647 for report of a

decision of the Mayor's and City of London Court in which Gray's Inn argued that its barristers were beneficiaries of the trusts on which it held its properties. Judge Stephen Terrell held that the Inn was a public charitable trust. There was no appeal from the decision.

20 At the time of writing the fate of this application had not been decided.

21 *The Bar on Trial*, op. cit. (note 11 above), chapter 3. The book is the work of ten young barristers. It is highly critical of the Bar. See similarly Mary Colton, 'The State of the Bar', 1977 (Bow Group). For similar proposals in the nineteenth century see Abel-Smith and Stevens, op. cit. (note 9 above), pp. 74, 217.

22 H. Kirk, *Portrait of a Profession*, 1976 (Oyez, London), p. 23.

23 M. Birks, *Gentlemen at Law*, 1960 (Stevens, London), pp. 146–7.

24 Ibid.

25 Ibid., p. 156.

26 H. Kirk, op. cit. (note 22 above), p. 36.

27 Ibid., p. 40.

28 In 1976 there were 29,406 solicitors with practising certificates and 27,700 members of the Law Society.

29 See *Law Society's Gazette*, 5 June 1974, p. 518.

30 Bar, *Evidence, Submission No. 7*, p. I.9, para. A.13.2.

31 Ibid.

32 M. Zander and P. Russell, 'Law Centres Survey', *Law Society's Gazette*, 10 March 1976, p. 210.

33 Ibid., Q.21.

34 Ibid., Q.22.

35 Law Centres Working Group, *Evidence*, para. 3.60, p. 47.

36 Zander and Russell, op. cit. (note 32 above), Q.24.

37 *Law Society's Gazette*, 31 August 1977, p. 698, para. 9.

38 The writer was involved in these negotiations on behalf of the Legal Action Group.

39 *Report of the Royal Commission on Assizes and Quarter Sessions*, 1969. Cmnd. 4153.

40 PIB, *Remuneration of Solicitors*, 1968. Cmnd. 3529.

41 PIB, *Standing Reference on the Remuneration of Solicitors, First Report*, 1969, Cmnd. 4217; *Second Report*, 1971, Cmnd. 4624.

42 PIB, op. cit. (note 40 above), para. 17.

43 Ibid., para. 36.

44 Ibid., paras. 50, 67, 86.

45 Ibid., para. 62. This recommendation was implemented in the Administration of Justice Act 1969, s.7(1).

46 Ibid., para. 6.

47 Ibid., para. 49.

48 PIB. op. cit. (note 41 above), para. 48.
49 The Solicitor's Remuneration Order 1970, S.I. 1970/2021; the Solicitors' Remuneration (Registered Land) Order, S.I. 1970/2022. See *Law Society's Gazette*, January 1971, pp. 2–5.
50 PIB, op. cit. (note 41 above), paras. 73, 75.
51 For the history of this, see Law Society's *Annual Report*, 1971–2, p. 1; *Law Society's Gazette*, 3 May 1972, p. 382; *Law Society's Gazette*, 21 June 1972, p. 549; Law Society's *Annual Report*, 1972–3, p. 1.
52 Monopolies Commission, *Report on the general effect on the public interest of certain restrictive practices in relation to the supply of professional services*, 1970, Cmnd. 4463, para. 19, p. 5.
53 Ibid., para. 349, p. 86.
54 Ibid., para. 351, p. 87.
55 Ibid., para. 352.
56 Ibid.
57 Ibid., paras. 353–5, pp. 87–8.
58 Law Society, *Annual Report*, 1970–1, p. 13.
59 Bar, *Annual Statement*, 1970–1, p. 13.
60 *Law Society's Gazette*, 24 November 1976, p. 990.
61 *Law Society's Gazette*, 6 October 1976, pp. 802–3.
62 Two chartered accountants, a sociologist, a trade unionist, the director of the Consumers' Association, a lay journalist, an academic economist, a former headmistress and a social administrator.
63 The director of the Legal Action Group and the former editor of the *New Law Journal*.
64 A High Court judge, a Queen's Counsel who was a member of the Senate of the Bar, and two practising solicitors one of whom was a Council member of the Law Society.
65 See p. 21 above.
66 The British Legal Association have, however, been doing their best to discredit the Royal Commission because of its membership. See *Solicitors' Journal*, Letters, 15 July 1977, p. 475; 29 July 1977, pp. 509–10; 5 August 1977, p. 525; 19 August 1977, p. 560; 26 August 1977, p. 576; and 9 September 1977, p. 604.
67 *Report of the Committee on Legal Aid and Legal Advice*, 1945, Cmnd. 6641, para. 129.
68 R. D. Abrahams, 'The English Legal Assistance Plan', *American Bar Association Journal*, January 1950, p. 31.
69 Legal Aid Act 1949, s.8(4).
70 Report, op. cit. (note 67 above), para. 187, given effect in the Legal Aid Act 1949, s.13.
71 See especially, *The Better Provision of Legal Advice and Assistance*, 1970; the *22nd Annual Legal Aid Report*, 1971–2, pp. 35–9; the

23rd Annual Legal Aid Report, 1972–3, pp. 31–7; the *24th Annual Legal Aid Report*, 1973–4, pp. 47–57; the *25th Annual Legal Aid Report*, 1974–5, pp. 41–50; and the *26th Annual Legal Aid Report*, 1975–6, pp. 60–3, 68–73.

72 House of Lords, *Hansard*, vol. 371, 15 June 1976, col. 1215

73 Law Society, *Evidence, Memorandum No. 3, Part 1*, p. 217, para. XX.18.2.

74 Ibid., para. XX.18.3.

75 Law Society, *Evidence, Memorandum No. 3, Part 2*, p. 22, para. I.12.1.(3) and pp. 177–8, para. XXII.1.2.

76 Lord Chancellor's Legal Aid Advisory Committee, *Evidence*, paras 25.17, 25.21.

77 Ibid., para. 25.21.

78 Ibid., para. 25.22.

79 Ibid.

80 See pp. 271–2 below.

81 *Sixth Report of the Common Law Commissioners appointed to inquire into the Practice and Proceedings of the Superior Courts of Common Law*, 1834, British Parliamentary Papers, vol. XXVI, p. 8.

82 Law Society, *Evidence, Memorandum No. 3, Part 2*, pp. 22, para. I.12.2.

83 Ibid., para. I.12.3.

84 Bar, *Evidence, Submission No. 7*, p. I.9., para. A.13.2.

85 Lord Chancellor's Advisory Committee on Legal Aid, *Evidence*, paras 25.24–5.

86 Ibid., para. 25.25.

87 Ibid.

88 NACAB, *Evidence*, p. 126.

89 Interview with Lord Denning, 4 February 1977.

90 Public Legal Aid Act 1972, s.4.

91 When the Legal Aid Services Society Act 1971 was enacted it provided for five lawyer members and five others to be appointed by the Lieutenant-Governor. Three of the first board were laymen. In 1975 the Act was amended to increase the Board to eleven and it was provided that the two new places would be reserved for laymen. (Letter of Mr Ronald J. Meyers QC, Executive Director of the Legal Aid Services Society, 27 April 1977.)

92 Letter to the writer from Mr Donald E. Jabour, Chairman of the British Columbia Legal Services Commission, 10 May 1977.

93 Letter to the writer from M. André Saint-Cyr, Secretary to the Quebec Commission des Services Juridiques, 30 May 1977.

94 Ibid.

95 Letter to the writer from Mr Calvin J. Clark, Provincial Director of the Saskatchewan Community Legal Services Com-

mission, 31 May 1977.

96 Letter to the writer from Mr Pat Somervell, Director of the Legal Aid Society of Alberta, 12 May 1977.

97 *Report of the Task Force on Legal Aid*, Ontario, 1974, p. 24.

98 Ibid., p. 27.

99 Ibid., p. 31.

100 See p. 85 above.

101 *Report of the Committee on Legal Aid and Advice*, 1978 (Ministry of Justice, Dublin).

102 Law Society Act 1970, s.13(1).

103 Ibid., s.26(1).

104 H. W. Arthurs, 'Counsel, Clients and Community', *Osgoode Hall Law Journal*, December 1973, p. 448.

105 Law Society Act, 1974, ch. 2, s.8.3(1).

106 California Business and Professions Code, s.6013.5.

107 H. W. Arthurs, op. cit., (note 104 above), p. 449.

9 The Need for Legal Services

1 *23rd Annual Report on Legal Aid*, 1972–3, p. 36, para. 23. (See to same effect *25th Report*, 1974–5, p. 49, para. 49.) The statement was endorsed by the Lord Chancellor Lord Elwyn-Jones in the House of Lords, *Hansard*, vol. 351, cols. 1079–80 and Vol. 371, col. 1214. See also Law Society, *Evidence, Memorandum No. 3, Part 2*, p. 182, para. XXII.6.1 ('The Law Society is quite sure that needs for legal services are not being met').

2 See generally Philip Lewis, 'Unmet Legal Needs' in *Social Needs and Legal Action*, (Martin Robertson, 1973) p. 73, and the *Law and Society Review*. Vol, 11 no. 2, 1977. See also Jonathan Bradshaw, 'The concept of need', *New Society*, 30 March 1972, p. 640.

3 M. S. Feldstein, *Economic Analysis for Health Service Efficiency*, 1968 (Markham, Chicago), pp, 193 et seq.

4 Stewart Macauley, 'Non-contractual Relations in Business: A Preliminary Study', 28 *American Sociological Review* 1963, p. 61.

5 A successful lawyer who was interviewed as one of a sample in a Detroit study of unmet need was contemptuous of the survey. The questions he thought could hardly apply to him since he obviously had full access to legal services. Yet during the interview it emerged that he had been cheated by a roofing contractor but had neither initiated legal action nor consulted anyone about doing so. (L. Mayhew and A. J. Reiss, 'The Social Organisation of Legal Contacts', 34 *American Sociological Review*, 1969, p. 318.)

6 Lewis, op. cit., (note 2 above), at p. 79.

7 Marc Galanter, 'Why the 'haves' come out ahead: Speculations on the limits of legal change', 9 *Law and Society Review*, 1975, p. 95. The advantages enjoyed by the repeat player identified by Galanter include: experience permits better planning for litigation; economies of scale; familiarity with and informal contacts with the decision-making agencies; the risk of litigation can be spread over many cases.

8 In personal injury cases, for instance, the plaintiff is under enormous pressure to accept the amount paid into court even if it is less than he thinks, and is advised, the case is worth – because of the pressure of the costs rule under which he has to pay the insurance company's costs from the date of payment-in if he is awarded less damages than the sum paid-in. See M. Zander 'Payment into court', *New Law Journal*, 3 July 1975, p. 638. See also J. Phillips and K. Hawkins, 'Some Economic Aspects of the Settlement Process: A Study of Personal Injury Claims', *Modern Law Review*, 1976, p. 497.

9 Lord Chancellor's Advisory Committee on Legal Aid, *Evidence*, p. 4, para. 1.2.

10 See J. E. Carlin and J. Howard, 'Legal representation and class justice', 12 *U.C.L.A. Law Review*, 1965, p. 381 (also published in V. Aubert (ed.), *Sociology of Law*, 1969 (Penguin, Harmondsworth), p. 332). This paper reviews surveys conducted in 1940, 1949, 1952 and 1963.

11 The first studies of the 'modern period' were G. M. Sykes, 'Legal needs of the poor in the city of Denver', 4 *Law and Society Review*, 1969, p. 255 and Mayhew and Reiss, op. cit. (note 5 above).

12 All previous studies must now give pride of place to the joint American Bar Association–American Bar Foundation study, *The Legal Needs of the Public: The Final Report of a National Survey* by Barbara Curran, 1977. The first results of the study were published in the Preliminary Report in 1974. This is the only study which is representative of the national population and it is also the most elaborate study to date. See also: for Australia, Michael Cass and Ronald Sackville, *Legal Needs of the Poor,* for the Australian Government Commission of Inquiry into Poverty, 1975; for the UK, B. Abel-Smith, M. Zander and R. Brooke, *Legal Problems and the Citizen*, 1973 (Heineman, London); for Holland, Kees Schuyt, Kees Groenendijk and Ben Sloot, *De weg naar het recht*, 1976 (Kluwer, Deventer); in English – *European Yearbook in Law and Sociology*, 1977, ed. Campbell, Blagvael, Schuyt (Martinus Nijhoff, The Hague).

13 M. Zander, 'Unrepresented Defendants in the Criminal Courts', [1969] *Criminal Law Review*, pp. 643–4; G. J. Borrie and

J. R. Varcoe, *Legal Aid in Criminal Proceedings, A Regional Survey,* 1970 (Birmingham University), Table 15, p. 34; Susanne Dell, *Silent in Court,* 1971 (G. Bell and Sons, London), Table 1, p. 11; M. Zander, 'Unrepresented Defendants in Magistrates' Courts 1972', *New Law Journal,* 23 November 1972, p. 1041.

14 M. Zander, 1969, op. cit., (note 13 above), Table 8; S. Dell, op. cit., (note 13 above), Table 6, p. 28; A. E. Bottoms and J. D. McClean, *Defendants in the Criminal Process,* 1976 (Routledge & Kegan Paul), Table 5.1, p. 105; M. Zander, 'The Unrepresented Defendant in the Magistrates' Courts 1972' *New Law Journal* 22 November 1972, p. 1040–1.

15 M. Zander, op. cit., (note 14 above), p. 1042. A study of a large sample of cases in New South Wales magistrates' courts found 'a clear association between legal representation and securing a less serious penalty' (J. Vinson and R. Homel, 'Legal Representation and Outcome', 47 *Australian Law Journal,* 1973, pp. 132–3.

16 K. Bell, 'National Insurance Local Tribunals', 1973, 4 *Journal of Social Policy,* p. 16; K. Bell, 'Research Study on Supplementary Benefit Appeal Tribunals, 1975, HMSO, p. 15; House of Commons, *Hansard,* vol. 855, 1 May 1973, *cols. 264–5.*

17 B. Abel-Smith, M. Zander and R. Brooke, op. cit. (note 12 above), pp. 120–45 – the figures are summarised in Table 29, p. 143.

18 B. Curran, op. cit., (note 12 above), p. 100.

19 In the study by Schuyt and colleagues in Holland it was found that 'the average number of legal problems is nearly the same for each (income) group' but 'for the different types of legal problem significant differences have been found'. The lowest income groups had more problems with social security, employment law, and rent; the higher income groups, and especially the highest, had more private law problems, more creditor problems and were more likely to be victims of crime (Schuyt *et al.,* op. cit. (note 12 above), Table 3). The measure of a legal problem for this study was what the interviewer or the respondent considered to be one.

20 B. Curran, op. cit. (note 12 above), pp. 100–2.

21 B. Abel-Smith, M. Zander and R. Brooke, op. cit. (note 12 above), Table 31, p. 153.

22 Ibid. See chapter 8.

23 My information is based on a preliminary paper on the results presented by Hazell Genn at a London seminar organised by the Legal Action Group on 20 May 1977, and subsequent discussions. I am most indebted to Ms Genn and to Donald Harris, Director of the Socio-Legal Centre, for permission to use their

results before they have themselves published them. Such generosity in the world of research is rare.

24 In the London study we reported pages of such reasons in relation to each problem area – B. Abel-Smith, M. Zander, and R. Brooke, op. cit. (note 12 above), pp. 181–7.

25 C. M. Campbell and R. J. Wilson, 'Public Attitudes to the Legal Profession in Scotland', undated, p. 16.

26 Unpublished survey conducted by Simon Roberts of the London School of Economics and reported at LAG seminar, 20 May 1977.

27 Gibson and Wilson, op. cit. (note 25 above), p. 7; B. Curran, op. cit. (note 12 above), p. 185; M. Cass and R. Sackville, op. cit. (note 12 above), p. 75.

28 M. Zander, 'Who Goes to Solicitors?', Law Society's Gazette, March 1969, p. 174.

29 See, for instance, the summary of five American studies in Carlin and Howard, op. cit. (note 10 above), Table 1, p. 383. See also M. Cass and R. Sackville, op. cit. (note 12 above), Table 13.4, p. 77.

30 Zander, op. cit. (note 28 above).

31 Campbell and Wilson, op. cit. (note 25 above), p. 7.

31a B. Curran op. cit. (note 12 above), p. 261.

32 Ibid., pp. 186–90.

32a Ibid., p. 193.

33 Ibid., Fig. 5.18, p. 198. (The exact figures are not given but they can be derived approximately from the line of the graph.)

34 Ibid.

35 Cass and Sackville, op. cit. (note 12 above), p. 77.

36 Figures obtained by comparing 27th Annual Report on Legal Aid 1976–7, Appendix 25 with 26th Report, Appendix 21.

37 American colleagues followed the same approach: – the War on Poverty; concern for legal services for the indigent; articles such as that of J. Carlin, J. Howard and S. Messinger, 'Civil Justice and the Poor', Law and Society Review, 1966, p. 9; or of E. and J. Cahn, 'The War on Poverty: A Civilian Perspective', 73 Yale Law Journal, 1964, p. 1317.

38 Carlin and Howard, op. cit. (note 10 above).

39 Table 8.1 above.

40 Curran, op. cit. (note 12 above), Fig. 4.26, p. 135. The extent of lawyer use varied from 850 lawyers consulted for the last 1,000 problems involving wills, 690 for divorce, 390 for acquisition of property (!), at one end of the spectrum to 90 per 1000 problems for wage collection, 80 for property damage and 10 for job discrimination. Out of 28 problem categories, lawyer use reached 400 consultations per 1,000 problems in only 5 problem

categories, more than 300 in 9 categories and 200 in 17 categories. (Table 4.41, p. 175, n. 109).

41 Cass and Sackville, op. cit. (note 12 above), p. 90.

42 Mayhew and Reiss, op. cit. (note 5 above).

43 Ibid., p. 311.

44 Ibid., p. 312.

45 Ibid., p. 313.

46 Ibid., p. 312.

47 Ibid., pp. 313–15.

48 For an elaboration of the theory by Mayhew, see his article, 'Institutions of Representation: Civil Justice and the Public', 1975, *Law and Society Review*, p. 401.

49 Abel-Smith, Zander and Brooke, op. cit. (note 12 above), Table 32, Table 7.1, p. 260–1.

50 Curran, op. cit. (note 12 above), Fig. 4.27, p. 137.

50aIbid., p. 261.

51 The ABA–ABF study found by contrast that no less than 38 per cent of respondents who bought property did not use lawyers. Instead they went to real estate agents (one third), financial institutions (28 per cent), title insurance companies (14 per cent), and miscellaneous others. Curran, op. cit. (note 12 above), p. 140.

52 P. R. Lochner, 'The No Fee and Low Fee Legal Practice of Private Attorneys', 1975, *Law and Society Review*, p. 436.

53 R. Hunting and G. Neuwirth, *Who Sues in New York?*, 1962, p. 65.

54 See Jack Ladinsky, 'The Traffic in Legal Services: Lawyer-Seeking Behaviour and the Channeling of Clients', 11 *Law and Society Review*, 1977, p. 207.

55 Abel-Smith, Zander and Brooke, op. cit. (note 12 above). These data have not previously been published, though a summary appeared in the book at p. 193.

56 Cass and Sackville, op. cit. (note 12 above), Table 13.6, p. 78.

57 Cited in Ladinsky, op. cit. (note 54 above), at p. 219.

57aCurran, op. cit. (note 12 above), p. 203. They accounted for 62 per cent of all lawyer-selections. See to same effect M. Murch, 'The Role of Solicitors in Divorce Proceedings', *Modern Law Review*, 1977, p. 627.

58 Proposed for instance by the Lay Observer, in his *Second Annual Report*, 1976–7. para. 29. See A. P. Dobson, 'Law Should be taught in School', *New Law Journal*, 8 September 1977, p. 875, and Michael Whincup, 'What should be taught in school?', *New Law Journal*, 20 October 1977, p. 1020.

59 Leon Mayhew, 'Institutions of Representation: Civil Justice and the Public', *Law and Society Review*, 1975, p. 401, 411.

60 Ibid., p. 412.
61 See M. Zander, 'The Unused Rent Acts', *New Society*, 12 September 1968, p. 366.
62 Charles Reich, 'The New Property', *Yale Law Journal*, 1963, p. 73.

10 Alternatives to Lawyers

1 National Consumer Council, *The Fourth Right of Citizenship: A Review of Local Advice Services*, 1977. (The Report is the source of a good deal of the factual material in this chapter. I refer to it simply as the NCC Report.)
2 For a description of the then existing facilities see Society of Labour Lawyers, *Justice for All*, Fabian pamphlet, 1968, pp. 24–31.
3 NCC Report, op. cit. (note 1 above), p. 1.
4 Ibid., p. 7.
5 See note 6 below.
6 The gradual decline can be seen from the following table showing unadmitted staff as a proportion of the total 'legal' manpower in three studies:

    1962(a)   50 per cent
    1968(b)   36 per cent
    1977(c)   25 per cent (or so)

(a) Hymans report, unpublished, on 'Undermanning of the Profession', Table 7; (b) PIB, *Standing Reference on the Remuneration of Solicitors, First Report*, 1969, Cmnd. 4217, Tables 2 and 3, pp. 29–30, (c) Law Society, information supplied informally to author in December 1977 from Remuneration survey then unpublished.
7 PIB, *Remuneration of Solicitors*, 1968, Cmnd. 3529, Table 3, p. 35.
8 Law Society, op. cit. (note 6(c) above).
9 Fellows must be over twenty-five, have worked for eight or more years in a solicitor's office and have passed three papers in the Fellowship Examination selected from a total of fourteen. Associates must have been employed with a solicitor for three or more years and have passed the Associate's Examination which consists of two papers in law and two in procedure. Students must be employed in a solicitor's office, be over seventeen and satisfy the minimum educational standards.
10 *Solicitors' Journal*, 19 August 1977, p. 560.
11 *Solicitors' Journal*, 17 December 1976, p. 841.

12 11 *Jurist* (1847) ii p. 274. In 1867 the *Law Times* complained of
    'this restless spirit of ambition on the part of solicitors' and
    warned that it would 'grow in proportion as they become more
    highly educated.... (T)his is an argument against making the
    ... examinations too stiff ... for who will perform the
    drudgery of the law?' (43 *Law Times*, 1867, p. 429).
13 *Solicitors' Journal*, 21 January 1977, p. 50.
14 The distribution of CABs is shown in the NCC Report, op. cit.
    (note 1 above), p. 3.
15 Annual Report of the National Association of Citizens' Advice
    Bureaux, 1975–6, p. 5.
16 NACAB, *Evidence*, p. 4.
17 Ibid., p. 49.
18 NCC Report, op. cit. (note 1 above), p. 61.
19 B. Abel-Smith, M. Zander and R. Brooke, *Legal Problems and
    the Citizen*, 1968 (Heinemann, London), p. 157.
29 Ibid., p. 188.
21 Ibid., p. 207.
22 *Report of the [Winn] Committee on Personal Injuries Litigation*,
    1968, Cmnd. 3691, para. 200.
23 G. Latta and R. Lewis, 'Trade Union Legal Services', XII *British
    Journal of Industrial Relations*, No 1, 1974, n. 17, p. 63.
24 The survey by Latta and Lewis showed that the largest firm by
    far, W. H. Thompsons, acted for 11 of the 49 unions studied
    (op. cit., note 23 above), n. 18, p. 63.
25 Latta and Lewis, op. cit. (note 23 above), p. 61.
26 Ibid., p. 56.
27 K. Bell, 'National Insurance Local Tribunals', 3 *Journal of Social
    Policy*, No. 4, p. 300, Table 4.
28 Latta and Lewis, op. cit. (note 23 above), p. 64.
29 The information in this section is based largely on the NCC
    Report, op. cit. (note 1 above).
30 There were, however, beginning to be signs of reluctance to
    maintain support at the local level. After the Conservatives won
    control in the spring 1977 elections in the West Midlands the
    local authorities decided to close all nine centres there (*Law
    Society's Gazette*, 31 August 1977, p. 706).
31 NCC Report, op. cit. (note 1 above), p. 22.
32 Ibid., p. 23.
33 Ibid.
34 Again, I have drawn heavily on the NCC Report for the facts in
    this section.
35 *Report of the Committee on Local Authority and Allied Personal
    Social Services*, 1968, Cmnd. 3703.
36 Ibid., para. 391, p. 124.

NOTES: 10 ALTERNATIVES TO LAWYERS

37 NCC Report, op. cit. (note 1 above), p. 28, citing an estimate of the Institute of Housing.

38 Ibid., pp. 28–9.

39 The Claimants' Union is an informal organisation consisting of separate and autonomous branches. In December 1977 there were some 117, There is a National Federation of Claimants' Unions but its hold on the separate branches is tenuous. There are no officers. The only condition for membership is to have been on supplementary benefit. The unions favour an aggressive style of advocacy – see Hilary Rose 'Who can de-label the claimant?', in M. Adler and A. Bradley (eds.) *Justice, Discretion and Poverty*, 1975 (Professional Books, London), pp. 143–54.

40 PHAS (Public Health Advisory Service) closed its doors in June 1977 for lack of funds but arrangements were made to keep many of its projects alive – see *Legal Action Group Bulletin*, June 1977, p. 124 and July 1977, p. 149.

41 John Ward, 'Equality of Information', *Municipal and Public Services Journal*, 17 May 1974.

42 NCC Report, op. cit. (note 1 above), p. 44.

43 Ibid.

44 'Social Work and the Delivery of Legal Services', unpublished at the time of writing but due to be published by the *Modern Law Review*. I am indebted to the author for permitting me to see the paper prior to publication.

45 Roger Lawrence, 'Welfare Advice and Advocacy', 1977 (NACAB Occasional Papers, No. 1), p. 20.

46 CCETSW, *Legal Studies in Social Work Education*, 1974.

47 Ibid., para. 2.16, p. 9.

48 Ibid., pp. 9–10.

49 Some LSE law students, for instance, undertake advocacy on a voluntary basis as members of the Free Representation Unit (see p. 317). In December 1977 the LSE Law Faculty agreed to a new course involving some tribunal advocacy in the social security field.

50 Cited by the writer in 'Clinical Legal Education', *New Law Journal*, 22 February 1973, p. 182.

51 Bell, op. cit. (note 27 above), Table 4, p. 300.

52 K. Bell, *Research Study on Supplementary Benefit Appeal Tribunals*, HMSO, 1975, p. 16.

53 NACAB, Administrative Circular, 5/1974, para. 10.

54 Chapeltown Citizens' Advice Bureau Leeds Tribunal Assistance Unit, *Progress Report – the First Six Months*, August 1976–February 1977, p. 6, para. 4.2.

55 Ibid., para. 2.2, p. 3.

56 Ibid., para. 4.7, p. 8; and para. 4.4, p. 7.

57 Ibid., para. 2.2, p. 3. See also Lawrence, op. cit. (note 45 above) and NACAB, 'Assistance to tribunal appellants', Feb. 1978.
58 NCC Report, op. cit. (note 1 above), p. 73.
59 Ibid.
60 Bar, *Evidence, Submission No. 13*, p. XX, 7, para. A.9.5(d).
61 Bell, op. cit. (note 27 above), vol. 4 No. 1, p. 16, Table 2; Bell, op. cit. (note 52 above), p. 15; House of Commons, *Hansard*, vol. 855, 1 May 1973, *cols. 264–5*.
62 All three studies cited in note 61 above show this.
63 *Legal Action Group Bulletin*, February 1974, p. 27. In its Evidence to the Royal Commission LAG proposed that the Legal Services Commission should be the national body to coordinate the tribunal advocacy scheme.
64 *24th Annual Report on Legal Aid*, 1973–4, p. 50, para. 33.
65 Lord Chancellor's Advisory Committee on Legal Aid, *Evidence*, p. 27. para. 24.3.
66 The Labour Party, *The Citizen and the Law*, June 1977, para. 15. The Labour Party and the TUC agreed policy on this issue after a series of meetings of a Working Party representing both sides, between autumn 1975 and summer 1977.
67 [1970] 3 W.L.R. 472.
68 *Mercy v Persons Unknown, The Times*, 5 June 1974.
69 For discussion of the relative merits of lay and lawyer advocates in tribunals see exchanges in the *Legal Action Group Bulletin*, March 1977, p. 70; April 1977, p. 79; May 1977, p. 118; June 1977, pp. 126 and 142; July 1977, pp. 151 and 169–70.
70 See *Solicitors' Journal*, 1972, p. 502; *Legal Action Group Bulletin*, 1973, p. 190; *Law Society's Gazette*, 8 May 1974, p. 427; *Legal Action Group Bulletin*, 1975, p. 65.
71 It was announced in October 1977, however, that the Nuffield Foundation and the Polytechnic of Central London would, at least for the time being, between them rescue the London, formerly the Westminster, Small Claims Court – see *The Times*, 18 October 1977, p. 3; *Legal Action Group Bulletin*, June 1977, p. 125.
72 County Court Rules, Order 19, rule 1(2). See Robert Egerton, 'Arbitration in County Courts', *Law Society's Gazette*, 12 September 1973, p. 2271 and JOT, 'Arbitration in County Courts', *Solicitors' Journal*, 1974, p. 43.
73 *Statistical Report on Arbitration in County Courts*, 1974, 1975, 1976.
74 Figures kindly supplied to the writer by the Lord Chancellor's Office.
75 Originally the procedure applied only to simple cases where the divorce was uncontested and was on the ground of two years

separation, and there were no children under sixteen.

76 See the somewhat disturbing results of the survey by Elizabeth Elston, Jane Fuller and Mervyn Murch, 'Judicial Hearings of Undefended Divorce Petitions', *Modern Law Review*, November 1975, Table 5, p. 618.

77 In *Buckland v Watts*, [1969] 2 All E.R. 985 the Court of Appeal ruled that although a solicitor could get his professional costs as a litigant in person, a lay person could not claim for either his time or his work. In *Malloch v Aberdeen (No. 2)* [1973] 1 All E.R. 304, the House of Lords held that a lay litigant in person could claim for costs incurred by a solicitor employed to assist him in the case.

78 There is a limit of £2 an hour for leisure time and the overall amount cannot be more than two thirds of the amount a solicitor could have recovered. The Rules do not apply to cases where the amount in dispute is under £100 where the ordinary no-costs rule (p. 215 above) operates to litigants in person just as to others.

79 See, for instance, the very useful proposals of an American expert, Professor John Payne, considered in *New Law Journal*, 17 November 1977, p. 1113. For a more radical treatment of this subject see Michael Joseph, *The Conveyancing Fraud*, 1976 (published by the author, 27 Occupation Lane, Woolwich, London S.E.18).

80 Thus the Mirror Group Newspapers in 1974–5 had some 100,000 letters in a fifteen month period addressed to Readers' Service and in 1976 had some 50,000 asking for help mainly on civil matters – Housing, Planning, Tax, National Insurance, Employment, Matrimonial and Consumer Law (Evidence of the Group to the Royal Commission).

81 Divided as follows: £44m. civil legal aid; £41m. criminal legal aid; £2m. law centres (central and local); £1.2m. (grant to CABs from central funds only); and £3.3m. consumer advice centres. (The Lord Chancellor's Legal Aid Advisory Committee's *Evidence*, pp. 28–9.)

82 NCC Report, op. cit. (note 1 above), pp. 62–3.

83 See, for instance, *26th Annual Report on Legal Aid*, 1975–6, pp. 67–8, para. 37, and the Committee's *Evidence*, pp. 30–41.

84 Lord Chancellor's Legal Aid Advisory Committee, *Evidence*, p. 34, para. 25.14.

85 NCC Report, op. cit. (note 1 above), p. 64.

86 Ibid., p. 64.

87 Ibid., pp. 65.

88 Bar, *Evidence, Submission No. 13*, pp. XX. 6–7, paras A.9.4–5.

11 The Future

1 There are some 34,000 solicitors and barristers compared with fewer than 100 public sector lawyers in England. In the United States there are currently some 430,000 private practitioners as against some 3,500 salaried lawyers working for the Legal Services Corporation, 900–1,000 in public defenders' offices and another 600 or so in various public interest law firms.

2 For details of such a proposal see *Report of the (Osler) Task Force on Legal Aid*, Ontario, 1974, pp. 95–101.

3 Preamble and Preliminary Statement, American Bar Association, *Code of Professional Responsibility*, 1970.

4 Earl Johnson Jnr, *Justice and Reform*, 1974 (Russell Sage Foundation, New York), p. 189.

5 For a favourable assessment of the achievements see E. Johnson, op. cit. (note 4 above), pp. 192–271; and *Balancing the Scales: Financing Public Interest Law in America*, a report of the Council for Public Interest Law, 1976, pp. 165–206. For a critical assessment of some of the claims made, see, for instance, S. J. Brakel, 'Styles of Delivery of Legal Services to the Poor: A Review Article', *American Bar Foundation Research Journal*, 1977, p. 219.

6 See G. W. Foster Jnr, 'The Status of Class Action Litigation', 1974 (American Bar Foundation); Allen D. Vestal, 'Uniform Class Actions', *American Bar Association Journal*, June 1977, p. 837; N. Williams, 'Consumer Class Actions in Canada: Some Proposals for Reform', *Osgoode Hall Law Journal*, 1975, p. 1; Bernard M. Dickens, 'Public Interest Litigation – Relator and Representative Actions', *Legal Action Group Bulletin*, November 1974, p. 273.

7 For an account of the origins of the 'Brandeis brief' see Alpheus Thomas Mason, *Brandeis*, 1956 (Viking Press, New York), pp. 248–51, excerpted in M. Zander, *Cases and Materials on the English Legal System*, 2nd ed., 1976, p. 435.

8 See Ernest Angell, 'The Amicus Curiae: American Development of English Institutions', 16 *International and Comparative Law Quarterly*, 1967, p. 1017.

9 For an account of the battles between the OEO Legal Services movement and the Nixon–Reagan forces see John R. Conyers, 'Undermining Poverty Lawyers', in Ralph Nader and Mark Green (eds.) *Verdicts on Lawyers*, 1976 (Thomas Y. Crowell, New York), pp. 129–43. For a view from the Nixon forces see Vice President Agnew, 'What's Wrong with the Legal Services Program', *American Bar Association Journal*, September 1972, p. 930.

10 See, for instance, Martin Partington, 'Some Thoughts on a Test Case Strategy', *New Law Journal*, 14 March 1974, p. 236.
11 B. Curran and F. O. Spalding, *The Legal Needs of the Public: Preliminary Report*, 1974 (American Bar Foundation), p. 94.
12 The other professional weekly, the *Solicitor's Journal*, only rarely publishes articles on aspects of legal services.
13 See note 49 in Chapter 7 above.
14 The problem of the small claim has caused increasing concern in many systems. If there is any solution to the problem, it must lie in special, low-cost systems for dispute settlements. But insofar as these succeed in avoiding costs in the form of fees paid to lawyers it is only because the burden of helping the parties to make their case is borne by the tribunal – either at the expense of the state or through the voluntary efforts of lawyers and other arbitrators.
15 For a pessimistic evaluation of the role of law in solving the problems of the poor and the disadvantaged, see, for instance, *Limits of the Law*, a publication of the Community Development Project, the Home Office, 1977.
16 Address by Clinton Bamberger Jnr to the National Conference of Bar Presidents, 19 February 1966.
17 There are a number of such evaluations. See, for instance: Geoffrey C. Hazard Jnr, 'Law Reforming in the Anti-Poverty Effort', *University of Chicago Law Review*, 1970, p. 242; Harry P. Stumpf, 'Law and Poverty: A Political Perspective', *Wisconsin Law Review*, 1968, p. 694; S. Krislov, 'The Right to Welfare', *Minnesota Law Review*, 1973–4, p. 211; Harry Stumpf et al., 'The Impact of OEO Legal Services', in Dorothy Buckton James (ed.), *Analysing Poverty Policy*, 1975 (D. C. Heath, Lexington, Mass.), but see Johnson, op. cit., n. 5 above.
18 House of Lords, *Hansard*, 15 May 1974, vol. 351, col. 1082.

Index